MUSICA RUSSICA

Russian Music Studies, No. 17

Malcolm Hamrick Brown, Series Editor

Chairman, Musicology Department
Indiana University

Other Titles in This Series

Choral Performance in Pre-Revolutionary Russia

by
Vladimir Morosan

MUSICA RUSSICA
Guilford, Connecticut

Second printing, revised and corrected

Produced and distributed by:

Musica Russica, Inc.
310 Glenwood Drive
Guilford, CT 06437

www.musicarussica.com

Library of Congress Cataloging in Publication Data

Morosan, Vladimir.
    Choral performance in pre-revolutionary Russia / by Vladimir
Morosan
    396 p. 15 x 23 cm
    Originally published Ann Arbor, Mich.: UMI Research Press, c. 1986,
in series Russian music studies.
    Includes bibliographical references and index.
    ISBN 0-9629460-2-8 (pbk)
    1. Choral music—Russia. 2. Performance practice (Music)—Russia.
I. Title.
ML 1537.M67 1994
782.50947—dc20   94–46533

Printed in the United States of America

To the Blessed Memory of
Klavdy Borisovich Ptitsa (1911–1983)
and
Ivan Alekseevich Gardner (1898–1984),
who inspired this work,
but did not live to see
its completion

Contents

Figures

Tables

Musical Examples

Preface

Russian choral singing has long been recognized as an art capable of beguiling those who hear its majestic sounds. The reactions of listeners, from Hector Berlioz (who marvelled at the Imperial Court Chapel in the nineteenth century) to packed houses that cheered Serge Jaroff's Don Cossacks in pre- and post-World War II Western Europe, have bordered on the wildly enthusiastic. Yet, of all the areas of Russian music, choral music and choral performance have been the least understood and have received the least attention from scholars.

To a large extent the reasons for this neglect are attributable to events that transpired in Russia after the Bolshevik Revolution of 1917. Throughout history, the most significant developments in Russian choral music had occurred in the area of sacred, liturgical music of the Russian Orthodox Church. After the Communist takeover, both the Church and its liturgical arts were for a long time subject to intense repression. Only recently have scholars in the Soviet Union been allowed to address topics dealing with the sacred musical heritage of Old Russia.

Historians of Russian music who have dealt with choral music in more than a passing fashion have tended to concentrate on the notation of the music and its style, leaving the questions of performance largely untouched. The present study seeks to fill a major void in Russian music history, not only for the benefit of the musicologist who desires to deepen his understanding of this all-important Russian genre, but also as an aid to the performer who may wish to perform the music.

Before undertaking the study of choral performance practice, a very important determination had to be made. When did choral singing, as it is commonly understood today, emerge in Russia? The fact that no previous study had ever addressed this question satisfactorily suggested that Part One of the present book be *historical*, assembling all available data, currently scattered throughout a multitude of primary and secondary sources, that deal specifically with the history and development of choral and vocal-ensemble performance in Russia.

The evidence drawn from a multitude of diverse sources—including church *typica* (books containing instructions for performing the liturgy), descriptions by foreign travellers and chroniclers, general social, political, and economic conditions, the numbers and sizes of extant manuscripts, and finally, the evidence drawn from the music itself—led to the conclusion that the consideration of choral performance practice in Russia should properly begin with the late eighteenth century, with specific attention paid to the late nineteenth and early twentieth centuries, when Russian choral performance developed into an independent and highly creative artistic phenomenon.

Due to a lack of basic information, Western performers who have aspired to perform Russian choral music have had to cope with the uneasy feeling that an essential component of a performance might involve something that was peculiar to or unique about the makeup of Russian choirs, the training of the voices and the conductors, or the ideals of choral sonority. Part Two of the present book seeks to determine whether such a notion has any justification.

The methodology used in Part Two is modelled on the approach taken by Robert Donnington in his ground-breaking studies of performance practice— *The Interpretation of Early Music* (London: Faber and Faber, 1975) and *A Performer's Guide to Baroque Music* (London: Faber and Faber, 1973). Taking up each element of performance—the choir, the conductor, and the music—I have assembled a multitude of relevant data from documents, textbooks, instructional manuals, concert reviews, extant recordings, and the scores themselves. Because in most cases the original sources speak best for themselves, and because they are not generally accessible to the Western reader, the quotations are offered in greater length and numbers than might normally be the case.

Previous English-language studies in the area of Russian Orthodox church music have inevitably devoted major sections to the intricacies of the liturgy. We may hope that with the appearance of Johann von Gardner's *Russian Church Singing*, Volume 1: *Orthodox Worship and Hymnography* (in English—Crestwood, N.Y.: St. Vladimir's Seminary Press, 1980; and in German—Wiesbaden: Otto Harrasowitz, 1976), this subject will pass into the category of "common knowledge," and will no longer require special treatment every time it arises in a scholarly treatise. In the present study only the major *musical* elements of the liturgy, as they pertain to the question of genre and style, have been summarized.

Acknowledgments

A number of organizations and individuals have made the writing of this book possible. I wish to thank, first of all, the Thomas J. Watson Foundation, the International Research and Exchanges Board, the Fulbright-Hays Doctoral Dissertation Research Abroad Program, the USSR Ministry of Culture, and the Moscow State Conservatory, for enabling me to do essential research in Soviet libraries and archives. Special thanks go to Ekaterina Alekseeva and Aleksei Naumov of the Glinka State Museum of Musical Culture in Moscow, to Professor Tatiana Vladyshevskaya of the Moscow State Conservatory, and to Professor Nikolai Matveev of the Moscow Theological Academy; to Nicholas Temperley, Ralph Fisher, John Hill, Louis Halsey, Alexander Ringer, Harold Decker, and James G. Smith, of the University of Illinois; to Evgeny Ivanovich Evetz, Director of the St. Alexander Nevsky Cathedral Choir in Paris; to John Casey and the entire staff of the Davidson College Computer Center; and to Malcolm Brown of Indiana University, whose encouragement and invaluable advice have significantly improved the final manuscript.

It would have been impossible for me to see this work through from its inception to the final revision of the manuscript without the infinite patience and unflagging support of my late wife, Zhenia. Her tragic and untimely death in an automobile accident occurred only a few months before the scheduled appearance of the book.

Two other individuals, neither of whom lived to see the publication of this book, deserve special mention: Professor Ivan Alekseevich Gardner, who for years virtually single-handedly carried the torch of scholarship in the field of Russian sacred music, and through whose inspired writings I first came to understand the issues at hand; and Professor Klavdy Borisovich Ptitsa, Chairman of the Choral Department at the Moscow Conservatory, who truly understood the significant role that sacred music had played in the choral culture of his country. It was he who said to me back in 1979: "Nowadays we have forgotten how to perform this music properly. So, Vladimir Petrovich, when you discover these secrets, please be sure to let us know."

Part One

The Historical Development of Choral Singing in Russia

1

The Period of Monophony and Early Polyphony

The Origins of Liturgical Singing in Kievan Russia

The question of when and under what circumstances choral or vocal-ensemble singing began in Russia cannot be determined with any degree of certainty. Most historians of Russian music agree that the beginning of choral music as a cultivated art form coincides with the establishment of Christianity as the official state religion in Kievan Russia by the Great Prince Vladimir in the year 988.[1] By that time the Christian liturgical ritual had already developed to an elaborate degree both in Byzantium (under whose authority the newly established Russian Church found itself) and in the Roman Church in the West. Included in that ritual as an immanent aspect of worship was singing in various forms—solo cantillation, and responsorial and antiphonal chanting by groups of singers.[2] The Christian culture also brought musical notation and a daily cycle of liturgical worship that provided the context for the practice, evolution, and transmission of musical forms.

The prevailing assumption among pre-Revolutionary historians of Russian music was that Russian liturgical singing in its initial form represented a wholesale importation of Greek Byzantine ecclesiastical music.[3] Only recently has this view been challenged by Johann von Gardner, who points out that the spheres of foreign influence in tenth- and eleventh-century Kievan Russia were by no means limited to Byzantium. Early Russian chronicles that mention the first arrival of Christian hierarchs and clergy in Kievan Russia[4] state that the Patriarch of Constantinople sent to Prince Vladimir the Metropolitan Mikhail, a Bulgarian by birth, together with four bishops, numerous priests, deacons, and *demestvenniki* (see page 10) "from among the Slavs." Thus, the singing they brought with them to Russia may have already been somewhat Slavicized. The Bulgarians and other Balkan Slavs, converted to Christianity some one hundred years before the Eastern Slavs in Russia, could have already introduced certain Slavic characteristics (arising from differences in texts, linguistic articulation, and ethnic musical sensibilities) into the original Byzantine forms of singing. Indeed, the first strong evidence of purely Greek Byzantine influence in Russia dates only from 1037, when the the Greek Metropolitan Theopemptes arrived in Kiev. From this point on, and for the next several hundred years, the Russian Church would be headed by Greek appointees from the Patriarchate of Constantinople, who undoubtedly brought with them a strong influx of Greek liturgical arts.

The earliest mention of church singers in the chronicles says nothing concerning their musical activities or the type of music they performed. The first reference to actual music is found in an oft-quoted passage from the *Stepennaia kniga* [The book of degrees] that purports to explain the origins of church singing in Russia. The passage reads as follows:

> Thanks to the faith of the Christ-loving Yaroslav [reigned 1010–1054] there came to him from Tsar'grad [Constantinople] three God-inspired singers with their families. From them originated in the Russian land angel-like singing, wonderful *osmoglasie* [singing according to the Eight Tones], and especially tripartite sweet-singing and the most beautiful *demestvennyi* singing to the praise and glory of God....[5]

The accuracy of this account began to be questioned as early as the seventeenth century.[6] Some writers have tended to dismiss the passage altogether: the references to specific types of singing were seen as grossly anachronistic, since both "tripartite" (three-voiced) and demestvennyi singing were developments contemporaneous with 1563, the date of the chronicle's final revision; the writer of the 1560s was perhaps trying to defend these innovations by underscoring the Greek origins of all liturgical singing in Russia. As Gardner points out, however, the main problem with the passage is that of terminology: since we do not know what the various types of singing were called in the eleventh, twelfth, and thirteenth centuries, we cannot evaluate the historical accuracy of the sixteenth-century terms. Thus, the only part of the account from the *Stepennaia kniga* that may be accepted without reservations is the arrival of three Greek singers in Kiev sometime during Yaroslav's reign, an event that is corroborated by other chronicles.[7]

The earliest surviving manuscripts containing liturgical hymns with musical notation date from the last years of the eleventh century or the first years of the twelfth. Semeiographically the notation falls into two categories: (1) *stolp* or *znamennyi* notation, and (2) *kondakarnyi* (kondakarian) notation.[8] Despite the continuing efforts of scholars, neither notation is as yet fully readable. Both notations are ideographic rather than diastematic in nature, and for this reason exact transcriptions may never be possible.[9]

The ideographic neumes of stolp notation (see ex. 1.1)[10] served as a type of shorthand to remind the singer of the contour of the melodic line; the notation does not indicate the exact size of the intervals or the modes or scales

Example 1.1.   Twelfth-Century MS in Stolp Notation Depicting a Cheironomic Hand.

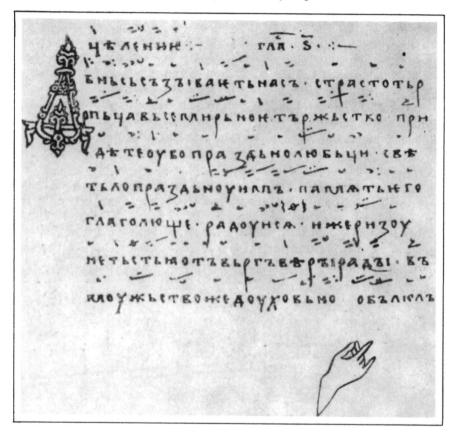

in which these intervals were executed. Similarly, no clues exist as to the pitch level at which the melodies were sung. Structurally the melodies are syllabic-neumatic, with only occasional melismas of more than three notes. Only one neume was written above each syllable of text; thus, melismatic passages can be recognized by the multiple repetition of a given vowel. Judging from the large proportion of signs indicating a repeated note, recitation on a single pitch prevailed.

The inventory of neumes from this period shows that some neumes of different shapes may have had the same diastematic meaning, but communicated more than purely intervallic and rhythmic information to the performer (for example, differences in dynamics or vocal articulation).[11] However, all clues to this aspect of the neumatic notation—even in later periods—have been lost.

While znamennyi chant in stolp notation can be found in manuscripts from the earliest times to the end of the seventeenth century, kondakarian singing with its notation was a phenomenon apparently limited to the eleventh, twelfth and thirteenth centuries. No manuscripts containing kondakarian notation dated after the thirteenth century have been discovered. Judging from the texts in the few surviving manuscripts, kondakarian singing was used in performing *kontakia*, long poetic homilies comprising an opening stanza (the *prooemion* or *koukoulion*) and as many as twenty-four additional stanzas (*oikoi*), each of which ended with the same refrain as the initial stanza. According to Gardner and other authorities, kondakarian singing is undoubtedly of Byzantine origin, although few Byzantine manuscripts with similar notation are known. The notation consists of two rows of symbols above a line of text—a lower row consisting of neumes in a one-to-one correspondence with the syllables of text (as in stolp notation), and a top row of occasionally spaced symbols, markedly different in appearance, known as "great hypostases" (see ex. 1.2).[12] Researchers who have attempted to decipher kondakarian notation[13] believe that these symbols point to the interpretation or technical execution of the melodic line notated by the lower row of neumes.

Example 1.2.   Early Twelfth-Century MS in Kondakarian Notation:
Troparion to the Holy Cross.

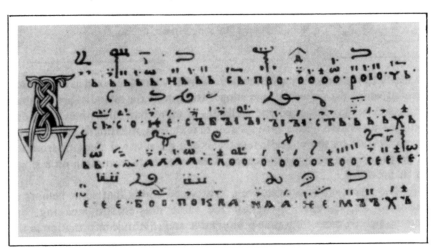

The structure of kondakarian melodies is extremely melismatic, as evidenced from long strings of repeated vowels in the text. In addition, the text occasionally contains interpolated syllables such as *ne, na, ane*, as well as entire Greek intonational formulas, *ananeanes, neanes, aneane*, etc., which suggests that the musical element in these hymns prevailed over the intelligibility of the text. The apparent complexity of kondakarian notation makes it even more difficult to imagine how this music may have sounded.

Despite the fact that the notation of both znamennyi and kondakarian singing reveals very little about the nature and technical execution of the music, some information concerning the performers in the eleventh, twelfth, and thirteenth centuries can be assembled from sources that describe the order and manner of Orthodox public worship. The main source of information concerning the liturgical ritual is the *typikon* (Slavonic: *ustav*), a term that may be translated as "use," having both a generic meaning (e.g., the typikon or use of cathedrals versus that of parish churches) and a more specific usage (e.g., the Typikon or Use of the Hagia Sophia Cathedral in Constantinople). The term also refers to specific manuscripts.

The Byzantine Greeks played an important role in establishing and organizing the early Russian Church. While the original chant melodies and notation may have undergone certain changes in being transferred to a different language and different ethnic musical sensibilities, the liturgical order (including the order of singing) remained Byzantine Greek, at least as long as Greek hierarchs from Constantinople headed the Russian Church. By correlating information concerning liturgical singing in Byzantium of the eleventh through thirteenth centuries with information found in early Russian uses, one may draw an approximate picture of a typical liturgico-musical establishment in Russia at this time.

The singing in the Byzantine church and in the early Russian church was performed by individuals ordained to minor clerical orders. As early as 360 A.D. the Council of Laodicea had decreed that "except for ordained singers standing on the ambo [a raised pulpit in the center of the church] and singing from a book, no one else is to sing in church."[14] This tradition was reaffirmed in Russia by a decree of the council in the City of Vladimir, held in 1274, which stated that "no one who was not specially ordained has the right to stand on the ambo."[15] At the same time, the special mention of this rule by the Russian council suggests that nonordained lay individuals may have been aspiring to perform musical functions reserved for clerics.

Byzantine and early Russian uses distinguish between ordained church singers (*psaltoi, pevtsy*) and sometimes an ensemble (*choros, lik*) on the one hand, and lay people (*laos, liudie*), who participated by singing short responses and refrains to hymns performed by a single singer, on the other hand. The exact nature of the laity's participation is not known; according to some sources the responses may have been spoken, not sung.[16] The participation of the laity is implied particularly in kondakarian singing, since the ending phrases of the hymns are not notated in the manuscripts. In Byzantine practice, the main portion of a hymn in kondakarian style was performed by a virtuoso soloist (the *protopsaltes*) standing on the ambo, while the ending phrases were sung by the entire congregation in the manner of a refrain.[17] Extensive participation by the congregation implies a certain amount of knowledge and education on the part of the laity; and, indeed, kondakarian singing was practiced primarily in large metropolitan cathedrals where Greek hierarchs followed the Use of the Great Church (Hagia Sophia in Constantinople), and where the congregation comprised the social elite.

The probability that kondakarian hymns (i.e., kontakia and certain other hymns) were performed by a soloist, rather than by a choir, is supported by the complexity of the notation and the highly melismatic character of the melodies. If the great hypostases above the melodic line of neumes were indeed directions for various types of vocal production and articulation or, possibly, ornaments such as tremolos, only performance by a soloist would do justice to these effects. Indeed, evidence of a flourishing tradition of solo singing in Kievan Russia may be found in Russian chronicles, which have preserved the names of some outstanding singers (*pevtsy gorazdye*), e.g., Manuil the Eunuch (who in 1137 became Bishop of Smolensk), Dimitri from Peremyshl', Luka from Vladimir, and Kirik from the Antoniev Monastery in Novgorod.[18]

The hymns that were not performed soloistically or by the congregation were presumably performed by choirs. In the early period these choirs stood on the right and left sides of the church in front of a low barrier, called a *kagkella*, which separated the sanctuary (altar) from the nave. (Later this barrier developed into the icon screen that is characteristic for Orthodox churches today.) In this position the choirs sang antiphonally, coming together in the center of the church at certain points during the service. Each choir was led by a *domestikos* (Slavonic: *demestvennik*), and both groups were coordinated by a *protopsaltes* (Slavonic: *nachal'nyi pevets*) or leading singer. The material sung by the choirs mainly comprised psalms performed antiphonally and hymns based upon or interpolated into scriptural texts: stichera, prokeimena, and kanons. The melodies were primarily syllabic or neumatic and were notated in stolp notation.

The existence of antiphonal choirs in Byzantium, both in the Cathedral of St. Sophia and at the Imperial Court, has been documented.[19] In the time of Justinian, for example, there were twenty-five singers on the staff of the Cathedral; the number of singers in other churches varied in proportion to their importance. With regard to Russia, however, the question of choirs is not at all clear. Much of the evidence that nineteenth-century scholars have cited for the existence of choirs is dependent upon terms whose initial meaning has changed over the centuries.

Two such terms are *kliros* and its derivative, *kliroshanin*—one who belongs to the kliros. The Russian word *kliros* (pl. *klirosy*; also *krylos*, *krylosy*, in some early sources) is taken from the Greek *kleros*, meaning clergy. In modern Russian the word has come to mean the special elevated platforms to the right and left of the icon screen where the singers of the choir(s) stand during the service. (The practice of placing the choir in a balcony over the west door dates from the late seventeenth century and is borrowed from Western tradition.) Hence, a kliroshanin in modern usage is a singer who stands on the kliros.[20] Originally, however, the association between singing and the kliros stemmed from the fact that the individuals who sang were all ordained clergy of minor rank (readers, singers), or clergy of higher rank (priests, deacons) who were not celebrating at a given service. The personnel of the performing unit, therefore, was not stable but changed from day to day.[21]

Earlier historians of church singing were misled by references in various chronicles to the initial establishment of klirosy in Russia. For example, the Chronicle of Nikon states that soon after the Christianization of Russia "Metropolitan Mikhail visited the land of Rostov, baptizing a multitude of people, ordaining priests and deacons, and establishing a kliros."[22] From this account Metallov concluded that from the earliest days of Christianity in Russia, choral ensembles (in the modern sense of the word klirosy) were established by the missionary hierarchs. On the basis of similar passages from other chronicles Metallov identified numerous klirosy from the pre-Tatar period: at the Kievan Cathedral of St. Sophia, the Novgorod Cathedral of St. Sophia, the Cathedral of Vladimir-on-the-Kliaz'ma, the cathedrals of Smolensk, Rostov, and also in various monasteries.[23] From a passage in the Lavrentiev Chronicle of 1175, which states that during the burial of Prince Andrei Bogoliubsky "the kliroshane carried [the body, first] into the temple, and [then], while singing over him, into the tomb," Metallov concludes that the principal function of the kliros was to sing.[24] Subsequent writers, paraphrasing Metallov or other sources, substituted the word "choir" for kliros, and so created an alleged network of choirs all over early Russia.

In challenging Metallov's position, Gardner cites evidence that defines a kliros as something much more than merely a group of noncelebrating clergy assembled for singing in church. According to this definition, the kliros in the early Russian Church was a body of high-ranking clergy who performed administrative, consultative, and judicial functions in the diocesan government.[25] This would, of course, account for their existence in the major cathedrals mentioned by Metallov, and would be a more likely reason for them to be mentioned in historical chronicles—as instruments of newly established ecclesiastical power. It is not inconceivable that on certain occasions, such as the state funeral of a prominent prince, these high-ranking church officials would also sing, insofar as singing was the province of every member of the clergy.[26] It is also possible that some members of the administrative kliros routinely sang hymns when they were not celebrating. However, says Gardner, "one must exercise caution concerning references to klirosy and kliroshane in the chronicles: in no way does this mean that one is dealing with ensembles of church singers."[27]

Another term that confuses the issue of whether choirs existed in the early Russian Church is *domestik* (and its related forms: *demestik, demestvennik, demestnik*). The various linguistic forms of this word in the early chronicles led Metallov to argue that domestiki (pl. of domestik) were leaders or conductors of choirs, while demestiki or demestvenniki were common singers who may not even have been ordained.[28] (Metallov derived the latter two terms from the Greek *demos*, meaning people or populace.)

Although he thoroughly repudiates Metallov's linguistic distinctions, Gardner believes that the arrival of domestiki in Russia implies the formation of collective bodies of trained and organized singers.[29] But Gardner's discussion of a domestik's function is not entirely consistent: on the one hand, he defines domestiki in terms of Greek Byzantine practice—as leaders of the right and left choirs, who conducted by means of cheironomy.[30] On the other hand, he states that the domestik was responsible for directing (not conducting) the musical aspect of worship, including congregational participation. According to the latter definition, a domestik could have exercised his functions without the presence of a choir. While the roles of the domestik and the protopsaltes were not, strictly speaking, identical, at times the domestik also functioned as the leading singer. To complicate matters further, some sources mention a *canonarch* (*kanonarchos, ustavshchik*), whose duties included executing the directions of the use accurately: e.g., ensuring that the readings and hymns were performed in the proper order, and determining the melody and style of performance (soloistic, antiphonal, responsorial, etc.) in which a given hymn would be sung.[31]

Certainly these closely related functions—selecting the hymn propers for a given day, determining the melody to be used, distributing the roles among the various singers and/or the congregation, and then actually beginning and conducting the singing—could have all been performed by a single individual who carried the title of domestik. However, the sources that discuss these various functions do not clearly establish the existence of choirs or define the relationship between the domestik and the choir. For the entire Kievan period there is only one known documentary account, dating from the eleventh century, that refers to collective psalm singing, possibly under the guidance of a domestik, in the somewhat specialized surroundings of a monastery: "When we begin the singing of psalms, we ought not interrupt each others' verses, which causes no small confusion in the singing, but should look to the side of the eldest [singer, on the right kliros], and without his beginning, it is not proper for anyone to begin."[32]

The early period has yielded no iconographic evidence that could shed light upon the question of choirs. Although Smolensky states that "the oldest drawings of Russian church singers always portray two groups of people standing on either side of the Royal Doors...,"[33] he neither identifies the drawings nor states how old they are. Findeizen, in his *Essays in the history of music in Russia*, shows several illustrations—decorative miniatures from sixteenth-century psalters—which depict groups of musicians.[34] These groups, however, are all allegoric portrayals, identified variously as "the angelic host" or "the assembly of the righteous," and comprise instrumentalists playing imaginative, if inaccurate, versions of various Biblical musical instruments. Thus, it remains for future researchers to discover iconographic representations of church singers that would provide clues to their numbers and positioning at liturgical services during the early period.

Even if one assumes that members of the kliros, high-ranking, noncelebrating clergy, participated in the singing collectively, and that ordained singers mounted the ambo not only individually but also in groups to engage in some type of collective performance, no information is available concerning the nature of these performances. Did the assembled voices perform the melodies in unison, following the leading singer or the domestik? Did they merely sustain a drone pitch (the *ison*, in Greek terminology) as a foundation for a soloist's melody? Or did they engage in some type of improvised heterophonic performance of the basic notated melody, as has been suggested by some historians?[35] The sources are silent concerning any or all of these possibilities, while past historians of Russian church music are either vague or speculative. I found only one mention of the possibility that Russian chant may have been performed with an ison; describing his impressions during a research trip to the Mount Athos monasteries, Smolensky writes: "Are there any indications that would point to performance [of Russian chants] by a protopsaltes with an accompanying ison? I think evidence ... can be found, ... most likely in those few pages in our singing-books that are still undecipherable, but which probably contain indications [i.e., symbols] similar to those the Greeks still use."[36] Elsewhere Smolensky states, however: "Our klirosy, though they are of more recent origin [than those of the Byzantine Church], undoubtedly arose under the influence of our [secular folk] choral singing, which in turn, developed upon the discovery of the artistic possibilities inherent in our native 'countervoices' (*podgoloski*)."[37] For Smolensky, therefore, choral ensemble performance is an a priori assumption, which he bases on a general predilection of the

Russian people toward collective singing, and from which he proceeds to make a number of other allegations concerning the interrelation between folk singing and the performance of Russian liturgical chant.

While the folk song may have indeed influenced the tonal structure of liturgical chant melodies over the centuries, one must be very cautious in assuming that elements from the secular (and mostly pagan) vocal music of the Eastern Slavs could have easily found their way into the Church. The Church, headed by the Greek hierarchy, resolutely opposed all secular music-making even outside the liturgical domain. Moreover, it already had an established body of music fixed in melodic content by the notation and in the manner of performance by the use, while the church canons restricted the execution of liturgical singing to ordained clergy. The above factors undoubtedly presented formidable obstacles to the infiltration of liturgical singing by secular folk elements.

Most historians of Russian music, however, have tended to disregard the above considerations and, like Smolensky, to accept the existence of choirs and choral singing in early Russia as a postulate. Findeizen, for example, writes: "Under [Prince] Vladimir a properly organized church choir was undoubtedly established...."[38] The Soviet musicologist and liturgist Nikolai Uspensky in his works on early Russian music continually employs the terms "chorus" and "choral culture" in reference to the tenth through thirteenth centuries.[39] The same is true of every pre-Revolutionary writer who dealt with the subject of early Russian chant.

In my opinion the use of these terms is inaccurate and unfounded, given the present state of knowledge concerning Russian liturgical singing during the period in question. Scholars who employ such terms are guilty of projecting conditions of the nineteenth and twentieth centuries—when choral singing was an established tradition in the Russian Orthodox church—back to a period when conditions were entirely different. The little that is known with certainty about the performance of early Russian liturgical chant may be summarized as follows:

1. Evidence from contemporaneous Greek Byzantine practice, from early Russian uses, and from the notation, suggests that the Byzantine tradition of virtuosic solo singing continued in early Russia

2. Similar evidence suggests that the congregation participated in performing refrains and responses, although the exact musical nature of this participation cannot be ascertained

3. The singing establishment at a cathedral or other large church included a canonarch, a leading singer, one or two domestiks, and an undetermined number of ordained singers, who on occasion were joined by noncelebrating higher clergy

4. The places designated for the performance of liturgical hymns were the ambo, an elevated platform in the center of the church, and the areas to the right and left of the Royal Doors that later came to be known as klirosy

5. There is no conclusive evidence that ordained singers were organized into choral ensembles, and the musical function of such ensembles, if they existed (e.g., unison singing, sustaining an ison, improvised heterophonic performance, etc.), remains undetermined.

The above information is not sufficient to answer definitively the question of whether choral ensemble singing began to be cultivated in Russian church singing as early as the eleventh, twelfth, and thirteenth centuries. Simultaneously, another important question is raised: Did the soloistic tradition, which definitely came from Byzantium, continue in Russia after the thirteenth century when chant-books were no longer written using the elaborate kondakarian notation?

The Period of the Tatar Yoke

By contrast with the pre-Tatar period (which, despite the scarcity of conclusive information, was evidently a time of considerable musical and cultural activity), the last half of the thirteenth century and most of the fourteenth century were undoubtedly times of cultural depression, when creative and artistic activity all but ceased. During this time Kievan Russia experienced devastating foreign invasions by the Mongol Horde from the east and by the Lithuanians and Poles from the west. Virtually all cities, including Kiev, the capital, were pillaged and burned to the ground. At the same time, the numerous feudal principalities carved from the Prince of Kiev's original domain engaged in constant civil war—often aided by either the Tatars or the Lithuanians—causing even greater destruction. Not until the end of the fourteenth century, after Prince Dimitri Donskoy defeated the Tatars at the Battle of Kulikovo in 1380, did cultural and creative activity resume.

The liturgico-musical manuscripts from the fourteenth and fifteenth centuries contain notation exclusively of the stolp variety; there are no known manuscripts with kondakarian notation. Because the notation does not exhibit any marked changes from the preceding period, it is no more decipherable than earlier stolp notation. While slight differences appear in the shape, syntax, and combinations of certain neumes, comparative analysis of manuscripts from the two periods shows that the melodic structure of chants remained essentially unchanged.[40]

The disappearance in this period of books containing kondakarian notation may be attributed to several factors. To the extent that kondakarian singing was directly of Byzantine origin, its use among the Russians may have decreased along with the general decline of Byzantine influence in Russian ecclesiastical affairs. The difficulties in travel and communication brought about first by the Crusaders' occupation of Constantinople (1204–61), then by the Tatar invasions of Russia (1237 and after), and by the Turkish invasions of Byzantium, diminished the Greeks' ability to control their Russian metropolitanate. Finally, in 1448, just five years before the fall of Constantinople, the Russian Church became *de facto* autocephalous, i.e., independent, headed by native Russian hierarchs rather than by Greek appointees from the Ecumenical Patriarchate.

Perhaps a more significant role in the disappearance of kondakarian singing in Russia was played by the liturgical reforms enacted by the council in the City of Vladimir in 1274. These reforms replaced the two uses employed theretofore in Russia—the Constantinopolitan Use for cathedral and parish churches and the Use of the Monastery of the Studios for monasteries—with the single Use of Mount Athos and Jerusalem (the Hagiooritical-Hagiopolitical Use) for both monasteries and cathedrals. Virtuosic solo singing had been most prominent in the Constantinopolitan cathedral rite, the Matins of which featured the singing of complete kontakia. By contrast, the Matins of the newly adopted monastic use emphasized the singing of kanons, while the kontakion was usually reduced to only its prooemion and a single oikos. In terms of textual structure, kanons were poetic elaborations within a given metrical framework on selected Biblical canticles. Musically, they employed the *automelon* (Slavonic: *podoben*), the singing a series of verses to a pattern melody. The melodies of kanons, therefore, had to be relatively short, syllabic in character, and easily memorizable.

A central question in the history of vocal performance in Russia is whether the style and manner of kondakarian singing continued, even though chant-books with kondakarian notation were no longer written. Smolensky has expressed the view that some kondakarian melodies continued to be used for hymns not affected by the liturgical reform, e.g., the communion hymns (koinonika), but were rewritten in stolp notation.[41] This possibility is supported by the continued presence in some stolp manuscripts of Greek musical terms (*aneanes, neanes,* etc.) interpolated into the texts. Moreover, stolp manuscripts of the fifteenth century began to exhibit the use of fitas (the Slavonic name of the Greek letter theta, θ), elaborate melismatic passages, to highlight key theological words and concepts within otherwise syllabic melodies. This phenomenon may be seen as the beginning of a fusion between the syllabic-neumatic style of the old stolp melodies and the highly melismatic style of kondakarian singing.

Gardner believes that the main distinction between kondakarian singing and stolp singing lay in the manner of execution—the method of vocal production, the nuances of dynamics and articulation, and other aspects of vocal technique—which stolp notation apparently could not express adequately. "If the melodic line of kondakarian singing," he writes, "were performed without the subtleties of articulation and the peculiarities of the kondakarian manner, but simply the way ordinary stolp melodies were performed, then the characteristic kondakarian neumes (of the top row, which most likely pertained to the manner of performance) become superfluous. And the melodies simplified in this fashion could then be notated in ordinary stolp notation."[42] The question remains, however, whether these melodies continued to be performed by a soloist or came to be sung in unison by a choir. If one assumes, as many historians do, that kondakarian notation was employed for solo singing while stolp notation was used exclusively for choral unison singing, the obvious corollary is that with the disappearance of kondakarian notation the practice of solo liturgical singing in Russia disappeared as well. However, it is unlikely that a firmly established legacy of solo singing received from the Byzantine Church would have been cast aside and replaced by choral unison singing in the absence of compelling internal or external influences. While the technical subtlety of the Byzantine manner of performance may have indeed been lost in the course of time, the practice of solo singing remained.

In fact, the prevailing socio-political and economic conditions in Russia during the fourteenth and fifteenth centuries favored solo over choral singing. The instability of life and the decimation of human resources brought about by the Tatar invasions made it extremely difficult to maintain organized musical establishments; and it was undoubtedly easier to find a single singer who knew the melodies and the notation than it was to find several singers who could perform as an ensemble. While some scholars mention the founding of schools in the late fifteenth century,[43] nothing is known concerning the nature of the curriculum or the role these schools may have played in the cultivation of liturgical singing. One source, in fact, speaks of schools in terms that are by no means complimentary: Gennady, Archbishop of Novgorod from 1485 to 1505, complained that the teachers are "ignorant *muzhiks* [boors, peasants] who, in the course of teaching their charges, corrupt the youngsters' speech." He also spoke disparagingly about the ordained singers of the time, calling them "stupid fellows" and lamenting that "in the entire Russian land great lawlessness and iniquity have arisen: impudent muzhiks are singing on the klirosy, reading Scripture and the Apostle on the ambo, and even going into the Altar."[44] These remarks suggest that not only had it become commonplace for incompetent nonordained singers and readers to perform in church, but even ordained singers did not measure up to expected standards. Early sixteenth-century Russia experienced a shortage of educated and well-trained individuals not only to serve as singers, but even as candidates for the priesthood. Gennady asked Metropolitan Simon of Moscow to plead before the Grand Prince for the establishment of schools where reading and chanting would be taught. Similar concerns were voiced by Ivan the Terrible at the Stoglav Council some fifty years later; and that Council decreed that schools should be established in the homes of priests and deacons to teach reading, writing, and singing.[45]

The only place where choral ensemble singing could have been cultivated systematically was in monasteries. The fourteenth and fifteenth centuries exhibited a tremendous growth of monasticism as people strove to find a structured way of life with a modicum of stability and security. Because monasteries at this time switched over to the Use of Mount Athos and Jerusalem, which did not expressly provide for participation by the laity, Gardner believes that monastic singing involved not only less congregational participation, but also less solo singing (although certain hymns continued to be sung by a single singer on the ambo). However, the entire brotherhood may have participated in singing certain responses, refrains, and psalms, as in the description of collective psalm singing cited earlier. By the same token, the relative stability of monasteries may have provided a haven for the systematic transmission of the soloistic art from one generation of expert singers to another.

In either case the fourteenth and fifteenth centuries probably did not witness the establishment of a systematically cultivated tradition of choral singing in Russia. Since the chronicles from this period do not specifically mention either the type of singing used or the manner in which it was performed, one may conclude that liturgical singing had become quite commonplace in Russia, and that no innovations occurred during this period that would have attracted the attention of the chroniclers.

The Singing Masters of Novgorod

The following two periods, encompassing the years 1480–1564 and 1564–1652, respectively, are of great interest to the historian of performance, since only in these periods does one begin to deal with transcribable examples of music. In addition, a good deal more information exists concerning composers and performers of this time.

The historical event that marks the beginning of the first period is the cessation of Tatar domination over the Prince of Muscovy, which resulted in the emergence of Moscow as the new center of political power in Russia. At the same time a significant musical event occurred in Moscow, one important enough to single out the year 1480 (or more probably 1479) as the beginning of a new era in Russian liturgical singing: the establishment of the first known corps of singers at the court of the Great Prince of Muscovy. Alfred Swan, however, has termed this period the "Novgorod period," since during this time a great school of chant composers, some of whom are known by name, arose in the city of Novgorod in the northwestern region of Russia. In the second of the two periods, which began in 1564, the activity of these Novgorod singing masters merged with that of the Great Prince's court singers, when Tsar Ivan IV (the Terrible) brought the Novgorodians to Moscow. For the time being, however, the activity of these two groups will be examined separately.

Although by the end of the fifteenth century Moscow had clearly established itself as the political and ecclesiastical center of Russia, Novgorod was, in many respects, better prepared to serve as a leader of the cultural revival in Russia after the Tatar domination. For one thing, it had escaped the devastating Tatar invasions due to its geographic location and the skillful diplomacy of its democratically elected princes. Furthermore, as a member of the Hanseatic League, it was in constant contact with Western Europe: the city had an entire foreign quarter inhabited by Western merchants, complete with a Roman Catholic church and Latin clergy. With the help of the foreign clergy, some Western theological treatises were translated into Russian; and Novgorodian singers may have learned something of Western musical theory from these sources as well. Unhampered by foreign invasions, these singers were also in a better position to preserve the musical heritage and practices of eleventh-, twelfth-, and thirteenth-century Kievan Russia, although they may not have been overly successful in that endeavor (see the comments of Archbishop Gennady cited on page 15). In any case, Novgorod was the home of the earliest creators of znamennyi (stolp) chant whose names have been preserved to this day.

An anonymous treatise from the second half of the seventeenth century relates that

> from Kiev all piety and the Orthodox faith went over to Novgorod the Great and from there to Moscow and the entire Russian land; and the faith began to spread along with God's churches, holy books, and divine singing. And when [we] began to learn from one another, then singing began to be spread....
>
> With our own ears we have heard of the old masters: I am speaking of Feodor the Priest, called Khristianin [the Christian], who had become famous here in the ruling city of Moscow and was artful in the singing of znamennyi chant; many learned from him, and his compositions are famous to this day. From his students who are known to us we have heard that he, Khristianin, would tell them about the old masters of Novgorod the Great: Savva Rogov and his brother Vasily, whose monastic name was Varlaam, Karelians by birth, and that later Varlaam was metropolitan in the city of Rostov; he was a pious and wise man and was artful in znamennyi singing and composed *troestrochnyi* and *demestvennyi* hymns as well. His brother Savva had students—the aforementioned priest Khristianin, Ivan Nos [the Nose], and Stefan, called Golysh [the Pauper].
>
> Ivan Nos and Khristianin lived in the reign of the pious Tsar and Great Prince of All-Russia, Ivan Vasil'evich [the Terrible, reigned 1533–84], whom they served in his beloved Alexandrov Sloboda; Stefan Golysh, on the other hand, was not there, but went from city

to city and taught in the Usol'e land [near the Ural mountains], and while in the employ of the [merchants] Stroganovs, he taught Ivan, called Lukoshko, whose monastic name was Isaia; and the master Stefan Golysh composed many znamennyi hymns. After him his student Isaia disseminated znamennyi singing extensively and perfected it.

And from those same students of Khristianin we heard what he had told them concerning the Gospel Stichera: that a certain wise and pious deacon in Tver' had set them to chant, while the Psalter was set to chant in Novgorod the Great...by a famous monk named Markel, called Bezborodyi [the Beardless]....He also composed a very artful kanon to [Saint] Nikita, Archbishop of Novgorod. The Triodia were set to chant and interpreted by Ivan Nos while he lived in Tsar Ivan Vasil'evich's suburb; and he also set to chant the stichera to many saints and the megalynaria [*velichaniia*]. The same Ivan set to chant the stavrotheotokia [*krestobogorodichny*] and the theotokia from the Menaion.[46]

This lengthy account contains much of what is known concerning an entire genealogy of two, possibly three, generations of the earliest known Russian chant composers. This is also the first mention of certain texts being set to chant (*raspety*, from the verb *raspet'*—to render in sung form), which suggests that theretofore these hymns had not been supplied with musical notation, but were sung to some simple pattern melodies transmitted in the oral tradition. Indeed, the term *znamennyi*, meaning "neumatic" or "neumed," originally distinguished composed chant melodies from those that were not notated.[47]

The turn of the sixteenth century brought about a reform in the system of neumatic stolp notation, as the melodies became much more extended and melismatic, with numerous inclusions of fitas. While the notation from the first part of the sixteenth century is still not entirely readable, the compositions of Feodor Khristianin and his contemporaries have survived in seventeenth-century manuscripts that can be deciphered.[48]

The reform of stolp notation, characterized by a proliferation of new neume symbols and their combinations, necessitated the compilation of the first *azbuki* (lexicons of neumes, the earliest of which dates from the late fifteenth century).[49] While these lexicons were little more than catalogs of neume symbols and their names, with little if any explanation of their execution, their appearance implies the beginning of musical schooling. Such schooling was most likely in the form of apprenticeship, since only with the aid of an instructor could the student learn how to perform a given neume. One such lexicon bears the title *Imena stolpovomu sii rech' diachemu* [The names of stolp singing, also called *d'iachii* singing], which suggests that stolp singing was the province of *d'iaki* (ordained chanters or clerics), as opposed to some other type of singing—perhaps nonneumed singing performed by the congregation.

This distinction brings up the question once again, by whom and in what manner—soloistic or choral—was stolp singing performed in the sixteenth century? One important aspect to be considered is the nature of the process involved in composing new stolp chant melodies, as described in a

seventeenth-century treatise: "the old masters who lived in Muscovy...
[under] Tsar and Great Prince Ivan Vasil'evich...[reigned 1533–84] sang the
kokiznik and *podobnik* by memory for the purpose of study; therefore they
knew the system of pitches [*soglasie*] and the neumes [*znamia*] extensively,
composing and setting the neumes [to new texts] by heart."[50] The
compositional process was, therefore, at least partly improvisational:
possessing a thorough knowledge of the musical vocabulary at his disposal—
the melodic formulae (*popevki*) contained in the kokiznik and podobnik—the
master singer-composer performed extemporaneously and, very likely, as a
soloist. From the passage quoted, however, one could surmise that this was
done only for the purposes of study or exercise, and that at some point the
melodies were written down so that an ensemble could perform them.

Another account speaks of a seventeenth-century singer-composer
named Login, who not only had an excellent voice ("beautiful, clear, and
loudly ringing; few voices such as his could be found at that time"), but was
also quite inventive in composing new melodies: "[He] taught his nephew
Maksim to sing [the same hymn] to seventeen melodies, according to different
neumes, and certain other hymns to five, six, nine, or even more chants."[51] In
spite of his inventiveness, Login was criticized by his monastery Superior for
the excessively free and grammatically incorrect treatment of the text in
performing the *Magnificat*: "In readings and prayers one says 'аврааму и
сѣмени' [to Abraham and his seed], and everywhere there is an *oksia* [a long,
sustained note] over the letter ѣ. . . . But you [in your ignorance] sing [this
word] as you pronounce it, and cry in a loud voice, 'аврааму и сѣмени,' and
put a *statia svetlaia* [a long, high note] over the letter и...and through this you
cause confusion and laughter among the brethren in God's church."[52] This
account clearly refers to Login's performance as a soloist during a church
service and not to a study exercise. By his station Login was a leading singer
(*golovshchik*), whose role included leading an ensemble. But the text "to
Abraham and his seed forever" is found at the end of the *Magnificat*, and not
at the beginning of a textual phrase. Therefore Login must have performed the
verses of the canticle as a soloist.

The same source from which the above excerpt is taken also implies the
existence of ensemble singing: "Having great artfulness in singing, [Login]
could set five, six, or ten different chants to the same verse of text, and he
taught many pupils [to do this]. But when his pupils would gather together,
not having rehearsed in their ignorance, there was general confusion and
discord...."[53] This is, quite possibly, the earliest unequivocal reference to
several voices actually singing (or, in this case, attempting to sing) the same
melody together. All previous references to ensembles or groups of voices,
such as liki or klirosy, make no mention of the roles executed by the various
performers.

The foregoing discussion makes it necessary to examine critically, and substantially modify, the widely held view that during the first six and a half centuries the liturgical singing of the Russian Church was primarily choral. The evidence clearly shows that as late as the seventeenth century (Login died in 1635) the traditions of solo and unison ensemble singing existed side by side. What remains to be determined is which categories of hymns and chants were performed by which forces.

A book of rubrics of the Novgorod St. Sophia Cathedral, dating from the late sixteenth or early seventeenth century, contains instructions that distinguish between performance by choirs (liki) and performance by ordained chanters or clerics (*d'iaki* or *podd'iaki*): for example, the rubrics for 25 September (St. Sergius of Radonezh) state: "the chanters sing verses to the saint, while the Mass (*obednia*) is sung by both choirs in strochnyi Moscow style." For 4 October the rubrics read: "the Mass is sung by the singers (pevtsy) of both choirs in strochnyi Moscow style."[54] Still another instruction makes it clear that the chanters sing on the ambo and not in the choir: "the singers sing the Liturgy in two choirs in strochnyi style (*v stroki*), while the chanters sing all ambo singing (*amvonnoe*) in demestvennyi style."[55]

Thus, the chanters who sang on the ambo in the center of the church are distinguished from the singers of the two choirs on the right and left of the icon screen. The word *chanters* is used in plural form, suggesting that several of them may have stood on the ambo simultaneously or that they may have taken turns. Nevertheless, two distinct styles of singing are mentioned: *d'iachee*,[56] also referred to as *demestvennoe* or *amvonnoe*, which, like kondakarian singing of old, was performed in the center of the church, and *strochnyi* singing, which was performed by the two choirs.

Thanks to the recent efforts of Soviet musicologists, most notably Nikolai Uspensky and the late Maksim Brazhnikov, a considerable number of znamennyi chants from the sixteenth and seventeenth centuries have been transcribed into modern notation, making it possible to examine the music for internal evidence that could offer some clues regarding its performance.[57] Unfortunately, none of these scholars considered the possible difference between solo and ensemble performance and, therefore did not supply information about the original sources that could have helped to differentiate the two styles. Nevertheless, the transcribed examples exhibit two basic styles of melodic structure: a syllabic style used primarily in psalm settings, known as "lesser znamennyi chant" (*malyi znamennyi rospev*), and a neumatic-melismatic style, abounding in fitas, known as "great znamennyi chant" (*bol'shoi znamennyi rospev*). The texts typically sung in great chant were stichera—poetic stanzas proper to the events of a given feast.

The chant composers mentioned earlier concentrated their efforts in the latter category of texts and chants, composing their own distinctive versions known as *perevody* (lit., translations or interpretations). The motivation for focusing on these particular texts may have been twofold: lengthy, elaborate melodies were traditionally used to achieve greater solemnity on festive occasions, and the poetic imagery found in stichera texts undoubtedly stimulated the composers' imagination. The individuality of musical treatment, the expressiveness of the music, the uniqueness of each composed melody, and the fact that these hymns were usually performed only once a year, all suggest that stichera settings in great znamennyi chant were performed, at least initially, by a soloist—most likely the composer himself. The composers certainly had the clerical rank of at least a clerk or chanter, so the type of singing they performed would appropriately be called "clerics' singing"—*d'iachee penie*. This distinction corresponds to the instructions in the book of rubrics cited earlier—that verses (stichera) to the saint of the day (the propers) were performed by the chanters, while the Mass (the ordinary) was performed by the choirs.

While nothing in the music of great znamennyi chant, as it has been transcribed by researchers, would automatically preclude ensemble performance, certain rhythmic complexities could present difficulties for an ensemble, especially in the case of hymns such as festal stichera, which were performed only once a year (see ex. 1.3).

Many melismatic chants found in sixteenth- and early seventeenth-century manuscripts contain *anenaiki* and *khabuvy*, seemingly meaningless syllables interpolated into liturgical texts and supplied with musical notation. Earlier, the presence of Greek musical terms (*ananeanes*, *neanes*, etc.) in the midst of liturgical texts has been a characteristic feature of kondakarian manuscripts, and may have meant something to Russian singers. However, by the sixteenth century the meaning was certainly forgotten; scribes continued to copy them into books simply by tradition. Gardner has found that anenaiki appear primarily in melismatic stolp and demestvennyi chants, and almost not at all in chants that are syllabic or neumatic in structure.[58] Thus, one more link is established between the florid, festive melodies of sixteenth-century great znamennyi chant, sung by clerics, and kondakarian singing of the eleventh through thirteenth centuries, which was most likely soloistic.

The other category of nonsense syllables, the khabuvy (sing. *khabuva*, also spelled *khebuve*, *khabuvu*) also occur in melismatic demestvennyi and stolp chants of the sixteenth and seventeenth centuries, and like anenaiki, can be traced backwards in time to kondakarian singing.[59] Of all the attempts to explain these bizarre, text-distorting inclusions, Gardner is perhaps closest to the truth when he regards them as the ultimate step in a process whereby aspirated articulation of melismatic passages evolved into fully written syllables. The term *khabuva* itself may have referred to a special vocal effect produced by closing and opening the mouth while vocalizing a melisma (known in Greek Byzantine terminology as *chachavouasa*); over the centuries

Example 1.3.   Faddei Subbotin—Sticheron to St. Michael the Archangel.
Transcribed by Maksim Brazhnikov, *Novye pamiatniki znamennogo raspeva*
[New monuments of znamennyi chant] (Leningrad: Muzyka, 1967).

(As you are a commander and a helper and the leader of angels...)

the meaning of this term was probably forgotten, but it continued to be copied faithfully into liturgical manuscripts.[60]

The continued inclusion of nonsense syllables in liturgical manuscripts serves as yet another reminder of the fact that in the conservative and tradition-bound Russian Orthodox Church established practices were not easily discarded, and major changes did not occur without powerful and compelling influences. As far as the Byzantine soloistic tradition is concerned, there is simply no persuasive evidence to suggest that in Russia solo singing gave way to unison ensemble singing at some given point during the first six centuries. The only evidence usually cited is the disappearance of manuscripts containing kondakarian notation. However, as the above discussion has shown, many essential features of kondakarian singing continued to exist in melismatic stolp and demestvennyi chants. Even Gardner, for all the significance he attaches to the disappearance of kondakarian notation, is forced to conclude that "one can hardly doubt that some thread from the tradition of kondakarian singing continued to exist in Russian liturgical singing even to the middle of the seventeenth century, as long as great znamennyi chant with its staffless neumatic notation remained part of the living performance tradition."[61]

If one approaches the study of early Russian chant solely from the point of view of paleography (as virtually all previous scholars have done), one may indeed conclude that the abrupt disappearance of kondakarian notation at the end of the thirteenth century signalled the end of an era. Likewise, new notations, the demestvennyi and *putevoi*, which appeared in the sixteenth century, may be viewed as harbingers of new genres or styles of chant. But if one shifts the point of view slightly to include traditions of liturgical performance, the two phenomena—kondakarian singing of the eleventh through thirteenth centuries and demestvennyi singing of the sixteenth and seventeenth centuries, with their respective notations—begin to appear as two visible ends of the same thread passing through the relatively obscure period of the fourteenth and fifteenth centuries. One must furthermore bear in mind that sources from the eleventh through thirteenth centuries give no clues regarding the names by which contemporaries designated the various types of liturgical singing. The term "kondakarian singing" (*kondakarnoe penie*) was coined by Dmitri Razumovsky only in the 1860s.

Demestvennyi Singing

The first mention of demestvennyi singing, in a chronicle entry dating from 1441,[62] significantly antedates the appearance of both its specific notation and manuscripts bearing the designation *demestvenniki*, i.e., collections of demestvennyi chants. Thus, as early as the mid-fifteenth century—and probably earlier—there was another type of singing besides stolp (znamennyi) chant.

The same confusion that accompanies the term *domestik* (*demestik, demestvennik*) in reference to church singers in Kievan Russia, exists with respect to the terms demestvennyi singing and *demestvo*. Basing his argument on premises that have since been proven erroneous, Razumovsky was the first to suggest that demestvennyi singing was intended for extraliturgical, household use, i.e., *cantus domesticus.*[63] His view was uncritically repeated by many writers after him. Yet, as Gardner points out in his monograph *Das Problem des altrussischen demestischen Kirchengesanges und seiner linienlosen Notation* (Munich, 1967), the evidence overwhelmingly indicates that demestvennyi singing was a liturgical genre, in many instances specifically intended for feasts and solemn hierarchal services. Demestvennyi singing differed from stolp chant in that the former did not follow the system of Eight Tones, which governed the melodic construction of stolp chants. Therefore it could achieve much more melodic and rhythmic freedom, as transcriptions of demestvennyi melodies demonstrate.

Gardner derives the adjective demestvennyi from the *domestiki* of the eleventh through thirteenth centuries: rather than *cantus domesticus*, he believes the Latin derivation should read *cantus arte domesticorum*—singing in the style of the domestiki.[64] The question thus arises of how and by whom demestvennyi singing, the other major category of Russian liturgical singing in the sixteenth and seventeenth centuries, was performed.

According to one line of thinking, the presence of a domestik implied the existence of an ensemble or congregation, which the domestik led. Yet, as mentioned earlier, the domestik at times functioned as the protopsaltes, a virtuoso soloist. The rubrics of the Novgorod Cathedral cited earlier assigned the performance of demestvennyi singing to the chanters, who, like domestiki or protopsaltoi of earlier periods, stood on the ambo in the middle of the church. This fact, coupled with the musical and textual features of demestvennyi singing—intricate melodic detail, considerable rhythmic complexity, anenaiki and khabuvy, and other links to the kondakarian tradition (see ex. 1.4)—suggests that, like great znamennyi chant, demestvennyi singing was probably performed by soloists.

Early Russian Polyphony

The same questions and problems that pertain to the performance of monody in the sixteenth and seventeenth centuries apply to the performance of early Russian polyphony. All the previous writers who assumed that the later Russian choral tradition could be extrapolated backwards in time to include

Example 1.4. Demestvennyi Chant—"Hymn to the Mother of God for Pascha."
Transcribed by Nikolai Uspensky, *Obraztsy drevne-russkogo pevcheskogo iskusstva* [Examples of the early-Russian art of singing] (Leningrad: Muzyka, 1971).

(Shine, shine, o new Jerusalem, for the glory of the Lord has shone on you. Exult now and be glad, o Zion...)

the performance of monody, applied the same reasoning to early polyphony. Perhaps they held that any vocal composition with more than one voice part could be termed "choral." However, as Manfred Bukofzer points out in his essay "The Beginnings of Choral Polyphony,"[65] a genuine distinction may be drawn between polyphony performed by a single voice per part, i.e., vocal-ensemble singing, and true choral polyphony. No writer in the field of Russian liturgical musicology has ever addressed this question with regard to early Russian polyphony.

Exactly when polyphony arose in Russia is difficult to determine. Although all the codices before the mid-sixteenth century and many thereafter contain only a single line of neumes, the possibility of nonmonophonic performance, with an ison or improvised heterophony, cannot be excluded. The first documentable occurrence of polyphonic performance dates from the 1540s: a book of rubrics for the Cathedral of St. Sophia repeatedly mentions singing *s verkhom*, i.e., with an added top voice.[66] The Stoglav Church Council, convened in 1551 by Ivan the Terrible, agreed to introduce Novgorod singing into Moscow and its environs, and in 1557 a number of Novgorod singing masters willingly or unwillingly came to Moscow. One of them, Vasily Rogov, mentioned in the genealogy of singing masters, was known as "a composer of *troestrochnyi* (three-voiced) and *demestvennyi* singing." Since, by the 1550s polyphonic singing is referred to as an already established phenomenon both in Moscow and in Novgorod, one may assume that it first appeared somewhat earlier.

A long-standing controversy exists concerning the provenance of Russian polyphony, with at least two opposing factions holding positions made famous in other fields of study by Slavophiles and Westerners. To enter into this discussion would be beyond the scope of the present study. It is noteworthy, however, that the earliest surviving evidence of notated polyphony stems from Novgorod, a city with abundant avenues of communication with Western Europe. As mentioned earlier, Novgorod singers and composers may very well have encountered the concept of notated polyphony and applied it to their own musical material. They did not, however, adopt either the staff or the mensural notation used in Europe at that time.

The manuscript sources of early Russian polyphony contain two distinct styles of writing, neither of which directly resembles contemporaneous Western European music. Strochnyi polyphony or *strochnoe penie* (lit., linear singing) comprises usually three (troestrochnyi), more rarely two or four, voices that closely follow the melodic contour and rhythmic motion of a given chant melody. The middle voice commonly carries the actual chant, the *cantus firmus*, known as the *put'*, meaning "way" or "path." The added voices are named according to their position in the vocal texture: *verkh*, meaning "top," and *niz*, meaning "bottom"; a fourth voice, when present, is called the *demestvo*. The principle of parallel motion is not followed strictly, however. The voices frequently come together in unisons or cross, which has led many writers to draw parallels between strochnyi polyphony and Russian folk heterophony, with its episodic deviations (countervoices) from the main tune.[67] But while strochnyi singing may have been improvisational at the outset, the compositional technique found in more advanced examples is far too calculated and controlled to be merely a notated version of improvised folk-style performance practice (see ex. 1.5).

Demestvennyi Polyphony

In addition to collections of monophonic demestvennyi singing, scholars have found demestvennyi manuscripts containing two, three, and, occasionally, four lines of neumes over a single line of text. Whereas strochnyi polyphony is essentially homorhythmic, the voices in the multi-linear demestvennyi manuscripts are largely independent of one another in terms of rhythmic and melodic motion (see ex. 1.6). The fact that highly dissonant combinations (e.g., strings of parallel seconds, fourths, and sevenths) would often result if the lines were performed simultaneously has led to two different avenues of thinking among scholars. While some maintain that the different lines represent alternative monophonic settings of the same text in different styles of chant,[68] others believe the manuscripts to be polyphonic scores. According to the latter viewpoint, the high degree of dissonance can be explained within a harmonic system based on superimposed fourths and fifths, rather than thirds, not unlike early melismatic organum in the West.[69] Until more insight is gained into the system of clefs and pitch notation used in Russian neumatic manuscripts, the question of whether multi-linear demestvennyi manuscripts indeed contain a form of polyphony may not be resolved.

The Tsar's Singing Clerics

As long as liturgical singing continued to have a purely utilitarian function, traditions of artistic performance were not likely to be cultivated. For such traditions to emerge, church singing needed to assume some extra-liturgical significance, whereby criteria of beautiful sonority, technical virtuosity, and emotional content would assume greater importance. The emergence of Muscovy as a political and ecclesiastical power, which resulted in increased pomp and ceremony at the royal court, provided the necessary stimulus in that direction. The fall of Constantinople, which brought about the vision of Moscow as the "third Rome," the emancipation from the Tatar yoke, the consolidation of fragmented feudal principalities under Moscow's leadership,

Example 1.5.   Troestrochnyi (Three-Voiced) "Cherubic Hymn."
Source: Nikolai Uspensky, *Obraztsy drevne-russkogo pevcheskogo iskusstva* [Examples of the early Russian art of singing] (Leningrad: Muzyka, 1971).
Transcribed by Maksim Brazhnikov.

(Let us [who mystically represent] the cherubim...)

Example 1.6. Three-Voiced Demestvennyi Polyphony: Festal Trisagion "*Elitsy vo Khrista*"
[As many as have been baptized].
Source: Nikolai Uspensky, *Drevnerusskoe pevcheskoe iskusstvo* [The early
Russian art of singing] (Moscow: Sovetskii Kompozitor, 1971).

(*As many as have been baptized into Christ, have put on Christ.
Alleluia.*)

and the annexation of the vast Siberian territories and resources, all pointed Russia towards becoming a major power, not only in Asia but in Europe as well. As the Muscovite rulers' sense of self-importance increased, the court ritual developed definite, fixed forms. These were patterned, in part, after the Imperial court of Byzantium, and also after Western-European courts. Emissaries to the West undoubtedly returned fascinated by the splendor of European courts. One such traveller, Dimitri Gerasimov, who visited Rome in 1525, is known to have admired Italian music during his stay there.[70]

The establishment of the first permanent corps of singers, the Tsar's Singing Clerics (*Gosudarevy pevchie d'iaki*),[71] at the court of the Grand Prince of Moscow, has been singled out as the beginning of a new era in Russian music. While the first documented mention of the Tsar's Clerics dates from the reign of Prince Vasily III (reigned 1505–33), both Findeizen and Gardner suggest that the founding of the singers' corps coincided with the dedication in 1479 of the Moscow Cathedral of the Dormition, built by the Italian architect Aristotle Fioravanti during the reign (1462–1505) of Prince Ivan III. Findeizen's discussion of the Tsar's Clerics' founding offers another example of loose and unwarranted assumptions regarding the origins of choral singing in Russia. Findeizen writes, "Now that he had a new edifice of church architecture so colossal for its time, could the Grand Prince have been satisfied with the performance of a numerically insignificant choir, as before?"[72] If Findeizen possessed information about the prior existence of a "numerically insignificant choir," he does not present a shred of evidence to that effect. Furthermore, his assumption that the Tsar's Clerics were a "choir" from the very outset implies the beginning in Russia of a specific genre of musical performance, an assertion for which concrete evidence has yet to be found.

More accurately, the Tsar's Singing Clerics should be regarded as the first musical establishment in Russia whose administrative structure can be deduced from surviving payment records and other documents. In pointing out that the Clerics were the first organization to sing church music under secular rather than ecclesiastical authority, Gardner suggests that the members may not have been ordained clergy. However, the fact that the members were called clerics (*d'iaki*), a term reserved for ordained lower clergy, contradicts his argument.

At the outset the Clerics' liturgico-musical functions were probably no different from those of any other ordained church singers—historical accounts singled them out merely because of their prominent position at the court. In time, however, their role expanded to include various nonliturgical musical events, such as providing vocal music at court feasts, participating in pageants and processions, and (especially in the seventeenth century) participating in productions of sacred dramas. By virtue of their presence at the court, the Tsar's Clerics may have come into contact with delegations of foreigners who visited the Prince. One noteworthy event that may have had some impact upon their activity was the arrival in 1490 of the Augustinian monk Johann Salvator, an organist brought to Moscow by the brother of Sophia Paleologos, the Greek wife of Prince Ivan III. Findeizen, in fact, credits the Clerics with introducing notated polyphony into Russian practice.[73] Later findings show, however, that polyphonic singing first arose in Novgorod and was brought to Moscow by Ivan IV as a novelty. Overall, the existing evidence does not support the view that the Tsar's Clerics instituted either monophonic or polyphonic *choral* singing in Russia, or immediately assumed the vanguard in the theoretical and practical development of liturgical singing, merely because they were organized administratively as members of the court staff.

Much of what is known concerning the organization of the Tsar's Singing Clerics throughout the early period comes from the research of Dmitri Razumovsky, published in his monograph entitled *Patriarshie pevchie d'iaki i podd'iaki i Gosudarevy pevchie d'iaki* [The patriarchal singing clerics and subclerics and the Tsar's singing clerics].[74] According to the earliest available data the total corps numbered thirty-five singers, divided into groups or teams known as *stanitsy*, each numbering five individuals. The teams were ranked in order of ability and salary, with the lowest teams evidently comprising trainees. During liturgical services the first team always stood on the right kliros, while the second stood on the left kliros. Thus, the minimum number of singers present whenever the Clerics performed was ten: five on each side when the singing was antiphonal, and ten when the singers congregated in the center of the church for certain hymns. Razumovsky implies that the remaining teams were also distributed between the two klirosy, although they may have also been responsible for performing in other court churches. There are no documented instances when all thirty-five performed simultaneously.

In 1589, following the establishment of the Russian patriarchate, a similar corps of singers, known as the the Patriarchal Singing Clerics and Subclerics (*Patriarshie pevchie d'iaki i podd'iaki*), was established. However, due to the chaotic events of the Time of Troubles, which soon followed, the earliest numerical data concerning this corps date from 1626–27, when the group numbered thirty. Like the Tsar's Clerics, the Patriarchal Clerics divided into teams numbering four or five singers. Razumovsky points out that under Patriarch Filaret, who held the office from 1619 to 1637, only two teams, with four singers in each, held the higher rank of clerics; the other singers were subclerics (or chanters, according to other sources).[75] Whether the difference in rank carried with it a different musical function remains unknown.

The information concerning the administrative organization and physical arrangement of the Tsar's and Patriarchal Clerics says nothing about the musical functions performed by the individual voices. Each kliros was presumably headed by a *golovshchik*, a leading singer, who may have either led the other voices in unison singing or performed soloistically over an ison. According to some accounts, the Tsar's Clerics were patterned after the musical establishment of the Byzantine emperors;[76] a typical Greek church ensemble would, in fact, consist of a soloist accompanied by four or five singers sustaining an ison.

The system of teams offers few immediate clues as to the number of singers involved in performing polyphony. Documents show that certain individual singers specialized in the performance of a given vocal line, and were termed *vershniki, putniki,* or *nizhniki,* depending on whether they sang the verkh, put', or niz.[77] In four-part polyphony the fourth part, called the *demestvo,* was performed by the domestik or demestvennik, who was also the leader of the ensemble.[78] However, the usual number of singers in a team (four or five) did not correspond exactly to the number of voice parts in most polyphonic scores (in most cases three, and more rarely, two or four). Thus, the balance of voice parts was uneven: an account dating from the reign of Tsar Feodor Alekseevich (who reigned 1676–82) indicates that each team in the Tsar's Singing Clerics consisted of a vershnik, two putniks, a nizhnik, and a demestvennik.[79]

If only one team per kliros performed polyphonic compositions at a given service, clearly the performance had the nature of vocal ensemble rather than choral singing. Razumovsky's hypothesis—that in addition to the first and second teams, the third, fourth, and others also participated—remains undocumented. Two additional factors support my view that early Russian polyphony and certain works of monody were performed by solo voices. The first stems from the aforementioned account in the *Stepennaia kniga* of the three Greek singers, who were credited with beginning "three-part sweet-singing and the most beautiful demestvennyi singing" in Russia. Whether or not the account is accurate historically, the concept of a single voice on a part was evidently not unfamiliar to the writers who completed the final version of the chronicle in 1563.

Far more compelling evidence for performance by solo voices, hitherto not considered by scholars, is the physical size of the neumed manuscripts. Although complete statistics on manuscript sizes cannot yet be compiled,[80] available information shows that an overwhelming percentage of Russian liturgical music manuscripts, especially after the fifteenth century, were extremely small. Table 1.1 lists the dimensions of manuscripts dating from the fifteenth to the seventeenth century found in the Findeizen Collection at the Moscow Conservatory.[81] More complete information, including the contents and the approximate date, is available for manuscripts found in the archive of Dmitri Razumovsky and Vladimir Odoevsky[82] (see table 1.2).

Table 1.1.   Dimensions of Neumed Manuscripts in the Findeizen
Collection

MS Number	Dimensions in cm
707	9.5 x 13.5
706	9.5 x 15.0
728	10.0 x 14.5
708	10.0 x 15.5
740	10.0 x 16.0
706	10.5 x 16.0
21260	10.5 x 17.5
737	13.5 x 20.0
721	14.5 x 18.5
736	14.5 x 18.5
21276	14.5 x 19.0
738	14.5 x 19.0
21053	15.0 x 19.0
729	15.0 x 19.5
713	16.0 x 20.0
21262	16.5 x 19.5
735	16.5 x 20.0
712	16.5 x 20.5
21052	18.0 x 20.0

Even this limited sampling shows that the prevailing size of neumed manuscripts was approximately 10 x 15 cm, hardly large enough for ensemble singing, especially considering the extremely small size of the written characters (see ex. 1.7). Only one reference was found to a "very large" demestvennyi book with neumes large enough for a number of singers to sing from it. However, the author of the reference, Smolensky, does not cite either the exact dimensions or the date of the manuscript.[83]

There is no evidence that manuscripts were produced in identical multiple copies for use by an ensemble. Although each manuscript in a given liturgical category (e.g., Heirmologion, Octoechos) followed a similar pattern of organization, the variants were sufficiently numerous to make the simultaneous use of several such manuscripts impossible. A passage from Aleksandr Mezenets's treatise of 1668, *Izveshchenie o soglasneishikh pometakh* [A report on the most-consonant markings], confirms that such discrepancies abounded: "As little-skilled masters began to correct znamennyi singing ... each in his own way, ... a great discord developed, so that in a single church not only three or more, but even two found it impossible to sing together."[84] The original Slavonic wording of the passage suggests that three singers constituted a desirable norm for unison znamennyi singing, but that

Table 1.2. Dimensions of Neumed Manuscripts in the Archives of D. V. Razumovsky and V. F. Odoevsky

No.	Contents	Date	Dimensions in cm
R-12	Oc,H, S	End 15th-beg. 16th c.	13.5 x 20.6
R-22	H, Oc, Ob	Beg. 17th c.	9.5 x 15.2
R-48	Octoechos	Beg. 17th c.	9.5 x 15.0
R-49	Oc, Ob	Beg. 17th c.	9.7 x 15.0
R-13	H, Oc, Ob, F	2nd quarter of 17th c.	10.2 x 17.8
R-14	H, A, Oc, Ob, S	2nd quarter of 17th c.	14.3 x 19.5
R-23	H, Ob, Oc, T	2nd quarter of 17th c.	15.5 x 20.0
R-24	H, Ob, Oc	2nd quarter of 17th c.	9.3 x 14.4
R-25	H, Ob, Oc	2nd quarter of 17th c.	10.3 x 15.7
R-26	H, Ob, Oc	2nd quarter of 17th c.	8.5 x 13.5
R-27	H, Ob, Oc	2nd quarter of 17th c.	9.5 x 14.5
R-28	H, Ob, Oc	2nd quarter of 17th c.	9.4 x 14.7
R-29	Various hymns	2nd quarter of 17th c.	14.2 x 19.0
R-30	Ob, Oc	2nd quarter of 17th c.	9.5 x 14.8
R-31	Triodia	2nd quarter of 17th c.	10.0 x 15.7
R-46	Liturgy	1642–45	9.3 x 12.0
R-32	Ob, P	Mid-17th c.	9.5 x 15.5
R-33	H,Oc, Ob, P	Mid-17th c.	10.4 x 16.0
O-7	H, Oc, Ob	Mid-17th c.	10.0 x 15.5
R-52	H, Theotokia	Mid-17th c.	10.0 x 15.5
O-10	H	Mid-17th c.	7.2 x 9.0
R-57	S	Mid-17th c.	9.8 x 15.3
R-59	Triodia	Mid-17th c.	14.8 x 19.4
R-62	Menaion	Mid-17th c.	16.0 x 20.8
R-63	Menaion	Mid-17th c.	15.3 x 20.0
R-64	Menaion	Mid-17th c.	15.3 x 20.0
R-65	Menaion	Mid-17th c.	15.7 x 20.1
R-66	Menaion	Mid-17th c.	15.7 x 20.5

Polyphonic Scores in Neumatic Notation

No.	Contents	Date	Dimensions in cm
R-79	P (2 pts.)	Mid-17th c.	9.9 x 16.0
R-80	T (2 pts.)	Mid-17th c.	10.4 x 15.8
R-78	Service to St. Dimitri	3rd quarter of 17th c.	15.2 x 20.0
R-81	Ob (2 and 3 pts.)	3rd quarter of 17th c.	9.2 x 15.0
R-83	S (2 and 3 pts.)	End of 17th c.	15.7 x 20.6
R-84	P (2 and 3 pts.)	End of 17th c.	15.7 x 20.5
R-82	P (4 pts.)	End of 17th c.	15.8 x 20.3

Key to abbreviations: Oc—Octoechos, Ob—Obikhod, H—Heirmologion, T—Triodion, P—Prazdniki (Feasts), F—Fitnik (Lexicon of *fita*'s), A—Azbuka (Lexicon of neumes)

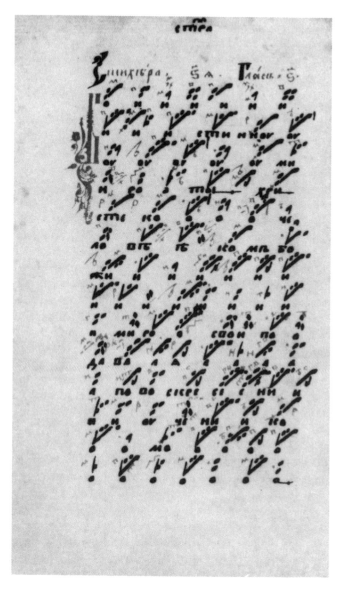

Example 1.7. Feodor Khristianin (Krestianin)—Great Znamennyi Chant "Gospel Sticheron." (original size)

prior to the corruption of the chant books by "little-skilled masters," the number may have been somewhat larger.

No significant enlargement occurs in the dimensions of polyphonic scores in neumatic notation. Looking at some of them, one indeed wonders how even three singers could have sung from a single book, to say nothing of a larger ensemble. As with monophonic manuscripts, no identical multiple copies of polyphonic scores are known to exist.

Summary

The roots of the Russian choral tradition are not to be found in the first six and a half centuries of Orthodox liturgical singing in Russia. So long as Russia remained an Eastern-oriented, theocentric society, fully cognizant of its Byzantine Orthodox heritage even after the fall of Byzantium, its musical development stayed within the boundaries of the Eastern Orthodox tradition. This tradition, even in today's Greek and Middle-Eastern Orthodox Churches, does not include choral singing in the Western-European sense of the word. Contrary to the beliefs of some Slavophile music historians, Russia before 1650 shows no evidence of indigenous cultural forces strong enough to have transformed a Byzantine tradition of soloistic monody into a tradition of choral singing. When the change to choral singing did occur, it was due to powerful cultural forces from the West, where choral part-singing was already a tradition of several centuries' standing.

To many historians of Russian music the above conclusion will appear revolutionary. However, it is the result of what I believe to be the first systematic attempt to correlate the available fragments of information pertaining to the performance of early Russian liturgical singing. While much of this information is admittedly fragmentary and incomplete, and the conclusions offered herein may be modified substantially by future discoveries, the existing evidence points strongly to a soloistic tradition and, at best, only circumstantially to choral ensemble performance.

2

The Introduction and Spread of
Choral Part-Singing

In the seventeenth century, increased contacts with Western nations (resulting both from Russia's rise as a political and economic power and from military confrontations with its neighbors) challenged many aspects of Russia's insular and theocentric culture. Among the areas affected most radically was that of liturgical singing. When Polish armies occupied Moscow during part of the period known as the Time of Troubles (1605–13), Russians heard, perhaps for the first time, organ playing and part-singing in the Western manner. The reaction of the Russian religious establishment at that time is summed up by the words of the venerable Patriarch Germogen of Moscow, who said: "The singing of the Latins I cannot bear to hear!"[1]

At the same time, confronted with a challenge from Western rationalistic ideas, leading Russian churchmen began to place more emphasis on the didactic side of worship, recalling the patristic admonition to "sing with understanding." In doing so, they came into open conflict with the singers of the time; for example, Archimandrite Dionisi, one of the most learned Russians of his time, accused his flamboyant singer Login of "not being learned in the dogmas of Orthodoxy" and of "calling grammatical science and learned philosophy heresy."[2] Another critic, the Monk Evfrosin, wrote in 1651: "Pay heed diligently to what the Holy Spirit says: He commands to sing ... not [merely] with noise and the ornamenting of the voice, but so that the singer would know what is being sung, and the hearer would understand the meaning.... We [however] only fill the air with shouting and whining.... In our singing we only decorate the voice and preserve the znamennyi neumes, while crippling the sacred words...."[3]

By the middle of the seventeenth century znamennyi singing had reached a crisis point (brought on, in large part, by the singers themselves), for it no longer fulfilled the didactic and aesthetic needs of the Russian Church. To carry out the badly needed reforms, a commission of "expert singers and composers," headed by the monk and scholar Aleksandr Mezenets, convened in Moscow in 1655. But an epidemic of the plague in 1655–56 interrupted the commission's work, and only thirteen years later did work resume. The result was a theoretical treatise entitled *Izveshchenie o soglasneishikh pometakh* [A report on the most consonant markings]. But in the intervening years an event occurred that shook Russian society to its roots, making the findings of Mezenets's commission largely superfluous. That event was the *raskol*, the schism that divided the Russian Orthodox Church and Russian society into two bitterly opposed factions.

The causes of the schism may be viewed on two levels. On the surface, it was generated by the opposition of certain priests and faithful to the reforms of liturgical books and church ritual carried out by Patriarch Nikon (patriarch from 1652 to 1658). On a deeper level, it was a rebellion of the old theocentric order against the increasing secularization of Russian life and society. The artistic legacy of the old order had already been challenged and criticized by writers in the first half of the century. After the religious schism, the liturgical arts suffered a division as well: the old forms retreated along with the exiled Old Believers (*starovery*), as the schismatics came to be called, into the impenetrable northern forests and distant frontiers, while the rest of Russia was left with a profound cultural and artistic vacuum. In the three or four decades that were to follow, the musical heritage of over six hundred years would be summarily swept aside and supplanted by foreign art forms that would dominate the nation's culture for the next two centuries. Znamennyi and demestvennyi monophony and indigenous Russian polyphony gave way to the "harmonious and graceful art" of *musikiia*, part-singing modelled after Western European polyphony.

The term *musikiia*, derived from the Latin *musica*, first appeared in Russia at the end of the sixteenth century, but according to lexicons of the time it originally applied only to instrumental music,[4] while liturgical chant was termed singing (*penie*). By the second half of the seventeenth century, however, this distinction ceased to be made, as the following passage from a preface to a theoretical treatise written around 1680 shows:

> I call all singing musikiia, especially that of the angels, about which one cannot say anything, for it is called heavenly musikiia [*musica divina*]. But he who has lost his reason and knows not the harmony of his own nature, says that church singing is not derived from musikiia and should not be called such.... [Yet] without musical knowledge he cannot understand anything in the churchly order of things or in hymns; [neither can he] write a single hymn without knowing the musical intervals. Another, a veritable fool, says that Russian neumes [*znamia*] are one thing,... while the signs of musikiia [i.e., musical notes] are another thing. Such a man is truly insane and speaks foolishness.[5]

The passage clearly depicts the magnitude of the gulf that existed between the concept of music in old Muscovy and the new theory and practice, which by 1680 had all but supplanted the former.

Part-Singing in Southwest Russia

The relatively speedy acceptance of Western-style part-singing in some quarters of Muscovite society was due, in part, to the fact that the new style had already gained a foothold in the southwestern region of Russia (known as the Ukraine) during the latter half of the sixteenth and the first half of the seventeenth centuries. Orthodox liturgical singing in southwestern Russia began to develop along a path different from that followed in the north-central part of Russia, when the region found itself separated both politically and ecclesiastically from the rest of the country. Originally the cradle of Russian civilization, Kiev and the surrounding territories, were repeatedly sacked by the Tatar invaders in the thirteenth and fourteenth centuries. As a result, the seat of ecclesiastical and civil authority was moved north, first to the city of Vladimir and then to Moscow. In the meantime the western principalities of Kievan Russia were conquered first by Roman Catholic Lithuania and then by Poland. By the fourteenth century, Orthodox churches in the Southwest gained ecclesiastical independence from the former Metropolitan of Kiev (who now resided in Moscow), when the Patriarch of Constantinople appointed a separate metropolitan for Galicia and Lithuania. Under the influence of Polish and Lithuanian Roman Catholic music, Orthodox liturgical singing in the Southwest began to evolve in a separate direction. A regional variant of znamennyi chant, known as Kievan chant, developed, displaying traits of Western mensural music. To date very little research has been done on the early stages of this evolutionary process. A clearer picture emerges only towards the end of the sixteenth century, as Orthodox lay brotherhoods (*bratstva*) began to arise in the region.

Even more than the Muscovites who came face to face with Western influence in the seventeenth century, the Orthodox living under the domination of Poland and Lithuania had to take stringent measures to preserve their religious and national identities. Under pressure to recognize Rome's ecclesiastical authority,[6] the Orthodox populace banded together into religious-cultural lay associations whose stated objective was "to unite the members of the Orthodox Church into a 'sworn bond and union of indissoluble brotherly love,' by concentrating in their hands the religious and patriotic upbringing of Russian youth, and to stand for the national identity of all that was Russian."[7]

The first brotherhood was formed in 1585 in the city of L'vov; other prominent brotherhoods arose in Kiev (1615) and Lutsk (1617), along with numerous similar organizations in smaller cities and villages. Realizing that education was a key factor in preserving cultural and religious independence, the brotherhoods made the establishment of schools a priority of the first magnitude.[8] The brotherhood schools attached special attention to the study of music, since the beauty and splendor of Roman Catholic liturgical polyphony were among the major factors that attracted Orthodox believers to Roman Catholicism and the *unia*. From the very outset the brotherhoods sought "to establish...[among the Orthodox] beautiful divine singing according to the order of musical consonances, [which would] put to shame the inanimate whining [i.e., organ playing] of the Romans."[9] In so doing, however, they suspected that they were going against established Orthodox traditions and practices, and therefore sought the dispensation of several Eastern Orthodox patriarchs. In his message to the Orthodox of Poland (i.e., southwestern Russia) Patriarch Meletios Pigas wrote in the 1590s: "What shall we say concerning music?... We do not censure either monophonic or polyphonic singing, as long as it is proper and decent.... As for the noise and droning of animate [*sic*] organs, Justin the Philosopher-Martyr condemns it; and it was never accepted in the Eastern Church."[10]

Conditions in southwestern Russia favored the development of harmonic singing. Because the region was close to the Balkan peninsula and to Greece, the Greek style of chanting with an ison (an intermediate stage between monophony and polyphony) was probably more familiar than in the north. The initial lack of educational institutions in the region forced singers to seek musical training abroad. In 1558 the Moldavian Prince Aleksandr wrote to the Orthodox in L'vov: "Send us four singers (*d'iaki*), fair youths, and we will instruct them in Greek and Serbian singing; and when they have mastered it, we will return them to you; just [be sure] they have good voices. We also have some singers from Peremyshl', who have been sent here for instruction."[11] Contacts with the West led to familiarity with Western European polyphony and to the adoption of five-line staff notation in place of the complicated and imprecise neumatic stolp notation, both for purposes of instruction and for liturgical use. While the exact date of its appearance is not known, staff notation was already used in a manuscript known as the *Suprasl' Irmologion*, dated 1601.[12]

Initially, the Orthodox borrowed the music of certain polyphonic hymns from the Roman Catholic repertoire in its entirety, adapting only the words.[13] However, eventually, the need to create additional polyphonic settings for Orthodox services stimulated compositional activity. The brotherhoods acted as collective patrons of the liturgical arts, commissioning new musical works and supporting conductors, teachers, and singers.[14]

The appearance of an extensive new polyphonic vocal literature raises the question of whether these works generated the beginning of a choral tradition in Russia. Fortunately, some sources are quite specific in this regard. For example, Point Seven of the direction given in 1586 to Feodor Ruzkevich, the music instructor at the L'vov Brotherhood school, states: "[The teacher must see to it]...that there be a strong bass with a good, steady voice, descants [i.e., boy sopranos] with exceptional, ringing voices, as well as an alto and a tenor."[15] The boy sopranos were evidently the objects of special concern, for the direction continues, "especially for the descants everything necessary must be provided, so that none of them might leave for want of something."

Thus, as early as 1586, a four-part vocal ensemble already constituted a norm, with a single singer per voice part for the lower three parts. This norm evidently persisted for at least a century: Zubritskyi's Chronicle of 1692 states that "the [L'vov] brotherhood [at that time] had four singers."[16] In other instances the number of singers may have been somewhat larger: when Metropolitan Mikhail Rogoza visited L'vov in 1591, he was greeted by children divided into three "choirs" (*liki*), which sang welcome verses. Isaevich suggests that the work may have been a twelve-part composition for three four-part choirs;[17] however, since the musical score is unknown, this assumption cannot be verified.

Kozytskyi's statement that the descants and altos were selected from among the young pupils in the brotherhood schools suggests that these parts were sung entirely by boys.[18] But his hypothesis is unquestionably true only in the case of the descants: the fact that at L'vov several descants were required to balance a single bass, tenor, and alto indicates that the latter part may have been sung by a high adult male voice. Indeed, many all-male monastic choirs, including that of the Kievo-Pechersk Monastery, were later famous for their *altists*, reflecting a practice that may well have originated in the early days of part-singing in southwestern Russia.

The aforementioned direction of 1586 also describes the manner in which the various elements of the service were distributed between the vocal ensemble and a chanter. Point Eight states: "When the teacher is in the choir [loft] singing the *iracteni* [a term the exact meaning of which has yet to be determined], he must leave on the kliros a person well capable of singing to the Tones (*na glas*) and to the automela (*na podoben*), and must see to it that there is no confusion [in the performance of the various parts of the service]."[19] Thus, in adopting part-singing from the Roman Catholics, the brotherhoods also adopted the practice of placing the vocal ensemble in an upstairs gallery or "choir" (*khory*) over the west entrance of the church. The ensemble sang only certain parts of the service (*iracteni*), while the remainder of the hymns, the changing daily propers sung to the Tones and other pattern melodies (*automela*), were sung by a chanter on the kliros. No mention is made of antiphonal singing between a right and left choir, as was traditional in Byzantium and in northern Russian churches of that time.

The change in the positioning of the singers was an important departure from the traditional Orthodox understanding of the function of church singing. As long as the singers remained on the *klirosy* at the front of the church, they functioned as coparticipants with the celebrating clergy in the performance of the liturgy. However, when the ensemble was removed to a choir loft, their role changed to that of musicians who merely accompanied or embellished the service.[20] This important change of perspective, which first came into the Orthodox Church in southwestern Russia under the influence of Roman Catholicism, was later destined to change the entire character of Russian liturgical singing.

Part-Singing in Muscovy

As the leaders of Muscovy sought to strengthen their native culture in the face of increasing influence from the West, they turned to their Orthodox brethren in the southwest for the necessary knowledge and education. Ironically, along with the fruits of learning, they ended up adopting the very elements of Western culture they were trying to counteract, just as the Southwesterners had done some fifty or sixty years earlier. Foremost among these cultural elements was music.

While Nikon, the future patriarch, was still Metropolitan of Novgorod (i.e., before 1652), he instituted Kievan and Greek[21] singing in his cathedral: "Expressing great concern for singing, he assembled klirosy of wondrous singers and exceptional voices [who produced] animate singing far better than an inanimate organ; and no one else had such singing as Metropolitan Nikon."[22] Nikon's accession to the patriarchate in 1652 coincided with the arrival in Moscow of several groups of singers from Kiev, who had been recruited by Tsar Aleksei Mikhailovich. Desiring to establish the same kind of singing as the Patriarch, the Tsar had dispatched the Priest Ioann Kurbatov to Kiev to purchase books and recruit singers. Kurbatov soon returned with a group of eleven singers, who, along with their leader, Feodor Ternopol'sky, were at once placed in the Tsar's employ. Although the names of the singers have survived, there is no way to determine whether they were all adults or included some boys among them.[23] This initial group soon returned to Kiev, but the same year two more groups (numbering six and seven singers, respectively) arrived in Moscow, appealing to "the Tsar's unutterable kindness and Orthodox Christian faith" to grant them employment.[24]

In the years that followed, a steady stream of southwest-Russian singers continued to flow into Muscovy. Some came by invitation of the Tsar, the Patriarch, and other influential personages.[25] Others came on their own initiative, seeking asylum from the wars and civil strife that continually beset southwestern Russia.[26] Still others were conscripted into the Tsar's service by military commanders, who had standing orders to seek out and recruit outstanding singers for the court.[27] Prominent courtiers and wealthy merchants recruited southwestern Russians for their households and churches as well. The most famous composer and theoretician of the new style, Nikolai Diletsky, was employed by the merchant Grigory Stroganov.

The new music brought to Moscow from southwestern Russia comprised hymns, psalm settings, and entire services in Western European motet style, which in Russia came to be known as the *partesnyi* (from the Latin *partes*, meaning parts) style. In many cases these works were in four parts, but just as frequently, in eight or twelve parts, while in some instances, the number of parts was as large as twenty-four and forty-eight. The appeal of this repertoire lay in massive sonorous effects (often imitating instrumental music), dancelike rhythms, and the display of vocal virtuosity in concertato passages. At the same time, these works often contained very little musical substance. As Preobrazhensky points out,

> creativity was simplified: the composer was not required, as before, to penetrate into the substance of znamennyi chant, to maintain a link with the internal content [of the text]. The new style freed the hands of any musically gifted singer to create melodies that had no connection with the melodic treasures accumulated over the centuries, but were naive in their simplicity and incredibly impoverished, both in rhythm and overall structure, compared to the objective yet profound znamennyi melodies.[28]

Quickly mastering the purely external aspects of the new compositional techniques, as outlined in Diletsky's treatise *Idea grammatiki musikiiskoi* [The idea of musical grammar],[29] native Russian composers—Titov, Kalashnikov, Redrikov, Bavykin, and a host of others—began to produce vast numbers of new works, including freely composed vocal concertos (see ex. 2.1),[30] four-part harmonizations of znamennyi, Kievan, and Greek chants (see ex. 2.2), and three-voiced *kanty* modelled after a Polish para-liturgical genre (see ex. 2.3). Summarizing Diletsky's impact on Russian church music, Preobrazhensky writes:

> By itself . . . [Diletsky's style] gives no reason to lament his influence upon our [Russian] singers: the collision of styles is an inescapable phase in the history of culture, and, for the most part, results in the triumph of the highest ideas of the time. The misfortune lay in the fact that Diletsky was not suited for the role that he was destined to play. . . . Much lower in stature than his Polish teachers, he brought to Moscow wares that were hardly so valuable as to warrant the Russians' exchanging their age-old treasures for them. . . . Diletsky's baggage was mere tinsel, which reflected the glitter of the latest Western schools of counterpoint, but had lost the main value of the latter, namely, the rigor of technique and the essence of style, in the long journey eastward. Diletsky was blinded by the freedom and external beauty of the contemporary style; but in enthusiastically propagating [it] he did not so much instruct and develop his students and followers as dazzle them.[31]

To perform works in the new concerted style Russian singers had to master a number of new techniques and concepts, including an entirely different system of notation, a system of intonation that admitted sharps and flats (in contrast to the essentially diatonic tonal system of znamennyi chant), and entirely new vocal registers and vocal techniques. Whereas the melodic

Example 2.1. Nikolai Kalashnikov (fl. ca. 1700)—"Cherubic Hymn" à 12.
Source: Nikolai Uspensky, *Russkii khorovoi kontsert* [The Russian choral concerto] (Leningrad: Muzyka, 1976).

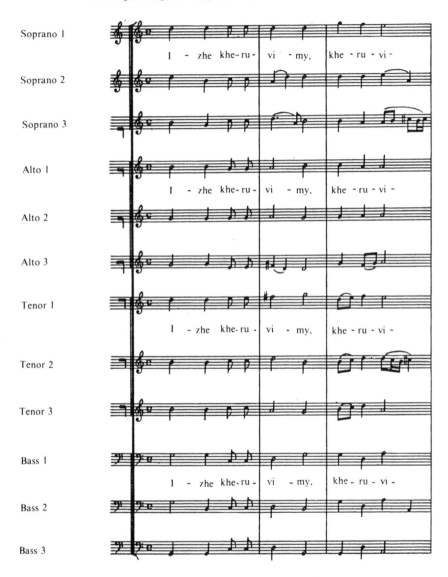

(*Let us who mystically represent the cherubim...*)

Example 2.1.   (continued)

Example 2.1. (continued)

Example 2.2. Harmonized Znamennyi Chant—Theotokion-Dogmatikon in Tone 5 (Late Seventeenth–Early Eighteenth Centuries).
Source: Nikolai Uspensky, *Obraztsy drevne-russkogo pevcheskogo iskusstva* [Examples of the early Russian art of singing] (Leningrad: Muzyka, 1971).

(In the Red Sea of old a type of the Virgin Bride was prefigured. There Moses divided the waters...)

Example 2.2. (continued)

– sa – sia   i – no – gda

ta – mo Mo – i – sei ra –

–zde – li – tel' vo – dy

Example 2.3. Sacred Kant—"*Vospoem pesn' novu*" [Let us sing a new song] (composed for the Victory at Poltava—1709).
Source: Vladimir Protopopov, *Muzyka na poltavskuiu pobedu* [Music for the Poltava victory] in *Monuments of Russian Music*, vol. 2 (Moscow: Muzyka, 1971).

(Let us sing a new song to the Lord God,
For He has poured out great bounties upon us today.
He did not let us be destroyed by the enemies
Who desired to deliver us all to death.)

motion of chant melodies was predominantly conjunct, the new style employed wide intervallic leaps and virtuosic, ornamental coloratura passages of eighth- and sixteenth-notes, requiring a vocal agility hitherto unknown in Russia. The rhythmic structure of the new music was also radically different, using regular periodic meters, proportional changes from duple to triple, and abrupt changes of tempo.

To Russian singers brought up in a tradition of monophony these complexities must have been utterly bewildering. Indeed, they expressed amazement at the process whereby "after beginning in a single voice, singing is composed in three and five degrees [i.e., in thirds and fifths], and thus has three voices, *niz, put'*, and *verkh*, each having its own sound and [yet] all harmonizing as one."[32] The immigrants from southwestern Russia could only partially compensate for the lack of local singers and teachers experienced in the Western polyphonic style. If this style was as widespread in Russia as presumed by some writers,[33] one might expect to find voluminous pedagogical literature dealing with the above questions. To date, however, the small amount of research that has been done in this area has discovered only one such pedagogical treatise, Diletsky's aforementioned *Musical grammar*, the greater portion of which deals with compositional technique rather than performance practice.[34] As a pedagogical tool for practical performance the treatise offered as little help to the uninitiated performer of its day as it does to the modern reader. The explanations of technical matters, such as note values, intervals, and proportions, could have been understood and mastered only if coupled with actual examples demonstrated by a teacher. The fact that Diletsky's treatise was so limited in its application suggests that the complex concerted style may not have been very widespread in Russia, and perhaps may have been limited to the Tsar's Singing Clerics at the Moscow court and a few establishments under the patronage of wealthy nobles and merchants who could afford to hire singers and teachers already well-versed in the Western European style.

Available information indicates that, at least at the outset, the new *partesnyi* style did not involve large choral ensembles. In southwestern Russia, where the style was first adopted from Europe, it was performed as vocal ensemble music with a single voice on a part. (As noted earlier, the L'vov Brotherhood maintained only four singers for *partesnyi* singing as late as 1697.) The data concerning the earliest groups of Kievan singers who came to Muscovy expressly to perform works in the new style also suggest that only a small ensemble was considered necessary to render the music: the first group, led by Ternopol'sky, consisted of eleven individuals. Soon after arriving in Moscow they sent for another singer from Kiev, bringing their number to twelve. With one voice to a part they would have been able to sing twelve-part compositions, which appear in great numbers in manuscripts from the period, providing they had boy descants among them. The other groups from Kiev numbered only six and seven singers, respectively. Since the music they performed differed considerably from the style familiar to native Muscovite singers, the newcomers could not have easily augmented their ensembles with local forces.

A passage from the instructions sent in 1657 by Patriarch Nikon to the Valdaisky Iversky Monastery in preparation for the visit of Tsar Aleksei stipulates the minimum requirements for forming an ensemble: "Select from among the brethren some good singers, [knowledgeable] in the *partesnyi* style, with beautiful voices, so that all the lines would be covered even in excess."[35]

But if some works were performed with "excess" voices per part, others were definitely executed by ensembles of solo singers. A description of a ceremonial meeting of the Tsar by the Patriarch reads: "Two of the Tsar's Clerics delivered a greeting: the demestvennik of the third team, Artemei Ievlev, and the putnik of the young [boys'] team, the little Dmitri Rostopchin."[36]

The numerous arrivals from the southwest eventually swelled the ranks of the Tsar's Singing Clerics and the Patriarchal Singing Clerics; registers of names from the second half of the seventeenth century abound with Ukrainian and Polish surnames. By the last two decades of the century the Tsar's Singing Clerics numbered between eighty and one hundred.[37] They rarely, if ever, performed simultaneously, however, but divided among the numerous court churches and private chapels that served the extended royal family.[38] The Patriarchal Clerics numbered forty-seven in the year 1700, but they were also divided into smaller contingents responsible for serving in several Kremlin cathedrals simultaneously.

The part-books used in the performance of partesnyi singing were not large: eight part-books from different sets belonging to Razumovsky's collection, dating from the early eighteenth to the late eighteenth centuries, all measure approximately 16 x 20 cm.[39] At most they could have been used by two or three singers at a time. Multiple copies of part-books have been discovered in only a few instances.

A few pieces of pictorial evidence further support the hypothesis that, originally, ensembles that performed partesnyi singing were small. A detail on an icon of the "Elevation of the Cross" found in the village of Sitikhovo near L'vov, dating from the late seventeenth century, depicts an ensemble of twelve men and boys with a conductor (see fig. 2.1).[40] The railings and arches indicate that the ensemble is in the rear gallery of a church.

A drawing in the 1681 MS of Diletsky's *Musical grammar* depicts a singing school of the time, showing a master and eight students, three or four of whom are young boys (see fig. 2.2).[41] The master's uplifted left hand and the part-books in the hands of the pupils suggest that singing is in progress. It is not clear, however, whether each singer is performing a separate part.

Another drawing, of a Palm Sunday procession, made in 1662 by the German Baron Meyerberg, shows several figures surrounding a replica of the scriptural fig tree mounted upon a carriage, followed by approximately twenty other figures—possibly singers—carrying palm branches (see fig. 2.3).[42] Adam Olearius, who described the ceremony, states that the fig tree was surrounded by six boys in white robes singing "Hosanna in the highest!" while those following the carriage included "a multitude of various clergy."[43] Which members of the group were ordained singers is impossible to determine either from the picture or from Olearius's description.

Until considerably more research is done on the topic, the question of

Figure 2.1. Performers of *Partesnyi* Singing.
Detail of icon from Sitikhovo, second half of seventeeth century.

Figure 2.2.   A Russian Singing School.
From 1681 MS of Diletsky's *Musical Grammar*.

Figure 2.3.   Palm Sunday Procession in Moscow, 1662.
Drawing by Baron Meyerberg.

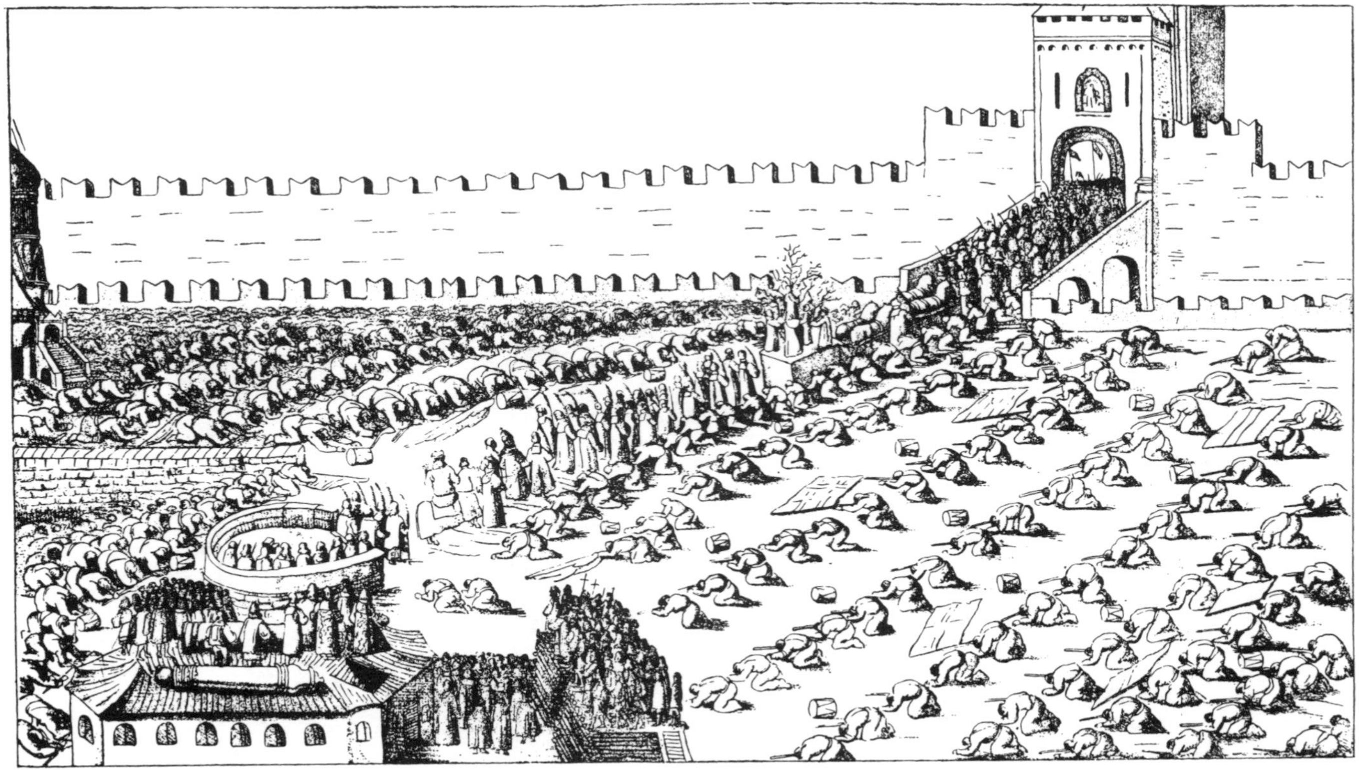

whether the partesnyi style was linked with the beginnings of choral part-singing in Russia will remain unresolved. Too little is known yet concerning the specific circumstances in which various types of works were performed to draw any definite conclusions with respect to techniques and traditions of performance. The biggest and most obvious change brought about by the new style was that, while one singer was sufficient to perform monophonic chant (possibly in a very elaborate and artistic fashion), partesnyi music required as many voices as there were individual parts in a composition. Beyond this requirement the actual practices may have been quite flexible and varied, depending on the circumstances and means of the particular establishment that employed the singers.

The Dichotomy between Partesnyi Singing and Chant

While Russian composers of the late seventeenth century displayed an extraordinary degree of adaptability, both in embracing an essentially alien style and in creating a vast new literature of their own,[44] their compositions were in many respects primitive and superficial, reflecting insufficiently mature compositional skills. Similarly, one wonders whether, in a short period of time, Russian singers were able to master the new vocal techniques and develop genuine artistry. The partesnyi style radically changed many aspects of church singing in Russia, but it certainly did not bring about a firmly established tradition of choral performance.

The introduction of freely composed musical "fantasies" into the liturgy profoundly affected the nature of church singing. As Diletsky's treatise clearly stated, the emphasis in freely composed works was to be on the music rather than on the content of the text. Beautiful sonority, which, in turn, depended on an effective technical rendition, thus became the central element in these works. Elaborate composed settings did not account for all of the musical elements of the the liturgy, however; a number of texts, primarily the changing propers of the day, continued to be sung in chant. Consequently, a dichotomy began to develop in Russian liturgical singing: freely composed works in the new polyphonic style took on the character of musical numbers inserted into the liturgical fabric of chants, which, by comparison, now seemed unadorned and artless. The polyphonic works were performed by a select group of singers specially trained for the purpose, while the chants were performed by one, or possibly two or three chanters[45] who became the "poor relations" of the church musical establishment. This dichotomy, which fully emerged in the first half of the eighteenth century but whose roots went back to the southwestern brotherhoods of the late sixteenth and early seventeenth centuries, was not without its critics. Leading opponents of Patriarch Nikon's innovations had accused him of "introducing Kievan partesnyi singing into the church, akin to secular voice-contorting singing, [freely] composed on its own terms rather than passed down by tradition from the saints—Latin and Roman whining in parts forbidden by the Holy Fathers." According to the critics, "The contortion and swaggering of the body [a reference to Diletsky's instructions that singers beat the *tactus* as they sing] and the excessive ornamentation of the singing . . . are more proper for jesters and players than for the church of God."[46]

Although the underlying musical principles and the aesthetic goals of composed partesnyi singing and chant were different, certainly the performance of znamennyi chant had not been totally devoid of technical or artistic considerations. Such a view did emerge, however, because of the magnitude of the stylistic differences between chants and free compositions, and the suddenness with which the two were brought into direct opposition. As a reaction to many partesnyi composers' obvious infatuation with trite technical effects and disregard for church order, the conservative faction took the position that church singing should not be (and, indeed, never was) concerned with beauty or technical refinement. This line of thinking, which may be traced from the seventeenth century even to the present day, had dire consequences for the future course of church and choral singing in Russia. Liturgical chants were effectively segregated from the mainstream of the culture's musical development and stigmatized as being altogether devoid of artistic value, while choral singing initially developed apart from the aesthetically enriching influence of the liturgy.

The most important consequence of the break between chant and composed polyphony was that the indigenous Russian chant heritage and its performance practice did not play a significant role in the emerging tradition of vocal ensemble and, eventually, choral performance. After the introduction of part-singing, the chants themselves in most instances were no longer performed in unison, but in simple three- or four-part harmony. The process of harmonizing was largely improvisatory: the main melody notated in the chant book was sung by the middle voice, a strong baritone. A higher voice added harmony, usually in parallel thirds, while the bass moved along the roots of triads suggested by the top two voices. A fourth voice, if present, sang a descant, filling in missing chord tones or sometimes doubling the melody an octave higher.[47] The number of singers could vary from two or three in a small church to several dozen in a large monastery or cathedral. Even though this manner of performance at times undoubtedly achieved a high degree of polish, the performers were not concerned with cultivating any particular artistic goals. In Gardner's words, "the focus of attention was not so much on the artistic technique as on the content of the singing itself . . . ,"[48] i.e., on executing the liturgical requirements of the service.

The technical aspects of choral ensemble performance in Russia, on the other hand, developed in the secularized environment of the Imperial court, particularly after the court's transfer to the newly founded capital of St. Petersburg. As Gardner points out, "For the Court Choir [as the Tsar's Singing Clerics were renamed by Peter the Great], the artistic-technical side of performance became paramount. This is understandable for a choir that, above all, had an important ceremonial significance and whose major concern was performance technique, regardless of the material being performed."[49]

The Court Choir under Peter the Great and His Successors

One of the steps undertaken by Peter to lessen what he felt to be the reactionary grip of the Orthodox Church on Russian society was the abolition of the patriarchate. The Church would henceforth be governed by a synod of bishops responsible to a secular court official, the ober-procurator, and, ultimately, to the sovereign himself. Because of the secular authorities' increased involvement in church affairs, and because of the growing importance of the court musical establishment, from this point on, the course and nature of church singing in Russia would be determined to a great extent by the concern (or lack thereof) expressed towards it by the ruling monarch.

Peter the Great was no great patron of church singing, but like all royal children, he had been trained in some of its practical aspects and frequently took part in singing the services. The focus of Peter's reign was on reforming Russia's society and updating its military and technological development, rather than on cultivating the arts. Of the hundred-voice corps of singing clerics that had served the various members of the extended royal family in the 1680s, only the largest contingent of twenty, attached personally to the Tsar, retained the title of the Tsar's Singing Clerics. As various members of the royal family died, their choirs were disbanded; and by the beginning of the eighteenth century only the Tsar's personal choir remained.[50] Peter, who led a spartan life and spent much of his reign in travels and military campaigns, did not see the need to maintain a large choir: through most of his reign the number of singers remained approximately the same—twenty-two in 1701–3, fifteen in 1711, twenty-two in 1716. Only in 1722 did the number increase to twenty-seven and then to thirty-four. In addition to performing at church services, the choir took part with increasing frequency in secular celebrations—masquerades and "assemblies"—which Peter introduced in imitation of Western European court customs. The music consisted of the aforementioned kants, often composed for the specific occasion.

The Tsar's choir at this time seems to have consisted of only tenors and basses. Payment records show that all singers received approximately the same remuneration, which suggests that they were all adult males. On certain ceremonial occasions, such as when the twelve-voice concerto *"Rtsy nam nyne"* [Say now unto us] by Vasily Titov[51] was performed as part of the thanksgiving service for the Poltava victory, boys were evidently added. However, much of the other music dating from Peter's reign—the kants and liturgical chant harmonizations—required only a male (TTBB) ensemble.

From Peter's death in 1725 and until 1732 the Court Choir numbered only fifteen singers.[52] In 1732 the practice began of bringing to St. Petersburg contingents of twelve singers from the Moscow Synodal Choir (formerly the Patriarchal Singing Clerics). These singers were attached to the Trinity Cathedral and did not necessarily serve at the court, but they may have augmented the Court Choir on ceremonial and extra-liturgical occasions.

In the reign of Empress Anna Ioannovna (reigned 1730–40) an organized campaign was begun to recruit young singers from the Ukraine, which had served as the primary source of singers since the mid-seventeenth century. An Imperial decree of 1730 reads: "Wherever you find singers in the Ukraine and in the cities of Malorossiia [Little Russia], recruit good young fellows, and having selected them, cause no offense to their families, nor subject [the latter] to taxes; [however, you must] not let good singers escape you."[53]

In 1738 another Imperial decree established the first school for the exclusive purpose of training choristers for the Court Choir. The school, located in Glukhov (at that time the residence of the Ukrainian Hetman and the administrative center of the Ukraine), may have actually been established several years earlier;[54] the decree of 1738 merely gave it official status and funding from St. Petersburg. Already in 1738 eleven young singers were sent to the court together with the precentor (*regent*)[55] Fyodor Yavorivsky. The purposes of the school are clearly spelled out in the Imperial decree:

> for the remaining [students] let another precentor remain, who shall be perfectly knowledgeable in four-part and partesnyi singing; and let there be established a small school into which [children of] clergy, cossacks, burghers, and others, up to twenty [students] at all times, would be recruited from all over Little Russia; see to it that they have the best voices, so that the aforementioned precentor might train them in Kievan and partesnyi singing; moreover, once knowledgeable foreign and Little-Russian masters have been sought out, let the students be also trained in string music, i.e., on the violin, gusli, and bandura, so that they would be able to play upon these instruments from [musical] notes; and once they are trained in singing and in string music, let them be sent, ten at a time, every year to the court of Her Imperial Majesty, and new ones recruited in their place.... [56]

With this kind of efficient system of recruitment the numbers of the Court Choir grew steadily; by 1752 the ensemble numbered forty-eight adults and fifty-two boys.[57] In 1768, according to Jakob von Stählin,[58] the Choir consisted of fifteen descants, thirteen altos, thirteen tenors, and twelve basses (a total of fifty-two), with almost as many trainees. Arriving in St. Petersburg with some musical training, the young singers were placed in the charge of experienced adult singers whose responsibilities, according to an instruction of 1749, included "to teach [the young ones] to sing in a 'mannered' style, and if any of the youngsters should be lazy in learning, punish them with the rod."[59] In addition to singing, the boys continued to study orchestral instruments. Somewhat later, in the 1770s, their education was expanded to include French, Italian, German, history, geography, arithmetic, and dramatics.

The Influence of Visiting Italian Maestri

The introduction in 1736 of Italian opera at the Imperial court began a new phase in the activity of the Court Choir. According to Metallov, the court singers first participated in an opera production in 1737.[60] The first clear record of their participation in an opera dates from 1742, when Hasse's *La Clemenza di Tito* was staged for Empress Elizabeth Petrovna's coronation. On that occasion fifty court singers were instructed to learn all the choruses in the opera with the Italian text transliterated into Russian.[61] The performance was evidently a success: as one contemporary relates, "After this these singers were invited to participate in all operas where there were choruses, and so mastered the music in the Italian taste, that they were unsurpassed in the singing of arias even by the best Italian singers."[62]

Through the remainder of the eighteenth century the Court Choir's musical development was shaped by a constant stream of Italian and German musicians invited to serve as *Kapellmeisters* at the St. Petersburg court: Francesco Araja (1735–38, 1744–59), Hermann Raupach (1755–62, 1768–78), Vincenzo Manfredini (1758–69, 1798–99), Josef Starzer (1760–70), Baldassare Galuppi (1765–68), Tommaso Traetta (1768–75), Giovanni Paisiello (1776–84), Carlo Canobbio (1779–1800), Giuseppe Sarti (1784–1802), Gennaro Astaritta (1784–89, 1795–1803), Domenico Cimarosa (1787–91), and Vincente Martín y Soler (1788–1806). Assessing the effects of more than a half-century of foreign influence upon the Court Choir, Metallov writes: "Upon the [operatic] stage the technical aspects of the vocal art were developed, various subtleties of vocal performance were studied, practical methods of voice training were mastered, ... accompanied by a loss of taste and attraction for the indigenous national style of singing that had been passed along from generation to generation."[63]

Peter the Great's daughter, Empress Elizabeth Petrovna (reigned 1741–62), was a great lover and patroness of church singing, studied it herself, and even participated in the choir at her private palace church. According to Stählin, Elizabeth did not allow much Italian music to be performed in church, even though Italian opera had already become a fixture in Russia.[64] On the other hand, the tastes of Catherine the Great (reigned 1762–96) were quite different in this regard. Stählin writes: "At daily services only a portion of the choir sings, and [the singing consists of] simple chant; but in the presence of the Empress and also on Sundays and feast days all the music is "figural singing," i.e., motets in ornate concerted style."[65] Catherine expressed regret that certain works composed by her Italian *maestri* could not be performed in church because they employed instruments. Her patronage of Italian music shaped the tastes around her so powerfully that even the members of the Holy Synod of Bishops (contrary to their monastic vows and hierarchal stature) attended performances of the Italian court opera, to the obvious delight of the Empress who once remarked, "The [members of the] Holy Synod were at yesterday's performance and laughed to tears along with us."[66]

In 1763, when Catherine ascended the throne, the Court Choir underwent an administrative reorganization and was renamed the Imperial Court Chapel (*Imperatorskaia Pridvornaia Pevcheskaia Kapella*). The choice of the term *kapella*, from Western European terminology was indicative of the prevailing views upon the nature and function of the Court Choir. Although the full details of this reorganization were not available for this study, it appears that as a result, the Court Chapel became an even more secular organization, subordinate to court officials, rather than to ecclesiastical authorities. Prior to the reorganization, from 1731 to 1749, the chief administrators of the Chapel had been the Hieromonks Gerasim and Iosif. As the extra-liturgical side of the Chapel's activities widened, the administration passed in 1749 to a nonclergyman—P. L. Chizhevsky, a former singer and rubrician (*ustavshchik*) who by then had the military rank of a colonel. The reform of 1763 created the post of Director of the Court Chapel, a civilian rank in the court administration; and the first to hold that post, from 1763 to 1796, was a former Chapel singer and precentor, Mark Fyodorovich Poltoratsky. At the same time, Empress Catherine instructed the new Italian *maestro di cappella* Baldassare Galuppi to assume artistic supervision of the Chapel.[67] Galuppi was evidently impressed with the Chapel Choir even before he took over as artistic director: upon hearing it for the first time, he is said to have remarked, "Un si magnifico coro mai non io sentito in Italia."[68]

On the basis of their study of the Imperial Chapel's archives[69] and other documents, Gusin and Tkachev observe that "from the first years of the reorganization [of 1763]...a noticeable change in [the Chapel's] repertoire and style of performance occurred in the direction of the Italianate style, which predominated at the court, and also penetrated into the main sphere of the Chapel's activity, church singing."[70] Galuppi and other foreigners in the service of the court even tried their hand at composing music for Orthodox services, using the latest Western European musical style;[71] and they continued the practice, established during the partesnyi period, of inserting sacred "choral concertos" into the services. While some concertos were based on liturgical or at least scriptural texts, such as the psalms, many were written on newly composed, quasi-religious texts that were as remote from traditional Orthodox hymnography as the music was from the old znamennyi chant.[72]

Excerpts from St. Petersburg newspapers and court journals show that in addition to church services the Court Chapel was active in extra-liturgical musical activities: "1762, February 9, the Court Singers performed Italian vocal and instrumental music. 1763, January 31, in the big opera house the Court Singers performed a Russian opera. 1764, March 7, . . . May 4, . . . May 20, . . . December 2, 5, and 6, the Court Singers performed music with the singing of arias."[73]

In the last quarter of the eighteenth century the Imperial Chapel began taking part in performances of Western European oratorios and cantatas: on 25 March 1774, they performed Pergolesi's *Stabat mater*, which was subsequently repeated a number of times; on 26 February 1779—Graun's *Te Deum*; on 5 March 1779—Hasse's *Salve regina*; and on 8 March 1779—Jomelli's *Passion*.[74] These performances, however, must have been of an occasional nature, for in 1782 Catherine issued an instruction making the Chapel's participation in operatic productions and concerts at the court mandatory.[75]

The broad spectrum of musical activities in which the Court Chapel participated under the tutelage of its Italian maestri helped to develop the ranks of well-trained Russian musicians—singers, instrumentalists, and even composers. At the same time, these musicians retained few, if any, links with their native musical culture—the ancient church chants and the equally ancient folk songs. Trained from earliest childhood in the Chapel's institutions, composers such as Dmitri Bortniansky (1751–1825), Maksim Berezovsky (1745–77), and Stepan Davydov (1777–1825), proved to be able students of Western European musical art; the former two were even sent to Italy to further their musical education. But as a consequence, their creative orientation and musical vocabulary were almost entirely European, as were the performance techniques mastered by the singers of the Court Chapel.

To what extent the performing traditions of the Imperial Court Chapel affected choral performance in the rest of Russia is the subject of some debate. On one hand, the Chapel was a closed, private establishment that primarily served the needs of the court. Most of its performances took place in court theaters and churches, or in private clubs such as the one formed in 1772 at the house of Kossakovsky in St. Petersburg. Thus, access to the Chapel's performances was limited to the highest echelons of St. Petersburg society.

On the other hand, the example of the Imperial court prompted many wealthy nobles and leading members of the church hierarchy to form their own choral and instrumental establishments, patterned after the Court Chapel. Some of these establishments were directed either by foreign

Kapellmeisters or by former musicians of the Court Chapel. An indication of the Chapel's influence outside its immediate sphere of activity is offered by Stählin:

> At the services of the...Russian Church,...[the singing is performed by] ordinary church chanters [*d'iachki*]...of whom there are two or three in each church. But at the Chapel of the Imperial court, in cathedral churches, monasteries, and house churches of noble families, in addition to these [chanters], there are usually special choirs of singers, called *pevchie*, who sing much more musically, in the style of motets....The [church] hierarchy—archbishops and metropolitans,...and archimandrites in their monasteries also maintain choirs of ten, twelve, and even twenty or more such musical singers....But it is impossible to imagine a more magnificent and perfect choir of church singers than the Imperial Court Chapel.[76]

In addition, Stählin mentions the existence of amateur choirs, composed mostly of young merchants and city-dwellers, which sang in churches where there were no professional choirs. In Stählin's words, these newly established choirs all imitated the style of the Court Chapel: "In a few years this 'improved' music [in the Italian style] spread from the court to other cathedrals and churches around the country."

The Moscow Synodal Choir in the Eighteenth Century

Not all church-music establishments in eighteenth-century Russia came under the influence of the Court Chapel's Italian style. The Patriarchal Singing Clerics evidently remained staunch adherents of the older, more liturgically oriented traditions. Well into the eighteenth century they remained an all-adult male ensemble,[77] and therefore did not have the descant and alto voices necessary to perform elaborate concerted compositions. At the same time, the Patriarchal Clerics suffered a tremendous loss of prestige during the eighteenth century, a fact symptomatic of the general decline experienced by the Church and its liturgical arts in the new Europeanized and secularized state molded by Peter the Great and his successors.

When Peter abolished the patriarchate in 1721, the Patriarchal Singing Clerics by a single legislative act were suddenly deprived of a patron and a reason for existing. In answer to what the Patriarchal Clerics' designation and duties should be, now that there was no patriarch, Peter wrote: "It seems they would be appropriately called the Singers of the Cathedral Church, and used wherever is seen fit, since, except for great feasts, I have no need of them."[78] Peter did not specify to which cathedral the singers were to be attached, or what their specific duties were to be. Of the forty-four singers that were on the staff in 1720, thirty-two were summoned to St. Petersburg, ostensibly to serve the members of the Holy Synod. The twelve singers remaining in Moscow were obviously in no position to continue a highly artistic tradition of singing, nor were the elaborate services that had taken place under the patriarch performed any longer. Three years later an Imperial order was issued to restore the ensemble to its former membership, whereupon inquiries were made regarding its makeup under the patriarchate. In 1725 the corps was reconstituted in Moscow at a strength of forty singers, divided, as before, into six teams, the first two with ten singers each, and the remaining four with five singers each. From the Patriarchal Clerics the singers were renamed the Synodal Singers (*Sinodal'nye Pevchie*), and assigned to sing in the Cathedral of the Dormition in the Moscow Kremlin. However, the singers' sense of purpose and discipline had evidently eroded considerably, necessitating, in 1727, the following instruction: "to come without fail to the Dormition Cathedral Church on Sundays and great feasts of the Lord and other major feasts for Vespers, Matins, and Liturgy, . . . and if any should not be there, to punish [them] severely."[79] In addition to the Dormition Cathedral, the Synodal Singers, in smaller contingents, had to sing in several other Kremlin churches and travel with the Metropolitan of Moscow, who until 1751 did not have his own personal choir. Furthermore, until 1763, they continued to bear the responsibility of serving in St. Petersburg in groups of twelve for a year at a time. Records from 1732 to 1763 contain numerous written requests from singers asking to be relieved of the year-long duty in the northern capital.

In 1763 the staff of the Synodal Choir was reduced to twenty-six singers, considered a sufficient number to serve the two Kremlin cathedrals—the Cathedral of the Dormition and the Church of the Twelve Apostles. Thus, the number of singers constituting an ensemble on each kliros could not have been larger than six or seven at any given time.

Exactly when treble boys' voices were introduced into the Synodal Choir is not clear. In 1752 a disciplinary reprimand noted that "only the old and the young come to services,"[80] but no details are given concerning the age of the "young" singers. A financial audit of 1763 showed that among the twenty-six singers were three *sopranist*s and two *altist*s.[81] How five boys' voices could have balanced twenty-one mature men's voices is difficult to imagine, unless the boys sang all together on one kliros in only one cathedral. An instruction from 1768 states that four adult singers were required to report daily to the Dormition Cathedral, while the boys were to report to the Cathedral of the Twelve Apostles.

The performances of the Synodal Choir at this time were far from exemplary, as evidenced from a rare "review" dated 8 August 1765: "During services the antiphonal [*krylosskoe*], plain [*prostoe*], and part [*partesnoe*] singing was executed very unharmoniously by reason of certain abrupt and wild voices, [which sang] so out-of-tune that no melody attributable to music could be discerned therein."[82] In 1767 twelve more singers were added to the Synodal Choir, bringing the total to thirty-eight. By 1782, twelve singers were under fifteen years of age, improving the balance of parts slightly but still considerably favoring the adult male voices. In 1804–5 the Synodal Choir was almost eliminated for economic reasons: a fire had gutted the wooden dwellings where the singers lived, and a capital outlay was required to construct new quarters of stone. "Long-standing tradition" was the only reason cited for continuing the Choir's existence.

The history of the Synodal Choir through the eighteenth century, culminating in its near demise, epitomizes the decline experienced by church-supported musical establishments at this time. In spite of its historical importance and stature, the Synodal Choir was reduced to a pitiful, subordinate position, forced to supply singers to St. Petersburg and having its staff increased and decreased arbitrarily by Imperial decrees and budget-minded bureaucrats. Under such conditions the Choir could hardly have cultivated or even maintained high standards of ensemble performance. There is no evidence that the Choir had a school, which would have disseminated its performing traditions beyond its immediate sphere of activity. Not a single prominent composer or conductor was associated with the Synodal Choir in the eighteenth century. Even the Choir's repertoire cannot be determined with any certainty.

However, what may have seemed a misfortune for the Synodal Choir at the time turned out to be a fortunate circumstance for the future of church singing in Russia. Neglected by the authorities in St. Petersburg, the Moscow Synodal Choir escaped the ubiquitous Western influence of the Imperial Court Chapel to some degree. Having no means of cultivating a technically oriented artistic tradition, the Choir concentrated on maintaining the liturgical side of its tradition, perhaps preserving some vestiges of native Russian singing style until the late nineteenth century, when it was once again thrust into a position of prominence.

Other Vocal Establishments in the Eighteenth Century

Information concerning eighteenth-century Russian vocal or choral establishments other than the Imperial Court Chapel and the Moscow Synodal Choir is very fragmentary. Towards the end of the seventeenth century some church hierarchs are known to have founded musical establishments modelled on those of the Tsar and the Patriarch, presumably for the purposes of liturgical singing—although some bishops (many of whom in the post-Nikon era were from the Ukraine) openly supported and cultivated concert-style partesnyi singing.[83] Few details are known concerning the numbers, composition, or repertoire of these archiepiscopal establishments. In 1721 an Imperial decree summoned the best singers from the cathedrals of Tver', Voronezh, Nizhnii-Novgorod, and Kazan', for service in St. Petersburg. Evidently the numbers in each ensemble were determined by a fixed budget, for the decree elicited complaints from diocesan archbishops who could not hire new singers, yet had to support the livelihood of those serving in St. Petersburg. The only other mention of archiepiscopal choirs occurs in Stählin's account cited earlier.

The other category of musical establishments in the eighteenth century were private chapels maintained by prominent nobles and courtiers. The present state of research in this area permits only a general description of these chapels, together with a partial list of noble patrons who maintained them. Very little is known concerning private chapels in the seventeenth and the first half of the eighteenth centuries. Only the Stroganov family is known for certain to have maintained a musical establishment at that time, although undoubtedly there were others. In the reign of Catherine the Great, however, a great vogue developed for keeping private chapels: according to Findeizen, many of Catherine's prominent courtiers—the Counts Pyotr and Nikolai Sheremetev, Grigory Orlov, Aleksei Razumovsky, and Grigory Potemkin—all maintained chapels, first founded in the 1760s or 1770s. (Potemkin employed Giuseppe Sarti as *maestro di cappella* for several years.) In addition, Findeizen lists about a dozen other lesser officials and nobles in the provinces who maintained both vocal chapels and orchestras.[84]

Factual information concerning the makeup, training, and repertoire of these chapels is very scarce. Generally, they were constituted from a small number of the patron's serfs and domestic servants, specially trained for the purpose by hired conductors who were almost without exception foreigners. Neither the conductors nor the musicians possessed any social status: the former were on a par with lackeys and cooks, while the latter were just a step above farm animals. Numerous accounts exist of serf musicians being rented, bought, and sold like any other personal property.[85] As a rule, the major concern of the household chapel was instrumental music; however, a certain number of musicians were also trained to sing. Newspapers of the time contain advertisements offering and requesting the services of singers for both church and domestic choirs. Some wealthy landowners evidently turned a healthy profit by training singers and leasing them on a yearly basis to various city churches.

As Findeizen points out, the domestic musical establishments were not natural manifestations of cultural and artistic growth in Russian society; they were merely slavish imitations of the almighty fashion of the Imperial court and its Chapel, and disappeared when the vogue for them passed. However, during the fifty years from aproximately 1775 to 1825, when these institutions were particularly widespread, they had a profound impact upon the status of church music and choral musicians in Russia.

With the exception of the Imperial Court Chapel, the Moscow Synodal Choir and the small number of archiepiscopal and monastic choirs, the domestic chapels were the only musical establishments where vocal ensemble and choral music was cultivated in Russia at the time. In all these institutions music was regarded from a purely practical, utilitarian standpoint: no opportunities existed to study music historically, theoretically, or in terms of aesthetics, whereby one could develop some notion of musical taste. In the case of private chapels, the factors that determined a patron's support of the arts were, more than likely, social prestige and an abundance of capital, rather than a genuine knowledge and appreciation of music. Patrons were seldom in a position to evaluate the qualifications of their conductors or to judge the artistic merits of their work; virtually the only qualification needed by a conductor was that he have a foreign-sounding name. The ready availability of performers under the patron's total control led to the spread of musical dilettantism and low-quality repertoire, which in church music became marked by total disregard for matters of style and liturgical propriety.

If the works composed by Galuppi, Sarti, and other Italians for church services at the court at least possessed a consistency of style and a high degree of musical literacy, the works produced by their provincial imitators were beneath all criticism from the standpoint of quality. Liturgical texts were set to arias from Italian operas with the orchestral accompaniment arranged for the remaining voices; grandiose concertlike settings, filled with meaningless vocal fioriture, appeared at the most solemn points in the liturgy. Many of these "essays" into the art of composition did not fulfill the most elementary standards of musical coherence and compositional technique. Some of the works written at this time, instead of composers' names, bear subtitles that aptly characterize their musical value: *"Otche nash"—ptichka* ("Our Father"—birdie), *"Kheruvimskaia"—veselaia* ("Cherubic hymn"—a merry song), *"Milost' mira"—s cherdaka* ("A mercy of peace"—down from the attic), etc.[86] In provincial churches these works gained such a strong foothold that many of them have remained in use to this day. Church choirs in parishes where everything, from the priest's and precentor's salaries to the maintenance of the building itself, was supported by the local landowner and "patron of the arts," had no choice but to sing these pseudo-musical creations, catering to the corrupt tastes of the time and perpetuating them for generations to come.

Another unfortunate effect of domestic chapels, which, like the low-quality repertoire, would persist throughout most of the nineteenth century, was the extremely low social status of both singers and precentors. Music-making in domestic chapels carried with it all the negative aspects of serfdom: compulsory service, harsh discipline, and total lack of respect for the individual. Only in a few exceptional instances were individuals with superior musical talent recognized and rewarded by emancipation: such were the cases of the composer Stepan Degtiarev (1766–1813), who for most of his life was a serf of Count Sheremetev, and the violin virtuoso Ivan Khandoshkin (1747–1804).

By far the greatest victims of the system were the young boys who constituted the soprano and alto sections of the choral chapels. Separated from their families, housed, clothed, and fed under conditions that were frequently unsanitary because of budgetary considerations, exposed to unsavory moral influences from the adult men in the choir, these boys were mercilessly drilled, often by means of the rod, to perform music they did not comprehend and for which they did not receive appropriate vocal or musical training. During their tenure in the choir they did not receive any significant general education; and when their voices changed, they were literally discarded and turned out into the streets without any means of earning a living. The more fortunate ones resumed singing, but even so, they remained on the lowest rung of the social and economic ladder. Throughout the nineteenth century, the term *pevchii* (choir singer) became synonymous with a social pariah—a person of low education, crude manners, tainted morals, and who was usually a drunkard.

The exploitation of child and adult labor was particularly prevalent in the "commercial" choral establishments that arose in the larger cities towards the end of the eighteenth century. As the demand increased for elaborate concert-style church singing, entrepreneurs known as *khorosoderzhateli* (lit. choir keepers) assembled large groups of singers and hired them out to various churches. In the nineteenth century some of these establishments numbered up to one hundred and fifty singers, though for singing in churches they divided into small contingents of ten to fifteen. The chief goal of the choir keeper was to make money, so it was not uncommon for the singers to rise at five or six in the morning and sing as many as two or three Divine Liturgies a day at different churches. Another profitable source of income was private offices: funerals, for which the singers had to accompany the casket from the church to the cemetery, on foot and bare-headed even in the bitter cold of winter; and weddings, at which the singers were expected also to provide musical entertainment at the wedding receptions which often lasted far into the night. Needless to say, this regimen was not conducive to either vocal or general health.

Contemporary accounts provide some insight into the level of choral singing produced by private entrepreneurial choirs and of the public's attitude towards choral church singing in the late eighteenth century. In a letter to his son, Bulgakov (Catherine the Great's Ambassador to Constantinople) describes a scene typical for Moscow at this time: "The splendid singers of Kazakov, who now belong to Beketov, sing in the Church of St. Dimitri Solunsky in Moscow. There is such a congregation, that the entire Tverskoi Boulevard is jammed with carriages. On a recent occasion the worshippers descended to such shamelessness, that they shouted *'fora!'* (i.e., bravo) in church. Fortunately, the owner had the good sense to lead the singers out, or even greater indecency would have ensued."[87] Another account, dated 1805, possibly referring to the same incident, contains an interesting detail—that private choirs at this time included women's voices:

> [In Beketov's choir] a certain girl by the name of Anisia (who was, incidentally, quite homely) distinguished herself by her beautiful voice and almost theatrical manner of singing. The choir was singing... *"Dostoino est"* [It is truly meet] and towards the end Anisia with her solo and, moreover, with her roulades so amazed both the pious and worldly listeners, that one of the latter, a certain Prince Vizankur—a baptized Hindu,... began to applaud in some kind of violent rapture.... The Chief of Police Alekseev made him leave.... [88]

Fascination with the Italian concert style had evidently undermined the long-standing tradition of restricting church singing to men and boys.[89]

As the above accounts show, the elaborate Italianate concert style found favor in certain circles of high Russian society. The question remains, however, to what extent Russian servant girls and peasant men and boys truly mastered the technical complexities of Italian bel canto and coloratura singing. Such mastery was possible in the Imperial Court Chapel perhaps; but elsewhere, in household chapels and city churches, attempts to imitate the court style frequently bordered on the grotesque, as the following report suggests:

> If, in singing the... fast-moving, jerky compositions [in the partesnyi and Italian style], they at least demonstrate some artistry, then it is not so repulsive—especially if the singers are Little Russians [Ukrainians] with naturally good voices. But now even our Great Russians—merchants, house servants, factory and textile workers, and various artisans,...—have taken to singing these same ridiculous works... and, at times, it is pathetic to listen as one Russian dolt, a bass, opening his huge maw, screams in rapid chatter, like a clanging tocsin; and if after a pause he has to take a high note, he does it so unskillfully, [that it sounds] like a neighing stallion; while on cut-offs he will cut so ungracefully, like a roaring bull.[90]

Another writer adds: "How much more beautiful and pleasant it would be to listen, if they would sing quietly, without torturing the voice; but our Russian rascals, unlashing their Adam's apples, scream at the top of their lungs."[91]

For all the enthusiasm they demonstrated towards the newly introduced activity of choral singing, the broad masses of Russians clearly lacked the sense of measure and culture necessary for genuine musical art. The old traditions of what was proper in church singing had been lost amidst the vast changes that occurred in Russia from the time of Peter the Great, while new standards of propriety had not yet had time to develop. Lacking technical refinement and good taste, the provincial choirs blatantly exploited the most obvious features of the Italian style: dramatic expression and vocal virtuosity. In some Russian choirs such manifestations of corrupt taste became so consistent that they took on the character of an identifiable style, a style marked by extreme and sudden changes of dynamics, bravura displays in the extreme upper registers (particularly by basses and tenors) or the extreme low registers (by bass "octavists"),[92] deafening fortissimo singing, and similar excesses.[93]

The Influence of the Imperial Court Chapel under Bortniansky

The first attempts to purge Russian church singing of the improprieties that had penetrated it occurred in the reign of Catherine the Great's successor, Paul I (reigned 1796–1801). In 1797 the Holy Synod issued a decree banning the performance of concerts on nonliturgical texts, and stipulating that only the prescribed communion hymn or a psalm be sung at that point.[94] In 1804 another decree was issued, this time by Emperor Alexander I himself (reigned 1801–25), charging diocesan hierarchs with the responsibility of seeing that the singing in their dioceses was performed properly.[95] These initial efforts to restore some measure of dignity to church singing were spearheaded by Dmitri Bortniansky (1751–1825), the first native Russian to achieve major stature as a composer in the post-Westernization era.

Bortniansky was connected in some fashion with the Imperial Court Chapel throughout his entire life. He began his musical education at the Chapel's preparatory school in Glukhov; and in 1758 (at the tender age of seven) was already sent to the court, where he became a member of a special select group of chamber vocalists (*kamer-pevchie*). After receiving his first lessons in composition from Galuppi, he was sent to Italy in 1769 to continue his musical studies. During the eleven years he spent abroad, at least three of Bortniansky's operas were performed in Italian theaters. Summoned back to Russia, he was appointed conductor at the Imperial Chapel as well as conductor at the court of Prince Paul, the heir to the throne. With Paul's enthronement in 1796, Bortniansky became Director of the Vocal Music and Manager of the Chapel, and, in 1801, Director of the entire Chapel musical establishment.

Bortniansky's appointment in 1796 as Director of the Vocal Music did not occur under very favorable circumstances. The following year the number of singers was reduced from eighty to twenty-four, with a simultaneous reduction in the salaries of the remaining singers. This may have been the result of Emperor Paul's manifest antipathy towards everything that had been advocated and patronized by Catherine. Bortniansky, in fact, was one of the very few individuals favored by Catherine who not only survived, but was actually promoted in Paul's administration. It is also possible that the measure was prompted by Bortniansky himself in an effort to phase out the Chapel's participation in opera productions. If, indeed, that was

Bortniansky's plan, it was successful: by 1800 a separate chorus was established for the court opera, while in 1801 the Chapel's numbers were increased to forty.[96] The newly reconstituted Chapel was no longer required to participate in theatrical productions.

During Bortniansky's tenure, the Imperial Court Chapel developed into an outstanding choral ensemble. By 1817 the number of fully salaried singers had increased to twenty-four boys and twenty-four men. In addition, there were sixty supernumeraries (thirty boys and thirty men), bringing the total to 108. Bortniansky possessed great administrative skills in addition to his musical abilities. During his tenure he succeeded in establishing a program of general as well as musical education for the boys of the Chapel, and made it possible for them to enter the civil service after their voices changed. Service in the Chapel under Bortniansky took on a measure of dignity and security that was quite unique for the choral profession in Russia at that time. Parents willingly consigned their children to the Chapel's ranks, so recruiting the best voices was never a problem.

Some writers have suggested that the Imperial Chapel under Bortniansky began to cultivate a specific style and manner of singing that was distinctly "churchly." Stepan Smolensky, who as Superintendent of the Imperial Chapel from 1901 to 1903 may have had access to specific documentary evidence (which he does not cite, however), states that Bortniansky trained the Chapel to sing sonorously, with thorough nuances and with excellent diction, while eliminating shouting and other grotesque effects.[97] Such attributes are certainly characteristic of a fine choir; but they do not in themselves define a "churchly" style. Nikolai Uspensky's observation (in reference to Bortniansky's activities) that "church music . . . has its own stylistic features and characteristic sound, as opposed to operatic singing, . . ."[98] while certainly true in a general sense, also does not give any clues as to what these distinguishing features may have been in Bortniansky's time.

In fact, Bortniansky's entire musical orientation—as a vocalist, conductor, and composer—was thoroughly Italian, and could scarcely have been otherwise in light of his training. What distinguished him from his Italian predecessors and their provincial Russian imitators was an attitude of reverence for the Orthodox liturgy and sensitivity to the bounds of good taste that should not be exceeded in church under any circumstances. On the strength of these qualities, coupled with an unquestionably well-polished compositional technique, Bortniansky succeeded in establishing himself as the sole authority and chief censor over all Russian church music.

The legal machinery set in motion by Bortniansky ensured that his compositions would continue to be the stylistic standards for Russian church music for nearly a century. In 1815 he compiled and published a two-voice setting of the Court Chant,[99] heretofore transmitted only by oral tradition, in order to encourage the "universal adoption of simple and standardized choral singing."[100] Concurrently, Bortniansky was to instruct all St. Petersburg precentors in the Court Chant. Singers from the Chapel were assigned to serve as precentors and singing instructors in other choirs. By 1824, twenty-two court singers were leading choirs in eight military regiments, nine institutes, the University, and four private chapels.[101]

Thus, under Bortniansky's administration the Imperial Court Chapel gradually expanded its role from being merely the private choral establishment of the ruling monarch to that of an institution actively influencing, and eventually controlling, church choral singing in the entire Russian Empire. As an authoritative musical-artistic entity with strong aesthetic appeal, the Chapel fostered the notion that singing in all churches should be choral; and by a series of legislative measures it acquired the legal means to define and enforce its standards for what that choral singing should be. The most important measure in this regard was a decree, issued on 14 February 1816, that gave Bortniansky as Director of the Imperial Chapel unprecedented powers of censorship over all music written for church use:

> The Emperor, on discovering that many churches use [manuscript] scores... that do not correspond to the sort of singing that is acceptable in churches, has supremely decreed: that henceforth the use of manuscript notebooks... is strictly forbidden, and everything sung in churches from [sheet] music must be in printed form, and must consist either of the personal compositions of the Director of the [Imperial] Choir,... Bortniansky, or the compositions of other famous composers, but the compositions of the latter may only be printed with the approval of Bortniansky.... The Director of the Ministry of Police [is instructed] to issue circulating injunctions to government authorities against the further publication of church-musical compositions without the approval of the Director of the Imperial Choir....[102]

The decree was prompted, at least in part, by Bortniansky's genuine desire to curtail the violations of liturgical propriety and the general excesses of the Catherinian epoch. At the same time, in the hands of Bortniansky's successors this decree was to have a profoundly stultifying effect on the creative development of Russian choral church music.

Outside the realm of church music Bortniansky continued the Imperial Chapel's extra-liturgical concert activity, which undoubtedly served to raise the level of its musicianship and vocal technique. No longer involved in operatic productions, the choir focused on performing Western European sacred choral masterworks: Haydn's *Creation* (1802) and *The Seasons* (1805), Mozart's *Requiem* (1805), Handel's *Messiah* (1806), Mozart's *Davidde penitente* (1807), Cherubini's first Mass (1810), Beethoven's *Christus im Oelberge* (1813), and one of Cherubini's Requiems (1820). In 1824 the Imperial Chapel gave the world premiere of Beethoven's *Missa solemnis*. In addition, the Chapel gave concerts of unaccompanied choral works in palace concert halls and in its own concert hall built in 1810 on Moika Street in St.

Petersburg. Beyond immediate court circles the Chapel's rehearsals on Saturday afternoons, which were open to the public, became important events in the musical life of the capital.

Summary

The period from approximately 1650 to 1825 was a time when choral part-singing became a relatively widespread phenomenon in Russia. However, it was introduced "from the top," i.e., through the Court Chapel. The royalty and aristocracy themselves never had a tradition of convivial vocal music-making, but relegated the performing function to the lowest servant classes. For a long time the educated middle classes and lay congregations in cities and villages did not participate in choral singing either. City dwellers turned their attention to instrumental music and sentimental solo songs (*rossiiskie pesni* and romances), while the rural peasantry remained totally out of contact with all traditions of art music. Conversely, the two spheres where the greatest amount of choral activity occurred, the Court Chapel and the domestic chapels, took no account of native Russian folk song or ecclesiastical chant. In the words of Preobrazhensky, "it is difficult to imagine two musical disciplines more drastically opposed . . . than Italian music of the eighteenth century and Russian folk singing."[103]

Thus, in its initial stages choral singing in Russia was not a natural phenomenon from either a sociological or cultural standpoint. Like an exotic plant transplanted into an alien environment, it flourished first in the rarefied atmosphere of the Imperial Court Chapel, tended by imported foreign caretakers. When it finally emerged into broader surroundings, the hybrid offshoots it produced were not necessarily beautiful or refined, even if they proved to be hardy and enduring.

Choral singing came to Russia from Western Europe at a time when the state of the art was in decline, both from the standpoint of composition and performance. As the wave of the Enlightenment swept Europe, church music, which had been the major arena for choral performance from the mid-fifteenth century, fell steadily into disrepute, and the church choirs and court chapels where choral singing had been cultivated disintegrated rapidly. The Italian *maestri di cappella*, invited to Russia for the sole purpose of producing operas, brought with them the musical style of the operatic stage, but they were certainly not equipped to impart the past riches of European choral church music. Through their limited involvement with Russian church music, they merely succeeded in demonstrating that the current Italianate style could be adapted in practice to choral forces without instrumental accompaniment. This unlikely union between the Italian secular style and the Orthodox

Church's demand for unaccompanied singing, which happened almost by chance, was the seed that produced the modern Russian choral style. In a strange twist of irony, within a few decades European choral establishments were looking to the Russian Imperial Chapel as a model for restoring their own traditions of choral performance.

3

The Emergence of a National Choral Style

From the death of Bortniansky in 1825 to the early 1880s, Russian musicians gradually mastered and internalized the Western European musical language, moving from imitation towards autonomous musical creativity that drew upon indigenous Russian musical material. The base of support for music and other arts, which had previously consisted almost exclusively of aristocratic court circles, gradually broadened to include a growing middle class of merchants and city dwellers. Musical institutions—including orchestras, opera theaters, and public concert societies—arose, catering to the aesthetic demands of this new audience, and conservatories opened to staff these organizations. In short, Russian musical life was developing a close resemblance to that of other European nations.

As Russia's musical culture became increasingly Europeanized, however, the choral culture suffered a concomitant loss of prominence. Whereas in the eighteenth century choral music had been the prime vehicle by which new and "progressive" foreign musical elements entered Russia, throughout most of the nineteenth century choral music played only a small and rather insignificant role in the emergence of a Russian national style. Church music in particular remained segregated from the vital developments that were occurring in other branches of Russian music.

As mentioned in chapter 2, in the seventeenth and eighteenth centuries the field of choral and vocal ensemble singing had split into two distinct and rarely interacting streams. One stream, by far the weaker of the two, was a continuation of the age-old, native Russian vocal genres—liturgical chant and the folk song. Although these genres were not cultivated in artistic performances, to the extent they were practiced in churches and social gatherings, they preserved the melodies as well as the rhythms, textures, sonorities, and methods of performance that were distinctively Russian. The other stream consisted of the technically polished but musically superficial style of choral part-singing in imitation of the Western manner. Even after a century and a half this style remained alien despite its widespread presence: both the literature and the function of choral part-singing were derived from foreign forms, fostering equally foreign performance techniques. A national school of choral performance could not emerge until Russian musicians, both composers and performers, came to recognize—either through instinct or through scholarly investigation—the unique characteristics of original Russian vocal forms and to develop a choral literature that embodied these forms.

The greater portion of the nineteenth century witnessed efforts in this direction in both church and secular choral music. Results appeared earlier in the secular field, since the secular folk song fortuitously entered art music by way of the developing Russian opera. The path of liturgical chant was more circuitous and thorny. The gulf between the aesthetic principles of chant and Western choral polyphony had become as immense as the differences between the theocentric world of Medieval Muscovy and the secularized, Europeanized Russian Empire of the nineteenth century. Merely to penetrate the neumatic notation of znamennyi chant required considerable effort, to say nothing of rediscovering the chant's structure and underlying aesthetic principles. Moreover, entirely new approaches had to be sought out for adapting this ancient melos to contemporary choral forms. Some efforts in this direction, such as attempts to apply the "strict style" of Palestrinian counterpoint to the chants, proved to be based upon faulty premises and led into artistic dead ends. Lastly, before newly fashioned artistic forms could become the basis for a living performance tradition, the technical side of choral performance had to be mastered more fully. The stylistic evolution of Russian sacred choral music during the nineteenth century has been discussed extensively elsewhere[1] and thus will not be described in detail here. Instead, the discussion will focus on the effects of these developments upon the area of choral performance.

The Imperial Court Chapel under Fyodor L'vov

After Bortniansky's death the directorship of the Imperial Court Chapel was assumed by Fyodor L'vov (1766–1836), who occupied the post until his death. In the late 1820s the excellence of the Imperial Chapel still inspired emulation not only in Russia, but abroad as well. In 1829 the King of Prussia, Friedrich Wilhelm III, wishing to pattern the reorganization of his own regimental choirs and the Berlin Dom-Chor after the Russian Chapel, dispatched to St. Petersburg one Captain Einbeck to observe and report on the Chapel's musical and administrative programs. Einbeck attended choir rehearsals, music lessons, and church services, and gave very high marks to the Chapel's activities. According to his report, the excellence of the Chapel was attributable to the following factors:

1. All singers had exceptionally fine voices
2. All voices were trained according to the best Italian method
3. All sections and soloists had a superb knowledge of their parts
4. The Imperial Chapel, as a special government-supported church choir, constituted a single artistic entity not affected by external circumstances, with the singers not having to devote their time to outside activities.[2]

Although Bortniansky had been dead for four years, Einbeck correctly attributed these qualities to the late Director's legacy.

Very shortly after Bortniansky's death, however, the situation changed for the worse. Fyodor L'vov repeatedly complained to the Emperor that "there are insufficient funds to give the young singers a decent education. The children are only taught to sing, without any other education. The [financial] situation of the singers is difficult, and the salaries are too small."[3] Even the musical training of the singers showed signs of deterioration. When in 1837 Mikhail Glinka, already a renowned composer, was appointed "*Kapell-meister* to the Chapel,"[4] he found that many singers could not read music. He writes in his notes,

> Shortly after my appointment I undertook to teach them music [i.e., sight-singing] and to correct their intonation. . . . When I arrived for the first time, chalk in hand, there were few volunteers; the majority of the adult singers stood at a distance with a skeptical air, and some even snickered. Ignoring this, I went to work with such energy and, I must say, such cleverness, that after a few lessons almost all the adult singers, even those who took other private lessons, came to my lectures.[5]

Thus, Bortniansky, despite his remarkable tenure, did not impart to his successor any firm pedagogical and methodological foundations that would have ensured the Chapel's continued excellence. After Bortniansky's death, which coincided with the end of Alexander I's reign, not only did the musical quality of the Chapel deteriorate, but Russian church music embarked upon a different artistic course, reflecting ideas expressed by Fyodor L'vov in his book entitled *O penii v Rossii* [Singing in Russia]:

> Italian singing . . . by its array of sounds leads a sensitive person to sweet self-oblivion. . . . [But] no learned complexity of voices and instruments will remind me why I am standing in God's temple. . . . Any honest thought is simple [and], therefore, convincing. . . . Sacred melodies must be, without exception, short and fixed invariably, so that they would become rooted in the memory and not distract one's attention with either novelty or variety; they must be simple and inspired by heart-warming fire, inflaming the heart and elevating the spirit![6]

In criticizing the artfulness of the Italian concert style L'vov advocated a return to the ostensible "pious simplicity" of native Russian chant, thereby steering choral church singing away from continued artistic development. As Preobrazhensky points out, the fact that a strong condemnation of the Italian style occurred within the Imperial Court Chapel, the very institution that had nurtured that style, would prove to be a significant factor in the future direction of Russian sacred music.[7] For while the Imperial Chapel rejected its own artistic accomplishments, no other musical institution in Russia could provide an alternative artistic direction. The only other tradition of choral performance of the time—the musically unsophisticated chanting of rank-and-file chanters (*diachki*) in improvised harmony—had been allowed to deteriorate for so long that it could not be the source of a well-ordered national tradition of church singing. Despite Bortniansky's accomplishments at the Imperial Chapel, it essentially became necessary to begin at the beginning: to establish Russian traditions of choral performance by developing an indigenous Russian choral literature, and by training ranks of Russian precentors and choral conductors. The burden of these formidable tasks fell largely upon Aleksei Fyodorovich L'vov (1798–1870), Fyodor's son, who in 1837 became Director of the Imperial Court Chapel.

The Imperial Court Chapel under Aleksei L'vov

The younger L'vov attained his high office not because he had any special expertise or interest in church music, but more as a result of his personal closeness to Emperor Nicholas I. An engineer and military officer by training, he had entered the Tsar's service as an aide in charge of travel and communications, and in 1833 won Nicholas's special favor by composing the hymn "God Save the Tsar," which became the Russian national anthem. Trained in music by private German tutors, L'vov became a highly accomplished amateur violinist. In the course of his travels with the Emperor he met the leading European musicians of his time, including Mendelssohn, Meyerbeer, Spontini, and Fétis, and received numerous awards and honorary memberships from various Western European musical academies. Predictably, his musical orientation and taste were totally Western European, with a strong predilection for German Romanticism; throughout his life he remained totally estranged from the concerns and achievements of the emerging nationalist movement in Russian music.

In selecting L'vov to be the new Director of the Imperial Chapel, Nicholas I was undoubtedly motivated by his own close personal ties with him and by L'vov's international reputation as a musician. Having a penchant for discipline and order in all things, Nicholas desired to establish a uniform standard of church singing throughout his realm (patterned, of course, after his own Imperial Chapel). He knew L'vov to be a faithful courtier and a reliable administrator to whom he could entrust this formidable task. The Tsar's personal support increased still further the vast influence, in the form of censorship powers, that L'vov possessed as Director of the Chapel.

In his monograph on Aleksei L'vov, Johann von Gardner identifies eight major points upon which L'vov focused his attention in the course of his directorship:

1. To raise the level of general musical education among the singers of the Imperial Court Chapel
2. To develop a systematic program for teaching the precentor's trade to capable singers of the Imperial Court Chapel as well as to candidates from regimental and diocesan choirs
3. To establish a strict and thorough control over the repertoire and quality of church choirs
4. To exercise strict censorship over all new music being composed for Russian church choirs
5. To bring all plain church singing [i.e., the daily chant propers] into uniformity, using the [harmonized] renditions of the Imperial Court Chapel as a model
6. To set in four-part harmony [for mixed voices] the entire yearly cycle of liturgical chants [as sung at the Imperial Court]
7. To set in four-part harmony the entire contents of the square-note chant books, making these settings mandatory and exclusive for all church choirs in Russia
8. To set down in musical notation chants still sung according to oral tradition in certain ancient monasteries and cathedrals, preserving them from being lost and corrupted.[8]

As Director of the Imperial Chapel, L'vov had the resources and the administrative power to carry out the gargantuan task of harmonizing the full yearly cycle of liturgical chants and disseminating the harmonizations. The actual work was executed by three of the Chapel's assistants—Ivan Belikov, Pavel Vorotnikov, and Gavriil Lomakin—following guidelines set down by L'vov. In his memoirs L'vov describes the limitations he imposed upon the artistic process: "Herein [there is] nothing of my own composition and, indeed, should not be anything besides the preserved chants and the correct application to them of four-part harmony."[9]

The hundreds of chant harmonizations poured from the same mold by L'vov and his assistants were, predictably, colorless and dull (see ex. 3.1). Moreover, the chants were not always rendered accurately or clearly, a point that raised the objections of some leading churchmen. The factor that

Example 3.1. Harmonized Court Chant—Vesper Psalm "*Gospodi, vozzvakh*"
[Lord, I call] in Tone 3.
Source: *Obikhod prostogo tserkovnogo penya, pri Vysochaishem
Dvore upotrebliaemogo* [The Common Chants of plain
church singing used at the Imperial Court]
(St. Petersburg: Pridvornaia Pevcheskaia Kapella, 1914).

(Lord, I call upon Thee, hear me. Hear me, O Lord.
Lord, I call upon Thee, hear me.
Receive the voice of my prayer, when I cry unto Thee.
Hear me, O Lord.)

ultimately determined the acceptance of L'vov's work, however, was the
opinion of Nicholas I. At a performance of the Imperial Chapel that included
some of L'vov's harmonizations the Emperor inquired, "Is this the unison
singing to which you are applying harmony?" "Exactly so," answered L'vov.
The Emperor took L'vov by the hand and said, "Here is the unity that I desire.
Thank you, thank you," to which L'vov replied, "I am your disciple. Your
approval is everything to me."[10]

L'vov's *Obikhod*[11] *prostogo tserkovnogo peniia, pri Vysochaishem
Dvore upotrebliaemogo* [The common chants of plain church singing used at

the Imperial Court] was published in 1848, and by Imperial decree was sent to all dioceses with the instruction that, whenever any member of the Royal Family happened to be present, it was to be used exclusively. Presumably, if a member of the royalty were not in attendance, the *Obikhod* did not have to be followed; however, L'vov agressively promulgated the adoption of it and the rest of the Chapel's repertoire throughout Russia by a series of other measures. Most effective in this regard was the Chapel's program of training and certifying church precentors (which will be discussed in detail in chapter 5).

Besides establishing strict control over the musical training and creative activity of church precentors, L'vov sought to control the repertoire of church choirs by actively exercising his powers of censorship. Under Bortniansky and Fyodor L'vov, enforcement of the Decree of 1816 had been largely left to diocesan bishops and individual parish priests. The prohibition against freely composed concerto-style works was evidently not too successful, for in 1850 the Holy Synod issued yet another decree prohibiting "the singing during Divine Liturgy of musical compositions [composed] in recent times, either printed or in manuscript, known as concertos, instead of the appointed Communion Verse."[12] But the most forceful legal statement of the official policy concerning church repertoire was written into the Imperial Codex of Laws, issued in 1846, which read: "New church musical compositions shall not be introduced anywhere in Orthodox churches without the prior approval of the Director of the Imperial Court Chapel, while those approved shall be used only in printed form and with the permission of the Holy Synod."[13]

With the same diligence and tenacity that characterized all his other undertakings, Aleksei L'vov assumed surveillance over the repertoire of church choirs in Russia, issuing "injunctions of the utmost strictness" and, at times, calling upon the police to enforce them. During his twenty-four years as Director, the only compositions added to those already approved under Bortniansky were his own.[14] The full consequences of the Chapel's censorship may be seen from a list of approved works published in 1871 (ten years after L'vov's retirement) which contains the works of only six composers— Bortniansky, L'vov, Maksim Berezovsky (one title), Makarov (one title), Gribovich (three titles), and Vorotnikov (thirteen titles).[15] The censorship process was so intimidating that individuals not connected directly with the Chapel did not even bother to submit works for consideration.

The tyranny of censorship, which continued under L'vov's successor, Nikolai Bakhmetev (1807–91, director from 1861 to 1883), was clearly a major factor that discouraged composers such as Dargomyzhsky, Serov, Borodin, and Musorgsky from writing anything for the Orthodox Church.[16]

The prevailing conservatism in the area of church repertoire extended to the Chapel's concert performances as well. Six concerts of Orthodox sacred music given privately at the court in the years 1847 and 1848 featured only the works of Bortnianksy, Galuppi, Sarti, Makarov, L'vov, and Vorotnikov. The same composers appeared on programs in the 1870s, with the addition of a few selections from the *Obikhod*.[17]

Outside the sphere of Russian liturgical music, the Choir of the Imperial Chapel continued to participate in performances of Western European cantatas and oratorios put on by the Philharmonic Society. In 1850 L'vov established an independent Concert Association within the Chapel for the purpose of "performing classical works to the highest possible perfection, directing the proceeds to [musical] artists' widows and orphans and to the furtherance of art." The programs included the finest examples of Western European music, both symphonic and choral-orchestral.[18]

The technical side of the Imperial Chapel's performances under L'vov was marked by a high degree of excellence, as evidenced by accolades from visiting foreign musicians. After hearing the Chapel in 1838, Adolphe Charles Adan called it "a wondrous vocal orchestra!... The doubling of the fundamental [by the octavists]... gives the ensemble a type of mellowness that is unknown in our vocal groups, [and] makes this choir resemble a grandiose organ, the magnificence and effect of which upon an impressionable listener's nervous system is beyond description."[19] Hector Berlioz, who visited Russia in 1847, was even more effusive:

> In our time we have no doubt that the Choir of Court Singers in Russia surpasses all choirs that exist at this moment in the entire world. The Chapel... performs works in four, six, and eight parts, sometimes in a rather fast tempo complicated by the difficulties of the figured style, at other times, in an extremely slow [tempo], with calm and divine expression that demands an assuredness and endurance of voices such as one does not often encounter, and which, in my opinion, surpasses everything that we have in Europe of this nature.... To compare the choral performance in the Sistine Chapel in Rome with these wondrous singers is the same as comparing a miserable little troupe of fiddlers in a third-rate Italian theater with the orchestra of the Paris Conservatoire. The effect of the music performed by this choir upon nervous people is irresistible. At those incredible accents you feel that you are being overwhelmed, almost to the point of pain, by a nervous state that you don't know how to control. Several times I attempted in these circumstances to remain calm, straining my will power, but I could never succeed.[20]

Robert Schumann in 1844 noted in his diary: "The Chapel is the most wonderful choir that we have ever had the occasion of hearing: the basses at times remind one of the low notes of an organ, while the descants have a magical sound, better than any women's voices. The subtlest nuances and shadings are mastered to the limit, at times even with too much refinement and detail...."[21]

What clearly impressed these Western European musicians was the sonority of the Chapel's choir. However, to conclude that the Chapel at that time cultivated performance techniques that were peculiarly Russian would be mere speculation. As mentioned above, the works performed in the 1830s and 1840s were none other than the Italianate compositions of Sarti, Galuppi, and Bortniansky and the German Romantic works of L'vov. These, by their texture and musical structure, demanded performance techniques no different from those applicable to any other works in the Western European style of the late eighteenth or early nineteenth centuries. In fact, the Chapel pointedly eschewed works of the nascent Russian school; it required great effort on the part of Dmitri and Vladimir Stasov to arrange a performance of the "Persian Chorus" from Glinka's *Ruslan and Liudmila* in one of the Chapel's concerts. [22]

Yet it was the Imperial Chapel that once again proved to be the model for the formation and training of Russian church choirs in the mid-nineteenth century, just as it had been during the reign of Catherine the Great. In 1853 L'vov published a monograph entitled *O tserkovnykh khorakh* [Concerning church choirs], in which he outlined, for the first time in Russia, the theoretical principles and requirements that should be followed by church choirs: "The fact that the liturgy of the Orthodox Church does not allow instrumental accompaniment is the reason that there are more church choirs in Russia than in any other country. There are a great many church choirs [and] their number is constantly increasing; all have the desire to sing, but very few know the direction in which to go to achieve the desired perfection...." [23] Indeed, beyond the Imperial Chapel, the status of Russia's choral culture in the mid-nineteenth century was very ambiguous. L'vov's observations regarding the number of choirs notwithstanding, choral singing in Russia did not enjoy the widespread popularity among various classes of society as it did in, say, Germany or England. Singing was usually not included in school curricula, and there was an almost total absence of qualified teachers and pedagogical materials.

Categories of Choirs in Nineteenth-Century Russia

Before the social reforms and the resulting cultural ferment of the 1860s, the only two types of choirs found in Russia were church choirs and theatrical choirs. The latter were either state-supported or, in the case of private theatrical enterprises, were among the performing forces engaged for specific productions. Despite the popularity of opera in Russia, operatic choirs were not always first-rate: in 1873, Tchaikovsky described the chorus of the Bolshoi Theater in the following terms: "The choruses [in Dargomyzhsky's *Rusalka*] could not be heard at all, and even when the hoarse sounds that emanated from them reached the ear, they only aggravated the auditory nerves.... Total disorder reigned in the ensembles; the orchestra played drably and poorly, while the choruses, as usual, sang with unmerciful discord...." [24]

Because the nature and activity of operatic choirs were narrowly circumscribed, they will be considered in this study only as an exception.

Choirs whose primary function was to perform at church services fell into several categories according to their economic status. The Court Chapel, which sang in the numerous court churches of St. Petersburg and its environs, was in a separate category both artistically and economically. The Moscow Synodal Choir (which sang in the Moscow Cathedral of the Dormition, the principal cathedral of the Russian Orthodox Church) also enjoyed state-supported status, but until 1886 its artistic importance was distinctly secondary.

On the next level were choirs attached to diocesan cathedrals, staffed and supported by diocesan treasuries. Monasteries and convents sometimes had organized choirs, although, with very few exceptions, monastic singing was on a very low level in the nineteenth century. Completing the category of "official," government or church-supported choirs were the choirs of various theological academies and seminaries, and the choirs of military regiments.

The next major category included choirs supported by private individuals—either wealthy nobility and aristocrats for their own household churches, or "choral entrepreneurs" (*khorosoderzhateli*), whose choirs were primarily commercial enterprises: the entrepreneur hired the singers (or, in the case of boys, housed, clothed, and fed them) and then entered into contracts with wardens of individual parish churches to supply the singing for church services and the private offices or needs (*treby*)—baptisms, weddings, funerals, etc.

Another category, which arose at the end of the eighteenth century but became widespread only towards the end of the nineteenth century, comprised "amateur" choirs at various parish churches. These sang Sunday services and certain major feast-day services, usually receiving some remuneration from the parish. Initially such choirs were found only in the major cities and included members of the middle-class bourgeoisie. After the emancipation of the serfs and the growth of city industry, however, similar choirs were organized in villages and factory towns, often as part of efforts to bring culture and musical education to the masses. Because the members were commoners from the worker or peasant class, the choirs were called "folk choirs" (*narodnye khory*), although they performed the same sacred repertoire as the other types of choirs described above. Folk choirs often functioned in conjunction with choirs at the local elementary or secondary school, particularly if the teacher of singing at the school was also the church precentor.

Aside from the Imperial Chapel and Count Sheremetev's private chapel, none of the above choirs was on a high artistic level in the first part of the nineteenth century. A Synod report dating 1835 states that the greater part of churches in Russia could not use the new four-part harmonizations issued by the Imperial Chapel because they did not have enough singers to cover four parts.[25]

In Moscow the Synodal Choir continued its meager and neglected existence after almost being eliminated in the early 1800s. The Choir's singing during this period is described exclusively in negative terms: out of tune, unbalanced, and containing noticeable blunders.[26] Metallov suggests that the main reason for the Synodal Choir's troubles was the forced introduction of compositions by Bortniansky, Degtiarev, and other Italianate composers, as well as L'vov's harmonizations written in a style totally unfamiliar to the Choir: "The Synodal Choir was, of course, not prepared [for these works], and in fact there was hardly a choir in Russia at that time capable of performing the 'concertos' of the Imperial Chapel's directors satisfactorily except the Chapel itself, which had all the necessary means and personnel for such singing."[27] Ironically these works were introduced in Moscow by precentors summoned from the Imperial Chapel to improve the Synodal Choir's quality. To achieve this end they were instructed specifically to learn no fewer than three of Bortniansky's concertos every four months.

Factors That Contributed to the Growth of the New Russian Choral School

The emancipation of the serfs in 1861 contributed greatly to the growth of choral singing in Russia. As idealists among the upper class turned their attention to educating the masses, they came to regard music as an important means of aesthetic education. Through church singing and the choral folk song, the two types of music closest to the populace, they felt they could help the Russian people establish an independent cultural identity. The nationalistic "choral movement" that began in the 1860s is an interesting and still largely unexplored chapter in the social history of Russian music. Though the nationwide achievements of this movement were not unequivocally successful by 1917 (when the Bolshevik Revolution radically reoriented all cultural and educational currents), within a few institutions headed by far-sighted and inspired individuals, a tremendous growth occurred in both the choral repertoire and the quality of choral performance, generating pride at home and envy in Western European capitals.

The growth of the "new Russian choral school" was aided by several important events in the area of sacred music:

1. The publication in the years 1867–69 of Reverend Dmitri Razumovsky's three-volume work, *Tserkovnoe penie v Rossii* [Church singing in Russia], the first major scholarly investigation into the essence and history of Russian liturgical singing

2. The gradual growth of public concerts of sacred music, beginning in the year 1864
3. The breaking of the Imperial Chapel's stranglehold on new liturgical choral composition—the result of Director Nikolai Bakhmetev's unsuccessful attempt in 1880 to block the publication of Tchaikovsky's *Liturgy*, Opus 41
4. The establishment in 1880 of Arkhangel'sky's Choir, the first independent professional choir in Russia, which several years later came to include women's voices
5. The appointment in 1883 of Mily Balakirev and Nikolai Rimsky-Korsakov to head the Imperial Chapel
6. The reform in 1886 of the Moscow Synodal School of Church Singing, together with the appointment of Vasily Orlov as the chief conductor of the Synodal Choir, and the appointment three years later of Stepan Smolensky as the School's director.

The Contribution of Liturgical Musicologists

Razumovsky's *Church singing in Russia* was a work of unprecedented scope and depth. Prior to that the only efforts in this field had been short monographs: Hieromonk Evgeny (Bolkhovitinov)'s *Istorichekoe rassuzhdenie voobshche o drevnem khristianskom bogosluzhebnom penii i osobenno o penii rossiiskoi tserkvi s nuzhnymi primechaniiami na onoe* [A historical discourse about ancient Christian liturgical singing], first published in 1799; Fyodor L'vov's *O penii v Rossii* [Singing in Russia] (1834); Vukol Undol'sky's *Zamechaniia dlia istorii tserkovnogo peniia v Rossii* [Comments on the history of church singing in Russia] (1846); and Ivan Sakharov's "Issledovanie o russkom tserkovnom pesnopenii" [An investigation of Russian church singing] (1849).

In 1866 Razumovsky was appointed to the Chair of Russian Church Music History at the newly opened Moscow Conservatory, a post he would occupy for twenty-three years until his death in 1889. Although *Church singing in Russia* contained some factual and methodological inadequacies, it brought the ancient Russian system of liturgical singing—znamennyi chant—to the attention of musicians at a time when the Germanophile tendencies of L'vov and Bakhmetev had all but obscured native forms of church singing. Moreover, Razumovsky's scholarship stimulated other researchers—Ioann Voznesensky, Stepan Smolensky, Vasily Metallov, and Antonin Prèobrazhensky, among others—who succeeded in laying the foundations of Russian historical musicology. In Gardner's words, "Razumovsky contributed a great deal to developing the principles that would guide the efforts to reinstate national and canonical elements in church singing, which so vividly characterize the so-called Moscow school of church singing. ... Without Razumovsky's contributions this phase [in the history of Russian church singing] could not have occurred."[28]

The Role of Public Sacred Concerts

Extra-liturgical performances of church music had occurred in the eighteenth and early nineteenth centuries in St. Petersburg, but they were usually given for private audiences. When Metropolitan Filaret of Moscow in 1864 gave his blessing for a public concert of sacred music, to be given jointly by the Moscow Synodal Choir and his own personal Chudov Choir, the event was considered so unprecedented that the Metropolitan received numerous letters of protest. To mollify the critics, no applause was permitted and the audience was required to stand at the singing of the Lord's Prayer. All in all, the concert was a success, opening the door to other public sacred concerts in Moscow. In each case, however, permission had to be obtained from church authorities, usually with some difficulty and only through highly placed connections. [29]

Despite their newly found popularity, sacred concerts in the 1860s and 1870s vividly demonstrated the malaise that had come to afflict Russian sacred music as a result of the Imperial Chapel's censorship and the lack of contact with the rest of the musical world. As the critic Hermann Larosch wrote in 1870: "Moscow has several fine choirs that give concerts and sing concert-style works in churches on major feasts. Under different circumstances these choirs could be genuine instruments of art: [they have] excellent voices, skillful execution of nuances, ... and good intonation.... But they are extremely limited by their musical environment and by their repertoire, [which] remains on the level of rank amateurism and dilettantism." Noting that in 1870 the Chudov Choir under Fyodor Bagretsov performed Palestrina's motet "*Sicut cervus*," Larosch continues:

> Palestrina sums up all that is lacking in our church music. Ignorant critics fail to understand that the [Russian church] music of Sarti and Galuppi and their Russian followers [e.g., Bortniansky, Vedel', Degtiarev, et al.] represents the worst examples of a fallen "Latinism"—external formalism without an inner warming spirit, worldly and secular content covered up with a "churchly exterior." This is what we have inherited and are imitating.... The entire style of our church music is in need of reform, but reform can only take place if composers would have freedom from the murderous monopoly of the Court Chapel.[30]

Within ten years the Chapel's monopoly was indeed broken. The sacred choral repertoire expanded, at first slowly, in the eighties and early nineties, and then in a veritable explosion of sacred choral composition that lasted until the October Revolution of 1917.

The programs of sacred concerts did not immediately embrace the new repertoire, however. As Aleksandr Nikol'sky points out, audiences at these concerts were not the same people that constituted the general concert-going public. Rather, they mostly included "partisan fans" of this or that choir, often from the wealthy but less than cultured merchant class.[31] Since the concerts were always a source of considerable income for their sponsors, the latter were at first reluctant to program new and innovative works that challenged the established standards of popularity. This prevailing attitude of conservatism on the part of both the public and the conductors was yet another obstacle that prevented serious composers from turning their attention to sacred music.

In time, however, the courage and willingness of certain individuals to take chances on innovative programming provided an important incentive for composers to write sacred music. In Smolensky's words,

> A vivid example before our very eyes: barely had the hope of being capably performed by the [Moscow] Synodal Choir glimmered before composers, when the entire lot of them, some writing for the church virtually for the first time, responded, e.g., Kastal'sky, Grechaninov, Ippolitov-Ivanov, Il'insky, Rachmaninoff, Chesnokov, and many others.... To what, if not to the concerts of the Synodal Choir, do we owe the appearance of such fresh forces and such vigorous compositions?...[32]

A major initiative in innovative programming was taken by Aleksandr Arkhangel'sky with his series of nine choral "historical concerts" given in St. Petersburg in the years 1888–90. The performance in 1891 of the first three programs in Moscow, attended by the city's leading choral conductors, prompted the Moscow Synodal Choir to give its own cycle of historical concerts in 1894–95 that were devoted entirely to the evolution of Russian sacred music (see table 3.1).[33] For the remainder of the pre-Revolutionary period sacred concerts served as the primary vehicle by which new sacred compositions were premiered and made popular. The most significant role in this area was played by the Moscow Synodal Choir. Other sacred works were premiered by Leonid Vasil'ev's private choir in Moscow, Chesnokov's amateur choir at the Church of the Holy Trinity, Anatoly P. Arkhangel'sky's Choir of Moscow (not to be confused with Aleksandr Andreevich Arkhangel'sky's Choir based in St. Petersburg), and the Choir of the Mariinsky Imperial Opera Theater in St. Petersburg.

The Collapse of the Imperial Chapel's Censorship

A notorious legal battle between the Director of the Imperial Court Chapel, Bakhmetev, and Tchaikovsky's publisher, the firm of P. Jurgenson, ended the Chapel's monopoly over the publication of sacred choral literature. This proved to be a turning point not only for composers of liturgical music, but also for the music publishing industry. In ruling in Jurgenson's favor, the Russian Senate clarified the earlier decrees of 1816 and 1846 concerning the censorship process with regard to musical compositions written on liturgical texts:

> In general, sacred musical compositions may be performed by private individuals in their homes [and], for the purposes of musical education and study of church and [other] sacred music, may be read through by musicians; such a reading, as well as performance [presumably, public performance], is permitted by law; therefore the review and approval of all sacred musical compositions in general shall reside with the [Office of] Sacred Censorship, just as musical compositions that are not sacred in nature are subject to the [Office of] Secular Censorship.[34]

The central issue of the case lay in the fact that Tchaikovsky had not requested approval of his Liturgy *for church worship*—a determination that remained with the director of the Chapel according to the Decree of 1816—but had submitted the work for routine approval by the Moscow Office of Sacred Censorship as a prerequisite for publication. The Office of Sacred Censorship was empowered to review only the correctness of the text, just as secular censors could only rule on the verbal text of secular musical works. The obvious conclusion was that neither the censor nor the director of the Chapel could legally object to the publication (and concert performance) of a sacred work merely on the grounds of musical style.

The Russian Senate's decision cleared the way for publication of numerous sacred choral works that had not been published previously due to the whims of the Imperial Chapel's director. Even so, the new freedom from censorship did not fully solve the problem of quality repertoire for the Russian Church. As Kastal'sky wrote as late as 1913, firms such as P. Jurgenson (the largest publisher of sacred choral music) were by no means selective in their choice of material:

> While the great talents pay attention to church music only in passing, here everyone who has the inclination rushes into this department, since the late P. I. Jurgenson and his successors, knowing the great need of church choirs, accepted and continue to accept without discrimination everything that these "creators" offer them, hoping thereby to enrich church musical literature at least quantitatively, if not qualitatively. The literature has become truly great and abundant, but... there is no order in it.... If the precentor conceives the audacious idea of selecting a repertoire of hymns that accord with moments of the liturgy, if he remembers that he is not an Italian or a German, and is ashamed of plastering the worshippers' ears with musical syrup in which the texts of prayers become stuck, and has scruples about stuffing them with musical rubbish—then he will find little that is of use to him in the huge piles of printed and written music paper.[35]

After the Imperial Chapel's censorship powers had been compromised, the Holy Synod of the Church attempted to retain some measure of control

Table 3.1. The Moscow Synodal Choir's Historical Concerts of 1895

CONCERT 1—February 3, 1895

a) *The first original compositions by Russian composers of the late 17th and early 18th centuries*

1. Bol'shoe mnogoletie — Vasily Titov
2. Blagoslovi, dushe moia, Gospoda — Vasily Titov
3. First litany, from "Sluzhba Bozhiia" a 4 — Anonymous
4. Svete tikhii a 12 — Anonymous
5. Nyne otpushchaeshi a 12 — Anonymous
6. Nebesa ubo dostoino da veseliatsia a 12 — Nikolai Bavykin

===========

b) *Compositions by Italian visitors; German compositions*

7. Otche nash — Sarti
8. Blagoobraznyi Iosif — Galuppi
9. Concerto "Bozhe vo imia Tvoe" — Sapienza
10. Concerto "Iz glubiny vozzvakh" — Maurer

CONCERT 2—March 3, 1895

The virtuosic and sentimental school of the Italians' students and followers

1. Concerto "Terpia poterpekh" — Degtiarev
2. Khvalite imia Gospodne — Esaulov
3. Dushe moia — Hieromonk Viktor
4. Concerto "Na rekakh Vavilonskikh" — Vedel

===========

5. Cherubic Hymn — Glinka
6. Tebe poem — Lomakin
7. Uiazvennuiu moiu dushu — L'vov
8. Concerto "Zhivyi v pomoshchi Vyshniago" — Bortniansky

CONCERT 3—March 20, 1895

Arrangements of ancient chants

1. Zadostoinik for the Meeting of the Lord — Turchaninov
2. Da molchit vsiaka plot' chelovecha — Potulov
3. Resurrectional Heirmoi in Tone 4 — Weichenthal
4. Dostoino est' — Arnold
5. Blazhen muzh, from *Vigil*, Op. 52 — Tchaikovsky

===========

Table 3.1. (continued)

Original compositions of the most recent years

6. Cherubic Hymn (G major)	—Rimsky-Korsakov
7. Selections from *Liturgy*, Op. 41	—Tchaikovsky
a. Cherubic Hymn	
b. Veruiu	
c. Tebe poem	
d. Dostoino est'	
e. Khvalite Gospoda s nebes	

over the music performed at church services. In 1901 the Synod instructed that upon review by the Office of Sacred Censorship, sacred musical works must be forwarded to the Supervisory Council of the Moscow Synodal School for an evaluation of their musical style and content. This unofficial censorship—which caused inordinate delays, violated copyright with regard to unpublished manuscripts, and sometimes ended in unexplained refusals—brought about a vigorous protest, launched in 1906 by the composer Grechaninov and joined by virtually every major composer of church music. Undaunted by the general abolition of censorship following the Revolution of 1905, the Holy Synod in 1911 decreed that only works found in a list compiled by a special review commission (including the noted composer Kastal'sky and the musicologist Metallov, among others) were permitted for performance during the liturgy.[36] None of these measures, however, could stem the tide of new sacred choral compositions. From the 1880s to 1917 the literature of Russian sacred choral music experienced a veritable renaissance. Altogether, the output of this "new Russian school" of sacred choral composition numbered over forty large-scale works and between nine hundred and one thousand shorter works by twenty-eight major composers (see table 3.2).

A. A. Arkhangel'sky's Choir

The formation in 1880 of Aleksandr Andreevich Arkhangel'sky's Choir proved to be an important event in the development of Russian choral culture. At first the choir numbered only twenty singers—six boys, eight men, and, significantly, six women. The unusual sonority of the women's voices and the highly polished interpretations attracted attention at the Post Office Church, where the choir sang. After a year or two, Arkhangel'sky was able to enlarge the choir to fifty—sixteen boys, sixteen women, and eighteen men—and began to prepare sacred and secular choral concerts, the first of which was given in 1883. In approximately five years all the boys were replaced by

Table 3.2.   The Sacred Output of the New Russian Choral School

Composer	Dates	Major Sacred Works	Small Sacred Works
Dmitri Vasil'evich ALLEMANOV	(1867–c.1918)	1 Oc	92
Aleksandr Andreevich ARKHANGEL'SKY	(1846–1924)	3 DL (66 Nos.) (14 Nos.) (14 Nos.) 2 ANV (74 Nos.) (15 Nos.) 1 LPG (11 Nos.) 1 Pan (12 Nos.)	78*
Evstafy Stepanovich AZEEV	(1851–c.1918)	—	88
Aleksandr Grigor'evich CHESNOKOV**	(1880–1941)	1 DL	24
Pavel Grigor'evich CHESNOKOV**	(1877–1944)	2 DL (10 Nos.) (12 Nos.) 2 ANV (10 Nos.) (23 Nos.) 1 LPG (9 Nos.) 2 Pan (11 Nos.) (11 Nos.)	192
Nikolai Semyonovich GOLOVANOV	(1891–1953)	—	23
Aleksandr Tikhonovich GRECHANINOV**	(1864–1956)	3 DL (13 Nos.) (13 Nos.) (15 Nos.) 1 ANV (10 Nos.) 1 PW (13 Nos.)	13
Mikhail Mikhailovich IPPOLITOV-IVANOV	(1859–1935)	1 DL (18 Nos.) 1 ANV (12 Nos.)	13
Georgy (Yuri) IZVEKOV	(fl. 1910)	—	31*
Viktor Sergeevich KALINNIKOV	(1870–1927)	—	24
Aleskandr Dmitrievich KASTAL'SKY**	(1856–1926)	1 DL (11 Nos.) 1 Pan (11 Nos.) 1 Wed (6 Nos.)	146
Nikolai Ivanovich KOMPANEISKY	(1848–1910)	1 DL (16 Nos.)	58*

Table 3.2. (continued)

Anatoly Konstantinovich LIADOV	(1855–1914)	—	10
Sergei Mikhailovich LIAPUNOV	(1859–1924)	—	6
Mikhail Aleksandrovich LISITSYN	(1871–c.1919)	2 DL	37*
Vasily Mikhailovich METALLOV	(1862–1926)	—	43
Aleksandr Vasil'evich NIKOL'SKY**	(1874–1943)	1 DL (15 Nos.) 1 ANV (9 Nos.) 1 LPG (7 Nos.) 1 Wed (9 Nos.)	78
Semyon Viktorovich PANCHENKO	(1867–1937)	1 DL (23 Nos.) 1 ANV (12 Nos.) 1 Pan (21 Nos.) 1 Wed (11 Nos.)	61*
Sergei Vasil'evich RACHMANINOFF	(1873–1943)	1 DL (19 Nos.) 1 ANV (15 Nos.)	1
Vladimir Ivanovich REBIKOV	(1866–1920)	1 DL 1 ANV (15 Nos.)	11
Nikolai Andreevich RIMSKY-KORSAKOV	(1844–1910)	—	40
Konstantin Nikolaevich SHVEDOV**	(1886–1954)	1 DL (13 Nos.)	15
Stepan Vasil'evich SMOLENSKY	(1848–1909)	1 Pan (9 Nos.)	9
Pyotr Il'ich TCHAIKOVSKY	(1840–1893)	1 DL (15 Nos.) 1 ANV (17 Nos.)	11
Nikolai Nikolaevich TCHEREPNIN**	(1873–1945)	2 DL (15 Nos.) (12 Nos.)	7
Nikolai Nilych TOLSTIAKOV	(fl. 1910)		10
Dmitri Moiseevich YAICHKOV	(1882–1953)	1 Oc	21

Key to Abbreviations: DL—Divine Liturgy; ANV—All-Night Vigil; LPG—Liturgy of Pre-Sanctified Gifts; Pan—Memorial Service (Panikhida); Wed—Wedding; Oc—Octoechos (Hymns that change according to Eight Tones)

Note: An asterisk (*) indicates that the number given is approximate. For composers marked with (**), only works composed before 1917 have been included.

women, liberating Arkhangel'sky from the thankless task of constantly training new boys to replace those whose voices had changed.

As an independent, noninstitutional choral ensemble, Arkhangel'sky's Choir achieved a remarkable continuity of tradition. Arkhangel'sky's uninterrupted forty-three-year-long (1880–1923) leadership of his choir was unique in the history of Russian choral performance. Singing in the choir was the main source of income for many of the singers; and in addition to its concert activities the choir generated income by serving churches in small contingents. Other singers held outside jobs but were still able to devote time to daily rehearsals. The continuity of membership was considerable—many singers sang in the choir for ten to twenty years—enabling the choir to develop a repertoire of unprecedented scope. Included were literally dozens of large-scale and small-scale works of Western choral literature, an ever-increasing number of Russian sacred and secular works, and numerous arrangements of folk songs. The advantages of working with capable and mature musicians were clearly demonstrated by the sheer amount of literature performed in the "historical concerts" of 1888 through 1890. "With its present makeup," wrote Nikolai Kompaneisky, "the choir is able to learn new works with almost the same rapidity as orchestral musicians, and can easily master the demands of its conductor. With this choir Arkhangel'sky . . . delights the audience with an unusual degree of polish and the independence of each singer's performance."[37]

Arkhangel'sky's historical concerts, while unprecedented in the sphere of choral music, were not a sudden occurrence. Rather, they were the logical outgrowth of a general movement in the last third of the nineteenth century, initiated by leading Russian musicians to raise the level of musical knowledge and sophistication of Russian audiences. In the 1885–86 concert season Anton Rubinstein presented a widely acclaimed historical series of piano concerts in St. Petersburg. The following season the repertoire included symphonic music as well. At the end of the final concert, devoted to works of the latest Russian composers, Rubinstein presented four Russian folk songs arranged and performed by Arkhangel'sky with his choir. This appearance inspired Arkhangel'sky to undertake, in the 1887–88 season, several choral concerts of a historical nature. The first concert consisted of some unison znamennyi chants and works from the Italianate period of Russian sacred music— Berezovsky, Vedel', Sarti, and Degtiarev; the second concert featured the first performance in Russia of Palestrina's *Missa Papae Marcelli*, while the third concert included several recent secular choral works by Russian composers— three choruses by A. Rubinstein, five by César Cui, three by Rimsky-Korsakov, and some folk songs arranged by Arkhangel'sky.

The success of these concerts prompted Arkhangel'sky to undertake a more ambitious cycle of nine concerts over three years. The goal was to familiarize Russian audiences with a broad spectrum of Western choral literature, most of which was totally unknown in Russia.[38] Thereafter Arkhangel'sky frequently featured Western compositions on one half of a program and Russian works on the other half.

Arkhangel'sky's major contribution to Russian choral culture was that he raised choral singing from its position as merely a servant of church ritual to the status of an independent musical art. He was also the first to disseminate genuine choral artistry outside the Russian capitals. In 1898 he took a contingent of thirty singers on a tour of twenty-eight cities in Russia and Poland. In 1899, the tour went to the Baltic provinces and Helsinki. Discontinuing his tours of Russia in 1901, Arkhangel'sky in 1907 took the choir to Germany, making it the first Russian choir to perform in Dresden, Leipzig, and Berlin. The choir made another trip to Dresden in 1912.

Arkhangel'sky's Choir was highly acclaimed by critics. As early as 1888 one reviewer in St. Petersburg noted: "The subtlety of nuances developed by Arkhangel'sky in his choir is remarkable. One gets the impression of a marvellous instrument, capable at times of superseding any orchestra by its performance—exactly the same impression produced by the marvellous choir of the Imperial Chapel."[39] In 1891 the Moscow critic Semyon Kruglikov wrote:

> In terms of its voices (men's and women's), the evenness of sonority, the absence of any rough edges whatsoever, ideal intonation, clarity in all types of difficult and fast-moving passages, the mellowness of full, sustained chords, Arkhangel'sky's Choir is one of the most disciplined we have ever heard. The entrances of all the voices are precise, displaying uncommon ensemble: the effect is that of a chord played by an organist when he suddenly presses several keys of a gigantic organ.... [40]

Ivan Lipaev, a Moscow critic whose standards for choral singing were always extremely high, gave Arkhangel'sky's Choir a generally positive review in 1897:

> The choir's transitions from nuance to nuance are highly developed, but [the conductor] is not above an occasional "effect," which is indicative of a predilection for a secular manner.... Particularly endearing in Arkhangel'sky's Choir are its diction, intonation, [and] the blend of the massed sound, and not only in the passages of barely audible, whisperlike pianissimo, but also in the mighty, deafening forte. At times it seems that the choir resembles some kind of instrument, such as an organ.... [41]

In 1898, the critic Mikhail Lisitsyn wrote:

> By his concerts in Riga, Revel [Tallin], Yur'ev, and Helsingfors [Helsinki], Arkhangel'sky not only destroyed... existing prejudices against Russian choirs, but also showed that choral singing in Russia can exist on a level no lower than in Europe. To what

extent [Arkhangel'sky] overturned foreigners' concepts of a Russian choir, which they had developed still from the concerts of D. A. [Agrenev-]Slaviansky, is indicated sufficiently by the Finnish newspaper *Nya Pressen* (no. 352, 1897): "We have never yet heard a choir that displayed such amazing virtuosity as this, equally in the areas of ensemble, purity of sound, nuances, and the ability to execute the most varied dynamic shadings. . . . We would like to call the singing of this choir ideal."[42]

Reviewers in Germany were equally enthusiastic:

> Human voices, that obstinate material, under Arkhangel'sky's direction acquire stability of intonation and a gradation of sound that not even a violinist or cellist can achieve. Considering all the variety and diversity of voices in Arkhangel'sky's choir, the unity with which volume is increased and decreased and the most subtle nuances are transmitted is amazingly precise and exhibits an all-conquering beauty. . . . We were surprised and pleasantly excited by certain novel and interesting interpretations of the choral works of our countrymen, most notably, J. S. Bach. . . . [43]

In St. Petersburg Arkhangel'sky devoted a great deal of his energy to raising the economic status of church choir singers. In 1902 he established the Church Singers' Benefit Association, whose pension fund income was generated by annual concerts given by the combined church choirs of St. Petersburg, usually numbering from five hundred to six hundred singers. Although these grandiose concerts did not always attain a high degree of artistic perfection, they remained popular until the October Revolution and greatly increased choral music's visibility in the capital.

M. A. Balakirev and N. A. Rimsky-Korsakov at the Imperial Chapel

In 1883 Mily Balakirev was appointed Superintendent of the Imperial Court Chapel. (The position of Director was eliminated that same year by an administrative reform.) Upon his appointment Balakirev invited Nikolai Rimsky-Korsakov to take charge of the Chapel's pedagogical activities. For the first time in over half a century the Chapel found itself headed by musicians of major stature, as it had been in Bortniansky's day.

Balakirev's appointment was hailed by some writers as an opportunity, indeed a mandate, to reform Russian church music in the light of the findings Razumovsky had made in his *Church singing in Russia*, i.e., to bring it into stylistic conformity with the ancient chants. The difficulty of such a task, however, did not escape even those who suggested the reform. Wrote Prince Nikolai Golitsyn:

> For two hundred years our Russian musical art . . . has been learning from Western Europe, which is foreign in nationality and in religion . . . The ears of the common masses are still not accustomed to this music, but the ear of the educated layers of society is so

spoiled by foreign music, . . . that to them our ancient church chants would sound crude and simply intolerable, and would only drive this layer of society even further away from the Church.

The second difficulty lies in forming church choirs that would thoroughly know, understand, and perform ancient church melodies with the appropriate artistry. Today's choirs, to a greater or lesser extent, are trained to perform Western European music . . . To transform them would be almost more difficult than to transform the music.[44]

Prior to their respective appointments neither Balakirev nor Rimsky-Korsakov had displayed much interest in church music; under Bakhmetev's repressive censorship policy any such interest probably would have been futile anyway. After coming to the Chapel, Balakirev wrote a few insignificant sacred works, devoting most of his energies to administrative duties. But he succeeded in broadening the church repertoire by relaxing the censorship: the published repertoire was enriched by the works of Gavriil Lomakin, Grigory L'vovsky, Arkhangel'sky, and Tchaikovsky's *Vigil*. Rimsky-Korsakov, on the other hand, composed more for the church, producing some works in a style thoroughly unusual for its time—with a variable number of voices in the choral texture, parallel voice-leading, octave doublings, unisons, and open fifths. Most of these works, however, remained within the confines of the Chapel and were published only after Rimsky's death.[45]

In an effort to upgrade the liturgical chant repertoire Balakirev and Rimsky-Korsakov collaborated on *Penie pri Vsenoshchnom Bdenii Drevnikh Napevov* [The all-night vigil in ancient chants], a collection of four-part harmonizations for mixed chorus in which the chant melodies were preserved without alteration and the harmonies were appropriately modal. But despite Rimsky-Korsakov's belief that in this work he and Balakirev had "opened everyone's eyes with regard to the proper and natural harmonization of common chants,"[46] the *Vigil* did not succeed in superseding the *Obikhod* of L'vov-Bakhmetev.

Of greater significance than their sacred compositions were Balakirev's and Rimsky-Korsakov's measures to improve the musical and pedagogical activity of the Imperial Chapel. Under Bakhmetev both the general education and the musical training of the Chapel's boys had been neglected. As Rimsky-Korsakov relates in his autobiography: "The illiterate boys, oppressed and ill-mannered, trained only so-so on the violin, cello, or piano, suffered an unfortunate fate upon voice mutation. . . . They were dismissed from the Chapel into the outside world, ignorant, and untrained for any work. Most often they became scribes, house servants, provincial choristers, or under the best circumstances, uneducated precentors or minor bureaucrats. . . . "[47] The educational reforms carried out by Rimsky-Korsakov and Balakirev (discussed in chapter 5) were significant for their time, although they still fell short of producing first-rate choral conductors in Russia.

The Decline of the Imperial Chapel

Although it continued to maintain a high level of musical performance, and continued to be headed by competent musicians, after the 1880s the Imperial Chapel never regained the position it had once enjoyed as the preeminent institution in Russia for the cultivation of sacred music. With the exception of Stepan Smolensky, who briefly occupied the post of Superintendent from 1901 to 1903, the musicians who headed the Chapel possessed neither the interest nor the special expertise needed to stimulate new creative directions in church music. Anton Arensky, who followed Balakirev as Superintendent from 1895 to 1901, was a thoroughly secular composer whose contribution to choral music in general was minimal. Moreover, because of his affliction with tuberculosis he spent much of his time at southern resorts, and therefore could not be actively involved in the Chapel's activities. After Smolensky's short-lived tenure, the post of Superintendent was eliminated altogether. Administrative and organizational decisions came to rest with the Head of the Chapel, formerly a ceremonial post, occupied from 1901 to 1917 by Count Aleksandr Dmitrievich Sheremetev, while the day-to-day supervision was assigned to the Assistant Head: from 1904 to 1906—Nikolai Klenovsky, from 1906 to 1912—Nikolai Solov'ev, and from 1912 to 1917—Khristofor Grozdov. The actual preparation and conducting of the choir was delegated to several choirmasters and their assistants—Evstafy Azeev, Pavel Tolstiakov (Dragomirov-Tolstiakov), Aleksandr Chesnokov (brother of Pavel Chesnokov), Mikhail Noskov, Pallady Bogdanov, and Mikhail Klimov.

The complicated administrative structure and the lack of consistent musical leadership did not fail to have an adverse effect upon the Chapel's musical activities. Once the most active choral ensemble in St. Petersburg, by the end of Bakhmetev's administration in 1882 the Chapel had ceased to make regular concert appearances. Balakirev, Arensky, and particularly Rimsky-Korsakov directed most of their attention to the Chapel's orchestral classes. Meanwhile, other choral ensembles—Arkhangel'sky's Choir and the Choir of the Mariinsky Opera Theater—assumed leading roles in choral performances. From 1888, the year that the *Russkaia muzykal'naia gazeta* (Russian musical gazette) began to provide regular coverage of concert life in the Russian capitals, through 1901 only one public performance by the Chapel is mentioned—a concert given in Moscow on May 24, 1896 under the direction of Stepan Smirnov. On that occasion Ivan Lipaev gave the performance a favorable review, noting the "unusual mellowness of sound, the [excellent] intonation, and the compactness [of ensemble]." The sonority is described as "massive and matted [in color]—a rare attribute." The diction was "gentle, but clear." On the negative side, the critic noticed slides in the tenor section and the excessive prominence of the octavists.[48]

That same year, however, when the Moscow Synodal Choir visited St. Petersburg, Smolensky wrote in his memoirs: "We were indeed very unpleasantly surprised by what we heard and saw at the Imperial Court Chapel. The constricted children's voices, the hoarseness of the octavists, insufficient purity of intonation, and an insufficient range in all types of nuances, surprised us no less unpleasantly than the works we heard (common [harmonized] chant, the compositions of Bortniansky, L'vov, etc.)."[49]

Upon taking over the Chapel in 1901 Smolensky found the technique of the Chapel even less satisfactory:

> The fast passages (in Kastal'sky's Serbian Chant "*Dostoino est*'" [It is truly meet]) had no lightness and no nuances whatsoever. The Chapel turned out to be thoroughly incapable of making crescendos and diminuendos even in the course of a single measure (in Adagio tempo), to say nothing of more subtle nuances; a *pp* was out of the question. . . . At rehearsal I took the risk of stopping Mr. Smirnov and requested . . . that the choir . . . make a large crescendo . . . to a good, full forte, . . . and then a big but gradual diminuendo to a sonorous piano. . . . [Under my direction] the singers finally heard a successful *pp* and thus were able to appreciate the beauty of this nuance.[50]

Smolensky's efforts to improve the Chapel's musical technique and to change its overall direction proved to be an exercise in frustration. During his tenure (in 1901) the Chapel celebrated the one hundred fiftieth anniversary of Bortniansky's birth, an event hailed as "the most festive celebration in seventy-six years since Bortniansky's death."[51] A concert in January of 1902 featured music by the Chapel's former directors in the first half and works of the new direction in Russian church music (Tchaikovsky, Kastal'sky, Rimsky-Korsakov) in the second. The critics noted that in this concert the singing of the Chapel was "better, freer, and more assured" than before. "Apparently the singers are developing their voices, not only learning the parts."[52] But the spirit of conservatism was evidently too much even for Smolensky to dislodge, and after two years he resigned his position in order to devote his time to scholarship and to his own Precentors' School in St. Petersburg.

Throughout the remainder of the pre-Revolutionary period the Imperial Chapel for the most part remained on the fringes of the burgeoning choral movement led by representatives of the new Russian school. Judging from reviews, it gave but one or two public concerts per year, featuring new works only occasionally. Reviewers criticized the limited public access to concerts, the often reactionary repertoire, the absence of a genuinely artistic conductor, and the lack of spontaneity and enthusiasm in the singers' performance.[53] The overall impression of the Chapel in those years is perhaps best summarized in the following review dating from 1916:

A spirit of formalism, inhibition, and required servitude seems to have permeated all the performers, beginning with the conductor [Mikhail Klimov]. Not a spark of living reaction to the religious ideas [embodied in the words], . . . not a drop of sympathy towards the works being performed!

[There is] much vociferation [*gromoglasie*], but no nuances of timbre, no flexibility of rhythm, no beautiful choral piano, no gentle pianissimo. The sopranos are weak, lacking brilliance; the altos are coarse and strident; neither [section] is in balance with the blaring basses and "sweetly singing" tenors. Is it really necessary for tenors in a church choir to emphasize their characteristic emotional timbre and attempt to emulate an operatic manner?!

How spiritless and "official" are all these mechanical climaxes and crescendos, the howls of the tenors, the deafening shouts of the basses, and the timidness of the boys at the slightest moments of challenge! While from the conductor there emanates only a formal, abrupt succession of tempos, nuances, . . . and the chilling reign of meter.[54]

The Rise to Preeminence of the Moscow Synodal Choir

Without question the supreme role in the development of the Russian school of choral performance in the late nineteenth and early twentieth centuries was played by the Moscow Synodal Choir and its fellow institution, the Moscow Synodal School of Church Singing. The Synodal School emerged as a new force in church music as a result of a thorough administrative reform enacted in 1886, which transformed what had been since 1830 a general four-year elementary school for the Choir's boys into an eight-year "middle school" whose stated purpose was "to train knowledgeable performers of Orthodox church singing for the Synodal Choir, as well as skillful precentors and teachers of church singing."[55] Concurrently, the number of adult singers was increased from twenty-four to thirty, while the number of boys was set at fifty. Most importantly, the singers' salary and upkeep were increased in an effort "to raise the moral level of the Synodal Choir, which must be an exemplary performer of church singing in general and a dedicated preserver of Orthodox church chants, and to give the younger singers the means to pursue church singing and other subjects thoroughly." This measure eliminated the necessity for the singers to hire themselves out for various private services—a practice that had contributed to moral and disciplinary problems.

Even without these private offices the full Synodal Choir sang a very busy schedule of services at the Cathedral of the Dormition in the Kremlin, as shown in table 3.3. Only in the summer, from Pentecost through Dormition, did the choir divide into three contingents and sing Vigils and Liturgies one group at a time. Services not sung at full strength and daily ferial services were sung by the men of the Synodal Choir and the all-bass choir of the cathedral clergy.

To oversee the educational and scholarly aspects of the Synodal School's work, a special Supervisory Council was appointed, which initially included

Table 3.3. Services Sung by the Moscow Synodal Choir at the
Dormition Cathedral

Liturgical Period	Services
From Dormition (August 15) To the Elevation of the Cross (September 14)	All-Night Vigils and Divine Liturgies
From the Elevation of the Cross To Palm Sunday (variable)	Divine Liturgies only
First Week of Great Lent and Passion Week	Liturgies of Pre-Sanctified and Grand Compline
Holy Thursday, Friday, and Saturday	All Services
Pascha (Easter)	Matins, Liturgy, and Vespers
From St. Thomas Sunday (after Easter) Through Pentecost	All-Night Vigils and Divine Liturgies

Reverend Dmitri Razumovsky, Nikolai Gubert (the Director of the Moscow Conservatory), and the renowned composer, Pyotr Il'ich Tchaikovsky. It was Tchaikovsky who in 1886 recommended that Vasily Sergeevich Orlov (1856–1907) be appointed chief precentor and conductor of the Synodal Choir, after which the Choir began its decisive rise to musical excellence. In reference to this appointment Tchaikovsky wrote to the Superintendent of the Moscow Synodal Chancery, A. N. Shishkov:

> At the present time, when . . . the Emperor himself [Alexander III] ardently supports the rebirth [of a national style in church music], when Russian composers are no longer discouraged from devoting their efforts and abilities to their Mother Church, . . . it is extremely important that the foremost choir in the capital [Moscow] be headed by a person who . . . has a substantial musical education, . . . experience in the technique of his art, and who can answer to the contemporary high demands in the field of church singing. . . . In my opinion no one fits the above requirements better than V. S. Orlov.[56]

In 1887 Tchaikovsky also recommended the appointment of Aleksandr Dmitrievich Kastal'sky (1856–1926), who had been his student at the Conservatory, as instructor of piano. In 1891 Kastal'sky became Orlov's assistant conductor.

The appointment in 1889 of Stepan Vasil'evich Smolensky (1848–1909) as Director completed the Synodal School's new leadership, which began to put into practice the ideas set forth in the reform of 1886. Before his appointment Smolensky had already distinguished himself with several publications in the field of liturgical musicology and as a pedagogue at the

Kazan' Teachers' Seminary. He came to Moscow deeply convinced of the historical and artistic value of the ancient Russian chants: just as the Mighty Five had used native folk melodies to create a national style of secular music, so he believed the chants could serve as a wellspring for a new style of native sacred music. At the same time, Smolensky's enlightened pedagogical ideas enabled him to change both the educational atmosphere and the musical direction of the Choir and the School. As Metallov notes in his commemorative monograph marking the twenty-fifth anniversary of the School's reform,

> [With Smolensky's arrival] began [the School's] new life, as the new leaders displayed the full array of their scholarly and musical knowledge, rich and broad experience and erudition, strong energy and talent; [they] set forth clearly established goals, made carefully thought-out plans, and demonstrated a sensitive, responsive spirit to the demands of contemporary times, coupling high aspirations in the field of church singing with uncompromising standards for [their own] service to Church and society and the purpose of the Synodal School and Choir....
>
> Heading this new movement...was Stepan Vasil'evich Smolensky. His right hand in carrying out the reforms...was V[asily] S[ergeevich] Orlov, while his other hand was A[leksandr] D[mitrievich] Kastal'sky.
>
> In no uncertain terms these were three powerful forces, who boldly and jointly directed the victorious and brilliantly successful triumphal procession of the Synodal School and Choir through the arena of church-musical activity....[57]

Another writer described the "triumvirate" of the Synodal School as "Smolensky—all thought, Orlov—all action, Kastal'sky—all inspiration."[58]

The Synodal School's new leaders directed their efforts along the following lines:

1. To improve both the attitude and the musical excellence of the singers
2. To propagate sacred choral literature of high quality
3. To deepen the scholarly understanding of Russian Orthodox church singing
4. To stimulate new compositions of liturgical music
5. To train highly qualified precentors who were both well-rounded musicians and outstanding specialists in their field.

As Smolensky relates in his memoirs, by 1889 when he became Director, "[the ensemble] of the Synodal Choir...was sufficiently satisfactory, both in terms of balance of voices and with regard to singing in tune. The choir's nuances were at times also sufficiently graceful, and the sonority was truly excellent. Orlov,...who had preceded me by three years, had succeeded in training the choir considerably by the time I arrived."[59] However, many choirs in Russia were trained to execute dynamics and nuances well. What was lacking, in Smolensky's view, was an intelligent approach to the music, as well as a sense of pride and dignity on the part of the choristers towards their art and towards their profession in general. Aleksandr Nikol'sky, who joined the Synodal Choir as an adult singer in 1894, describes the kind of attitudes Smolensky set out to eliminate:

> Being in a [professional church] choir sometimes leaves a peculiar stamp upon a person, which is expressed in his manners, bearing, jokes, etc. There are sarcastic expressions, such as "a chorister's 'refinement,'" "a chorister's joke," and so forth. Those familiar with the nature of these "choristers' peculiarities" will no doubt agree that they...exude something more appropriate to a tavern—a kind of tradesman's sassiness. In view of this, it goes without saying that all measures must be taken to eliminate this spirit from our church choirs. One would like to see in each singer more dignity and overall uprightness than he normally displays.[60]

In his memoirs Smolensky describes the long, hard battle he waged to raise the "level of upbringing" of the adult choristers and to enact a new discipline based on respect and camaraderie among the boys. Concurrently, he and Orlov strove determinedly to raise the level of the Choir's musical sophistication by involving them in extra-liturgical concert performances and the study of Western choral classics. In 1891 the Synodal Choir participated in a performance of Mozart's *Requiem* under Vasily Safonov, Director of the Moscow Conservatory—evidently the first time the Choir was permitted to engage in such an extra-liturgical event. Afterwards, Safonov wrote to the Ober-Procurator of the Holy Synod, Konstantin Pobedonostsev:

> Permit me to offer my sincere gratitude for the permission given to the Choir of the Synodal School to participate in the performance of Mozart's *Requiem* at the Symphonic Meeting of March 15. The participation of this choir imparted a special charm to the performance of this immortal work. The superior contingent of voices and exemplary preparation of the Synodal Choir greatly alleviated my difficult task. Without exaggeration I can say that Moscow for a long time will not forget the performance of the *Requiem* by such opulent vocal resources.[61]

Smolensky claims to have played a leading role in stimulating Orlov's interest in Western European choral literature. Perhaps such an assessment displays a measure of conceit on Smolensky's part. Be that as it may, Orlov and the Synodal Choir did, in fact, devote a great deal of time to studying Western contrapuntal masterpieces, a practice that could not have failed to affect their approach to Russian choral works. Smolensky writes:

> The last links in our plan [to raise the Synodal Choir's technique and artistic level] were courses for the adult singers and a number of works such as Mozart's *Requiem*, Beethoven's *Mass in C major*, the entire *Musica sacra* anthology, several Masses of Palestrina, his eight-

voice *Stabat mater,* Josquin des Prez's *Stabat,* Lasso's *Penitential psalms,* etc. This plan
was accomplished over several years and culminated during my administration by our
learning all the choruses in Bach's *B-minor Mass.* . . . The study of these works . . .
extraordinarily raised the cultural level of the Synodal Choir, which began to sing with
intelligence and developed marvellous vocal technique. The beginning of this perfection
dates from the winter of 1893/94, when it awakened the talent of Kastal'sky, and then
Chesnokov, who began composing under the influence of ancient chants and the examples
of the old masters.[62]

In the meantime [1896] the Synodal Choir's technique continued its rise, for having
mastered the entire *Musica sacra* collection, we learned Palestrina's famous Pope
Marcellus Mass, which opened our eyes to a number of things, since we were already
accustomed to singing from scores [as opposed to parts]. . . . Upon learning this Mass the
Synodal Choir developed into a first-class choral artist, whose technique, as I can recall,
was higher than anything I had ever heard in my life. Within the Choir there arose a most
noble awareness of their mastery, which had nothing in common with conceit, but on the
contrary, embodied the kind of humility characteristic of a good artist; also—a remarkably
refined sense of discipline, and an entirely unexpected improvement in the life-style,
behavior, and attitude of the singers toward their work. . . . It is not difficult to imagine how
the technique and literacy of the Synodal Choir progressed after such preparation.[63]

As mentioned earlier, the historical concerts given in Moscow by
Arkhangel'sky's Choir inspired Smolensky to undertake a similar series with
the Synodal Choir (see table 3.1). Smolensky writes,

The historical concerts were the Synodal Choir's first serious debut, for these concerts
displayed the Choir's ability to perform works of all styles and periods as well as its
considerable choral technique; some works were included in the program specifically with
the view of demonstrating the Choir's easy conquest over all technical difficulties. The
historical concerts stimulated interest towards the Synodal Choir in St. Petersburg; that is
the only way to explain the Choir's trip there for a concert in [Ober-Procurator]
Pobedonostsev's hall, which took place 7 March 1896.[64]

After the historical concerts the Synodal Choir initiated a steady stream
of public appearances, which, beginning in 1897, came to feature new works
by Kastal'sky and other composers associated with the Synodal School. From
1897 to 1917 the Choir gave no fewer than sixty-two concerts, in which close to
one hundred works were premiered. (Table 3.4 lists the most important
concert programs given in Moscow during this period.) This fact alone singles
out the Moscow Synodal Choir as the ideal choral ensemble of its time, and
the one for which most choral composers conceived their works.[65]

To reform the entire style of Russian church music was not an easy
matter. The success of this undertaking must be credited to the tireless energy
and far-sightedness of the Choir's precentor, Vasily Orlov. Nikolai Kochetov,
a long-time colleague, describes Orlov's contribution in the following terms:

Vasily Sergeevich ... was a fighter—strong and persistent—and this is what made his name glorious and ineffaceable in the annals of Russian church music. ...

To realize how strong must have been his own personal artistic convictions, how great was his faith in the rightness of his cause, to what extent he was able to subordinate any personal successes to the success of his beloved and revered true, genuine art, we need only recall the attacks he was forced to endure. ...

On one hand [we had] music that was foreign [in style] to our Church, to its indigenous melodies; on the other hand—a dilettantism devoid of any serious significance. Upon this dualistic foundation was reared the taste of several generations. Sweetness and sentimentality were accepted as genuine religious feeling, and external opulence of sonority as real beauty. When national consciousness arose in the field of music, the tastes had already been formed, and the sympathies had been defined. Properly directed efforts, designed to bring our church singing into accord with the historical order of the Orthodox Church, were condemned as innovations. In reality, however, these things were not innovations, but attempts to restore the positive aspects of our ancient heritage. And this task was undertaken not by dilettantes, but by real musicians, who in their service to Russian art wished to make their contribution to church musical literature as well. "Not churchly, not pious," was the response of people who fancied themselves connoisseurs of church music. ...

And so ... Vasily Sergeevich gradually but persistently began to reeducate the public away from its mistaken notions. ... Whenever a new, vital, and excellent composition or [chant] arrangement would appear, he would include it in a program, encouraging composers in this fashion to continue their work. To be sure, he received some support in this from the audience, very tentative at first, as well as from his colleagues, his superiors, and the press, and this support inspired him. But how many protests he had to endure! ... [66]

Indeed, Orlov did receive support from music critics, most notably from Nikolai Kashkin and Ivan Lipaev. The latter called attention both to the unprecedented artistic level that the Synodal Choir had achieved and to the overall cultural significance of the Synodal Choir's activities. Lipaev wrote in 1897:

The large makeup of the Choir is superbly balanced by Orlov. The character of the performance is strictly defined, enclosed within a framework of simplicity and naturalness, which achieves a naïveté that harmonizes well with compositions of church music. ... Herein lies the secret: [Orlov] has limits that he does not exceed. [67]

Two years later Lipaev wrote: "In recent years the Synodal Choir has tried to demonstrate particularly vividly what kind of singing is needed in the Orthodox Church, how it should be performed, and how to stimulate the enthusiasm of composers who desire to tackle the serious task of cleansing our church music from [foreign] accretions." [68]

In April of 1899 the Moscow Synodal Choir astounded music critics in Vienna, where it gave a concert after singing at the dedication of the Russian

Table 3.4. Major Concerts by the Synodal Choir at Which New Works Were Premiered

Works marked with an asterisk (*) denote premieres; works marked (**) are likely to have been performed for the first time in a concert setting.

SACRED CONCERT—1897

*1.	Cherubic Hymn	—Vargin
*2.	Molitvu proliiu	—Il'insky
3.	Vizhd' tvoia prebezzakonnaia dela	—L'vov
*4.	Cherubic Hymn (Znamennyi Chant)	—Kastal'sky
*5.	Miloserdiia dveri	—Kastal'sky
6.	Pomilui mia, Bozhe	—Poluektov
7.	Bozhe, pesn' novu	—Bortniansky
8.	Tebe poem	—Smolensky

SACRED CONCERT—March 15, 1898

1.	Tebe odeiushchagosia	—Turchaninov
2.	Uslyshi, Gospodi	—L'vov
3.	Cherubic Hymn	—Azeev
4.	Dushe moia	—Hieromonk Viktor
**5.	Cherubic Hymn (Moscow Dormition Cathedral Chant)	—Kastal'sky
**6.	Sam edin esi bezsmertnyi	—Kastal'sky
7.	Miloserdiia dveri	—Kastal'sky

SACRED CONCERT—December 14, 1900

1.	a. Troparion to the Nativity (Unison)	—Znamennyi Chant
	b. Kontakion to the Nativity (Unison)	—Znamennyi Chant
	c. S nami Bog (Unison)	—Znamennyi Chant
**2.	a. Troparion to the Nativity (Znamennyi)	—Kastal'sky, arr.
	b. Kontakion to the Nativity (Znamennyi)	—Kastal'sky, arr.
	c. S nami Bog (Znamennyi Chant)	—Kastal'sky, arr.
**3.	Blazhen muzh (Moscow Dormition Cathedral Chant)	—Kastal'sky
**4.	Blagoslovi, dushe moia, Gospoda	—Grechaninov
**5.	Cherubic Hymn ("Streletskii" melody)	—P. Chesnokov
6.	Svete tikhii	—Tchaikovsky
7.	Zadostoinik to the Nativity	—Turchaninov
8.	Gospodi, spasi	—Azeev
9.	Cherubic Hymn	—Tchaikovsky

Table 3.4. (continued)

SACRED CONCERT—November 3, 1902

1.	Sticheron for the Elevation of the Cross	—Komarov
2.	Gospodi, spasi	—Komarov
3.	Cherubic Hymn (No. 3)	—Azeev
4.	Blazhen muzh	—Moscow Chant
**5.	V pamiat' vechnuiu	—Kastal'sky
**6.	Theotokion-Dogmatikon in Tone 5	—Kastal'sky
**7.	Great Doxology	—P. Chesnokov
8.	Blazheni iazhe izbral	—Kopylov
9.	Cherubic Hymn (No. 3)	—Tchaikovsky
**10.	Se nyne blagoslovite Gospoda	—Ippolitov-Ivanov
**11.	Se chto dobro	—Ippolitov-Ivanov
**12.	Svete tikhii	—Grechaninov
13.	Blagoslovi, dushe moia, Gospoda	—Grechaninov

SACRED CONCERT—November 16, 1903
(All-Kastal'sky Program)

1.	Blazhen muzh (Moscow Dormition Cathedral Chant)	
2.	Dostoino est' (Serbian Chant)	
**3.	Tebe poem (Znamennyi Chant)	
4.	Sam edin esi bezsmertnyi	
**5.	Blagoobraznyi Iosif	

(Nine other compositions and chant arrangements.)

SACRED CONCERT—December 13, 1903

**Liturgy*, Opus 18   —Panchenko

(Also works of Ippolitov-Ivanov.)

SACRED CONCERT—April 11, 1904

*1.	Cherubic Hymn ("Sofroniev" Melody)	—Kompaneisky
*2.	Dostoino est'	—Vik. Kalinnikov
*3.	Angel vopiiashe	—Lisitsyn
*4.	Pokaianiia otverzi mi dveri	—Lisitsyn
*5.	Cherubic Hymn	—Grechaninov
*6.	Svete tikhii	—Kastal'sky
*7.	Nyne otpushchaeshi	—Kastal'sky
*8.	Otche nash	—Keneman
*9.	Veruiu	—A. Chesnokov

Table 3.4. (continued)

SACRED CONCERT—November 5, 1906

**1.	Svete tikhii	—Tolstiakov
2.	Vo tsarstvii Tvoem	—P. Chesnokov
3.	Razboinika blagorazumnago	—P. Chesnokov
4.	Sam edin esi bezsmertnyi	—Kastal'sky
5.	Blagoslovi, dushe moia, Gospoda	—Kastal'sky

============

**6.	Blagoslovi, dushe moia, Gospoda	—Nikol'sky
**7.	Cherubic Hymn	—Il'insky
**8.	Milost' mira	—Nikol'sky
9.	Otche nash	—Grechaninov
10.	K Bogoroditse prilezhno	—Grechaninov

SACRED CONCERT—December 10, 1906

**1.	Cherubic Hymn	—N. Tcherepnin
**2.	Dostoino est' (Athos Chant)	—Yaichkov
**3.	Sovet predvechnyi	—Nikol'sky
**4.	Ot iunosti moeia	—Kastal'sky
**5.	Vnushi, Bozhe, molitvu moiu	—Grechaninov

============

6.	Nyne otpushchaeshi	—P. Chesnokov
7.	Khvalite imia Gospodne	—P. Chesnokov
8.	Milost' mira	—P. Chesnokov
**9.	Cherubic Hymn	—Chelishchev
*10.	Sacred verse in memory of Father Amvrosy, Elder of the Optina Hermitage	—Shvedov

SACRED CONCERT—December 14, 1908

1.	Vecheri Tvoeia tainyia	—L'vov
2.	Dostoino est' (No. 2)	—L'vov
3.	Cherubic Hymn	—L'vov
*4.	Blago est' ispovedatisiia	—Shvedov
*5.	Slava...Edinorodnyi Syne	—Vik. Kalinnikov
*6.	Khvalite imia Gospodne	—Nikol'sky
*7.	Theotokion-Dogmatikon in Tone 3	—V. S. Orlov
*8.	Gospodi, vozzvakh; Dogmatikon; Troparion in Tone 7	—P. Chesnokov
*9.	Arkhangel'skii glas	—Tolstiakov
*10.	Bogoroditse devo	—Tolstiakov
*11.	Dostoino est'	—N. Tcherepnin

Table 3.4. (continued)

SACRED CONCERT—November 8, 1909
(Program showing two contrasting directions in Russian church music: the Western and the National Russian.)

1. Blazhen muzh boiaisia Gospoda	—Bortniansky
2. Heirmoi "Pontom pokry"	—L'vov
3. Khvalite Gospoda s nebes	—Arkhangel'sky
4. Khvalite imia Gospodne	—Tchaikovsky
5. V molitvakh neusypaiushchuiu	—Rachmaninoff
6. Cherubic Hymn	—N. Cherepnin

============

1. Ne rydai mene, Mati	—Turchaninov
2. Sticheron for the Elevation of Cross	—Komarov
3. Voskliknite Gospodevi	—Grechaninov
4. Cherubic Hymn (B minor)	—P. Chesnokov
**5. Angel vopiiashe	—Tolstiakov
**6. Veruiu (No. 3)	—Kastal'sky
7. Kto Bog velii	—Smolensky

SACRED CONCERT—March 10, 1911, in St. Petersburg

*Selections from *Liturgy*   —Rachmaninoff

============

(Second half devoted entirely to works of Kastal'sky.)

Concerts Celebrating 25th Anniversary of the Reform at the Moscow Synodal School of Church Singing

CONCERT 1—November 5, 1911

*Cantata *Stikh o tserkovnom russkom penii*   —Kastal'sky

CONCERT 2—November 6, 1911
(Works by graduates of Moscow Synodal School.)

1. Cherubic Hymn ("Raduisia" melody)	—P. Chesnokov (1895)
**2. Plotiiu usnuv	—N. Kovin (1896)
**3. Dostoino est'	—A. Chesnokov (1899)
**4. Khvalite imia Gospodne	—N. Tolstiakov (1903)
**5. Cherubic Hymn	—K. Shvedov (1904)
**6. Blazhen muzh	—A. Vorontsov (1905)
**7. Plachu i rydaiu	—I. Sokolov (1907)
**8. Svete tikhii	—V. Stepanov (1908)
**9. Two Exaposteilaria	—N. Golovanov (1909)
**10. Theotokion-Dogmatikon in Tone 2	—A. Chugunov (1910)

Table 3.4. (continued)

SACRED CONCERT—February 19, 1912
(Concert Marking 300 Years Since the Death of Patriarch Germogen.)

*1. Blazheni iazhe izbral	—Kastal'sky
*2. Zastupnitse userdnaia (text by Germogen)	—Ippolitov-Ivanov
*3. Troparion to St. Dionisy	—Ippolitov-Ivanov
*4. "The Reading of Patriarch Germogen's Message to the Traitors of Tushino"	—Kastal'sky
*5. Sacred Verse (text by Germogen)	—Ippolitov-Ivanov

SACRED CONCERT—November 24, 1913

(First half devoted to works of Tchaikovsky.)
============

*Selections from *Liturgy*   —Shvedov

SACRED CONCERT—January 15, 1915

**1. Edinorodnyi Syne	—Krylov
**2. Cherubic Hymn	—Krylov
**3. Angel'skii sobor	—Nikol'sky
**4. Ot iunosti moeia	—Vik. Kalinnikov
**5. Dostoino est'	—P. Chesnokov
**6. Khvalite Gospoda s nebes	—P. Chesnokov

============

**7. Elitsy vo Khrista	—Golovanov
**8. Edinorodnyi Syne	—Golovanov
9. Velichit dusha moia Gospoda	—P. Chesnokov
**10. Voskresenie Khristovo videvshe	—Vik. Kalinnikov
11. Angel vopiiashe	—P. Chesnokov
**12. Blazheni vsi boiashchiesia Gospoda	—Nikol'sky

SACRED CONCERT—March 10, 1915

All-Night Vigil, Opus 37   —Rachmaninoff

(Repeated December 18, 1915, April 25, 1916, and at least three other times.)

Table 3.4. (continued)

SACRED CONCERT—March 6, 1916
(All-Kastal'sky Program)

1. "Gospodi vozzvakh," Sticheron, and Troparion for Dormition
2. Deva dnes'
3. Blagoobraznyi Iosif
*4. Razboinika blagorazumnago
*5. Selections from *Bratskoe pominovenie* (Requiem)
    a. So sviatymi upokoi
    b. Pokoi, Spase nash
    c. Vechnaia pamiat'
6. Slava...Edinorodnyi Syne
7. Veruiu (No. 1)
8. Veruiu (No. 2)
9. Sam edin esi bezsmertnyi
10. Nyne otpushchaeshi
11. Dostoino est' (Serbian Chant)
12. Svete tikhii (No. 3)

SACRED CONCERT—March 13, 1916

1. Se chto dobro	—Ippolitov-Ivanov
2. Utverdisia serdtse moe vo Gospode	—Ippolitov-Ivanov
3. Razboinika blagorazumnago	—Shvedov
4. Dostoino est'	—Shvedov
5. Svete tikhii	—Kastal'sky
6. Selections from *Bratskoe pominovenie*	—Kastal'sky
a. So sviatymi upokoi	
b. Pokoi, Spase nash	
c. Vechnaia pamiat'	
7. Blagoobraznyi Iosif	—Grechaninov
8. Khvalite imia Gospodne	—Grechaninov
**9. Blazhen muzh	—Vik. Kalinnikov
**10. Veruiu	—Vik. Kalinnikov
11. Svete tikhii	—P. Chesnokov
12. Se Zhenikh griadet	—P. Chesnokov
13. Egda slavnii uchenitsy	—P. Chesnokov

embassy church (see table 3.5). The *Neue Wiener Tageblatt* singled out the "unheard-of subtlety of nuances," while the *Volksblatt* noted that "the ensemble is so good that one seems to be listening to an excellent organ." The *Neue Musikalische Presse* wrote: "What the Moscow Synodal Choir gave us was an experience the likes of which is not soon forgotten.... We have nothing equal to this Synodal Choir, nor anything even resembling it; it would behoove us to ponder the reasons why we do not, and how we could."[69]

In the ensuing years the Synodal Choir continued to receive accolades from Lipaev: reviewing a concert of March 1900, he called the choir "unique in the mellowness of its sound [and] astounding in the variety of all possible musical nuances.... This choir may serve as ... an ideal."[70] A year later he wrote: "From time to time, one hears in the sound something instrumentally symphonic, [an] immaterial [quality], which carries the imagination away into the soaring vaults of the church.... This, in my opinion, is the type of choral singing desirable for our church choirs...."[71] Concerning the significance of Orlov's innovative programming Lipaev wrote in 1903: "The Synodal Choir has set itself the goal of familiarizing a broad spectrum [of the public] ... with works of composers having the most diverse intentions and directions.... One cannot help but welcome this attitude towards creativity, since only with this kind of tolerance and freedom can our church singing develop."[72]

Immediately following Orlov's death in 1907, when Kastal'sky took over as principal conductor of the Moscow Synodal Choir, the exemplary qualities of the Choir evidently suffered. A review from 1907 notes that the singing was marked by "a great warmth and breadth in comparison to past concerts [under Orlov]." However, "the descants stuck out from the rest of the choir, destroying the fullness of the ensemble, and the entire choir displayed a sort of indifference towards its task...."[73] A year later another reviewer wrote: "At the concert on March 25 [1908], the Synodal Choir was unrecognizable. There was no tuning, none of the ensemble that amazed us formerly. Individual voices stick out among the descants, and even more so, in the basses...."[74] The reviewer recommended that Kastal'sky set aside his superior rank and turn the choir over to a more talented conductor.

The Synodal Choir's technical mastery returned to its previous level under its new conductor, Nikolai Danilin, a graduate of the Moscow Synodal School, who was Orlov's student and in many respects his follower. In March of 1911 the Choir performed excerpts from Rachmaninoff's newly composed *Liturgy* in St. Petersburg. In the review, Lisitsyn noted that the performance under Danilin "reminds one of the Choir's past glory under Orlov, [displaying] mobility, subtlety of interpretation, and virtuosity in emphasizing various voice parts"; in Lisitsyn's opinion, however, the sound of the descants was "a little too open," and the accents in certain places "excessive."[75]

Table 3.5. The Sacred Concert Performed by the Synodal Choir in
Vienna

1.	Veruiu	—Tchaikovsky
2.	Tebe odeiushchagosia	—Turchaninov
3.	Dostoino est' (Serbian Chant)	—Kastal'sky
4.	Tebe Boga khvalim	—Rimsky-Korsakov
5.	Cherubic Hymn	—Glinka
6.	Svyshe prorotsy	—Balakirev
7.	Gospodi pomilui	—L'vovsky
8.	Volnoiu morskoiu	—Grechaninov
9.	Vysshuiu nebes	—P. Chesnokov
10.	Ne imamy inyia pomoshchi	—Kastal'sky

Another reviewer noted that the sections in the choir were uneven in quality: "the sopranos are the best, followed by the altos, the tenors, [while] the basses are the worst." Other criticisms included "sforzandi that were too frequent and too intense" and the "overindulgence in piano and pianissimo singing. . . . One gets the impression that . . . the choir is singing con sordino." But the same reviewer noted that the diction was "exceptionally clear and precise" and that "Danilin has . . . comprehensively mastered the method of the late V. S. Orlov."[76]

Still another review called the concert "a rare treat," noting that the "the children's voices [were] crystal-clear and unusually beautiful; the artistic level of the performance, the dynamic flexibility and *messa di voce*—marvellous; the pianissimo—ideal in its lightness; the clarity, the intonation, the flexibility of the cantabile—on a rare level." All this, says the reviewer, makes the Synodal Choir "an ideal instrument for Rachmaninoff's music, [with its] fragile, airy gentleness and gracefully etched texture."[77] The same "crystal-clear sonority, flawless intonation, and vocal 'orchestration' " were singled out by Grigory Prokof'ev in a review of Rachmaninoff's *Vigil*, premiered on March 10, 1915 by the Synodal Choir under Danilin.[78]

Undoubtedly the Moscow Synodal Choir's greatest and most significant artistic triumph was its 1911 tour to Western Europe. (Table 3.6 lists the three different concert programs the Choir performed on tour.) The numerous reviews from this tour indicate what aspects of the Choir's sound most impressed foreigners. The Italian reviews, from Rome and Florence, tended to be brief and not particularly analytic: *Popolo Romano* called the performance "remarkable in terms of sonority and gentleness."[79] *Il Messagero* noted the "wonderful purity of the voices and the remarkable nuances."[80] *Natione* in Florence wrote: "The Russian singers amazed everyone by the beauty of their voices [and] a remarkable purity and gentleness of tone."[81] Similar accolades appeared in *La Tribuna, Il Corriere di Roma, La Giornale d'Italia* (Rome), and *Il Nuovo Giornale* (Florence).

Figure 3.1.   The Moscow Synodal Choir on Stage at the Augusteo Hall in Rome, May 13, 1911.

Table 3.6. Concert Programs Performed during the Synodal Choir's European Tour of 1911

PROGRAM 1

The Development of Early Russian Polyphony

1.	a. "Vonmi nebo" (unison)	—15th century
	b. "Na reke Vavilonskoi" (2–voice)	—16th century
	c. "Na verbe posrede eia" (3–voice)	—17th century
	d. "Vospoite nam" (4–voice)	—Early 18th c.
2.	Mnogoletie	—Vasily Titov

The Italian Influence

3.	Otche nash	—Giuseppe Sarti
4.	Kto Bog velii (2 choirs)	—Bortniansky
5.	Tebe odeiushchagosia	—Turchaninov

The Period of General-European Influence

6.	Vecheri Tvoeia tainyia	—L'vov
7.	Cherubic Hymn	—Glinka
8.	Gospodi pomilui	—L'vovsky

The Contemporary Period

9.	Svete tikhii	—Tchaikovsky
10.	Chertog Tvoi	—Rimsky-Korsakov
11.	Deva dnes')	—Kastal'sky
	S nami Bog)	

(Program performed on May 16 in Rome, and May 29 in Dresden.)

PROGRAM 2

The New National Direction in Russian Church Music of the Recent Period

1.	Svete tikhii (No. 2)	—Kastal'sky
2.	Blagoobraznyi Iosif	—Kastal'sky
3.	Tebe poem	—Kastal'sky
4.	Excerpts from *The Play of the Fiery Furnace*	—Kastal'sky
5.	Sam edi esi bezsmertnyi	—Kastal'sky
6.	Milost' mira; Tebe poem	—Vik. Kalinnikov
7.	Volnoiu morskoiu	—Grechaninov
8.	Arkhangel'skii glas	—Tolstiakov
9.	Tebe poem	—P. Chesnokov
10.	Kto Bog velii	—Smolensky

(Program performed on May 19 in Rome, and May 30 in Dresden.)

Table 3.6.   (continued)

PROGRAM 3

1.	Cherubic Hymn	—Arensky
2.	Vo tsarstvii Tvoem	—Rachmaninoff
3.	Edinorodnyi Syne	—Rachmaninoff
4.	Da ispolniatsia	—Rachmaninoff
5.	Tebe poem	—Rachmaninoff
6.	Cherubic Hymn	—Grechaninov
7.	Khvalite imia Gospodne	—P. Chesnokov
8.	Tebe poem	—Shvedov
9.	Nyne otpushchaeshi (No. 1)	—Kastal'sky
10.	Dostoino est'	—Kastal'sky
11.	Veruiu (No. 3)	—Kastal'sky
12.	Svete tikhii (No. 3)	—Kastal'sky

(Program performed on May 21 in Rome, May 22 in Florence, and May 31 in Dresden, with minor modifications.)

(Programs composed of the above selections were also given on May 8 and June 2 in Warsaw, and May 26 in Vienna.)

The Vienna reviewers were more loquacious:

The nuances of piano, which approached total incorporeity, were incomparably marvellous.... Equally incomparable were the sounds of the gentle children's voices and the strong basses. These basses particularly attracted attention today [as] on several occasions they easily reached low E [*sic*], which for our German singers is so formidable. (*Neue freie Presse*)[82]

... the gentle, seemingly unearthly sound of the children's voices against the underpinning of the famous Russian basses sounded like the flute registers of the organ against the bass pedals. (*Neues Wiener Journal*)[83]

Fresh, unexhausted vocal material, instrument-like clarity of intonation, nuances that are gently shaded dynamically and full of power, rhythm that is both subtle and firm, various characteristic shadings of sound—these are the rare qualities of the Moscow Synodal Choir.... The even crescendos, reminiscent of instrumental effects,... enticed everyone into a rapturous mood of mystical ecstasy. (*Die Zeit*)[84]

The extraordinary gentleness of nuances, particularly the sudden pianissimos,... deserves total admiration.... For its almost unearthly gentleness the choir is indebted to its soprano voices. (*Deutsches Volksblatt*)[85]

The most extensive reviews came from the three concerts in Dresden:

One may praise the perfection of the dynamics, the broad crescendos, the gradual diminuendos to *ppp*, which did not, however, cease to be sonorous, etc., etc., all of which can be described in technical terms. But in the final analysis only one phrase describes all of this: a miracle of sound. (*Dresdner Anzeiger*)[86]

While the basses, who frequently descend extremely low without the slightest difficulty, sound full and mellow, like ideal organ pipes, and the tenors are extremely beautiful, it is the boys' voices that are utterly astounding, for one would think that nothing like this could even be possible. The best of them sound like first-class female singers of the bel canto tradition, and one cannot even imagine that these are boys' voices.... In all Germany, among the Catholic and Protestant church choirs, there is not a single one that can be compared even most distantly to this Russian choir, simply for the reason that in Germany there are no such voices.... (*Dresdner neueste Nachrichten*)[87]

Connoisseurs of music are amazed by the Russian singers' uncommon specialized training. Such discipline we cannot find even in the best German choirs; what is particularly remarkable and amazing is that the children's voices have such a high level of vocal culture.... Evidently the Moscow Synodal School still cultivates the old Italian method of singing. The art of sound production and breathing have been applied here to choral singing and are evidently cultivated in close connection with ancient tradition. (*Dresdner Journal*)[88]

All the listeners agreed unanimously that until now, we have not had the occasion to hear anything this perfect in the area of a cappella singing. The art of breathing and vocal production, inherited from old traditions and cultivated systematically and consistently, are manifest in the singing of this choir in an entirely unique way. In short, one can say that these three evenings were a genuine triumph of vocal music and may become a significant turning point in the history of musical evolution. We live in an epoch when instrumental music is overvalued, and all our musical-educational institutions are following this one-sided path all too willingly, bringing about results that are quite disturbing ([Richard] Strauss, Reger). How beneficial for its music has been Russia'a conservatism, which was noted already by Bismarck! (*Dresdner Zeitung*)[89]

Other reviews from Dresden noted the beautiful bel canto, the prevalence of legato, and the continuity of the text declamation within the musical line.[90]

The reviews clearly show that the Moscow Synodal Choir was in every respect the preeminent choir in Russia in the last decade of the nineteenth and the first two decades of the twentieth centuries, and was the foremost interpreter of sacred choral music composed by the new Russian school.

Secular Choral Music; The Choir of the Free Musical School

As mentioned earlier, secular choral literature in the first part of the nineteenth century was limited almost exclusively to opera choruses. The development of unaccompanied secular choral literature was significantly retarded by the lack of independent, nontheatrical choral organizations that would perform such works. One reason independent choirs had difficulty existing prior to the political reforms of 1861 was that a meeting of a choral class or choral society was considered an "assembly," permission for which had to be obtained on every occasion from the police. Only institutional or staff choirs of churches and theaters were exempt from this rule. Thus, choirs whose main interest lay in secular choral singing for cultural edification or recreation, were practically nonexistent in Russia before the 1860s.[91] The first such group was formed in 1862 at the Free Musical School in St. Petersburg by Mily Balakirev and Gavriil Lomakin (1811–85).

When the Free Musical School first began, Lomakin viewed its main purpose to be the development in Russia of choral singing as a cultural activity. The School provided the first opportunity for educated amateurs to make music, a need that was in no way fulfilled by the recently founded St. Petersburg Conservatory. The School's choral class met three nights a week, with a general rehearsal on Sunday nights, and included solfege, voice training, church chant, music theory, and violin instruction for potential teachers of singing. During Lomakin's eight-year association with the School his course was attended by hundreds of students. Most of them had had no previous training in music, however, and the course did not produce any outstanding figures in the field of choral conducting.

More lasting was the influence of the concerts given by the three hundred-voice choir of the Free Music School. As Lomakin himself relates, "Before that [first concert, on February 25, 1863] little attention had been paid to choral singing, but since the public performance of the Free Music School's choir, one notices how those in the choral profession, out of a sense of competition, have begun to seek the greatest possible perfection, thereby greatly uplifting this area of the arts."[92] At first Lomakin's choral programs consisted of Western works. But beginning in 1863, as Balakirev assumed a more active role, the programming changed to include more music of the Russian nationalist school, featuring opera choruses by Glinka, Dargomyzhsky, Rimsky-Korsakov, and Borodin. The technical side of the chorus' performances received enthusiastic reviews from critics. Aleksandr Serov wrote:

> The singing of the chorus [displayed] crescendos from a barely audible pianissimo, almost whispered by the great mass of voices, to a deafeningly loud forte; there was distinctness and clarity in every sound,...thousands of nuances,...a complete fusing together of the mass of voices into a single entity, obedient to the slightest gesture of the conductor's hand; the union of the performers with the will of the conductor was absolute,...as one heard the strains of genuine musicality—sincere, warm, and [filled with] pure love towards the activity at hand, which one so rarely encounters in St. Petersburg,—and the results were marvellous![93]

Recent Soviet writers (e.g., Daniil Lokshin) have singled out the choir of the Free Musical School under Lomakin as "the leader not only in repertoire but also in the style of performance. The singing of the choir embodied the best national realistic tendencies,...which garnered the support of only the progressive contingents in Russian society."[94] According to Vladimir Stasov, however, "despite the overall excellence of Lomakin's performances, they were characterized by an excessive sweetness and affectation. . . . " Only under Balakirev's influence did performances become "genuine, powerful, fervent, and energetic." Stasov continues:

> Little by little not only Russian solo singers, but the Russian chorus and orchestra as well, developed their own unique manner and character, which we ourselves do not always recognize due to our habitual closeness to them, but which undoubtedly are manifest. . . . That which is "our own" in the orchestra and chorus developed little by little from the time of Glinka and Dargomyzhsky, and was preserved to the greatest degree and most authentically in the performances of the Free Musical School.[95]

In 1874, after Balakirev left the Free Musical School, his place was taken over by Nikolai Rimsky-Korsakov, who divided his attention equally between the School's choir and orchestra. The first concert under Rimsky-Korsakov's direction, on March 15, 1875, featured choruses from Bach's *St. Matthew Passion* and a *Kyrie* by Palestrina. The following year the program included works by Palestrina, Allegri, and excerpts from Bach's *Mass in B Minor* and Handel's oratorios. Rimsky-Korsakov's direct association with the choir prompted him to compose a number of choral works, including the *Six Unaccompanied Choruses*, Opus 16, and the *Four Variations and Fughetta on a Russian Song Theme*, Opus 14. Other works specifically completed for concerts of the Free Musical School included the Polovetsian dances and the closing chorus from *Prince Igor* by Borodin, and the Persian dance from *Khovanshchina* by Musorgsky.[96]

In 1881 Rimsky-Korsakov relinquished his leadership of the Free Musical School once again to Balakirev, who retained this position until 1908 even while serving as Superintendent of the Imperial Court Chapel. The School continued to exist until 1917, headed by the composer Sergei Liapunov.

I. A. Mel'nikov's Free Choral Class Conducted by F. F. Bekker

The Free Musical School's most active period ended in the 1880s. In the 1890s the role it had played in stimulating the composition and performance of new choral works was assumed by the Free Choral Class founded in 1890 by Ivan Mel'nikov and conducted by Fyodor Bekker. Mel'nikov, a well-known opera singer and a one-time student of Lomakin, first came into contact with choral singing through one of the several German *Liedertafeln* that functioned in St. Petersburg at the time. Wishing to further the cause of amateur, recreational choral singing in Russia, he financed the Choral Class and invited Bekker to be the conductor.

Bekker had begun his activity as a choral conductor in 1888, when he gave a concert of sacred music with the chorus of the Mariinsky Theater. The attention of critics was attracted by the vividness of his interpretation: "As cold and dull, despite its technical mastery, as was the performance of the Imperial Court Chapel at its last concert, so the performance of the opera chorus glistened with rich color, life, enthusiasm, and feeling," wrote the critic Nikolai Sokolov.[97] Bekker's approach to choral interpretation may be summed up in the following fashion: "The main feature in choral singing a cappella must be the proper and sensible declamation of the text. The music does not suffer on account of the text, but is explained by the word. The singers must become so absorbed by the sense of the words and the music...that the performance has the spark capable of electrifying the listener."[98]

Despite the fact that in 1894 Bekker suffered a slight stroke which affected his personality in an increasingly adverse way, his concerts continued to receive plaudits from reviewers. Sergei Rybakov wrote in 1897 that

> such tuning, cleanliness, and expressiveness can be achieved only by a first-class artist-conductor.... The choir has mastered the most subtle nuances of performance, from barely audible pianissimo to a mighty fortissimo.... Bekker at times underscores the meaning of the text a little excessively, as a result of which the performance takes on a certain dramatic quality,... in comparison with traditional performance [of sacred works].[99]

Bekker's approach was not beyond criticism, however. An anonymous reviewer wrote in 1898:

> Mr. Bekker conducts in a fashion that is not only singular, but marvellous as well; he controls his choir totally. Laying aside his baton, he conducts with both arms, his head, and even facial expressions,... each work on the program—from memory.... [However,] Mr. Bekker sometimes becomes too carried away by mere beautiful sonorities, changes of tempo that are often sudden and completely unnecessary in a given work, and especially, by dynamic [contrasts] of forte and piano.... This is highly effective, but clearly contradicts the sense of the composition.[100]

Like the choir of the Free Musical School, Bekker first began by programming Western choral works, many of which were first-time performances in Russia. Beginning with the 1893/94 season, the programs were increasingly devoted to Russian choral works. Composers who wrote works specifically for the Free Choral Class included Tchaikovsky, Cui, Arensky, Grechaninov, and Taneev.

Bekker left the Class in the 1898/99 season due to his deteriorating health, and the Class ceased to exist in 1901 despite attempts by several other conductors to continue the enterprise.

The Russian Choral Society of Moscow

The first secular chorus in Moscow, the Russian Choral Society, was formed in 1878 by Karl Albrecht, and remained for many years the only group of its kind. The members were amateurs in the true sense of the word, receiving no remuneration and paying membership dues instead. The concerts, which took place usually only once a year, were referred to as "open meetings."

The Russian Choral Society was very slow to assume a significant role in propagating secular choral music in Moscow. From the time of its founding and until the 1897/98 season its performances evidently did not merit much attention from the musical press. That season the musical directorship was taken over by Mikhail Ippolitov-Ivanov, who improved the sound and technical execution of the choir and introduced some innovative programming—works by Rimsky-Korsakov, Borodin, Grechaninov, and Cui, among others. By the third season under Ippolitov-Ivanov, the critic Lipaev noted a significant improvement: "In contrast to the past, the choir of the Society has travelled far on the road towards perfection: ... the discipline deserves positively the highest praise.... Under Ippolitov-Ivanov's talented guidance the choir is striving towards performance that is artistic and exemplary."[101] At the same time, Lipaev asks why the Choral Society does not perform more works of a folk character, and states furthermore, that one public performance a year is not sufficient to stimulate any serious interest in secular choral singing.

In 1901 the Society's performance, under assistant conductor Fyodor Keneman, was called "a pitfall from the past twenty years," and no reviews appeared dating from 1902 or 1903. In 1904 the Society celebrated its twenty-fifth anniversary, but no reviews are found from 1905 to 1908. In 1908, once again under Ippolitov-Ivanov, the program included seven premieres—works by Grechaninov, Chesnokov, Kalinnikov, and Zolotarev. The performance was judged by one critic to be "satisfactory but not exemplary."[102] The next two seasons were quite similar—several novelties, but performances described as "lackluster," "uninspired," and "monotonous." Ippolitov-Ivanov gave way to S. Pototsky in 1911, Sergei Vasilenko in 1912, Nikolai Golovanov in 1913, and himself returned again in 1914. But with the exception of the performance under Golovanov, the Society's activity was summed up in 1914 by the critic Grigory Prokof'ev: "year-in, year-out, the same dull singing, the same dull programming."[103]

The inertness of the Russian Choral Society in Moscow undoubtedly accounts, in part, for the relative dearth of Russian secular choral repertoire, particularly by Muscovite composers. Among the composers of the new Russian choral school the sacred output generally outnumbers the secular by a ratio of between five and ten to one.

D. A. Agrenev-Slaviansky's Cappella

Professional choirs, whose repertoires included some sacred works, but which were organized primarily as secular business enterprises, were also late in developing in Russia. The two most prominent groups in this category were Dmitri Agrenev-Slaviansky's Cappella, established in 1868, and Arkhangel'sky's Choir, founded in 1880. The activity of Agrenev-Slaviansky (1836–1908) and his choir is one of the most controversial chapters in the development of Russian choral culture. As Lokshin points out, "no other musical ensemble or solo performer simultaneously elicited so many inordinately enthusiastic and highly negative opinions."[104]

Dmitri Aleksandrovich Agrenev (the pseudonym "Slaviansky" was added later), gifted with a natural voice, received a smattering of musical and vocal training in Moscow and St. Petersburg, and then furthered his vocal studies in Italy for several years. Instead of pursuing a career as an opera singer, he turned to performing Russian folk songs, first as a solo performer, and then, beginning in 1868, with a choir that initially numbered approximately twenty-five men and women and eventually as many as sixty men, women, and boys. In the next forty years Agrenev and his choir visited four continents and gave close to fifteen thousand concerts of Russian and other Slavic folk songs. In 1869 he gave one hundred seventy-five concerts throughout the United States, while in 1885 he toured Europe extensively, giving one hundred fifty concerts in Germany alone. Before that the only Russian choral ensemble that had toured outside Russia had been Prince Yuri Golitsyn's serf choir, which had toured England and America in the 1850s and 1860s.

On the positive side, Agrenev propagandized the Russian folk song in places where its musical value and potential had not yet been recognized. (In 1865 Russians living in Berlin implored him not to include any folk songs on a concert program, saying, "Have you no shame? You will embarrass all of us and yourself.") The German court critic, Heyer, praised Agrenev, noting that "he sang in a unique, inimitable, and purely national manner, and expressed that sadness and boldness found [alternately] in Russian songs."[105] Even Agrenev's critics among more serious Russian musicians admitted that he was the first to turn the attention of the Western European public to Russian folk songs.[106]

The reaction of Westerners was quite enthusiastic: "The melodies of the Slavs, so varied in nature—at times profoundly sad, at times light and graceful—but always filled with real and genuine emotion, elevate the soul and gladden the heart," wrote the *Leipziger Nachrichten*.[107] "Agrenev-Slaviansky with his wonderful tenor elicited a torrent of applause by his performance of the Russian boatmen's song [*"Ei, ukhnem"*].... Despite the fact that everything was performed in a foreign language, the effect upon the public was obvious from the innumerable compliments," wrote the *New York Herald*.[108] In France *Le Figaro* printed the words and music to *"Ei, ukhnem"* after Agrenev's performance, which prompted Charles Gounod to hyperbolize, "If I were forced to listen to the boatmen's song *'Ei, ukhnem'* every day for as long as it would take me to drink the entire Volga, even then I would not get tired of this wonderful melody.... If I were younger and should contemplate writing another opera, I would fill it entirely with authentic Russian tunes."[109]

The negative side of Agrenev-Slaviansky's activity lay in the fact that neither his selection of repertoire nor his manner of performance embodied the best traditions of Russian music. Though he was the first to write down numerous genuine folk songs, his performances and published collections presented these songs in thoroughly inappropriate and distorted arrangements, together with trite, sentimental songs that had nothing whatsoever to do with genuine folk song. As Sergei Taneev justifiably pointed out, "The arrangements of these songs not only are inappropriate to their character, but are made with an extremely unskilled hand, which reveals in their author insufficient familiarity with the most basic elements of music."[110] Comparing genuine folk songs as performed by a peasant chorus with ostensibly similar songs performed by Agrenev's choir, Hermann Larosch noted that "an entire abyss separates [the former] from the confections served up by Mr. Slaviansky's chorus."[111]

Equally dubious was Agrenev-Slaviansky's approach to performance: the choir appeared on a stage designed to look like a Russian boyar palace, in stylized boyar costumes of the sixteenth or seventeenth centuries. With this outfit Slaviansky himself wore white kid-gloves studded with numerous gaudy rings. As for the singing, critics described it as "mannered," "filled with various audacious effects,"[112] consisting of "endless *ff* and *pp* ... never a mere *mf*."[113] As more thoughtful critics perceived, all these outward effects were concocted merely for the purpose of showmanship and to cover up for the essential lack of musical content. Tchaikovsky perhaps said it most eloquently when he wrote: "If Slaviansky is acknowledged to be some kind of hero, holding high the banner of Russian music, then I maintain that such assertions can be made only by individuals who know neither music in general nor the Russian [folk] song in particular... This exploitation of [low-brow] patriotism from beyond the Moskva River has nothing in common with music whatsoever!"[114]

Peasant Folk Choirs

In connection with the secular choral folk song, special mention must be made of peasant folk choirs. Such groups had existed in Russia since time immemorial as distinctive elements of Russia's folk musical heritage, in which collective, heterophonic singing was more prominent than the solo song or instrumental music. In their indigenous form the makeup of peasant choirs was variable and flexible, as was the nature of the musical performance itself—numerous local variants of basic song prototypes sung with embellishments improvised in the course of the performance. Peasant choirs and their songs occasionally caught the attention of "academic" musicians: they are mentioned in the notes and memoirs of such musicians as Aleksei L'vov, Yuri Arnold,[115] and of course, the composer Modest Musorgsky who perceptively distilled elements of folk heterophony for use in his works. In every case sensitive musicians were captivated by the spontaneity and directness of the expression, as well as by the freshness of the musical language. L'vov, for example, described the singing as follows:

> Many times I have had the opportunity to hear Russian songs sung by [folk] songsters, and the same songs sung by [trained] choir singers. The first sang by ear and, so to speak, according to natural instinct; the latter sang according to the laws of art. I could not help but give preference to the former. In their performance, uninhibited by conditioned rules, there was an obvious strength, a fire, and an occasional burst of inspiration; by contrast, the choir singers sang correctly, but feebly and drably; it was clear that the requirements of music constrained them.[116]

Through the nineteenth century various attempts were made to write down Russian folk songs and to utilize them in works of art music.[117] However, it was not until the very end of the nineteenth century or even the first decade of the twentieth century that *choral* folk singing with its complete, heterophonic texture became the object of widespread interest in Russian musical circles, largely through the efforts of the Commission for Musical Ethnography of the Russian Geographic Society. In 1911, spurred by this interest, Mitrofan Piatnitsky gathered in Moscow a group of peasant singers from the Voronezh, Riazan', and Smolensk districts for the purpose of presenting peasant songs in their authentic folk form to concert audiences. Thus began a process whereby, in the words of Boris Asaf'ev, "what used to be everyday life became a [musical] style."[118] It is important to recognize the relative lateness of this phenomenon in pre-Revolutionary Russia. The folk chorus as an organized—and often professional—entity properly belongs to the Soviet period, when it assumed a position of prominence as a separate category distinct from the "academic" choirs, which continued to cultivate the traditions of choral art music. In the present study references to this post-Revolutionary category of folk choir will be made only insofar as they offer illuminating comparisons with the art tradition on points that are a frequent source of confusion to Western performers.

Perceptions of Russian Choirs outside Russia

Agrenev-Slaviansky's Cappella and the Moscow Synodal Choir epitomize the two opposite extremes of Russian choral performance at the turn of the century: the first—cheaply effective but musically vacuous, the second—founded upon the highest principles of musical artistry. Unfortunately for Russian choral art, far more people both in Russia and abroad heard Slaviansky than heard the Synodal Choir. As a result of this, Russian choral performance came to be regarded in a decidedly one-sided fashion. As late as 1928, when the Leningrad Cappella (the former Imperial Court Chapel) was touring Western Europe, the conductor Mikhail Klimov noted in his diary that "many of the concertgoers [in Germany] expected to hear 'light' music and to see 'Russian dances' but instead found themselves at a serious concert. This once again confirmed my observation that for most rank-and-file Germans a 'Russian choir' is a cabaret act with obligatory prancing in sarafans and costumes *à la mouzhik*. This view of Russian choirs has been cultivated among the Germans by various 'Don Cossack choirs,' 'Ukrainian choirs,' and so forth...."[119]

Before the Revolution a few Russian choirs had formed outside Russia. One such choir, numbering twenty-one men and women, performed in 1913 in Geneva under Vasily Kibalchich, a one-time assistant to Arkhangel'sky. The traits singled out by Swiss reviewers are remarkably similar to those characteristic of the best choirs in Russia: "ultimate balance of sonority, a great variety of nuances, [and] legato—a wonderful sostenuto [that] creates the impression of organ playing."[120]

Another choir was formed in 1912 at the Russian Cathedral of St. Nicholas in New York City, composed of professional male choristers from Russia and boys from the local Russian community. The choristers and the conductor, Ivan Gorokhov, were brought from Moscow through an endowment by Charles Crane, an American businessman who had developed a fascination with Russian choral music while travelling in Russia. The reviews of the choir's performance in 1913 resemble the accolades bestowed upon the Synodal Choir by European reviewers:

> "Perfection" is a word that must be used with circumspection, but if ever it was in place, it is with reference to the performance of this choir. Where nearly all choirs of the English Church fail—in ensemble enunciation—the Russian choir was perfection itself. The utter accuracy with which thirty or more voices pronounce together long passages of unmeasured declamation is astonishing. In tonal modulation every shade is under the absolute control of the director. Phrases shade off into nothing as from the most delicate violin bow under a master hand. The pianissimo which the choir obtains is softer and more perfect than one could believe possible. But perhaps the most amazing miracle ... is its attack ... [when] the whole choir, in the same instant, strikes its chord, so true and perfect in intonation, that it varies not a hair's breadth while it is being held.[121]

After the Revolution, when the tide of emigration swelled the ranks of Russian choirs abroad, few representatives of the best traditions of Russian choral performance were among them. None of the leading figures associated with the Moscow Synodal School or Choir emigrated; those musicians who did emigrate (e.g., Grechaninov and Rachmaninoff) were not outstanding choral conductors. The prominent conductor among Russian émigrés with roots in the Moscow Synodal tradition was Sergei Jaroff (1896–1985). (He entered the School in 1906 and was still a boy soprano during the 1911 European tour.) But he and his Don Cossack Choir elected to travel the path of showmanship that had been blazed by Agrenev-Slaviansky.

In Russia, meanwhile, the events of the October Revolution and the virtual destruction of the Orthodox Church in the 1920s and 1930s led to the dissolution or reorganization of all institutions engaged in the cultivation of the choral art. Some pre-Revolutionary ensembles, e.g., Arkhangel'sky's Choir and the Imperial Chapel, begat "socialistic offspring." However, the reorientation of these institutions and the change of repertoire—from sacred, liturgical works to revolutionary and "mass" songs—was so drastic that little, if any, continuity of tradition remained. My personal observations over the course of several stays in the USSR suggest that, although some present Soviet choirs are outstanding in their own right, none of them embodies the best traditions of the pre-Revolutionary choral school. Thus it has become the task of scholars to reconstruct as well as possible on the basis of available sources this remarkable chapter in the history of choral performance—seemingly so close in time to the present day, yet in many respects less understood than the performance of Renaissance polyphony.

Part Two

Choral Performance in the Late Nineteenth–Early Twentieth Centuries

4

The Choral Instrument in Russia

As the historical survey in the first three chapters has shown, only in the late nineteenth and early twentieth centuries did choral singing in pre-Revolutionary Russia mature as an art and take on qualities that may in some instances be identified as distinctively Russian. The examination of the practical side of Russian choral performance appropriately begins with a consideration of the choral instrument itself—how it was conceptualized in theory, and how it was constituted in practice.

The choral literature of the new Russian school was created by composers working in close contact with specific choirs that served for them as tangible "sonorous laboratories." Thus it would seem essential, in speaking of a given choir, to make reference to the style of music it performed. At the same time, almost paradoxically, both the historical events and the theoretical works on choral singing of this period justify the examination of the choral instrument on its own terms, initially apart from the music. "The performance, the interpretation of a work, must not be confused with choral sonority per se: good choral sonority can be accompanied by an anti-artistic, even illiterate interpretation," wrote Pavel Chesnokov in the opening paragraphs of his book, *Khor i upravlenie im* [The choir and how to direct it].[1]

To be sure, the vast growth of choral culture and repertoire in Russia from the 1880s to the 1910s created the need for analyzing and systematizing choral performance techniques. As Nikolai Kovin wrote in 1916, "contemporary choirs [are presented] with a series of new problems in terms of technical preparation....Conductors...are no longer satisfied with former stereotypes of performance and are demanding [of their singers] the execution of different, more serious and complex tasks.... The time has come to raise the question about the...means for choirs to acquire [necessary] performance techniques."[2] But there is conclusive evidence that the leading Russian choirs developed their technical mastery even before the stylistic revolution of the 1880s and 1890s and thus were already prepared for the explosion of new repertoire in the decades that followed. Indeed, without these technically superior choirs composers would have been less inclined to compose as they did.

As Aleksandr Nikol'sky has suggested, Russian choirs in the 1870s and 1880s focused on developing the purely technical side of their performance due to the restricted circumstances under which they worked and performed: in church services and in occasional concerts of sacred music. The repertoire sung on these occasions was so common and familiar to the "audiences" of church-goers, that the only difference and source of possible interest was the degree of technical excellence displayed by a given choir on a specific occasion.[3] The success or failure of a particular choir depended largely upon the benevolent, if subjective, judgment of a limited coterie of "choral connoisseurs."

Even as the focus of choral performances in the 1890s and 1900s shifted in the direction of new repertoire and attracted the attention of serious music critics, choral sonority and technical virtuosity continued to be held as parameters of highest importance, no less crucial than what was actually being sung. In Chesnokov's aforementioned book, technical excellence of the "instrument" is the sine qua non in the very definition of a chorus. The opening sentence reads: "What is a chorus, and what is not a chorus but only an assemblage of singers? What is choral sonority, and what is merely the sound of human voices?..." In Chesnokov's opinion, good choral sonority requires three elements: ensemble, tuning, and expressive shading (nuances). "This position," he continues, "must be the first principle, the cornerstone, in the foundation of choral science. Based on this we can determine precisely what is a chorus: an assembly of singers whose sonority displays a strictly balanced ensemble, precisely regulated tuning, and artistic, distinctly worked out nuances."[4]

Chesnokov presupposed, of course, that the component elements of his ideal choral instrument—the individual voices—were appropriately selected and trained. Before examining further the various concepts of choral sonority in Russia, we must take a closer look at those all-important component elements—how they were trained, selected, and postioned during performance.

Vocal Pedagogy in Russia

The question of the role played by vocal pedagogy in shaping the nature of the Russian choral instrument is quite problematic. Neither the solo vocal methods intended primarily for artists of the operatic stage nor the general music textbooks for elementary and secondary schools (most of which contained sections on singing) directly address the subject of choral voice training. Pedagogical materials dealing specifically with choral voices did not appear until the 1910s.

Although musical monuments attest to a continuous tradition of liturgical vocal music in Russia dating back to the tenth or eleventh century, they provide no information concerning the nature of the vocal style or traditions of vocal training. Consequently, writers who have attempted to identify some theoretical basis for the development of a native Russian vocal school have resorted to more or less imaginative speculation.[5]

Vsevolod Bagadurov, for example, points to the centuries of experience in unison chant singing, which, in his words, "trained one from an early age in long-winded and calm breathing, developed the ability to sustain a sound of a given timbre and to control the dynamics of piano and forte without forcing, and developed breath support necessary...to sing legato, lento, and sostenuto."[6] (As will be noted in chapter 7, the slowness of tempo in chant performance remains an unproven postulate.) Nikol'skaia-Beregovskaia points to the various genres of the Russian folk song, "which gradually developed the indigenous national traditions of vocalism and performance style that became the basis for the Russian professional school of choral singing."[7] Bagadurov, however, appears to be closer to the mark when he observes that "at the time when Italian opera appeared [in the mid-eighteenth century],... Russia did not have any accumulated vocal-pedagogical experience, [methodological] observations, or traditions of performance" that can be identified from documentary sources.[8] Indeed, it remains somewhat of a mystery how Russian singers managed to negotiate the complex vocal roles of Italian opera seria without extensive vocal training in so foreign a style.

The tunefulness and melodism (commonly referred to as cantilena in Russian sources) inherent in the Russian lyric folk song (*protiazhnaia pesnia*) may have served as a common ground with the Italian bel canto style introduced by the imported *maestri di cappella* at St. Petersburg. But any specific training methods introduced by the Italians evidently remained in the purely practical sphere and were not set down in written form. The first written vocal methods in Russia—those of Mikhail Glinka and Aleksandr Varlamov—did not appear until 1835 and 1840, respectively; Glinka's method, however, remained unpublished until 1903.

Varlamov's and Glinka's association with the Imperial Chapel has led some writers to conclude that their vocal methods served as the point of departure in the development of a uniquely Russian choral school. The merit of this claim, however, is open to question.

Of the two, Varlamov's method is more comprehensive (as is suggested by its title, *Polnaia shkola peniia* [The complete school of singing]). Varlamov began his singing career as a boy chorister in the Imperial Court Chapel in 1811, when Bortniansky was director; and in his memoirs Varlamov describes how the seventy-year-old Bortniansky once illustrated a certain vocal passage in a "gentle falsetto." While in the preface to his method Varlamov states that he "made use of the best works in this field and, particularly, the inspired works of [his] famous teacher, D. S. Bortniansky,"[9] passages from the memoirs suggest that much of his information on European styles of singing was accumulated during a ten-year-long tenure as precentor of the Russian embassy church in The Hague, where he was sent at the age of eighteen. It was here that he became familiar with contemporary opera (mainly of the French variety), met various famous singers, and took part in performances of vocal chamber music. Characteristically, most of the technical terms employed in his treatise are French. Bagadurov, the leading expert on Varlamov's vocal method, states that "[it] does not depart from the well-known European methods of [Louis] Hérold and Mannstein [Heinrich Steinmann]."[10]

Upon his return to Russia, Varlamov successfully petitioned to rejoin the Imperial Chapel as a singer and teacher of singing. From January 1829 to November 1831 he trained boy soloists to sing trios for hierarchal services. After two years, however, he was released from the Chapel and spent the remainder of his career as assistant conductor in the Moscow Imperial Theaters and as a private vocal pedagogue. By all appearances, Varlamov's tenure at the Chapel was not particularly distinguished; in 1848, when he again petitioned to return to the Chapel, the request was denied.[11]

Varlamov's vocal method contains little that is applicable specifically to training choral voices. Bagadurov characterizes it as "mostly reflecting the stylistic requirements of the [vocal] chamber music of the time—Varlamov's own, and that of his predecessors and contemporaries."[12]

Mikhail Glinka, whose compositions earned him the sobriquet "father of Russian music," was also a singer and vocal pedagogue. During three years spent in Italy (1830–33) he studied singing with Eliodoro Bianchi, Andrea Nozzari, and Mme. Fodor-Mainvielle. In 1835 he produced his *Uprazhneniia dlia uravneniia i usovershenstvovaniia gibkosti golosa* [Exercises for steadying and perfecting the flexibility of the voice][13] for Osip Petrov, the famous operatic basso who premiered the role of Ivan Susanin in the opera *A Life for the Tsar*. Some twenty years later a virtually identical set of exercises was written for the soprano A. Kashperova, which suggests that they were a standard set of vocalises used by Glinka. Glinka's method does not address a number of important questions with regard to vocal pedagogy such as classifying voices, blending registers, breathing technique, and phonation. Designed to improve an already well-trained voice, it provides only limited insight into Glinka's manner of training voices—certainly not enough to serve as the basis for an entire "Russian school of voice," which is what Kompaneisky and others have attempted to evolve from it.

Glinka's basic premise is that all voices have sounds that are produced without any exertion, the so-called "primary" tones, and others, which require an unavoidable exertion of the chest and tension of the throat. Accordingly, the singer must first master the primary, natural tones and then gradually progress to the other sounds. Writers who regarded Glinka as the founder of a peculiarly Russian school of voice training seized upon the coincidental fact that untrained folk singers usually begin their singing within the natural, "primary" tones. But in fact, Glinka himself clearly relates his method to the Italian school, when he admits "tormenting [his students] with abominable Italian music in order to develop the voice."[14]

Glinka's association with the Imperial Court Chapel was hardly more substantive than Varlamov's. Appointed to the post of *"Kapellmeister"* in 1837, he worked briefly to improve the singers' musicianship. He then went to the Ukraine to recruit voices, and resigned in 1839 mainly because of personality clashes with the new Director of the Chapel, Aleksei L'vov.

Very little new material in the area of vocal pedagogy appeared between the publication of Varlamov's *Complete school* in 1840 and the 1880s, despite the emergence of a Russian nationalist school of composition in the intervening half-century. Some writers have pointed to a passage in a letter from the composer Dargomyzhsky to the famous Russian singer Liubov' Karmalina as evidence for the existence of a peculiar Russian school of singing. Written in 1860, the letter reads: "If you preserved in [your] singing the direction given to you here by Russian composers (who worked so diligently with you), I am not suprised at your successes [abroad]. The naturalness and noble character of the Russian school cannot fail to produce a positive reaction amidst the extravagance of the Italian, the shouting of the French, and the mannerism of the German schools."[15] It appears, however, that Dargomyzhsky was referring more to the manner of interpretation and possibly stage deportment than to actual differences in vocal production. By itself the above excerpt cannot stand as proof of a distinctive Russian school.

In 1880 the St. Petersburg Conservatory adopted Bronnikov's *Uchebnik peniia* [Textbook of singing], a compiled work that "drew the best from each of the methods" of Hérold, Lablache, Duprez, Garcia, Panofka, Cinti-Damoreau, and Vaccai, among others.[16] Influential vocal methods were also published by Stanislav Sonki (1853–1941), a student of Lamperti; Aleksandr Dodonov (1837–1914), a student of Garcia and Lamperti; Ippolit Prianishnikov (1847–1921), a student of Sebastiano Ronconi (among eighteen other teachers); and Caspar Křižanovsky (1861–1928), a student of Bucci, Giraldoni, and Cotogni.[17] As may be seen from the authors' backgrounds, they were all products of the Italian or French vocal schools (mostly the former), and were hardly in a position to develop any peculiarly Russian techniques in their methods.

Vasily Karelin (1869–1926) was perhaps the first to discuss certain traits peculiar to Russian singers. Writing in 1912, he noted that Russians, especially men, tend to speak and sing with a low-lying larynx and a dark timbre, which he attributed to the underdevelopment of the sphincter muscle. This makes it difficult to train baritone and bass voices properly. By contrast, Russian sopranos and tenors in choirs tend to sing with the throat closed and the larynx in a position close to swallowing, a practice which makes the proper training of the voice "hopeless." That staple of Russian choirs, the bass octavists, Karelin viewed to be "abnormal in the manner of vocal production"—with the larynx turned downwards and the vocal folds overcrossing. The attainment of a proper sound and function by octavists, in Karelin's opinion, is impossible.[18]

Vocal pedagogy at the newly established Russian conservatories in St. Petersburg and Moscow was based entirely on Western European methods. The most prominent pedagogues in St. Petersburg were Camillo Everardi and Henrietta Nissen-Saloman (1819–79), whose method was based on that of Garcia. At the Moscow Conservatory vocal pedagogy was headed from 1869 to 1887 by Giacomo Galvani (1826–89) and was based entirely on Italian music. Other pedagogues in Moscow included Aleksandra Aleksandrova-Kochetova (1833–1902), a student of Teschner in Berlin and Ronconi in St. Petersburg; Varvara Zarudnaia-Ivanova (1857–1939), a student of Everardi; and Umberto Masetti (1867–1919), the teacher of the famous soprano Antonina Nezhdanova (1873–1950). As the critic Nikolai Kashkin observed, "Our conservatories have not given us anything resembling an independent school of singing."[19]

Vocal Training in Choirs

Written theoretical methods in the area of choral voice training developed even more slowly than in solo vocal pedagogy: works such as Kovin's *Preparing the voice and ear of choral singers*[20] and Nikol'sky's *The voice and ear of the choral singer*[21] appeared only in the second decade of the twentieth century. Prior to the appearance of written choral methods, vocal training in Russian choirs was evidently shaped by the high degree of continuity found in most institutional or private choral establishments. A type of apprenticeship system, whereby younger and less experienced members learned from the older members, is already in evidence in the division of the Tsar's Singing Clerics and Patriarchal Singing Clerics into teams of various ranks, with the lowest-ranked teams consisting of trainees. Jakob von Stählin speaks of an apprenticeship system in the Imperial Chapel under which the young trainees arriving in St. Petersburg from the school in Glukhov were placed in the charge of experienced adult singers who taught them to sing according to the proper Italian manner.[22] A similar type of tutorial system (without the rod!) is described by Findeizen at the Moscow Synodal School at the end of the nineteenth century.[23]

Major establishments maintained a "teacher of singing" (*uchitel'peniia*), who was responsible for teaching both the existing repertoire and new pieces to the new singers. In smaller choirs this function was performed by the precentor himself. The manner in which the note-learning process was accomplished undoubtedly had a marked effect upon Russian choral performance. Almost without exception, notes were learned with the aid of a violin—an obvious legacy of the Italians. (More rarely, the assisting instrument was a harmonium.) The violin was considered to be an essential tool for a precentor: all students in the Imperial Chapel's precentors' courses instituted in 1852 by Aleksei L'vov (himself a first-rate violinist) had to own a violin and were expected to know how to play it. Wrote Pavel Vorotnikov, one of L'vov's assitants at the Chapel: "The violin has all the necessary qualities for supporting singing [at rehearsals]. Under an [expert] bow it can produce sounds quite similar to the human voice and, by the same token, becomes a good model for singing."[24] Vorotnikov did not recommend the piano for this purpose, while the harmonium in his opinion was not suitable because of its mechanically produced sound. Violin playing was introduced by Lomakin and Balakirev into the curriculum of the Free Music School specifically as "the main tool for [future] teachers of church music."[25] The curriculum of the Moscow Synodal Choir included eight years of violin, from the Second through the Ninth Grades (along with ten years of piano and six years of cello).[26]

As the earlier discussion of solo vocal pedagogy suggests, when it came to adopting a systematic method for training voices, Russian choral establishments had only Western European vocal methods at their disposal. According to Einbeck, who observed the Imperial Chapel in 1829, one of the main reasons for the choir's excellence was that "all voices were trained according to the best Italian method."[27] During the late eighteenth and early nineteenth centuries the Chapel produced a number of outstanding opera singers, among them such names as Orlov, Demidov, Labetsky, Fyodor Nikol'sky, Evsiutin, Grigory Klimovsky, Sobolev, Krupitsky, and Nikolai Ivanov.[28] In the 1830s, according to Rosliakov, the chief voice teacher was one Rubini.[29] Other voice teachers from 1825 to 1880 were Piccioli, Tombroni, Faciotti, Disciani, and Cavalli,[30] whose names clearly betray their nationality and likely vocal methodology.

Although establishments such as the Imperial Chapel evidently used some system of training their choristers, the very idea of training voices for choral singing in church was not universally recognized. As G. Serebriakov observed, as late as 1907 many church choir directors did not concern themselves with vocal training because, in their opinion, a trained voice with vibrato was useless for church singing. "In most choirs," he says, "the sopranos are dull [because] their voices have no forward projection, the basses sing with an unpleasant and ugly timbre, the altos are either hoarse or nasal, while the tenors sing with either a closed sound or falsetto." According to Serebriakov, such famous choral conductors as Arkhangel'sky, Yakov Ternov (conductor of the Metropolitan's Choir in St. Petersburg), and Evstafy Azeev (one of the principal conductors of the Imperial Court Chapel), did not have the slightest notion about vocal training.[31]

In 1909, Nikolai Kochetov (son of the singer Aleksandrova-Kochetova) delivered a report on the subject of choral voice training to the Second All-Russian Convention of Choral Conductors. He observed that many Russian church choirs persistently sing out of tune—the result of singing slightly nasally and with a constricted throat, habits brought on by the constant demand to sing softly and to observe the most subtle nuances. This manner is mistakenly considered to be part of the style in church singing, and has led to the view that training voices for church singing is somehow different from vocal training for secular singing. But healthy and normal singing, said Kochetov, is the same for church singing, secular choral singing, and solo singing. The real distinction of a churchly style lies in avoiding the mannerisms and excessive nuancing encountered in secular singing. Kochetov recommended that the Convention endorse the position that vocal training for church singing and secular singing follows identical principles.[32]

The following year, the Third Choral Convention heard a controversial report from Viacheslav Bulychev, entitled "Choral singing as an art." Under the present circumstances [in Russia]...," said Bulychev,

> the phrase "vocal training for choral singers" has a strange ring to it.... We have no choral singing as an art. What we call choirs and choral singing today are only signs of a strongly developed desire for such art, but it is not the art itself.... Show us at least one textbook of choral singing! Indeed it is impossible to name a single good textbook of choral singing in Russia...[other than] various solfege [methods], which mainly serve to develop the ear, but are composed quite illogically at that. Even foreign texts are virtually non-existent,... the only one being Franz Wüllner's *Chorübungen der Münchner Musikschule*,... the first part of which has been translated into Russian by Professor A. A. Il'insky.... But special questions pertaining to choral singing and its pedagogy still await their resolution in the future.[33]

Bulychev's lecture was not well-received. Several insulting remarks followed, and the lecturer left the convention in protest. The question of choral voice training did not reappear on the agenda.

Although Bulychev set forth very high standards for truly "artistic" choral singing, he was overstating the case by saying that Russia had no choral singing as an art. Certainly the Moscow Synodal Choir came very close to meeting his criteria, even though it had attained them only within the last decade of the nineteenth century. But within the walls of the Moscow Synodal

School itself the question of vocal training was subject to some debate, as is indicated by Semyon Kruglikov's argument to the Procurator of the Holy Synod Chancery, Prince Shirinsky-Shikhmatov, for additional funding:

> The quality of the Choir depends directly not only on its preparation [and] ensemble, but also on the freshness and beauty of its voices. To maintain the proper choral timbre and intonation, it is extremely important that these voices, in addition to the pleasant qualities imparted by nature, have the skill to produce the sound [properly] and regulate the breathing correctly, i.e., that they be trained to a certain extent.... For this reason I believe that training the young [boys'] voices as they enter is beneficial to the Choir.... [34]

The Moscow Synodal School did, in fact, adopt a method of voice training for newly accepted boys, and eventually made vocal pedagogy an integral part of the curriculum in the Ninth Grade. From 1892 to 1901 the voice teacher was V. S. Tiutiunnik, a singer with the Moscow Imperial Opera; he was followed by P. V. Vlasov, a graduate of the Synodal School. The curricular materials employed in the Ninth Grade courses on vocal training and the methodology of vocal development included the vocal methods of Abt and Marchesi, the vocalises of Concone, Garnault's book on the physiology of speech and singing, and other texts by Prianishnikov and Sonki. [35] As practical materials for study the curriculum suggested art songs by Russian composers, the folk song collections of Balakirev, Rimsky-Korsakov, and Liadov, and melodic chant formulae drawn from Metallov's *Osmoglasie znamennogo rospeva* [The Eight Tones of znamennyi chant] and the square-note chant books published by the Holy Synod. [36]

Just as Western choral part-singing was adopted by the Russians as their own and eventually synthesized into a vehicle for intensely national musical expression, so the Western vocal techniques of bel canto found receptive adherents among Russian singers in the "academic" choral tradition. The search for a peculiarly national Russian school of singing, whether solo or choral, did not yield any convincing results in the early twentieth century and is unlikely to do so in the future. The remarkable results achieved by leading Russian choirs are more the product of naturally talented vocal material, rigorously selected and systematically trained according to principles held in common both in Russia and in the West.

The Numerical Composition of Choirs

With regard to the size of the performing forces, the scholar of Russian choral performance of this period is in a fortunate position: sources indicating the numerical composition of specific Russian choirs are extensive and, one may assume, accurate. The practical figures, furthermore, correlate with ideal proportions for the balance of voices given in several theoretical manuals that were written as aids for workers in the expanding field of choral singing in late nineteenth-century Russia. In some cases, of course, the numbers represent minimums to be striven for in small provincial cities or villages. However, the theoretical numbers take on greater significance because their authors— L'vov, Lomakin, Chesnokov, Kastal'sky, and Kovin—were practicing composers and conductors themselves, involved directly with performing the music and eminently qualified to determine minimum numerical requirements from their own experience. Detailed information is also available concerning both the size and repertoire of choirs conducted by such master-conductors as Chesnokov and Danilin. Taken together, these data help to establish the acceptable numerical limits for performing Russian choral music of various genres.

The first attempt to define the size of a chorus theoretically was made by Aleksei L'vov in his work *O tserkovnykh khorakh* [Concerning church choirs], written as part of his effort to bring uniformity into Russian church choral singing, following the express wishes of Tsar Nicholas I. According to L'vov:

> The minimum size of a choir of adult singers is eight people, i.e., two first tenors, two second tenors, two first basses, and two second basses.
>
> The minimum size of a choir of adults and children [i.e., boys] is ten: three descants, three [boy] contraltos, two tenors, and two basses.
>
> A full choir...consists of the minimum numbers of singers quadrupled, i.e., twelve descants, twelve altos, eight tenors, and eight basses.[37]

These proportions differed only slightly from the numerical composition of the Imperial Chapel itself: in 1829, during Fyodor L'vov's tenure, the Chapel consisted of twenty-five descants, twenty-five altos, eighteen tenors, and twenty-two basses, of whom seven were octavists.[38] In 1853, Aleksei L'vov reported to Fétis that the Chapel consisted of fifty boys and forty men, without, however, specifying the number in each section.[39] In considering these numbers, one should bear in mind that the Imperial Chapel often had to provide singing in several court churches simultaneously. Moreover, in a given church the choir was divided into two groups—a right choir and a left choir—according to the church use. The singers may have joined together for certain important hymns, but even this possibility was determined by the architecture of a given church; in the eighteenth and nineteenth centuries many churches were built with widely separated balconies, which effectively prevented the right and left choirs from joining together.

Like many of L'vov's other administrative measures, his definition of the composition of a church choir came under criticism from leading churchmen.

Filaret, the Metropolitan of Moscow, took apart L'vov's treatise point by point, stating in part: "This number of singers [i.e., forty] in a choir is arbitrary and can rarely be applied in practice! Diocesan choirs are staffed by twenty-four singers. The few choirs that have a larger number of singers often divide into smaller contingents because they must sing simultaneously in several churches."[40]

Lomakin in his *Kratkaia metoda peniia* [A brief method of singing] gives twelve as the minimum number of singers in a mixed choir, but in slightly different proportions than L'vov: four descants, three altos, two tenors, and three basses. For all-male or all-female (e.g., monastic) choirs the proportions are: three first descants or tenors, three second descants or tenors, and four altos or basses; for a children's choir—ten first descants, eight second descants, and twelve altos.[41] Lomakin spent much of his career as conductor of the private chapel of the counts Sheremetev. In 1822, when Lomakin first came to that choir as a boy, the group numbered thirty singers; later, under Lomakin's direction, the choir numbered sixty boys and men (the subdivision into sections is not known).[42]

The number of singers considered necessary to constitute a church choir remained small into the last quarter of the nineteenth century. In 1875, in his *Obshcheponiatnoe rukovodstvo k izucheniiu notnogo tserkovnogo khorovogo i odinochnogo peniia* [A common-sense manual of choral and solo church singing] Ivan Kazansky wrote: "The average number of individuals making up a chorus is twelve: namely, four descants (two firsts and two seconds), the same number of (or at least three) altos, and the same number each of tenors and basses. This number of voices will constitute a relatively full chorus capable of performing absolutely everything. A choir of thirty ... [is] the fullest choir."[43]

As the nineteenth century drew to an end, the theoretical size of a choir increased, reflecting the demands of the new repertoire. However, the increase was not as large as the musical scores, replete with divisi and octave doublings, might suggest. In 1907 Vasily Zinov'ev's *Prakticheskoe rukovodstvo dlia nachinaiushchego uchitelia-regenta* [A practical manual for the beginning precentor] specified eight sopranos, six altos, six tenors, and eight basses—a total of twenty-eight. These figures also served as proportions for the balance between sections in larger or smaller choirs.[44]

In Kastal'sky's *Obshchedostupnyi samouchitel' tserkovnogo peniia* [A popular self-instructor of church singing], his only published theoretical work dealing with the performance of church singing, the basic definition of a "choir" is very broad: "If many are singing (eight to ten) it is called a chorus."[45] The manual is deliberately directed at the most uneducated village reader, and Kastal'sky probably did not expect that his works would be performed by so small a choir. Elsewhere in the manual he states that if the choir is "not too small—say, twenty or so [singers]," divisi and doubling of parts should be used in singing simple litanies and responses.[46]

Kastal'sky's unpublished notebook entitled "Metodika prepodavaniia shkol'nogo khorovogo peniia" [The methodology of teaching choral singing in the schools], under the heading "The size of the choir," contains more specific numbers: six basses (two of them octavists), five tenors, seven altos, and nine sopranos (five firsts plus four seconds). "For a full chorus (with doublings) no fewer than twenty-seven singers are required."[47]

The first comprehensive theoretical work on choral conducting to be published after the stylistic revolution in Russian choral music was already well on its way was Nikolai Kovin's *Upravlenie khorom* [Choral conducting].[48] In this work Kovin, a graduate of the Moscow Synodal School and a teacher of choral conducting at Smolensky's Precentors' School in St. Petersburg, reflects the demands of the new choral style. He distinguishes between a "large mixed chorus, . . . which has good, sonorous, well-developed voices, to whom are accessible all the notes of their range without difficulty" and a "small mixed chorus—a type of choir that has appeared only recently— in educational institutions, villages, and small towns, . . . distinguished not so much by the number of voices, as by their quality. . . . Voices in a small mixed chorus, even if they are naturally good, are generally untrained."[49] While he is reluctant to prescribe any specific figures for the number of singers in a chorus, Kovin states that "with equally good voices the numerical proportions of the sections will be approximately as follows: twelve descants, and nine each of altos, tenors, and basses."[50]

The most complete and well-argued discussion of the number of singers in a chorus is found in Chesnokov's *The choir and how to direct it*. The minimum number in each section is derived from his basic definition of "choral" singing—that no singer is ever left singing alone, without having to blend and tune with other voices. Thus, the minimum number of voices per section is three: when one singer takes a breath, two other voices remain to carry the part. Based on this requirement Chesnokov builds his totals: a small mixed choir must be made up of twelve singers, but such a choir cannot execute divisi and is limited strictly to four-part literature. The minimum number for what Chesnokov calls a "full mixed choir—a choir that, with very few exceptions, can perform virtually all [Russian] choral literature" is twenty-seven: three first sopranos, three second sopranos, three first altos, three second altos, three first tenors, three second tenors, three baritones, four second basses, and two octavists. "The regrouping of the bass section," says Chesnokov, "occurs because the bass, as the fundamental [voice], must be slightly strengthened. As far as the section of octavists is concerned, here one may make an exception to the rule that 'the minimum number of singers in a section is three. . . .'"[51]

Proportionately increasing the number of singers per section, Chesnokov obtains the composition of a "large mixed chorus": six S1's, six S2's, six A1's, six A2's, six T1's, six T2's, six B1's, eight B2's, and four octavists, for a total of fifty-four. "To this mighty chorus is accessible all choral literature."[52] While admitting that these numbers may appear to be somewhat arbitrary and overly theoretical, Chesnokov points out that they are the result of many years' observation and experience. He also does not set any upper limits for a large mixed chorus, but states that beyond a certain limit, the sonority simply increases in decibel level but not in quality.

The relationship between the theoretical figures given above and actual practice has already been mentioned in the case of the Imperial Court Chapel and the Sheremetev Choir. The numerical composition, if not the musical quality, of the Imperial Chapel remained stable throughout the nineteenth and into the twentieth century. In 1910 the Chapel consisted of ninety boys, including trainees, and thirty-six adult males;[53] in 1916, there were sixty regular boys, twenty to thirty boy trainees, and thirty-eight men.[54] However, the Chapel continued to serve several different court churches, appearing in concerts with its full complement of voices only once or twice a year.

Statistical information on other church choirs in St. Petersburg appeared in a survey made in 1910 by the journal *Khorovoe i regentskoe delo*. Altogether, twenty-two choirs were surveyed of which nine were professional. The numerical makeup of the four most important choirs is given in table 4.1. For church services these choirs probably divided into two choruses of equal size. In some cases, such as at the Cathedral of the Alexander Nevsky Lavra, the joining of the two choirs was impossible because they stood in balconies to the right and left of the nave. The survey concluded that in many cases the size of the choir was acoustically insufficient for the size of the church. The amateur choirs in particular were quite small, numbering from eight to thirty singers. Even Arkhangel'sky's professional choir, which altogether numbered between sixty-five and seventy singers, served six different churches in contingents of fifteen, ten, twelve, twelve, ten, and eight singers.[55]

Additional information on choirs that performed in concerts as well as in churches is found in the *Musical handbook* for 1914: K. K. Biriuchev's Choir (sixty men and women), V. V. Pevtsova's Choir (sixty singers), M. P. Rechkunov's Choir (twenty men and twenty women), the Bratsky Chorus under Anastas Nikolov (sixty men and women), and Count A. D. Sheremetev's Choir (ten sopranos, ten altos, ten tenors, ten basses), reorganized, now with both men's and women's voices after being disbanded in the late nineteenth century.[56]

In Moscow, the Synodal Choir gradually increased in numbers as it gained in status and prestige. Whereas from 1767 to 1857 the Choir had numbered thirty-eight singers, in 1857 the number was increased to fifty-

Table 4.1.   The Numerical Makeup of Church Choirs in St. Petersburg in 1910

Choir	Type	Sopranos	Altos	Tenors	Basses	Total
St. Isaac's Cathedral	Professional	18(b)	12(b)	8	12	50
Kazan Cathedral	Professional	20(b)	12(b)	11	15	60
Izmailovsky Regiment	Military	25(b)	15(b)	17	20	77
Alexander Nevsky Lavra (Metropolitan's Choir)	Professional	35(b)	30(b)	16	16	97

(b) = boys

four—thirty boys and twenty-four men. Throughout this period the Synodal Choir had been responsible for providing singing not only in the Cathedral of the Dormition, but also in the Church of the Twelve Apostles and in various other court churches in the Kremlin. The administrative reform of 1886 increased the number of boys to fifty and the number of men to thirty; and the Moscow Synodal Choir existed in this form until its dissolution immediately after the October Revolution of 1917.[57] When the Choir sang at full strength in the Cathedral it usually divided into two equal choirs of forty singers each. Only forty singers went in 1899 to Vienna for the dedication of the embassy church; and the same number went in 1913 to Leipzig for the blessing of a monument.[58] In both Vienna and Leipzig the Choir not only sang church services but also performed concerts. Hence, forty singers was evidently an acceptable minimum, even for concert performances of works in the new style. In 1912, twenty-three members of the Choir travelled to Nice for the dedication of a church, but no information is available concerning what they performed on that occasion. Of course at its most important performances— the history-making concerts at the Synodal School and the European tour of 1911—the Choir appeared in its full complement of eighty voices (though only seventy made the European trip).

The Moscow Chudov Choir, the personal choir of the Metropolitan of Moscow (named after the Chudov Monastery, formerly located in the Kremlin but destroyed after the October Revolution) numbered twenty-four singers from the time it was formed in 1750 until well into the nineteenth century. In 1868, at the height of its glory under Fyodor Bagretsov, the choir numbered between one hundred and one hundred twenty singers; thereafter the number decreased to thirty-four.[59] By 1914, the number of singers had increased once more to over one hundred, although the choir had lost much of its former significance. (I did not find a single review of the Chudov Choir or its activities after the 1870s.)

It is difficult to say exactly how many singers other professional church choirs in Moscow employed at a given service. Available sources give only the total number of singers maintained by various choral entrepreneurs: Leonid Vasil'ev—one hundred eighty, Fyodor Ivanov—two hundred, Anatoly Arkhangel'sky—ninety to one hundred, A. A. Andreev—sixty, and so forth.[60] With the exception of Vasil'ev's and Ivanov's choirs, which occasionally gave concert performances, these large groups seldom performed as a whole, but divided into smaller contingents to sing in several different churches. Among other Moscow choirs, the choir of Christ the Savior Cathedral numbered fifty, and probably did not divide into smaller groups. I. I. Yukhov's Choir, which made numerous gramophone recordings in the first two decades of the present century, numbered thirty men and women. The amateur choir of the Church of the Holy Trinity "na Griaziakh," conducted by Chesnokov from 1902 to 1913, consisted of forty-two singers in 1904: ten women sopranos, seven women altos, twelve tenors, and thirteen basses.[61] With this choir Chesnokov performed numerous works in the new style, including first performances of his own compositions, particularly from his opuses 27 and 33, "for small chorus." (A partial listing of this choir's repertoire appears in table 4.2.)

A particularly interesting source is a complete, service-by-service listing of works performed by the choir of the St. Paraskeva Church (located in what was known before 1917 as the Okhotnyi Riad), directed by Nikolai Danilin after the Bolshevik Revolution, when the Moscow Synodal Choir was disbanded. The listing, which runs from August of 1924 to May of 1928, shows that with a choir of twenty-three to thirty singers Danilin continued to sing the highly challenging repertoire of the Synodal Choir—works by Kastal'sky, Grechaninov, Chesnokov, Rachmaninoff, and other composers of the new Russian school.[62] To be sure, conditions for church choirs were by no means optimal after 1917 and Danilin's number of singers may well have been determined by the church's budget. But even if the number of singers were fixed, Danilin still retained discretion over his choice of repertoire; the fact that such a sensitive and demanding artist continued to perform these works with a relatively small number of singers suggests that extremely large choirs are not necessary to render works of the new Russian choral school properly.

Little detailed information is available concerning the numerical makeup of secular choirs. No figures could be located for the Russian Choral Society in Moscow, for example. Numerical data for Mel'nikov's Choir in St. Petersburg shows that between 1894 and 1900 the group fluctuated from one hundred fifty to three hundred singers: for example, in the 1896/97 season the choir numbered twenty-six first sopranos, twenty second sopranos, nineteen first altos, twelve second altos, twenty-five first tenors, twenty second tenors, seventeen first basses, and eleven second basses.[63] Due to the educational nature of the group, the personnel changed from year to year. Arkhangel'sky's

Table 4.2. The Concert Repertoire of Pavel Chesnokov's Amateur Church Choir

SACRED CONCERT—April 10, 1905

1. Litanies — Smolensky
   a. Great
   b. Augmented
   c. Supplication
2. Cherubic Hymn (from *Liturgy*) — Tchaikovsky
3. Slava...Edinorodnyi Syne — Grechaninov
4. Cherubic Hymn — Grechaninov
5. Tebe poem (Znamennyi Chant) — Kastal'sky
6. Otche nash — Tchaikovsky
7. Dostoino est' — Tchaikovsky

===========

8. Great Litany — Tchaikovsky
9. Se nyne blagoslovite Gospoda — Ippolitov-Ivanov
10. Tebe odeiushchagosia — Turchaninov
11. Veruiu — Grechaninov
12. Vo tsarstvii Tvoem — Panchenko
13. Milost' mira — Kastal'sky
14. Voskliknite Gospodevi — Grechaninov

SACRED CONCERT—April 13, 1906

1. Se nyne blagoslovite Gospoda — Ippolitov-Ivanov
2. Tebe poem (Kievan Chant) — P. Chesnokov
3. Gospodi, spasi...Trisviatoe — P. Chesnokov
4. Otche nash — Tchaikovsky
5. Angel vopiiashe — Tchaikovsky
6. Tebe odeiushchagosia — Turchaninov

=============

7. Cherubic Hymn (Greek Chant) — L'vovsky
8. Vo tsarstvii Tvoem — Panchenko
9. Slava...Edinorodnyi — Grechaninov
10. Tebe poem (Serbian Chant) — Kastal'sky
11. V chermnem mori (Dogmatikon in Tone 5) — Kastal'sky
12. Paschal Stichera — Smolensky

SACRED CONCERT—December 21, 1908

1. Cherubic Hymn — Muzichesku
2. Cherubic Hymn — Glinka
3. Gospodi spasi...Sviatyi Bozhe — Tchaikovsky
4. Gospodi spasi...Sviatyi Bozhe — P. Chesnokov
5. Milost' mira (Serbian Chant) — Kastal'sky

Table 4.2.   (continued)

6.	Vo tsarstvii Tvoem	—Vik. Kalinnikov
7.	O Tebe raduetsia	—P. Chesnokov
8.	Veruiu	—Tchaikovsky
9.	Vskuiu mia otrinul esi	—Arkhangel'sky
10.	Se chto dobro	—Ippolitov-Ivanov
11.	K Bogoroditse prilezhno	—Grechaninov
12.	Blazheni iazhe izbral	—Tchaikovsky

SACRED CONCERT—March 19, 1909
(Concert devoted entirely to Chesnokov's own works.)

1. Blagoslovi, dushe (at Liturgy)
2. Slava...Edinorodnyi Syne
3. Gospodi spasi...Krestu Tvoemu
4. So sviatymi upokoi
5. Cherubic Hymn ("Raduisia" melody)
6. Milost' mira (E minor)
7. Angel vopiiashe (w. soprano solo)
8. Gospodi spasi...Elitsy vo Khrista
9. Tebe poem (Kievan Chant)
10. O Tebe raduetsia
11. Chertog Tvoi
12. Razboinika blagorazumnago
13. Na rekakh Vavilonskikh
14. O vsepetaia Mati

Choir, after the first few years, numbered from sixty to seventy singers, although it frequently toured with as few as thirty.

The figures cited above indicate that by the nineteenth century the four-part mixed choir had become standard in Russian choral practice. Most choirs included soprano and alto parts sung by boys (later by women). The all-male (TTBB) chorus tradition was not as widespread as the large number of émigré male Russian choirs would suggest. All-male choirs and all-treble choirs (SSAA) were found primarily in schools and monasteries.

The only type of choir whose makeup differs substantially from well-known Western equivalents is the peasant folk chorus, which, as mentioned earlier, developed into a stylized professional ensemble after the October Revolution of 1917. The following description of the folk chorus should dispel any possible confusion between this type of choir and the various church and professional "art" choruses discussed thus far in this chapter.[64]

The usual size of a Russian folk chorus is between fifteen and twenty singers. Some of the professional folk ensembles in the Soviet Union, such as the Piatnitsky Chorus or the Northern Chorus (*Severnyi Khor*), are slightly larger, numbering between twenty-five and thirty singers. The balance of voice parts in a folk chorus reflects the fact that the choral sonority is built around the timbres of the altos in the women's group and the timbres of the high baritones in the men's group. Thus, in a folk chorus with eight or nine altos, it is sufficient to have two or three sopranos while in the male contingent, eight or nine baritones and basses are effectively balanced by three or four high tenors. Low bass voices or octavists play no part in a folk chorus. In general, the composition of folk choruses is marked by a great degree of flexibility: the numbers given above could easily be modified, for example, to ten to twelve altos, two or three sopranos, and only five men singing a single voice part.[65] Similarly, some folk choruses approach the "academic" chorus in terms of vocal makeup and working range. Much depends on the texture of the piece being performed, which in turn is determined by myriad local and regional performing traditions. Elsewhere in this chapter various other specific features of the folk chorus will be described; however, one must bear in mind that the folk chorus had no influence whatsoever upon the composition or sonorous ideal of Russian choirs in the nineteenth and early twentieth centuries.

The Positioning of the Singers

The sources that contain information about the numerical makeup of choirs in the late nineteenth and early twentieth centuries also describe the way they were positioned. Kovin, for example, suggests several ways of arranging the choir on a kliros or in the choir loft, depending on the architecture of the church and the circumstances of the performance.[66] Under the optimal conditions of a concert stage, Kovin, Kastal'sky, and Chesnokov all favor the arrangement shown in figure 4.1.[67]

The important thing, according to Chesnokov, is that the highest and lowest voices be grouped towards the center, while voices that usually function as harmonic fillers are placed on the outside. Kovin also gives another arrangement, shown in figure 4.2. The sections at the rear should be raised "at least by a head" over those in front of them, [68] and "passageways should be left between the rows, so that the conductor can conveniently distribute the pitches"[69] without the audience hearing. (The Moscow Synodal Choir's practice of taking the pitch inaudibly particularly impressed Western European reviewers.)

Arranging the singers in distinct sections obviously placed great emphasis on blend within a given section, a principle articulated early on by Aleksei L'vov: "In general rehearsals, [the precentor] should see to it that no voice...overpowers another, since choral singing is perfect only when the listener, hearing all the singers, does not discern any one individual voice."[70]

Figure 4.1.   The Scheme for Positioning a Chorus Recommended by Chesnokov.

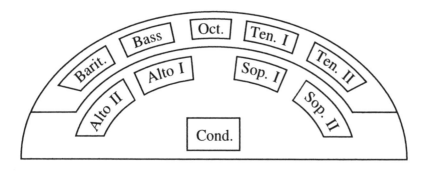

Figure 4.2.   Another Possible Scheme for Positioning a Chorus.

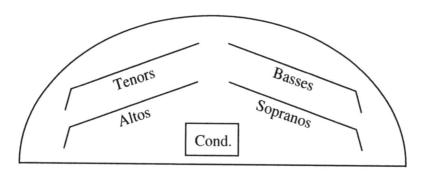

Generally speaking, Russian choirs adhered to positioning by sections and did not experiment with the placement of singers. There is evidence, however, that the Moscow Synodal Choir occasionally performed in a formation that alternated the boy sopranos and altos and the tenors and basses, as shown in figure 4.3.[71]

The Characteristics of Choral Voices

The question of vocal timbres and ranges is somewhat more problematic to investigate than the numerical makeup of choirs. As comparative studies of vocal pedagogy have shown, the terminology employed to describe various aspects of vocal sonority is highly individualized and subjective.[72] This subjectivity is reduced slightly whenever a writer relates his descriptive terms

Figure 4.3.   An Arrangement Used on Occasion by the Moscow Synodal Choir.

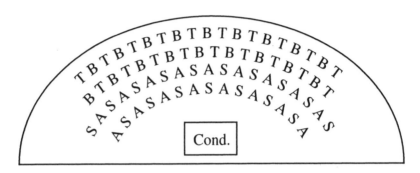

to specific physiological functions, but even physiological functions are sometimes couched in abstract or obscure terms.

One of the earliest general descriptions of desirable vocal qualities appears in an instruction issued in the 1830s by the Imperial Court Chapel to its precentors sent to the Ukraine to recruit voices: "The voice of the auditionee must be even from the first to the last note [of the range], capable of taking each note of the diapason softly, increasing it in volume, and ending softly once again, demonstrating the natural freedom without which no voice can have genuine merit...."[73] Another general statement appears in an instruction issued in 1836 by the Synodal Chancery in Moscow to the Moscow Synodal Choir. It states, in part, that the singers should not pronounce words through the teeth or into the nose "in a provincial manner."

> A good method of singing demands that every singer ... pronounce the words as clearly and precisely as possible, for church music properly serves to express the word.... Good taste demands that in church singing two extremes be avoided:... excessive affectation, which is appropriate for the theater, and crude shouting, to which are particularly prone [choirs of] the wealthy who have no taste or education. Good voices, concord among them, balance in volume, trueness of pitch, simplicity inspired by piety, clear, distinct, and cultured pronunciation of words—this is the perfection in church singing to which the choir should aspire.[74]

The statement that singing not be "in the nose" is interesting in light of a description of an Old Believers' choir in an article by Valentin Moshkov entitled "Nekotorye provintsial'nye osobennosti v russkom narodnom penii" [Some provincial peculiarities of Russian folk singing].[75] The writer likens the timbre of the singers to the Near-Eastern nasal manner of singing heard in Jewish synagogues. Although the Instruction of 1836 did not specify the type of vocal timbre desired in church singing, it evidently preferred a "cultured," Europeanized manner of singing to a "provincial" style.

The desirable qualities of choral voices are described more specifically in the manuals of Lomakin and Kazansky, which date from the 1860s. Kazansky writes: "The voice must be pure, rounded, and precise,...mobile and mellow,...[capable of] producing notes of the shortest duration....[It] should not be blatant, but full, sonorous, and gentle,...having an identical [quality] throughout both the high and low range. The voice should maintain its integrity [both] in forte and piano."[76] Lomakin states essentially the same criteria, but places them in the context of vocal training: "The student must at the very beginning of study master a vocal sound that is accurate, rounded, and mellow, and not allow himself to sing with a constricted, nasal, or throaty voice.... Particular attention must be paid to the mellowness and flexibility of the voice...."[77]

The most frequently employed terms to describe a desirable vocal timbre are "resonant" and "ringing." A physiological explanation of what is a "resonant" timbre is found in N. Vitashevsky's *Shkol'noe prepodavanie khorovogo peniia* [Teaching choral singing in the school]: "The sound is at its fullest, most 'rounded,' most resonant, when the sound-forming column of air is directed at the middle of the hard palate. If [it is] directed at the soft palate, the timbre is muted, with insufficient resonance; by contrast, if it is directed at the aperture of the lips, the sound is too shrill, though not devoid of resonance."[78] While Vitashevsky speaks specifically of boys' (or children's) voices, Dmitri Allemanov in his *Metodika tserkovnogo peniia* [Methology of church singing] makes a more general statement: "The best vocal tone occurs when the sound is felt in the middle of the mouth (with the stream of the sound-bearing air current striking the hard palate). Dull sounds result when the sound current is directed to the soft palate; flat sounds—when the current does not strike the palate at all but simply escapes from the throat out the opening of the teeth."[79]

Kastal'sky illustrates the desirable "placement" of timbre by means of an easily reproduced example: "[While singing the 'ah' vowel] maintain the throat as if you are blowing to warm up a window pane that has frosted over.... Sing a note of medium pitch ... and try to feel it resonate in the chest; the sound should come straight out the mouth (without the teeth getting in the way), and feel as if it is striking the top front teeth.... The rounded roof of the mouth behind the front teeth is called the hard palate; it is here that the sound strikes upon emerging from the throat."[80] Down-to-earth as Kastal'sky's description may be, it suggests that he favored a timbre that was more "forward" or "open," focused on the hard palate closer to the front teeth. This preference, at least with respect to treble voices, is confirmed by a comment found in his "Methodology," where he complains about "the poor manner of placing the high register of children's voices—into the head (a type of cuckoo-bird timbre), as a result of which the sound comes out lifeless."[81]

Specific statements by various Russian choral conductors show that they did not agree upon the ideal type of choral voice. Fyodor Bekker, for example, insisted that his singers sing with a "clear and beautiful sound" and avoid sounds that were "open" or "throaty." At the same time, the singer must "distinguish clearly between a bright and dark sound," depending on the content of the text.[82]

Arkhangel'sky began his rehearsals by practicing "closed sounds," which he always demanded in choral singing. In Arkhangel'sky's words, "a closed sound has a 'depth' that is very convincing and full of perspective." The desired position of the vocal mechanism was achieved by having the singers close their mouth and, tightly clenching the teeth and lips, sing on the pitches of a song, pronouncing the words mentally but naturally. In normal singing the vocal mechanism was to maintain the position it had had with the mouth closed. Throaty sounds were "absolutely inadmissible on any letter or syllable," and the sound must reside "exclusively in the chest." Arkhangel'sky also regarded tremolo as a major shortcoming in a voice. "This must not happen! The voice must sound like a string [of an instrument]."[83]

One of Nikolai Danilin's students, Klavdy Ptitsa, describes his teacher's preferences for choral voices in the following terms:

> Among women's voices Nikolai Mikhailovich preferred light sopranos, capable of precise intonation and without the wide, "thick" sound that blends with difficulty within a section. In the first altos he primarily used voices with a straight, "boy alto" timbre, while in the second altos he liked a velvety and saturated timbre. He considered voices with a rapid tremolo particularly dangerous for the chorus. Among the voices he considered unsuitable for choral singing were most baritones; thus he recruited the first bass section extremely carefully, preferring light basses.[84]

Pavel Chesnokov favored a more closed, "covered" sound than his colleagues at the Moscow Synodal School, Kastal'sky and Allemanov, advocated in their physiological descriptions:

> Sound that strikes the hard palate directly tends to be reedy,... open, "white." [Such a sound] is not permissible in the chorus. By contrast,... sound that strikes the soft palate,... acquires a matte shading,... which is then [additionally] resonated in the mouth, assuming a roundness, fulness, density, and dimension.... This closed sound should be demonstrated often to the singers.... [Nevertheless,] the skillful and controlled *opening* [of the sound], i.e., moving the point of focus towards the hard palate, creates a majestic effect that cannot be achieved with any other manner of sound production.[85]

In addition, Chesnokov identified a "semicovered" sound (*prikrytyi zvuk*), which contained more audible breathiness than tone: "By means of a semicovered sound the most rigorous pianissimo may be easily achieved."[86]

Concerning the selection of voices Chesnokov makes the general statement that "One should...avoid voices with strong vibrato,...since they destroy sectional blend."

Chesnokov developed the theoretical aspects of "voicing" a choir to a great degree of complexity, describing the timbres of the various sections in terms that border on the ideally abstract. His presentation is best perceived in tabular fashion (see table 4.3).[87]

Interestingly, in describing vocal timbres, Chesnokov makes no distinction between female voices and boys' voices. As for the timbre of second basses, which, Chesnokov says, "is so commonly known, that one hardly needs to expound upon it," it is noteworthy he employs the term "bright," contradicting the widely held notion that Russian basses are dark and hooty.

Chesnokov's description correlates with Vitoshinsky's observation about basses in central Russia: "Abroad, Russia is famous for its basses. But the bass in Great Russia is always a little blatant, somewhat raspy.... Southern basses do not have this natural propensity to be blatant or coarse...." According to Vitoshinsky, the quality of northern basses may be attributed to the fact that "among Great Russian singers the opinion persists to this day that, in order for the voice to be strong and pleasant, a good bass must unfailingly and abundantly 'pour it down the necktie' [i.e., drink vodka—V. M.]."[88]

The distinction between "academic" and "folk" choruses described earlier is made even more apparent by differences in the sonorities and ranges of the various sections. Concerning the two most important sections in the folk chorus, the altos and baritones, Anna Rudneva says:

> ...the timbre of the first altos must be ringing, bright, clear, [and] free from excessive vibrato or matte shading.... The distinctive...ringing quality (*zvonkost'*) [is achieved] within the chest register. The upper head register of the alto voice is hardly used.... Such voices are very similar in timbre to boys' voices.... The sopranos...must [also] be similar in timbre to boy sopranos, but their main distinguishing characteristic is the almost total lack of vibrato—a straight, somewhat shrill sound.

In drawing the analogy to boy sopranos and altos, Rudneva does not specify whether she is referring to raw, untrained boys' voices or voices that have undergone some systematic training, which would undoubtedly alter the quality. Concerning the male voices, she continues: "[The joint section of] baritones and tenors [is] strong, ringing, and 'rich' in timbre.... The two or three high tenors who sing upper countervoices sing with a sound similar to boy altos. The basses [often] sing the tenor part in falsetto or join the baritones [while] maximally lightening the sonority of their voices."[89] Each section in a folk chorus generally sings in a limited range of no more than an octave;

Table 4.3. The Timbres of Choral Voices according to Chesnokov

Voice Part	Range	Characteristic Timbre
1st Soprano	f″—a″	Strong, bright, brilliant, silvery
2nd Soprano	c″—g″	Rich, solid, saturated
1st Alto	g′—c″	Rich, solid, saturated
	b—f′	Somewhat lacking in lustre
2nd Alto	g—c′	Strong and thick
	c′—f′	Full, thick, solid
1st Tenor	e′—a′	Light, bright, brilliant
2nd Tenor	g—c′	Rich and thick
	d—g	Strong and solid
Baritone	B—f	Solid, thick, somewhat lacking in lustre
	g—c′	Strong and bright
	c′—e′	Brilliant
2nd Bass	Throughout	Strong, powerful, dense, saturated, yet bright
Bass Octavist	G,—C	Not strong, but deep, mellow, velvety
	C—G	Strong, but often heavy and coarse
	A—c	Heavy and unpleasant
	above d	Poor

consequently, the entire chorus has a much more limited diapason as well, emphasizing the two octaves on either side of middle C and avoiding the extremes. Thus, Russian choral folk singing makes *no use* of low bass voices, in either the second bass or the octavist ranges. This fact is often ignored by those scholars (particularly in the Soviet Union) who attempt to derive the Russian artistic choral tradition from folk roots or to trace Russian church chant and folk singing to common sources.

The Bass Voice in Russian Choral Singing

Much has been said of the important role played by low basses in Russian choral singing. However, for decades the only specific guideline available to Western performers was N. Lindsay Norden's dictum that "It is customary, in Russian church music, for the octavo-bass to double the written bass when harmonically possible. This is, perhaps, the chief element in rendering this music, and should be given the necessary preparation."[90] This statement, splashed indiscriminately over most of Norden's editions, has justifiably raised doubts among more perceptive writers. For example, Elwyn Wienandt and Robert Young write: "Whether such knowledge was general—or accurate—is doubtful."[91] The question of Russian basses, and particularly the octavo-bass, requires closer examination.

The prominence of the bass voice among the Russians has been noted for a long time. In the mid-seventeenth century, Deacon Paul of Aleppo, who travelled to Muscovy with Patriarch Makarios of Antioch, wrote:

> The singing of the cossacks [in the south] gladdens the soul and drives away sorrow, since their melody is pleasant.... These others [the Muscovites], on the other hand, perform singing without any schooling; however it comes out, it is all the same to them, and they are not ashamed of it. [They consider] the best voice [to be] coarse, deep, and bassy—one that brings no pleasure to the listener. Just as we would consider such a voice to be a shortcoming, so they consider our high chanting indecorous.... They all perform [ekphonetic] reading in the same fashion.[92]

There is no documentary evidence that pinpoints when the practice of doubling the bass line an octave lower in choral singing originated in Russia. In the four-part Baroque-style polyphony that prevailed in Russia from 1650 to the coming of the Italian opera in 1735, the bass lines sometimes provide the harmonic foundation in the manner of basso continuo. Yet at other times they are extraordinarily florid, filling in intervals with rapid eighth- and sixteenth-note runs that seem to defy the heaviness of the low bass voice. (One can hardly imagine that these lines would have been performed with octave doublings.) More than likely, the practice of doubling was introduced in the eighteenth century by the Italian composers at the St. Petersburg court, who transferred many stylistic features of the contemporary instrumental style (including the doubling of the bass line by cellos and double basses) to the realm of unaccompanied choral music. Until the coming of the Italians, Russian music theorists still employed the hexachord system; hence, the term *octavist* (as well as the term *basso profundo*, sometimes used to describe the voice) probably originated with the Italians. Once the need for extremely low voices became dictated by the style, the Imperial Court Chapel and its imitators among the choirs of the nobility used their ample recruiting resources to find the necessary voices.[93] Dmitri Rosliakov, who was a boy soprano in the Imperial Chapel in the 1830s, tells the story of how a member of the Imperial Guard, a certain Kartushin, answered Emperor Nicholas I's greeting in such a strong and low voice, that the latter immediately ordered him to report to the Chapel.[94]

Towards the end of the nineteenth century octavists were undoubtedly a familiar phenomenon in many Russian choirs, but not so familiar that they didn't merit more discussion by writers and critics than any other section in the choir. V. M. Orlov says that "[the octavist] is a rather rare voice. With his low velvety sounds...[he] unites the entire choir and gives it a great deal of beauty. Oftentimes one such voice is sufficient for a chorus. There are [however] among them very strident [voices],...which should be controlled as much as possible, because they are not always pleasant to the ear."[95] Similar sentiments are expressed by Kovin, who writes:

A full sonority of the lowest notes in a chord sung by the second basses and octavists tremendously beautifies and enhances the sound of the choir (in slow tempos). [Just as a] modern orchestra introduces low-sounding instruments into each group,...[so] in a chorus one should not disregard the number of second basses, as some choir directors are inclined to do for fear that the section will predominate over the others. One can always contain basses that are singing too loudly and too coarsely.[96]

While Kovin maintains that "the timbres of baritones, basses, and octavists are sufficiently different to be considered separate voice parts," Chesnokov writes that "the octavist section in essence is not a separate section; this beautiful sounding part is really to some extent a luxury in a chorus (albeit one that is almost indispensable). This part must be used with great care, without excesses; otherwise the beauty of its sound will be depreciated and will even become tiresome."[97]

In the journal he kept while conducting the choir at the Church of the Holy Trinity, Chesnokov expresses further thoughts concerning the octavists:

Octave [doubling] is a luxury in the chorus, but one that is often used without due consideration for the proper place and time; hence, it does not produce the effect that can be achieved when it is used skillfully. Composers today, as in former times, for some reason have not paid the necessary attention to this mighty and effective element of the choir. This leaves only the conductor to bring this aspect of the choir to order, using the [octavists] in the most favorable sonorities and circumstances. With this in mind I mark all pieces for the octavists and absolutely forbid them to take liberties with their contra-octave tones.[98]

Chesnokov's comments suggest that, while the sonority of the octavists is indeed important in Russian choral performance, it should be used with discretion and good taste. Discriminating critics in the late nineteenth century, such as Ivan Lipaev, frequently singled out the misuse of octavists as a cheap device characteristic of the more vulgar church-choir practices. In a review of a 1896 performance of the Imperial Court Chapel in Moscow, he writes that "The octavist displayed what choir singers call an 'uncommon *basse contre*.'"[99] In a critique of Leonid Vasil'ev's Choir in 1901, Lipaev notes that "the choir cannot part with certain things that are peculiar to church choirs...an octavist who sometimes roared 'as a lion after its prey.'"[100]

Boys' versus Women's Voices

In the late 1800s and the early 1900s Russian choral circles engaged in a lively controversy over the question of boys' versus women's voices in church choirs. While the credit for introducing women permanently into the church choir is generally given to Arkhangel'sky, there is evidence that female voices were used nearly a century earlier in private serf choirs. Referring to the peasant girl Anisia in Beketov's Choir, who enraptured the Moscow congregation in 1805, Prince Vladimir Odoevsky reported to the Minister of Education that, "To perform the church music of Galuppi, Sarti, Kerzelli, and others, women's voices were needed. [Odoevsky neglects to explain why.] The nobility established choirs, and since it was forbidden to bring women onto the kliros, servant girls were shorn, dressed in men's clothing, and made to sing in church."[101] As the nineteenth century progressed, there is no evidence, however, that women participated in church choirs until Arkhangel'sky's innovation in 1880.

Contrary to the opinion of some Western scholars, the Orthodox Church never imposed a canonical prohibition against women singing in church.[102] The apostolic injunctions that women be silent in church (e.g., I Corinthians, 14:34–35 and I Timothy, 2:11–12) were interpreted to mean that women should not teach or preach, but not as forbidding them to sing. The reason women for a long time did not sing in church choirs had more to do with the Orthodox custom of having men and women stand separately in church: if those in the congregation had to stand separately, it would not be proper for women to stand together with men in the choir. Also, the practice of not ordaining women even to minor holy orders effectively excluded them in the days when most of the singing was performed by ordained clerics. However, by the time Arkhangel'sky broached the subject in 1880, choirs composed of laypersons had become commonplace, and he had no difficulty obtaining permission from church authorities to employ women in his church choir.

In the climate of social reform towards the end of the nineteenth century—and particularly after the Revolution of 1905, which gave life to the trade union movement—the question of women's versus boys' voices in church choirs came to be approached more from a socio-economic than from a canonical standpoint. Was it cheaper in the long run to pay a higher salary to a trained woman chorister than to house, clothe, feed, and educate (however minimally) a boy soprano or alto, who, after finally mastering the necessary repertoire, underwent a voice change? Could women be expected to work the long, gruelling hours that choristers in entrepreneurial choirs worked? Finally, would the presence of women in church choirs serve to improve the low moral standing and drunkenness that was characteristic of professional male choristers, or, on the contrary, would women choristers also succumb to these negative social influences?

An opinion poll conducted in 1907 by the journal *Muzykal'nyi truzhennik* [The musical worker] brought responses from many prominent composers and conductors in the choral field. While some replies addressed the subject exclusively in the light of sociological considerations, others contain observations that pertain more specifically to choral performance.

Most clearly in favor of boys' voices is Vasily Sergeevich Orlov, who states that boys can and must continue to sing in exemplary choirs such as the Moscow Synodal Choir and the Imperial Court Chapel, where they receive proper education and care. A reform of these choirs, says Orlov, would be unrealistic. [103]

Kastal'sky's position was not as clear-cut:

> Speaking ideally, in church choirs the clear sound of male children's voices, devoid of any passionate nuances, is preferrable to the timbre of women's voices. But...[with the presence of] mature and knowledgeable [women] participants, who are more capable of feeling the idea and spirit of the works being performed, the artistic side of the performance can only gain, provided that the women adhere to the same choral discipline expected of the other members. [104]

In terms of musical aesthetics, Nikolai Kompaneisky preferred boys' voices:

> From the standpoint of musical interest boys' voices have certain substantial qualities that are preferable over women's voices. The timbre of a boy's voice, especially an alto, has a penetrating quality that makes it easier to emphasize a given voice part, [while] on high notes boy sopranos are much truer to the pitch than women. [Moreover,] boys' voices have less vibrato, and the character of the timbre is serene and devoid of passion, which is more appropriate to a religious atmosphere. [105]

However, as a fervent defender of church singers' social and economic rights, Kompaneisky felt the question ultimately had to be decided on the basis of sociological considerations.

The ability of mature women to express the meaning and content of a musical work, which Kastal'sky saw as a positive aspect, was a source of concern to Aleksei Karasev, who wrote:

> It is highly regrettable that many mixed choirs with women's voices have recently developed the manner of singing with vibrato....The choir sings as if in a fever....Such singing, of course, cannot be conducive to the "laying aside of all earthly cares,..."—the retreat from everyday concerns to which we are invited in the church. If to this one adds singing with "scoops" upward or downward, the impression is that of a bad operetta or even a gypsy chorus. The singing of boys may not always express religious feeling, but at least it does not display any secularized emotionalism in the performance. [106]

Stepan Smolensky appeared to be of two minds on the subject. In 1905 he wrote to a student of his that "of course, boys' voices are much more mobile than women's voices. . . . But with good training there is very little difference between a choir with women and a choir with boys."[107] Two years later, however, in response to the questionnaire, Smolensky came out much more strongly in favor of women's voices, with the added suggestion that boys and young girls sing alongside mature women. "The opinion that boys' voices have some special beauty which does not exist in female voices is mere prejudice," he concludes.[108]

Clearly on the other side of the argument were Rimsky-Korsakov, who "greatly preferred" the sound of women and men to the sound of boys and men, and Grechaninov, who wrote:

> Boys are incapable of the same deep feeling and inspiration of which adults are capable. Deep religious ecstasy, mysticism, the inspired prophetic word, . . . which so often are found in our church works, . . . to all these things the child's heart remains indifferent. . . . Performance by children will always be objectively cool, naive (granted, occasionally beautiful in its naivete), but in most instances completely insufficient to convey the necessary mood, and inappropriate to the content of what is being performed.[109]

It is not surprising, therefore, that many of Grechaninov's compositions were premiered not by the Moscow Synodal Choir but by Leonid Vasil'ev's Choir, which by the year 1908 (and possibly earlier) had a mixture of women's and boys' voices in the soprano and alto sections.[110]

Most of the other respondents to the poll come out in favor of introducing women into church choirs, either exclusively or in combination with boys, which is, in fact, what gradually occurred in Russian choirs over the first two decades of the twentieth century. However, the Moscow Synodal Choir and the Imperial Court Chapel, which served as ideals of choral sonority for many composers, continued to use exclusively boys' voices until the October Revolution.

Concepts of Choral Sonority

Additional insights into the overall sonority of Russian choirs may be found in critical accounts of actual performances. One of the earliest sources in this category is the report of Paul Einbeck, sent to St. Petersburg in 1829 to observe the Imperial Chapel:

> The seven octavists among the twenty-two basses serve as the foundation of the choir; the tenors have beautiful, mellow voices, the altos are weak and gentle, while the sopranos' voices are sweet and buzzing. The balance within the ensemble is such that the bass is the loudest, the tenor—somewhat softer, the alto—still softer, and the soprano—the softest.

> Fortes, pianos, and all dynamic nuances in general are executed for the most part by the male voices; the top voices act in a very restrained fashion, only to heighten the effect somewhat.[111]

This "pyramidal" concept of choral sonority may also be found in more recent times, in descriptions of some Scandinavian choirs (and their followers in the United States, such as Olaf and F. Melius Christiansen) and the Westminster Choir under the direction of John Finley Williamson.

While remaining at a high level of excellence, the sound of the Imperial Chapel apparently changed somewhat over the course of fifty years, particularly with regard to the execution of dynamics. As Stepan Smolensky relates in his memoirs:

> In 1875, when I was already...a sufficiently experienced precentor, I purposely spent one-and-a-half months in St. Petersburg and visited the [Imperial Court] Chapel at every rehearsal, studying the procedures of Aleksandr Ivanovich Rozhnov and listening to the beauty of the choral sound [produced by] exemplary voices. The Chapel at that time sang absolutely entrancingly—precisely, in tune, rhythmically, and with an entire scale of the most amazing nuances. I particularly liked its fortissimo—deafening in volume, clear in sound, [but] without the least amount of shouting and absolutely uniform in all the voice parts. Moreover, the Chapel's choral sound was inimitably mellow—the result, of course, of its excellent voices. Finally, the Chapel's *ppp* was somehow magical, remarkably light and mobile.[112]

A different concept of choral sonority prevailed in the Moscow Synodal Choir under Vasily Sergeevich Orlov. Aleksandr Nikol'sky, who was himself a singer in the choir, describes the sound of the various sections in considerable detail:

> Orlov had a marked distaste for "lugubrious" basses and "soaring" tenors. From the basses he demanded a baritonal timbre and complete mobility of sound; any attempt to "deepen" the tone elicited a sharp reprimand from him. The bass sound in the Synodal Choir, light and simple in tone, resembled that of a cello.
> From the tenors Orlov demanded gentleness rather than power; the timbre of the tenor section approached falsetto, although it was certainly not true falsetto. In general, the tenors and basses were a rather homogeneous section, freely and easily moving from the low to the high register, just as a cello does.
> The altos of the Synodal Choir lacked resonance and strength of tone, but tended to be gentle and weak, appropriately complementing the first sopranos via the second [sopranos]. In their homogeneity of timbre, all the children's voices resembled the sound of a violin.
> Thus in its overall sound the Synodal Choir approached a string quartet, where the basses were the cello, the tenors—the same cello in its middle register, the [boy] sopranos and altos—the first and second violins, respectively. Herein lay the source of the exceptional *transparency* of the choral ensemble and the lightness of sound that were characteristic of the Synodal Choir.

With the second basses and octavists Orlov strove to achieve a velvety sound—full and rich, but by no means shrill; the octavists, doubling the first basses, lightly shaded the main bass line, but by no means stood out from the choir "to amaze the world." The octavists did not double the bass part throughout, but only in places indicated by the composer or allowed by Orlov.[113]

A similar homogeneity of choral sonority was sought after by Arkhangel'sky, although, as the following review by Ivan Lipaev points out, these efforts adversely affected the sound of some sections: "In his apparent desire to make the sound of the entire choir as 'spherical' [and] compact as possible, Mr. Arkhangel'sky has overlooked the following: that while his altos sing openly and transparently, the sopranos [both sections composed of women] produce a lot of hooty and heady sounds, ... muted in sonority and lackluster in quality, which becomes particularly noticeable in comparison to the luminous tones of the altos and tenors."[114]

Orlov's and Arkhangel'sky's approach to choral sonority was by no means universally accepted in Russia. To cite Nikol'sky once again:

> For [Orlov's] critics, the voices and [their] role in the choir were both distorted: the basses were too weak and colorless, the tenors sang in falsetto, the altos lacked power, and the sopranos sounded mournful....
>
> In many fine choirs the treatment of the voices is entirely different: each section is asked to deliver a maximally large and highly individualized tone quality. The basses are powerful, especially when supported by imposing octavists; the tenors sing with a broad and free sound; the altos are ringing and sturdy; the sopranos sound bright and full. Such a choir is a conglomerate of four distinct timbres; it sounds colorful, rich, and, at times, captivatingly forceful. The piano of such a choir is merely quiet singing next to a monumental forte.
>
> One may love and admire this type of sound, but it is by no means the only one that is possible or legitimate.[115]

It is precisely the latter approach that is described in a review of the Russian Orthodox Cathedral Choir in New York under Ivan Gorokhov, a precentor who, although he was imported from Moscow, evidently did not adhere to Orlov's principles:

> The deep bass of the choir ... gives the ensemble the dignity and impressiveness which is given to an organ choral by the pedals. But when the music had a polyphonic emphasis, its meaning was more completely given than would have been possible with any instrument of group of instruments, because each set of voices was *so distinct in quality* [my emphasis] that it could maintain the full integrity of its part against the others. The adult voices had all the dignity and richness of the brass section of an orchestra without any of its roughness or mechanical quality; the boys' voices ... seemed to contain all that is lovely in the tone of the clarinets and flutes.

At the same time, the diversity of timbres in the Cathedral Choir did not prevent it from displaying "qualities of ensemble [in which] it was agreed that it had no equal in this country, and few equals in the world."[116]

Around the turn of the twentieth century some highly sophisticated and idealized theories of choral sonority emerged in Russia. The author of one such theory was Viacheslav Bulychev, who had caused a furor at the Third Convention of Choral Conductors in 1910 with his lecture on "Choral singing as an art." Bulychev argued that, because Russia, unlike Western Europe, had never experienced a "golden age" of choral polyphony, its artistic capital was not yet spent. Consequently, he saw great potential for the future of choral singing in Russia, which, he believed, would exploit the full potential of the human voice in ways it had never been used before. Although he made no direct reference to the composers of the Moscow Synodal School, he recognized the direction in which some of them were moving in their compositions:

> At present we can [already] perceive the desire [on the part of composers] to diversify choral sonority by deliberately exploiting the natural variety of timbre found even within each vocal category.... Ultimately, [these efforts] will find their expression in the form of vocal *symphonism*, whose embodiment will be the *symphonic choir*.
>
> The essence of this symphonism, like instrumental symphonism, would lie in the fact that in [performing] polyphony we would employ not only pitches of different levels, but also the differences in their timbres. The difference may be either *natural* or *artificial*. The first would be the result of natural, unchanging attributes of various voices, while the second would result from artificial vocal techniques, such as "open" and "closed" sounds, singing with the mouth closed, doubling male and female voices at the octave ..., the crossing of voices..., and many other things....
>
> In a word, the symphonic chorus would be an enormous living organ, whose every pipe would be a thinking being, capable of melding into a single purpose with its conductor and responding to the most difficult artistic and technical demands.
>
> The symphonic chorus, as the highest form of vocal ensemble, would strive to employ all possible sonorities of human voices, uniting them in the most diverse harmonic, rhythmic, dynamic, and—most importantly—coloristic combinations....
>
> Thus far no one has heard such a choir. But let us bear in mind that every member...[must be] a *musically educated* virtuoso singer....[117]

Closely related to Bulychev's vision is the "registro-timbral" system (*registro-tembrovaia sistema*) developed theoretically by Chesnokov in his book, *The choir and how to direct it*. The simple classification of voices into the four common categories of a mixed choir, argues Chesnokov, does not fulfil more complex artistic demands. To satisfy these demands a more complex form of vocal organization is needed in the chorus.

The basic assumption underlying the registro-timbral system is that within each vocal category (soprano, alto, tenor, bass), one can identify at least three subcategories. "Only that which lies in the natural register [of each voice] can be sung well, and only when nuances are . . . assigned to the choral subgroup that has all the required attributes can they be executed successfully, easily, and correctly."[118]

In the registro-timbral system the entire choir is divided into a "heavy" and "light" group, and each voice part is subdivided further into three subcategories; thus, the first soprano section is divided into subgroups A, B, and C, the second sopranos into A, B, and C, and so forth. Each singer is then assigned according to the range in which his or her voice displays its most characteristic timbre; the criteria for classifying voices are similar to those given earlier in table 4.1, with a few additional refinements. Using Chesnokov's previously established criterion for the number of voices in a section, the total number of singers in a choir of this type is eighty-one: nine singers each in every section from the first sopranos through the baritones (in descending order), twelve in the second bass section, and six octavists. On stage the group would be positioned as shown in figure 4.4: each subgroup of three singers forms a triangle on specially constructed riser platforms, which in turn rise towards the rear of the stage.

With this kind of choir at his disposal, the composer or the conductor must then determine the "timbrization" or "vocal orchestration" of each piece of music. In his book Chesnokov gives an example of such timbrization for the opening phrases of Sergei Taneev's chorus, "*Voskhod solntsa*" [The rising of the sun].[119]

Chesnokov considered the registro-timbral system and timbrization of choral music a thing of the future, although he undoubtedly conceived it on the basis of his practical experience as a choral conductor and composer. In the Soviet Union his system did not find a practical following; I found only a few published works scored according to Chesnokov's system, by his friend and colleague, Aleksandr Nikol'sky.[120]

Chesnokov's scheme could be realized only in circumstances where one had a virtually unlimited pool of voices from which to choose; perhaps he envisioned such a possibility in the rarefied atmosphere of the Soviet professional choral establishment. There is evidence, however, that Chesnokov did not develop his ideas about choral singing in an abstract, ideal context, as did Bulychev. Early in his book Chesnokov sets forth what indeed appears to be a very high standard for an ideal choir:

. . . we see first of all the concentrated attention of the singers towards their own section . . . , the striving of each individual to *blend* with his section both in *volume* and in *timbre.* . . .

[Each section in turn] . . . strives to balance in volume with the other sections. . . . Each singer and each section, listening intently to their neighbors and the other sections, tune their sound in relation to the others with absolute correctness and precision. . . .

[Finally,] . . . each singer is tightly bound to the conductor: the conductor's will is his will; the singer does not attempt to make a single sound without observing the conductor and

Figure 4.4.   The Positioning of a Chorus Using the Registro–Timbral System.

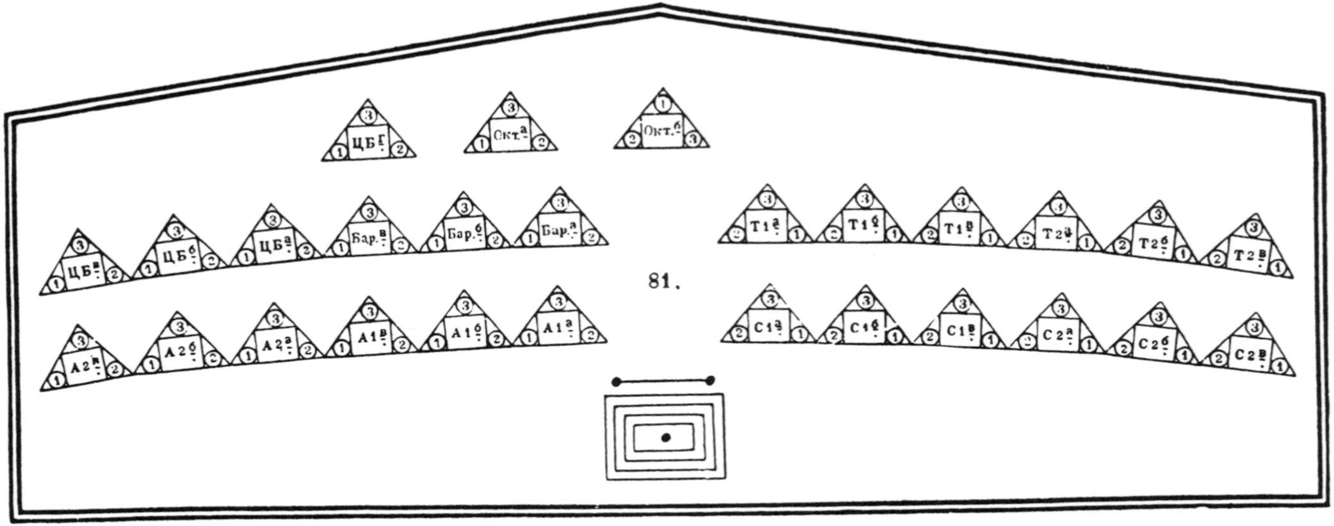

81.

without being in constant communication with him; in this communication and guidance lies [the singer's] strength. Such communication and melding of the singers with the conductor establish an extraordinarily sensitive mutual understanding: the slightest direction of the conductor is immediately accepted and executed by every singer, every section, the entire choir; the conductor's glance, facial expressions, [and] inner movements of artistic sentiment immediately find reflection in the feelings of the singers. From this most subtle mutual understanding are born...[the most delicate ensemble] nuances....

"Having thus analyzed the sonority of an imaginary exemplary choir," concludes Chesnokov, "we establish the three most important composite elements of choral sonority: ensemble, tuning, and nuances." [121]

Chesnokov's analysis, while interesting on its own terms, would remain merely theoretical and (since it appeared in a book published only in 1940) would apply only peripherally to the present study were it not for a remarkable handwritten note found in Chesnokov's personal copy of the book, now located in his archive. After the word "imaginary" there appears an asterisk and the following note in the margin: "For me, however, this choir is not imaginary, but real: one that existed in Moscow on Bol'shaia Nikitinskaia Street (today Gertsen Street), next to the Moscow Conservatory. This ideal chorus (S. V. Smolensky, ([Administrative] Director; V. S. Orlov, Conductor)... served for me as a concrete model in the writing of this book. One can only lament that this choir was dissolved in the first days after the revolution...." [122]

Thus, for Chesnokov, the Moscow Synodal Choir embodied the highest imaginable ideals of choral sonority. Indeed, as pointed out earlier, under Vasily Orlov the sound of the Synodal Choir was in many respects unique among choirs in Russia. But as we conclude this examination of Russian choral sonority, we must bear in mind that it was for the Synodal Choir under Orlov (and later, Danilin) that numerous composers of the new Russian choral school conceived their works; and it was Orlov and Danilin who first gave these works a definitive interpretation.

With the dissolution of the Moscow Synodal Choir after the October Revolution, the sacred choral music of the new school lost its true original interpreter. The approach to choral sonority in most Russian émigré choirs, as well as in most Soviet choirs today, is almost diametrically opposed to that of the Synodal Choir. Consequently, these choirs hardly do justice to the music of the late nineteenth and early twentieth centuries. What apparently distinguished the Synodal Choir from its contemporaries was that its sonority did not call attention to itself in a purely technical sense, but allowed the music to occupy a position of central importance. By contrast, the most striking feature in the performances of most Russian choirs over the last sixty years [123] has been the technical aspect of the sonority, whether it be the deafening fortissimos of the Soviet academic choirs and their incredible bassi profundi, or the astonishing tenor falsettists of the Don Cossacks. This approach to choral performance harks back to the church choirs of the 1860s and 1870s and to choirs like Agrenev-Slaviansky's Cappella, and arbitrarily ignores the finest achievements of the Russian choral tradition, both in terms of literature and in terms of performance practice.

5

The Choral Conductors

The subjective and idiosyncratic stamp that nineteenth-century conductors tended to place upon their musical performances is well known, and is the result of the new perception of the conductor as an artist whose creative methods were worthy of description and critical analysis. The study of choral performance in the nineteenth and twentieth centuries allows one to examine documentary evidence pertaining to specific conductors—something that cannot be done for earlier periods of music history. Like the discussion of vocal training and choral sonority in the preceding chapter, the current chapter aims to place Russian choral conductors in a familiar context and dispel some of the mystique with which interpreters of Russian choral music have been heretofore surrounded.

Choral performance in late nineteenth-century Russia was an evolving art, and although it lagged somewhat behind developments in instrumental and operatic music, it was not immune to trends in those areas. Having for centuries embodied ideals of objectivity and anonymity in serving the Church, Russian choral music after the coming of the Italian style increasingly developed features that invited and demanded subjective interpretation. Unfortunately, the low level of culture and musical training that overwhelmingly typified church musicians in the first half of the nineteenth century encouraged subjectivity that was unmitigated by the most elementary standards of good taste. There was some improvement as the century progressed, but the church precentor's prerogative for subjective interpretation largely remained. When the precentor's profession, through fortunate circumstances, came to include such natural geniuses as Aleksandr Arkhangel'sky and Vasily Orlov, the image of the choral conductor as a creative artist was reinforced, as statements from contemporary sources indicate.

In his *Prakticheskoe rukovodstvo dlia nachinaiushchego uchitelia-regenta* [Practical manual for beginning precentors] Vasily Zinov'ev writes: "The precentor is a magician, to use a somewhat elevated phrase; his hand or tuning fork is a magic wand, which out of indifferent, lifeless lines [of notes] conjures up wondrous living images."[1]

"The precentor is the soul of the chorus...," writes Chesnokov, "and having worked out the external side to perfection (ensemble, tuning, nuances), the precentor...[must have] the ability and the talent to breathe life into what is being performed, imbuing and inspiring the choir by the force of his talent with whatever [emotions] he is experiencing at the moment....[Ultimately] performance, just like composition, is a creative act."[2]

Kompaneisky notes the subjective impact choral conductors have upon both musical works and choirs: "Successful methods for training choirs have not yet been worked out theoretically; they remain personal secrets invented by the talent of the conductor.... Each choir has its own specific qualities, sings in its own manner, and has its own positive and negative aspects; for this reason the conductor imbues each work not with the absolute nuances indicated by the composer in the score, but with those that the choir can execute with the greatest advantage for itself."[3]

Extreme subjectivity of interpretation became the subject of growing criticism at the turn of the century, however. Speaking at the First All-Russian Convention of Theatrical Workers, held in Moscow in 1901, the conductor P. A. Shchurovsky argued that "the changing and revision of nuances according to the taste of the conductor, in total disregard for the markings of the composer, is inadmissible. The fallacy of such procedures is so evident that it requires no argument; yet how often our critics interpret such folly as a sign of the conductor's talent!"[4]

Nevertheless, because conductors such as Arkhangel'sky, Orlov, Chesnokov, and Nikolai Danilin, were the first interpreters of the vast new choral literature created for their choirs, the magnitude of their artistic stature made them the standard bearers and trend setters in their field. Before discussing each conductor's individual artistic traits and interpretive principles, the overall educational and musical influences that shaped the creative personalities of choral conductors in Russia will be examined.

The Training of Choral Conductors in Russia

Little information is available about the training of conductors before the mid-nineteenth century. Prior to that time Russia had no specialized institutions that taught the theoretical and practical musical subjects necessary for a church precentor or a teacher of singing. Rudiments of church singing were taught in various institutes and theological seminaries. More advanced musical training, primarily in secular music, could be obtained at the Academy of Fine Arts and the Theatrical Institute. Most musical studies, however, were carried on with private tutors, the majority of whom were foreigners (Bortniansky, for example, had studied with Baldassare Galuppi and Hermann Raupach, who were *Kapellmeisters* at the Imperial Court; Aleksei L'vov received his musical training from private German tutors). Most conductors of privately owned choirs around the turn of the nineteenth century were foreigners who did not have any special knowledge of Russian church singing.

The first concrete development in the training of choral conductors for the Russian Church occurred in 1847 when a program was established at the Imperial Court Chapel to educate and certify church precentors. The program was part of Aleksei L'vov's wider efforts to bring all church choral singing in Russia under his administrative and artistic control. By decree of the Holy Synod three ranks or degrees of certificates were established. A precentor with a certificate of the third (lowest) degree was empowered "to instruct a choir in plain singing [according to the *Obikhod* of the Imperial Chapel], but was prohibited from teaching the . . . music composed by the most recent composers, or, moreover, from composing new music for the church." A precentor of the second degree was permitted "to teach not only the plain singing, but freely composed works as well (but only those approved by the censors of the Chapel)." The holder of a first-degree certificate, in addition to the rights and privileges of the two lower categories, also had the right "to compose new choral music for liturgical use, with the stipulation that each piece should be submitted to the Court Chapel for preliminary examination [and approval] prior to being performed in church."[5]

That same year another Synodal decree instructed all diocesan bishops to send either their precentors or experienced singers with the potential of becoming precentors to the Imperial Chapel for training. The recipients of the Chapel's certificates were required to report to St. Petersburg every four years for recertification, and agreed to adhere strictly to the rights granted by their degree; failure to comply could result in a loss of certification.[6]

The rigor of the certification system was not matched by the practical training, however. Aspiring precentors did not go through any structured curriculum or special courses. Each student simply made arrangements with one of the Chapel's assistant conductors or singers and studied with him until the appropriate examination could be passed. The absence of a systematic curriculum perhaps explains the lack of specific information concerning the nature of the precentors' training. The only surviving documentary evidence is an announcement of the courses, dating from 1848, which states that prospective students had to be at least eighteen years of age and had to own proper clothing, a violin and bow, and a tuning fork. They also had to know how to read music and had to have had "a certain amount of experience in church music." Tuition was three hundred rubles per year for the first degree, one hundred fifty for the second, and thirty for the third. Certificates could also be obtained without studying at the Chapel at all, but simply by travelling to St. Petersburg and passing the appropriate examination.[7]

Some indication of what prospective candidates for certification may have been expected to know is found in L'vov's book *Concerning church choirs.* According to L'vov, a precentor had to know

1. How to select voices
2. The scale of all notes
3. All tonalities or modes
4. How to give pitches by means of a tuning fork
5. How to pronounce words and their [component] sounds correctly and properly
6. The table of chords
7. [How to recognize] correct and incorrect sequences of pitches [i.e., voice leading]
8. The division of notes into measures of various lengths.

Furthermore, he had to have facility in reading notes. "It is useful," adds L'vov, "to know some kind of musical instrument at least well enough to be able to check and assist the singers."[8]

Ultimately, the Chapel's precentors' courses accomplished little to raise the level of artistic choral singing in Russia. The most tangible result was the widespread adoption of the Chapel *Obikhod* for plain church singing, which, in fact, may have been L'vov's chief objective in instituting the courses. But the courses were hardly successful in disseminating the artistic aspects of the choral art: as far as is known, no provision was made for the students to attend rehearsals or performances of the Court Chapel Choir regularly, while those who received certification by examination perhaps never even heard the Choir. Only a few members of the Chapel itself received certificates: of four hundred thirty-five certificates granted over a period of more than thirty years, only six went to the Chapel's own teachers of singing. The result, in the words of one critic, was "an abundance of ignoramuses bearing diplomas from the highest church-musical institution in the land."[9] Wrote Rimsky-Korsakov, upon becoming Assistant Director (under Mily Balakirev) for Musical Pedagogy in 1883: "The entire curriculum, both in the instrumental class and the precentors' program, set up by the author of 'God Save the Tsar' [i.e., L'vov] was no good. Everything had to be revamped or, better yet, created anew."[10]

During Rimsky-Korsakov's and Balakirev's tenure, the Chapel's precentors' courses were upgraded to a five-year program that included a comprehensive curriculum of musical studies equal to a conservatory course in music theory. While a student had to go through the full five-year course to become a "teacher of church singing and music theory" (first degree), diplomas could still be obtained by examination. Between 1886 and 1904, four hundred seventy-five diplomas were granted: thirty-eight of the first degree, two hundred twenty-seven of the second degree, and two hundred ten of the third degree.[11]

Nevertheless, the program established by Rimsky-Korsakov in 1884 (and revised in 1891) was criticized because it included no voice training or pedagogical methods: students did not gain sufficient practical experience in conducting a choir since they had the opportunity to conduct on only two or three occasions a year; students did not acquire sufficient technical mastery of the violin or piano; moreover, students still could not attend rehearsals of the Chapel Choir and heard it only several times a year.[12] Even if the musical training had improved somewhat, the prestige of the Chapel's diploma remained dubious. A former member of the Chapel, Vasily Zolotarev, who later became a composer, wrote in 1891 to his mentor, Balakirev: "Here [in Rostov-on-the-Don] I attend church.... The singing is terrible—theatrical. The tenors rise on their tippy-toes, the basses bulge their neck veins, the boys squeal like cats whose tails have been stepped upon. Virtually all the conductors claim to have 'diplomas from the Chapel'—which is very, very doubtful. Looking at these 'nurslings of the Chapel,' one could get the impression that the Chapel is the disseminator of some kind of caterwauling. Truly!..."[13]

Despite these shortcomings, the Chapel was the only institution in Russia at that time where an outsider, i.e., someone who was not a member of the Chapel, could obtain any kind of training in choral conducting. The Moscow Synodal School, for all the excellence of its curriculum after Smolensky's reforms, taught only its own members. In 1907 the Imperial Chapel followed suit and closed its doors to outside students, henceforth allowing only its own singers to receive conductor's training. This prompted Smolensky, who now lived in St. Petersburg, to open his private Precentors' School (*Regentskoe Uchilishche Smolenskogo*) in order to continue offering the training formerly available at the Chapel—but with special attention to music of the new Russian national style. Smolensky's School, continued after his death in 1909 by his students and followers, remained as the only institution open to the general public where the choral conductor's art could be studied.

In the newly established Russian conservatories and specialized music schools choral training was practically nonexistent. Although some institutions issued diplomas to choral conductors, they had no resident choirs for the students to conduct; only for the final examination would a church choir be hired for that purpose. The conservatories offered no studies in the methodology of conducting or in the history and literature of choral music.[14]

Given the scarcity of opportunities for formal training in choral conducting and the lack of a clear-cut methodology for teaching it, the practical musical experience obtained within the walls of a given institution became paramount. "The best choral conductors are brought up in the choirs in which they sing," wrote Kastal'sky in his notes on pedagogy.[15] Without question, the institution that produced the leading interpreters of the national Russian choral style was the Moscow Synodal Choir and School.

Some scholars have suggested that because the Synodal Choir was never under the musical direction of foreign *maestros*, it preserved the ancient traditions of church singing practiced in the Moscow Dormition Cathedral from the time the Choir began singing there in 1589 as the Patriarchal Singing Clerics.[16] Ancient variants of certain Cathedral chants may indeed have been preserved by the choir of cathedral clergy, composed entirely of basses, which continued to sing certain portions of the services in unison; however, the checkered history of the Synodal Choir, particularly in the eighteenth century and through most of the nineteenth, does not support the hypothesis that any unique performing traditions were preserved. The situation was particularly unstable in the middle decades of the nineteenth century: between 1830 and 1850, the Choir had at least six conductors, none of whom were in any way outstanding. From 1849 to 1868 the Choir, like all other cathedral choirs, was required to send two of its most capable singers to the Imperial Chapel for training as precentors.[17] This fact alone undermines theories concerning the artistic self-identity of the Synodal Choir. But the status of the Choir had sunk so low that from 1845 to 1874 there are no records as to who the conductors were; it is only known that a certain Zveryov died in 1874 while occupying the post of precentor.

In 1874 the Synodal Choir finally received its first conductor with some specialized academic and musical training—Dmitri Vigilyov, a graduate and former precentor of the Moscow Theological Academy, who, nevertheless, had to obtain certification from the Imperial Chapel. Vigilyov headed the Synodal Choir until 1886, the year the Synodal School was reformed academically and Vasily Orlov was appointed principal conductor of the Choir.

Until the reform of 1886, the curriculum did not include any specialized training in choral conducting. Only with Stepan Smolensky's appointment as director in 1889 was a four-year precentor's course fully implemented in Grades 5 through 8 for the teen-age choirboys undergoing vocal mutation. The curriculum was revised slightly in 1892 and again in 1897, expanding the scope of the musical studies and adding one more grade at the elementary level, making the entire educational program nine years in duration. The curriculum as it stood after the revision of 1897 is shown in table 5.1.[18] Prominent choral musicians who graduated from the Synodal School under this curriculum included Pavel Chesnokov (1895), Nikolai Kovin (1896), Nikolai Danilin (1897), Aleksandr Nikol'sky (who received his diploma by examination in 1897), and Mikhail Klimov (1900).

Table 5.1.   The Musical Curriculum of the Moscow Synodal School—
1897–1910

Church singing—4 years (including history of church singing and staffless neume notation in the last two years)

Solfege—4 years (plus 5 years on elementary level)

Choral score reading at the keyboard—4 years (plus 3 years on elementary level)

Harmony, counterpoint, and form—4 years

Piano—4 years (plus 3 years on elementary level)

Violin—4 years (plus 3 years on elementary level)

String ensemble playing and conducting of choral works—4 years

Cello—4 years

The policy-makers of the Synodal School were not entirely in agreement concerning the type of preparation needed by church precentors. Smolensky clearly favored a more general and multi-faceted musical training, a stance that led to repeated clashes with the church authorities overseeing the School and ultimately resulted in his dismissal from the post of director. However, Vasily Orlov, who suceeded Smolensky as director, at first regarded the preparation of precentors in a narrower, more practical scope. He argued in 1900 that

under the present system, it is rather difficult to imagine the [adequate] preparation of highly qualified precentors. To remedy this unfortunate situation...students in the Synodal School must participate in the rehearsals and services continuously, throughout the entire [nine-year] course. This length of time will enable them to learn the techniques and methods used by an experienced choral conductor to achieve various practical results...[and] to learn the church services practically.... [19]

The differences of opinion between Smolensky and Orlov reflected a basic dissimilarity in their approach to choral conducting. While Smolensky's broad education and erudition undoubtedly included a competency in music, he certainly was not a distinguished conductor, despite some experience as a church precentor in his earlier days in Kazan'. Consequently, he adhered to the view, held widely at the time, that to be a church precentor did not require any specialized preparation in conducting technique. As he wrote in his *Kurs khorovogo tserkovnogo peniia* [A course in choral church singing],

> To direct a [church] choir is not difficult. To achieve this skill one must have—besides a thorough knowledge of harmony, the order of services, and the common cycle of church hymns—the ability to exercise self-control and to remain calm, unhurried, and confident while giving precise directions. It is by his directions that a precentor gives the choir a unanimity of performance and melds it into a single entity. . . .
>
> The precentor's specific duties include: (1) giving the pitch, (2) marking the time, and (3) indicating the nuances.[20]

Smolensky was not alone in this view. Similar views were expressed by K. Veber, A. Maslov, and V. M. Orlov.[21]

In contrast to the above position, V.S. Orlov, the innately gifted conductor, sensed that the art of conducting involved specialized skills and techniques which could be transmitted to students as much through practical observation as through formal instruction. The nature of Orlov's own training in conducting is unknown; he probably learned through observing precentors such as Zverev and Bagretsov, and while playing the bassoon in the orchestra of the Moscow Conservatory. (Orlov's overall musical background will be discussed in greater detail below.) Perhaps for this reason Orlov believed that students who did not sing in the Choir while their voices were changing should still attend rehearsals and services.

In the six years that he was director of the Synodal School, Orlov moved towards reconciling his initial narrow views concerning the precentor's art with Smolensky's vision of a broad musical curriculum. Shortly before his death in 1907, he proposed yet another curriculum revision, one that he did not live to see enacted but which became the core of the new curriculum adopted in 1910. In this report he wrote:

> The Synodal School must remember its duty to supply its graduates . . . with all the requirements necessary to gain a reputation as superb musicians in the musical world and, particularly, as specialists in church singing. . . . Such an individual must, first of all, have a solid musical education; he must be experienced technically . . . on the level currently demanded in [choral] church singing . . . [and be] an intelligent interpreter of all music and particularly—of church music, both as a conductor-performer and as a pedagogue. . . .
>
> The insufficient circumstances in the School's curriculum are sensed by the students themselves. The transfer [or continuation] from our school to the conservatory has in recent times become commonplace. . . . They run away from us in search of knowledge, and they run away from us in search of status. . . . Hence we must overhaul our programs so that they could impart a complete body of knowledge, first and foremost in the area of the school's specialization. And along with knowledge, we must provide some status—at least that of a "free artist" [*svobodnyi khudozhnik* (an official social rank in Imperial Russia bestowed upon graduates of conservatories and other advanced fine arts institutions)].[22]

Thus, the curriculum revision of 1910 (shown in table 5.2) came to include specialized courses in choral conducting technique, but only after a slow process of evolution.

Table 5.2.   The Musical Curriculum of the Moscow Synodal School—
Revision of 1910

Music Theory

Elementary music theory—2 years (Grades 2 and 3)
Harmony—3 years (Grades 4, 5, and 6)
Counterpoint in strict style—1 year (Grade 7)
Counterpoint and fugue in free style—1 year (Grade 8)
Musical form—3 years (Grades 7, 8, and 9)
Solfege—7 years (Preparatory through Grade 6)

Church Music

Church chant—8 years (Preparatory through Grade 7)
History of church singing, including ancient notations—2 years
   (Grades 8 and 9)
Canonical chant—1 year (Grade 9)

Conducting

Methodology of teaching church and school choral singing—1 year
   (Grade 9)
Choral score reading at the keyboard—6 years (Grades 4 through 9)
Conducting and ensemble playing—5 years (Grades 5 through 9)

Voice and Solo Instruments

Voice training—3 years (Preparatory, Grades 1 and 9)
Theory of voice training—1 year (Grade 9)
Piano—10 years (Preparatory through Grade 9)
Violin—8 years (Grades 2 through 9)
Cello—6 years (Grades 4 through 9)

Music History

General history of music—2 years (Grades 8 and 9)
Russian folk music—1 year (Grade 9)
History of the arts—1 year (Grade 9)

Of particular interest was a course entitled "Methodology of choral singing and conducting." Judging from the syllabus, the course offered a very detailed study of the organizational, technical, and musicianship skills involved in conducting a choir. There was, however, no single text available for this course: none of the texts listed as resources dealt directly with the topics covered. [23]

The other course where conducting techniques were mastered was entitled "Conducting and ensemble playing." Introduced by Smolensky, it gave student conductors the opportunity to gain practical experience in a laboratory situation. "A strange and unusual class," wrote the critic Nikolai Findeizen, "—with a string quartet playing choral scores under rotating student conductors."[24] Judging by Findeizen's remarks, this approach was thoroughly unique and unprecedented, and distinguished the Moscow Synodal School from other institutions where church music was taught. Having students play rather than sing was necessary, first because most of the students' voices were changing at the time, and also in order to render all four parts of the choral score. The fact that string instruments were used becomes all the more significant in light of Nikol'sky's description of the Synodal Choir's ensemble sound as "resembling a string quartet." Obviously, the choice of the medium for the student conducting laboratory was not arbitrary and, moreover, reinforced an already existing sound ideal.

In the conducting course, beginning with the fifth grade, the students started out by learning basic conducting techniques, including conducting unbarred, recitative-style hymns and easy compositions in homophonic style. In addition, they had to be able to sing one part of the choral score while playing another part on the violin. With each year the works studied in this fashion became increasingly complex, including, in the eighth grade, the Bach motets, and in the ninth grade, Mozart's *Requiem,* Bach's *Mass in B minor,* and Mendelssohn's *Elijah.* In addition to the ensemble laboratory, more advanced students conducted a student choir in rehearsals and services at a small church directly across the street from the Synodal School, and also on occasion conducted string orchestra and a secular chorus at the School.[25]

In 1913–14, a final curriculum revision, which transformed the Synodal School into an "Academy of Church Singing" equal in stature to the Conservatory, introduced one hour of orchestral conducting in the ninth year in addition to choral conducting, as well as highly specialized courses in the aesthetics of Orthodox liturgical singing and the musical forms associated with Orthodox worship.[26]

A curriculum very similar to that of the Synodal School was offered by Smolensky's Precentors' School, established in 1907 in St. Petersburg. And in 1911, the Imperial Chapel adopted a curriculum that was virtually undistinguishable from the Synodal School's 1910 revision.[27]

The Role of the Conductor

At the end of the nineteenth century, faced with the demands of the new choral repertoire, Russian choral conductors began to recognize the need for systematizing a technique of conducting gestures. Apparently, this need was not universally acknowledged: as late as the 1900s, stubborn old traditions and practices necessitated such seemingly self-evident arguments as the following:

Figure 5.1. The Faculty of the Moscow Synodal School (ca. 1911). Seated in the Front Row (l. to r.): Nikolai Kashkin, Aleksandr Nikol'sky, Rev. Dmitri Allemanov (?), Nikolai Danilin, Filip Stepanov (from the Synodal Chancery), Aleksandr Kastal'sky, Rev. Vasily Metallov, Viktor Kalinnikov.

> Indeed, what can the precentor of a choir use to communicate a sense of inspiration as well as a correct and unified rhythmic interpretation? [He may use] his own voice, an instrument, but most importantly, of course, of the movement of the hand. The hand can show everything: the nuances of execution, changes in tempo, and the relative strength of accents.... The choir must *never* be left to its own devices,... but all [aspects of the performance] must come from the precentor.[28]

> Often the precentor waves his hand unevenly: where the sound is to be sustained longer, he holds the hand, and where the sounds move quickly, he waves faster. [But]... one should wave evenly with the hand (this is more correct and more convenient); the notes themselves will show how they are to be sung.[29]

> The impression that church hymns lack a [measured] rhythm has brought about chaotic time-beating in the performance of these hymns, and thereafter, in conducting everything else.[30]

> It is a rare precentor who does not violate the generally used conventions of hand gestures, which, as we know, are specific and strictly defined for every meter. Such gestures have the merit of being a *common language* by means of which the rhythm is precisely regulated.[31]

Even these arguments were not universally accepted. As late as 1910, V. M. Orlov offered the following curious advice: "If during the singing the precentor wishes to reduce the sound of the choir, he should not say '*ts*,'... as many do, but *should say* [my emphasis] '*tishe*' [quiet], '*eshche tishe*,' [still quieter], 'piano,' [or] 'pianissimo....' In church, so as not to distract the worshippers, he *may* [my emphasis] express his wish by means of some hand gesture, but only one that is proper."[32]

Smolensky's Precentors' School, as an institution intended to serve outside students, provided the impetus for the publication of the first important work on conducting technique—Nikolai Kovin's *Choral conducting*.[33] In this work the modern-day understanding of a choral conductor was articulated for the first time in Russia:

> Few people link the concept of "precentor" with that vast array of practical skills, knowledge, and inborn talent that make the precentor the mind, will, and soul of the chorus. The precentor's most direct and most elevated function is to understand the piece [of music], illumine it with this understanding, communicate it to the choir, and, having fused the latter into a single organic entity, summon all the individual conceptions and skills of the singing body to the collective task of performance.[34]

Side by side with the conductor's role as an artist there are aspects of his everyday work, particularly in church, that do not demand such constant tension: "Besides the poetic, artistic element, conducting also contains a prosaic element—the technique," writes Kovin.[35]

The text goes on to discuss the various skills necessary for a conductor: giving the pitch, indicating tempo and meter, showing the initial attack and internal cues, conducting unsymmetric and unbarred rhythms (a major section); finally, some rehearsal techniques and procedures are described. A separate section is devoted to the proper use of a supporting instrument in rehearsals, at which point Kovin challenges the established practice of using the violin:

> In working with a chorus it is very difficult—I would say, even impossible—to get by without the aid of an instrument.... The requirements placed upon the instrument in this situation are unfortunately satisfied least by the one instrument most widely used in choirs—the violin. Often its use is indeed dictated by necessity, lack of funds, [and] the organizational instability of many of our choirs. [But] this instrument, so beautiful by itself, and capable, in good hands, of conveying the most subtle intonations [and] the most intimate moods and emotions, can only be used to teach individual parts to the chorus, and only partially at that. One might use it, for example, to point out faulty intonation to a singer. But what will guarantee that the singer will not forget this purely mechanical demonstration, if he is not shown the other parts in relation to which he must tune his own voice?...
>
> The most suitable instrument [for the choral rehearsal] is the piano. Its relatively short sounds, clearly defined and distinctly separated by the striking of the hammers, only show the singer the pitch level; after that it is up to the singer to supply the necessary corrections of intonation, making sure that the sound is beautiful, steady, full, and proper in character.... [36]

Kovin saw his brief (fifty-one-page) work as "only an attempt to systematize the essential rules and principles that make up the primer, the indispensable first steps, of the technique involved in the complex and living field of choral conducting." The problems of artistic conducting, however, far exceed the limits of a manual of conducting technique. "To solve them," concludes Kovin, "one must turn to the living examples of major artist-conductors and to a thorough exploration of the sacred choral literature." [37]

The Early Conductors: Lomakin, L'vovsky, and Bagretsov

Just as nothing is known concerning the training of Russian conductors before the mid-nineteenth century, no information survives regarding the conducting activities of the first generation of Russian choral composers— Bortniansky, Artemy Vedel' (1772–1808), Stepan Degtiarev (1766–1813), Stepan Davydov (1777–1825)—who were also church precentors and orchestral *Kapellmeisters*. Accounts of Aleksei L'vov as a performer are limited to his violin playing, which was acclaimed as virtuosic.

The first choral conductors whose activities have been to some extent documented are Gavriil Lomakin (1811–85) and Fyodor Bagretsov (1812–74), who rose to prominence in the 1830s and 1840s, and Grigory L'vovsky (1830–94), whose activity began in the 1850s. Bagretsov's and L'vovsky's lives were the subjects of monographs by admiring contemporaries, while Lomakin left a sizable autobiography.[38] While it is difficult to evaluate how much influence these three individuals had on succeeding generations, the prominence of the posts they occupied and the acclaim they received from contemporaries suggest that their legacy could not have gone unnoticed by the next generation of choral conductors, who founded the modern Russian school.

The son of a serf on the Sheremetev estate, Lomakin began his musical career as a boy soprano in the Sheremetev Chapel at the age of ten. The first guiding musical influence in his life was probably the Italian *maestro* Antonio Sapienza (1755–1829), a well-known composer and opera conductor, who was also Count Dmitri Sheremetev's voice instructor.[39] Sapienza was not long at his post and in 1830 the nineteen-year-old Lomakin became the Chapel's teacher. In his formal music training, Lomakin was largely self-motivated; his autobiography mentions violin lessons with a member of the Count's orchestra and piano lessons with a theater musician named Vasilevsky. Later he studied music with Kossov, a student of pianist John Field, and with the composer Adolphe Charles Adan, who visited Russia in the 1830s. His expertise in conducting, however, seems to have been developed largely on his own through practical experience with the Sheremetev Chapel: having no suitable textbooks or methods to teach singing, he made up his own vocalises and exercises, and taught the singers to read pitches and rhythms while beating time. "After a few years," he writes, "the children, as well as the adults, read difficult works *à livre ouvert*. Confidently reading notes and rhythms and firm in their intonation, they handled their voices so well that at the sign of their teacher, they softened or increased their sound gradually and uniformly. Out of this unified concord resulted an ensemble whose singing resembled that of a monolithic entity."[40]

Apparently, such flexibility and variation in dynamics was an innovation at the time; upon hearing Sheremetev's Choir under Lomakin, the Director of the Imperial Chapel, Aleksei L'vov, remarked: "One ought not perform church music with such expression," after which the Count ordered that all singing be performed in the Imperial Court manner—"without any nuances." Nevertheless, Lomakin was invited to the post of teacher of singing at the Imperial Chapel, but his attempts to introduce his teaching methods there met with failure. After spending nearly twelve frustrating years at the Chapel, he left in 1859, channeling his energy once again into Sheremetev's Choir and the new enterprise of the Free Musical School, which he cofounded with Mily Balakirev in 1862.

In 1857 Lomakin travelled to Germany and France, where he heard the best choirs in Europe, including the Berlin Dom Chor, and "obtained many techniques and pointers, which he later used in his own choirs."[41] But even before this visit, Sheremetev's Choir under his direction had attained great proficiency, earning numerous accolades from Western European musicians (including Berlioz and Liszt). Prince Grigory Volkonsky compared Lomakin's choir favorably to the Sistine Chapel Choir, noting that the singing of the latter was "cruder and less harmonious." The critic Vladimir Stasov considered the choir to be superior even to that of the Imperial Chapel. Reviewing a private concert given in 1856 at the Count's palace, he wrote:

> We will cite here two facts that best of all attest to the substance and stature of the school through which every member of the Sheremetev Choir must pass: we have on numerous occasions witnessed how this choir, *a prima vista*, has performed difficult and complex works of the ancient masters by sight, without any preparation. We have also witnessed how, after stopping, the conductor would tell some section, say, the tenors, from which place and measure to begin, and all the other voices would enter correctly in their places, without any special instructions. And if the first fact is indicative of an excellent school and proper method of teaching, the second bespeaks of the attentiveness and perceptiveness to which the ear of every choir member's ear has been trained. Such a phenomenon among little children, the sopranists and altists, is so rare, that it would be the envy of any German choir.... [42]

The concert activity of Sheremetev's Choir was largely limited to private performances, through which Lomakin could hardly have exercised much influence on other musicians and conductors. A new opportunity to transmit his expertise to a much wider audience was presented by the Free Musical School, in which he headed the choral class and the choir. Recognizing this fact, Stasov wrote: "Let Lomakin, then, who surpasses everything that we have yet seen in this department, prepare his heirs in the area of conducting.... For so long the business of conducting has gone on so-so, half-heartedly, that the time has come to try something different: conscious skillfulness, preparation, and education based on experience and observation...." [43]

Despite the admiration and friendship of many major Russian composers, among them Glinka, Serov, and the "Mighty Five," Lomakin had but one indirect musical "heir." This was the conductor Fyodor Bekker, who in 1880 completed the St. Petersburg Conservatory in the voice class of Ivan Mel'nikov, a one-time student of Lomakin. There is no evidence, however, that Bekker himself ever worked directly with Lomakin. He began his career in 1869, at the age of eighteen, as a chorister and minor soloist in the Mariinsky Opera Theater; Lomakin left the Free Musical School in 1870 and, after a few more years of work with the Sheremetev Chapel (which was temporarily disbanded from 1872 to 1874), suffered a serious downturn in his health, which substantially limited his musical activities throughout the remainder of his life.

Difficult as it is to assess the degree of Lomakin's influence in the field of Russian choral performance, several significant factors in his background must be noted. There is no evidence that in any of his early musical education he came into contact with any distinctly Russian performing traditions, such as those of folk choruses. His teachers—from Sapienza and Adan, to the *Kapellmeisters* of the choirs in Berlin and Dresden—were foreigners. Moreover, most of the choral music upon which he honed his performing skills with Sheremetev's Chapel consisted of works by Western European Renaissance and Baroque masters—Durante, Leo, Lotti, Arcadelt, Palestrina, Carissimi, Nanini, and J. S. Bach, among others.[44]

Lomakin's approach to choral performance apparently placed great emphasis on dynamic nuances, which subjected him to criticism from L'vov but earned him accolades from St. Petersburg music critics. His association with the Free Music School and the composers of the "Mighty Five" in the crucial 1860s—when a new style of Russian secular music was being born—may have served to make dynamic variety and flexibility, and the vividness of emotional expression engendered by such variety, important aspects of the emerging Russian choral style. Whether or not Lomakin was directly responsible for it, performances by Russian choirs after him displayed a vast array of dynamic subtleties and effects. It was this aspect of Lomakin's interpretation that was emulated by Fyodor Bekker, whose Free Choral Class also stimulated the composition of many new choral works, particularly secular ones. The mere fact that both Lomakin's and Bekker's choral classes were attended by thousands of singers at various times undoubtedly had an effect on subsequent choral performance in Russia.[45]

After the Imperial Chapel and Sheremetev's Choir, the next most prominent positions in St. Petersburg's church choral circles belonged to the choirs of the Alexander Nevsky Lavra (the Metropolitan's Choir) and St. Isaac's Cathedral, both of which were headed for close to forty years by Grigory L'vovsky . Unfortunately, L'vovsky's biographer, Aleksei Karasev, did not live in St. Petersburg and was acquainted with his subject mainly through correspondence and numerous choral compositions and chant arrangements. Thus, aside from some information on L'vovsky's musical training and a few citations from manuscript notes, Karasev's biography sheds very little light upon L'vovsky's activities as a choral conductor.

A native of Kishinev in Moldavia, L'vovsky was educated in the local theological seminary and, apparently on the strength of his natural talents, was appointed precentor of both the seminary choir and the archiepiscopal choir. When the Imperial Court Chapel's precentors' courses were instituted, he was sent to St. Petersburg for further musical studies—particularly in violin, for which he had a special gift. Upon receiving his diploma from the Chapel, he returned to Kishinev for three years, but was then summoned to St.

Petersburg to become precentor of the Alexander Nevsky Lavra, and soon afterwards, of St. Isaac's Cathedral, which was consecrated in 1858. Working in St. Petersburg, he continued studies in music theory and counterpoint with Zaremba, professor of theory at the St. Petersburg Conservatory, and through private research. The promise of an outstanding career as a violinist was destroyed in 1863, when L'vovsky developed rheumatism and lost full use of several fingers on both hands.

The little that is known regarding L'vovsky's approach to choral performance is found in some manuscript notes he left behind. Apparently a man of great personal piety, L'vovsky had a strict, purist approach towards both the performance and the composition of sacred music. He wrote:

> Not enough attention is paid to the performance of church singing as a service to God.... One must be particularly careful [with composed part-singing] always to maintain a good sense of taste, for from the sublime to the ridiculous there is but one small step.... The goal of church singers is not at all to caress the ear and play upon the emotions, but rather, to attend to the meaning and spirit of the hymn (whether composed or otherwise [i.e., a chant]), and not only to the sonority.... [46]

L'vovsky evidently represented the "strict" school of church choral performance which believed that church hymns should be rendered in a neutral fashion, without much variety of dynamics, articulation, or expression. This approach to church singing, advocated earlier by Aleksei L'vov, came to be regarded as a trademark of the "St. Petersburg style," fostered by the Imperial Chapel. [47] It should be noted, however, that L'vov's dictum in particular may have referred initially to plain church singing— simple chant harmonized in four or more parts, as opposed to composed (*partesnyi*) part-singing of such composers as Bortniansky, Degtiarev, and L'vov himself. Certainly L'vov's original compositions did not lack expression or dynamic variety. Throughout the remainder of the nineteenth century, however, the purist views expressed by L'vovsky in the passage above continued to hold sway in certain quarters of the Russian choral profession.

Other prominent choral conductors in St. Petersburg during the latter half of the nineteenth and the early twentieth centuries included Aleksandr Rozhnov, precentor and head teacher of singing at the Imperial Chapel from 1861 to 1878, Stepan Smirnov (1847–1903), who held the same post from 1878 to 1903, and Evstafy Azeev (1851–1918), who was a conductor both at the Chapel and at the Mariinsky Opera Theater. Another important figure was Yakov Ternov, L'vovsky's successor in the Metropolitan's Choir. However, few documentary accounts have survived of their conducting activities, which, for the most part, were narrowly confined to the Imperial Chapel's and the Metropolitan Choir's official duties.

In Moscow the chief figure in choral circles in the mid-nineteenth century was Fyodor Bagretsov, the precentor of the Metropolitan of Moscow's Chudov Choir. Bagretsov sang in the Chudov Choir as a boy and, like Lomakin and L'vovsky, acquired a piecemeal musical education: music theory with Daniil Kashin (1770–1841), a music teacher at the Moscow University; singing with Nikitenko, a singer in Sheremetev's Chapel; and violin with Johannis, a *Kapellmeister* at the Moscow Bolshoi Theater. In 1835 he was appointed "travelling precentor" to a contingent of the Chudov Choir that accompanied Metropolitan Filaret on his travels to St. Petersburg. While in St. Petersburg, Bagretsov frequented performances of Sheremetev's Chapel, which in the 1830s was directed by Pietro Antonio Sapienza (the younger, 1794–1855), who shared the conducting duties with Lomakin. According to one of Bagretsov's contemporaries, it was from Sapienza that the former acquired "the manner of interpretation and the understanding of the [choral] field."[48]

In 1840, upon his appointment as head precentor of the Chudov Choir, Bagretsov undertook to change the style of performance from one that was "blatant and extravagant" to a "quiet and intelligent [style], . . . impeccably in tune, neither drawn out nor hurried."[49] Bagretsov's admirers credited him with developing Moscow's musical taste in the area of church singing: "Many works performed heretofore received a totally different interpretation in Bagretsov's hands. It was he who introduced and interpreted [the works of] Bortniansky, which had hardly ever been performed [in Moscow] before. . . ."[50]

Indeed, Bagretsov appears to have been the first Russian choral conductor who became somewhat of a cult figure; in the eyes of his devoted followers he could do no wrong. This makes it difficult to assess the objectivity of passages such as the following one by Zipalov:

> Bagretsov's method of teaching [his singers] was marked by the sincerity of his verbal explanations, which commanded the singers' attention, a profound intelligence, the ability to discern the composer's intentions, and the ability to express [his own] intentions by means of musical terms, which in his practical usage acquired unusual vividness. . . . He had the ability to attend to specific minute points that others passed by without noticing. . . .
>
> In Bagretsov's interpretation everything was carefully thought out, [consistent] in terms of style, impeccable from a technical standpoint, [but, in addition] he displayed what may be called *creativity in performance* . . . expressed in minute brush-strokes that cannot be transmitted by any musical markings and in which genuine art truly finds its origins.[51]

Judging from the words of Urusov, another of his chief admirers, Bagretsov employed a good deal of rubato and other liberties in his interpretation:

> The rhythm of the piece and the notes themselves he regarded as servants, necessary to express the full depth of the text. . . . His spirit and emotions did not settle into precast, notated metronomic cells. and for this reason one did not hear in the singing of his choir a

cold, mechanical, abrasive calculatedness and automatic monotony of rhythm, but rather, something vital, infinitely varied, flexible, and gentle, which enveloped the listener in warmth, penetrating within and elevating him to prayer.

On occasion Bagretsov was known to change note values in works to achieve the desired effect.

Bagretsov was one of the first Russian choral conductors whose conducting manner has been described by eyewitnesses. According to V. M. Orlov, Bagretsov invented a new entire system of hand signals to communicate with his choir,[52] which Zipalov describes as follows:

> In conducting the choir Bagretsov did not use commonly accepted visual techniques of conducting—overt gestures of the hand; all the force of his control over the choristers resided in unnoticeable [presumably to the audience] and extemely moderate movements of the hand, with no display or posturing, which exerted an inner influence upon the choir that inspired the performers.... Bagretsov's external conducting was accomplished through movements invisible to the congregation and by means of his eyes....

The statement concerning the eye contact is puzzling, in view of the fact that

> ... Bagretsov, being genuinely devout, stood facing the altar and would not allow the singers to face away from it either.... Even on the concert stage [he] always stood in a space between the two halves of the choir, *facing the audience*, with the choir behind him.

It is not known whether the special conducting gestures pioneered by Bagretsov were adopted by others. However, he was definitely one of the last church precentors who conducted with his back to the choir. According to Zipalov,

> The manner of conducting, so indecorous and indecent in an Orthodox church, whereby the musical sense of a piece is expressed by means of overt, abrupt, and sudden hand movements, and which brings into play theatrical affectation, was begun in Moscow and became widespread from the time of ... V[asily] S[ergeevich] Orlov, and unfortunately, became firmly entrenched among all graduates of the [Moscow] Synodal School, who in the process of conducting permit themselves to wave their hands, clench and unclench their fists, etc., as well as [employ] bodily movements, which are absolutely inadmissible in church during worship [and] cause laughter and dismay among the congregation....
>
> [Similarly, in concerts,] choral conductors today, in imitation of orchestral conductors, stand with their back towards the public.

Bagretsov's thirty-four-year leadership of the Chudov Choir established him as the foremost representative of "traditional" Moscow church singing, in the minds of both his admirers and critics. Among his critics (posthumously) was Smolensky, who objected to "the highly popular and widely sung compositions of Bagretsov...[and others], which have filled our churches with the most intolerable vacuousness, shouting, and illiteracy."[53] Yet one cannot dispute the accuracy of the statement made in 1899, on the twenty-fifth anniversary of Bagretsov's death, by the music critic Semyon Kruglikov: "The fruits of Bagretsov's labors have been consciously or unconsciously used by dozens of precentors throughout our vast homeland. They are either his direct students or those who have heard the singing of the Chudov Choir under Bagretsov."[54]

Vasily Orlov, who sang in the Moscow Synodal Choir as a boy in the 1860s, undoubtedly observed Bagretsov, since the Chudov Choir and the Synodal Choir sometimes sang together or antiphonally in the same church. The precentor of the Synodal Choir at the time, Zveryov, was also among Bagretsov's students. One must be cautious, however, in attributing any direct influence of Bagretsov on Orlov; aside from the marked difference in conducting styles between the two, Bagretsov's followers were among the most stalwart opponents of the new direction undertaken by the Synodal Choir under Orlov and Smolensky.[55] Evidently, Bagretsov's legacy had little in common with the style of music and interpretation promulgated by Orlov.

The St. Petersburg School: Aleksandr Andreevich Arkhangel'sky

The most prominent figure upon the choral scene in St. Petersburg towards the end of the nineteenth century was Aleksandr Arkhangel'sky (1846–1924), who was responsible for establishing Russia's first independent professional (or semiprofessional) choir. Although Arkhangel'sky's name appeared in literally hundreds of concert announcements and reviews, it was only recently (1974) that he became the subject of a well-documented scholarly monograph.[56]

Born in a village near the city of Penza, Arkhangel'sky was enlisted as an alto soloist in the local archiepiscopal choir. While a student at the Penza Theological Seminary he studied violin for seven years with the concertmaster of the Penza Opera Theater, as well as theory and harmony with the amateur composer Nikolai Potulov (1810–73), who had an estate near Penza. Studies in conducting and singing were taken up with one Pyotr Fedotov, formerly a tenor recitalist (a student of D. Franzoni) and the conductor of the local chapter of the Russian Musical Society.

Upon graduating from seminary in 1868, Arkhangel'sky became precentor of the bishop's choir and the seminary choir, but in 1870 departed for St. Petersburg, determined to pursue a higher education. Unsure of his calling, he tried the Medical Institute and the Institute of Technology, in the meantime studying piano with a professor of the St. Petersburg Conservatory (for a total of ten years) and singing with G. Zanetti. In 1872 Arkhangel'sky passed the examination for a diploma of the Imperial Court Chapel, which enabled him to seek employment as a church precentor in the capital.

Figure 5.2.   Aleksandr Andreevich Arkhangel'sky (1846–1924).

Although he held a number of church positions from 1873 to 1880, he had to take on a job as a government office worker to supplement his income.

Working as a hired precentor in choirs over which he had no real artistic control proved to be highly unsatisfying to Arkhangel'sky. So, in 1880, he organized his own choir along professional lines—a bold step whose significance was discussed in chapter 3. Arkhangel'sky's was the first choir in Russia composed of mature and knowledgeable adults, a circumstance that undoubtedly affected his approach to rehearsal and performance. He expected his singers to be accomplished, independent musicians. Rehearsals did not involve any collective voice training or vocalization; every singer was expected to come to rehearsal already warmed up. Maintaining a strict discipline in the choir, Arkhangel'sky demanded from each singer an impeccable knowledge of his or her part, including all nuances and subtleties. Each learned piece had to be "turned in" individually to the conductor.

Some of Arkhangel'sky's specific views on the role of the singer and his relationship to the conductor were recorded in the course of rehearsals with the Russian Student Chorus in Prague:

> Do not be timid, sing out!... Get accustomed to a bold, independent sound, but take care that it corresponds in volume to what is required....
>
> Remember some necessary conditions in the relationship between [the chorus and] the conductor. You must not wait for the conductor to invite you to begin; instead, you must invite the conductor by your attitude of preparedness, as if saying: "We are ready! Begin!" In a disciplined choir it cannot be otherwise. It is [as essential] as oxygen....
>
> The conductor is not a metronome. His movements bring to life and animate the piece and its characteristic features. Remember the previous instructions of the conductor, but also watch for a certain amount of creativity in the course of the concert.... [57]

The above remarks indicate that Arkhangel'sky, more than other Russian choral conductors of his time, allowed singers to exercise a measure of independence and initiative, as might well be expected in working with an all-adult group. This corresponds with an observation made by the Soviet choral conductor Klavdy Ptitsa that "there is an opinion that during a performance it is valuable for the singers to be in a state of freedom, when the conductor merely reminds [them] about what has been accomplished at rehearsals, while the choir creates. Such views at that time [early twentieth century] were characteristic of the St. Petersburg school. [Vasily] Orlov and [Nikolai] Danilin represented the opposite direction." [58]

Aside from what has already been cited from concert reviews about the sonority of his choir and about his preferences in the area of vocal sound, the notes from the sessions with the Russian Student Chorus offer a few additional insights into Arkhangel'sky's views and techniques:

The most important thing is that the singing be pliant: smooth, coalescent, and connected. For this to occur, all measures must be joined in a special way: do not breathe between the last note of the preceding measure and the first note of the next measure.... When you are not taking a breath, do not separate the notes. See to it that the melody moves smoothly and fluidly to the greatest extent possible....

Remember, pianissimo must be your [constant] preoccupation; forte will always come out. "More sonorously" does not mean "more loudly," but rather, "with greater clarity"— then it will be heard.... Don't forget: a chorus always benefits from soft singing; then mezzo-forte and forte-fortissimo will be much more effective, even though you will not expend great energy [to achieve] it.[59]

The only thing mentioned about Arkhangel'sky's conducting gestures is that they were "economical and restrained, without 'flailing about,'" and that he used his face and fingers to interpret subtle details.[60]

Arkhangel'sky's pedagogical activity was limited to work in several secondary schools, where he was a teacher of singing. Thus, his activity as a conductor did not translate directly into specialized pedagogical work. Although he had a number of assistants who ran part rehearsals and conducted small contingents of the Choir in various churches, the only familiar name among them is that of Vasily Kibal'chich, who achieved some prominence in Western Europe and the United States with his "Russian Symphonic Choir."

The Moscow School: Vasily Sergeevich Orlov

Vasily Sergeevich Orlov (1856–1907) was unquestionably the initiator of a new era in Russian choral conducting. He merits this distinction not only because of the prominent role he played in raising the Moscow Synodal Choir to an unprecedented level of excellence and because he served as the mentor and model for an entire generation of Russian choral conductors, but also because of his remarkable qualities as a musician and interpreter of choral music. Orlov's artistic stature came to be recognized during his lifetime in a number of reviews and articles, and his untimely death in 1907 was marked by the publication of a commemorative anthology entitled *Pamiati V.S. Orlova* [V.S. Orlov: In Memoriam].[61] Many of his creative principles were discussed in great detail in an article by Aleksandr Nikol'sky, who was one of Orlov's students at the apex of the latter's career. These materials offer many valuable insights into the life and work of this remarkable artist.

Orlov's musical career, like that of many other church musicians, began when, at the age of eight, he was placed in one of the private choirs serving Moscow churches. From there he was transferred to the Synodal School—at that time only a four-year, elementary-level institution—which he completed in 1871, at the age of fifteen. Nikolai Kashkin, who taught music theory at the

Figure 5.3.   Vasily Sergeevich Orlov (1856–1907).

School, recalls that Orlov stood out among his fellow students by "the extraordinary seriousness and intelligence of his studies."[62] In 1873 Orlov expressed the desire to enter the Moscow Conservatory, but since he had no money, he had to compete for one of several scholarships available for students studying wind instruments. Those who passed the examination were assigned the instrument by the Director, Nikolai Rubinstein. Orlov was given the bassoon.

At that time the number of students at the Conservatory was relatively small, and they received a lot of personal attention from the faculty members. Orlov, who had studied with Tchaikovsky, attracted everyone's attention by his promise and ability in the field of church singing. Even while a student at the Conservatory, he was recommended by Kashkin and Rubinstein for several teaching and conducting positions. In 1880, with the workers' choir at Mamontov's Printing House, Orlov performed Tchaikovsky's *Liturgy*, Opus 41, satisfactorily negotiating the novelties and complexities of the notorious composition. "Had he in this case asked the advice or opinion of experienced musicians," writes Kashkin,

> anyone, of course, would have told him that such an undertaking was entirely out of the question with the choral resources at his disposal; V. S. Orlov, however, didn't ask anyone, but simply learned the Tchaikovsky Liturgy, and all we could do was listen and marvel at the results of his labors, for indeed everything was sung quite satisfactorily....
>
> The main result of this achievement was that...from this time on, in the eyes of musicians, V. S. Orlov acquired the stature of a person sufficiently capable and qualified to stand at the head of any church choir whatsoever.[63]

Upon graduating from the Conservatory in 1880 with a diploma that granted the rank of "free artist," Orlov obtained a precentor's diploma from the Imperial Court Chapel and became the precentor of Smirnov's private church choir (which, upon Smirnov's death in the early 1880s, came under the aegis of the Russian Choral Society of Moscow). Simultaneously, he became second assistant to Vigilyov, the conductor of the Moscow Synodal Choir. In his work with the Choral Society Orlov displayed a remarkable ability to gain the respect of his singers and to assert his authority without being overbearing. His success endeared him even further to Tchaikovsky, who was closely involved with the Choral Society. Thus, when in 1886 the position of head conductor of the Synodal Choir became vacant, Tchaikovsky unhesitatingly recommended Orlov out a field of several candidates:

> In the musical circles of Moscow Vasily Sergeevich Orlov enjoys such a superior reputation as a musician in general and as a specialist in church singing in particular, that I can limit myself to only a few words in offering my recommendation.... In my opinion, no one fulfills the stated requirements better than Vasily Sergeevich—a marvellous musician,

practically familiar with his field, ... [and] an intelligent person, inspired, moreover, by a great love for the work—who would, if appointed, establish the Synodal Choir on an appropriate level of excellence and would undoubtedly justify the hopes placed upon him. I permit myself boldly, decisively, and ardently to recommend Vasily Sergeevich Orlov to your attention. [64]

Besides a fortunate combination of natural talent, initiative, and intimate familiarity with the field of church singing, Orlov possessed a musical education on the conservatory level—something which no church precentor in Russia had hitherto received. Even though the conservatory did not have any specialized courses in conducting, Orlov undoubtedly picked up a substantial amount of technique simply from playing in the conservatory orchestra. What is more, he certainly had a wider scope of musical knowledge and a more solid theoretical background than most church precentors. Orlov's close colleague Kastal'sky recalls:

> In Orlov's rendering, ... everything sounded not only interesting, but often wondrous! His remarkable musical instinct and sensitivity enabled him to uncover the salient features of [all] church music—Western European as well as Russian. With what boundless devotion to his beloved work did he study with the [Synodal] Choir the works of Palestrina, Orlando Lasso, and Josquin, the Requiems of Mozart and Schumann, Bach's *Mass in B minor*, Beethoven's *Mass in C major*, and others! And all this merely to improve and develop the Choir, to raise its level.
>
> Almost everything I wrote for the Choir he performed with a careful attention that left nothing further to be desired. [65]

Orlov's erudition and highly developed musical taste not only made him a foremost interpreter of newly composed works, but also enabled him to set new standards in the performance of choral music. Writes Nikolai Kochetov:

> The singing of the Synodal Choir was called "unchurchly." How was this "unchurchliness" manifested? Only in the fact that the choir under V. S. Orlov sang in an exemplary musical fashion.... "They sing well, but there are no [real] voices," others said. The Synodal Choir had voices to be sure, but what V. S. Orlov feared most, what he rejected with every fiber of his musical being, was the showing-off of voices and the cheap effects of purely external sonority. For him the chorus was first and foremost a chorus, where the individual disappears in the total mass, concerned above all with fulfilling the overall majestic, stately character of our church service, while rejecting all that is crude, blatant, or overtly virtuosic. Herein originates the restraint in the singing of the Synodal Choir under Orlov—strict, stately, and devoid of the slightest affectation.
>
> If in the West the organ earned its undisputed position of prominence as the instrument least of all bound to the earth with its turbulent emotions and passions, so the Russian Orthodox choir will be all the better the less it reminds one of a sentimental *romance* or an operatic choral number. One would think that these are all unarguable truths, but in reality it was not so; and having brought the Synodal Choir to an exemplary [manner of] performing church hymns, Vasily Sergeevich had to work long and hard to accustom

listeners to this strict and unfamiliar manner. But this manner in turn was destined to open composers' eyes with regard to what type of music and what type of choral singing ought to occur in the Orthodox Church, and in accordance with these ideals they began to create their compositions.[66]

The above words eloquently describe the significant role played by Orlov during his career as conductor of the Synodal Choir and, later, as Director of the Synodal School. Indeed, Orlov's struggle was all the more significant because it concerned a field that encompassed much of what was indigenous and distinctive in Russia's musical culture—the choral singing of its Church. Clearly, the fruits of misguided and corrupt taste could not be rooted out all at once, but to Orlov largely belongs the honor of establishing and defining the ideal. (This ideal would have left a much greater mark on Russian choral church singing had the tradition not been disrupted by the Communist takeover.) Moreover, by linking the works of the new Russian choral school so closely with the masterpieces of Western choral art, Orlov pointed out their essential kinship in the artistic realm.

Orlov not only played an important role in reforming the repertoire and style of Russian choral music, but was also the mentor of an entire generation of Russian choral conductors. These include Nikolai Danilin (1878–1945), Pavel Chesnokov (1877–1944), Mikhail Klimov (1881–1937), Nikolai Golovanov (1891–1953), Vladimir Stepanov (1890–1954), and many others.

A number of Orlov's artistic principles and rehearsal techniques have been described in various reviews and monographs.[67] His long-time associate, the critic Semyon Kruglikov, characterized his manner of conducting in somewhat critical terms:

> The external manner of Orlov's conducting in church was not a thing to emulate. His conducting gestures were too large and expansive. In church one prefers to see more modest and restrained movements, ones that are almost unnoticeable. . . . But something else was more important. Orlov mysteriously discovered a sure way to obtain from the choir everything that he desired, to compel the choir to do exactly what the conductor asked of it. In this respect . . . [he] was a rare master of his art.[68]

In a positive vein, reviewers in Vienna noted that Orlov conducted "least of all with his arms, but amazingly indicated all the nuances with his eyes," producing what the writer called *ein innige Kontakt* with the singers. Moreover, Orlov "mouthed all the words, which is why the singers did not even for a moment take their eyes off his mouth."[69]

The critic Ivan Lipaev compared Orlov to the great orchestra conductor Artur Nikisch: ". . . both in external gestures and in his talent of searching out the most important elements of the score, Orlov may be compared only to Nikisch."[70]

The most extensive descriptions of Orlov's methods of work, along with observations of his character and temperament, have been given by Nikol'sky. Orlov's personality apparently exhibited a remarkable dualism:

> Pleasant and attentive, . . . at times he carried himself so timidly and shyly, that one could only marvel, for in front of the choir, as a conductor, this man was absolutely transformed: his gaze became steely and commanding, the face took on an expression of strength and power; the intense, erect figure, the stroke of the hand—all called to order and submission, summoning within the singers the ultimate willingness to perform everything that he, Orlov, demanded. . . . At the moment of creative inspiration he literally became transfigured, standing there before the choir—all power, strength, fire!
>
> Overall, the choir appeared to be a monolith; the oneness was granitelike. At the moment before the singing began no singer dared to take his eyes off the face of the conductor, or to shift from one leg to another; all stood planted there, holding their breath, as if enchanted by their leader.

Nikol'sky also describes Orlov's method of learning a new work with the choir. The process consisted of at least three stages. The initial read-through on solfege syllables was followed by a period of singing through the work daily with the text, accompanied on the piano, with Orlov watching not only for mistakes in the notes, but also for the slightest defects in intonation. "I am just a choral tuner," Orlov would say jokingly. Already in this rough stage he gave instructions regarding various nuances, but these might be changed from day to day. "It was as if he were 'feeling about' [for the nuances]," writes Nikol'sky, "not establishing them definitely, but nevertheless training the choir to execute them." By the end of the first stage, the choir had complete command of the notes, sang the piece in tune, and had been exercised in its ability to perform the slightest nuances and gradations of volume.

In the second stage, still using the keyboard, Orlov began to establish a more definite interpretation of the work, in individual passages and as a whole.

> Here his niggling with regard to intonation knew no bounds! Precise choral diction and the overall character of textual expression became the objects of intense working out. It was both fascinating and highly instructive to observe how, little by little, phrase after phrase, he persistently outlined the piece, creating its character like an artist with a brush. Out of the notes, nuances, and sounds of each voice part appeared a vivid musical image of what the piece ought to be in an excellent rendition. These images were often of great intensity, vividness, enchanting beauty, and expressiveness, revealing Orlov to be a profound and sensitive artist-musician of major stature. This [quality] manifested itself equally in interpretations of common, hackneyed [church] pieces, which had for a long time been interpreted in various ways by other conductors, as well as in the interpretation of brand new works by some new composer. Vasily Sergeevich created the prototypes for the interpretation of a vast number of pieces—old and new—prototypes that were beguiling in the genuineness of their expression and compellingly evoked unconscious emulation.

The final phase consisted of singing through the pieces a cappella for several rehearsals. "To an outside observer these rehearsals would have appeared as public performances.... The creative intensity of the chorus was such that after this the concert itself would appear easy: the work was all behind us, and in the concerts the chorus revelled in its own artisticity.... But Orlov was never fully satisfied, always finding some new shading, some new musical idea to introduce at the next rehearsal."[71]

Elsewhere, Nikol'sky criticizes Orlov's penchant for extremely quiet singing:

> It is very important to consider the reasons why Orlov always makes [the choir] sing in half-voice. By doing this he apparently achieves not one goal, but several: (1) In quiet singing neither the chest nor the throat becomes fatigued, which saves the voice...; (2) Obviously, [by preventing] fatigue, [he prevents] the voices from being ruined...; (3) Finally, quiet singing results in in-tune singing....
>
> To some extent, however, extremes are always harmful.... In this instance, the Synodal Choir sings some pieces in tune and some not...: because [in rehearsals] exclusively soft singing is practiced, the choir sings in tune only those places that are intended to be performed *p* and *pp*, but cannot sing in tune when *f* and *ff* are called for.... [Also,] quiet singing does not develop the singers' voices, and this results in [what appears to be] a serious shortcoming in the Choir.... Indeed, does one perceive power in the voices of the Synodal Choir? No! Listening to this choir one constantly wants to do something to increase its [volume], to make it more powerful.[72]

Predominantly quiet singing was practiced primarily at rehearsals. In performances the Synodal Choir was capable of considerable dynamic variation. Nikol'sky continues:

> The crescendos of the Moscow Synodal Choir were rarely gradual; more often the increase in volume came in bursts, moving quickly from piano to a powerful forte. Similarly, the diminuendo in most cases was...a rather fast change from forte to piano. Of course, this was not because Orlov could not teach his choir to increase and diminish its sound gradually, but for a more profound reason: as a device expressing a surge of religious feeling, the crescendo must not be strictly gradual, for such controlled gradation would contradict the elemental nature of emotion.

Orlov had a specific manner of dealing with diction. The description below evidently pertains not only to common hymns in recitative style (which, according to Nikol'sky, Orlov did not find particularly inspiring), but to other works as well:

> Orlov demanded a certain choppiness of text. The shout "Shorter!" with regards to the manner of enunciating the text, constantly accompanied the learning of a new piece. The goal, however, was not mere choppiness for the purpose of intelligibility.... By some indescribable means Orlov achieved a character of enunciation that was optimal for purposes of expressiveness.... This was not merely passive delivery of the text, but "living words".... In this area his secret died with him.[73]

Orlov's manner of musical interpretation was not without critics, of course. Some accused him of stifling the vocal and personal initiative of the singers. Others considered his performance "machinelike," "dry," and "lifeless." Still others criticized the extreme virtuosity of the Synodal Choir's nuances and the abrupt accents produced by diminishing the sound too quickly.[74] But even his critics recognized Orlov's historic accomplishments in promoting the works of the new Russian choral school. Nikol'sky summed up these accomplishments best, when he wrote: "Orlov was an unparalleled interpreter of the works of the new school. In these works there was so much that was new, both in terms of the compositional technique and in the character of the music itself, that one had to be an extraordinarily gifted performer to be their [first] interpreter, and to give these works the success that they were destined to have in Russian society. This was particularly true with respect to the works of Kastal'sky...."[75]

Aleksandr Dmitrievich Kastal'sky

After Orlov's death in 1907 the position of head conductor of the Moscow Synodal Choir was assumed by Aleksandr Kastal'sky (1856–1926), who was next in rank at the Synodal School after Orlov. However, despite the fact that Kastal'sky had been Orlov's close collaborator for close to twenty years, and from 1903 was his assistant conductor, he clearly did not have his predecessor's gift. In 1904, while visiting Moscow, the composer and critic Nikolai Kompaneisky made the following comparison between Orlov and Kastal'sky (the former conducting the right choir and the latter the left):

> Orlov reigns over the singers and conducts with authority. When the singers show the least sign of faltering, confronted with some unusual rhythm in the znamennyi chant, he forces them to follow by a sudden energetic gesture. [By contrast] Kastal'sky appears to be a weak conductor. His movements lack energy. When unusual rhythms arise, he seems to leave the singers to their own devices, but they clearly perceive his thought in the light movement of his hand and his intense gaze . [Consequently,] the singing of the left choir is much calmer and clearer.[76]

Another visitor from St. Petersburg, the Reverend Mikhail Lisitsyn, noted: "I cannot acknowledge Kastal'sky to be a true conductor.... His psyche is entirely too much that of a composer—mild, artistic, and feminine...."[77] Moscow critics, who had actively followed the rise of the Synodal Choir to excellence under Orlov, were even more direct. Ivan Lipaev called Kastal'sky "absolutely unemotional and dull as a conductor,"[78] while a certain A. L—n wrote: "Let A. D. Kastal'sky (who conducted the choir) not take offense at us: he has done a great deal for church music as a composer, but as a conductor he could do the reverse. To save the [Synodal] Choir's greatness he should select . . . as his assistant someone who is a conductor by calling and not merely by [official] rank. . . . "[79]

Nikolai Mikhailovich Danilin

The visible deterioration of the Synodal Choir's quality under Kastal'sky ended in 1910 when he became Director of the Synodal School, a role for which he was eminently more suited. The position of principal conductor was then turned over to a man who not only was a worthy perpetuator of Orlov's legacy, but may well have been the greatest Russian choral conductor in the first part of this century—Nikolai Mikhailovich Danilin (1878–1945).

Danilin, unlike his predecessors, was entirely the product of the new, reformed Synodal School. Born into a poor peasant family, he entered the Synodal School in 1890, displaying an outstanding voice of solo caliber, natural musicality, a keen ear, and an astounding musical memory. All these qualities endeared him to Orlov, and he quickly became the latter's favorite student. Graduating from the Synodal School in 1897 with a gold medal, Danilin joined the School's faculty in 1901 as a teacher of solfege. In 1902 he was appointed assistant conductor to Orlov, and at the same time entered the Musical-Dramatic School of the Moscow Philharmonic Society. Here, he specialized in piano and graduated with a gold medal. It was at this time that his friendship with Sergei Rachmaninoff began, a relationship which, in the future, would lead to numerous exchanges of expertise.

Appointed the principal conductor of the Synodal Choir, Danilin was not long in re-establishing the standard of excellence the Choir had known under Orlov. During the Choir's trip to St. Petersburg in the early spring of 1911, Lisitsyn noted that its singing "reminded one of the past glory under Orlov."[80]

Danilin was destined to conduct the Synodal Choir for only eight years. In 1918 the Choir was dissolved, while the Synodal School was renamed the "People's Choral Academy." Deprived of his foremost "instrument," Danilin worked for a time as chorus master at the Bolshoi Theater (1919–24), conducted choirs at the churches of St. Paraskeva and St. Trifon (1924–28), and briefly headed the State Academic Cappella (formerly the Imperial Court Chapel) (1935–36) and the State Chorus of the USSR (1937–39). Concurrently, he taught on the choral faculty of the Moscow Conservatory. According to those who knew him, Danilin was a private, retiring man. A bachelor, he had no heirs and died leaving few worldly possessions. The little that is known about him and his methods of work comes from reviews during his Synodal Choir period, from a monograph written in 1970 by one of his

Figure 5.4.   Nikolai Mikhailovich Danilin (1878–1945).

most devoted students, the late Klavdy Borisovich Ptitsa (1908–83),[81] and from various fragmentary reminiscences of contemporaries and students that are still in the process of being systematized.[82]

Danilin's first artistic triumph, which won him the accolades of such luminaries as Nikisch, Perosi, and Toscanini, as well as critics in Italy, Germany, Austria, and Poland, occurred during the 1911 Tour of the Synodal Choir to Europe. (Many of the laudatory reviews of this tour have already been cited.) Specifically with regard to Danilin and his conducting, the *Dresdner Neueste Nachrichten* noted that he conducts "without a baton, with uncommon calmness, technical precision, and rhythmic power.... The singular unanimity between the conductor Danilin and his choir clearly demonstrates their uncommon dedication to art. This is true self-sacrifice, when no commotion, no earthly cares can distract them even for a second from their objective."[83] The *Warszawski dnewnik* wrote: "The most gifted N. M. Danilin played upon it [the choir] as upon an obedient, homogeneous instrument, which responded to a mere glance from him, to his slightest gesture. In other words, this was not conducting, but exquisite molding, which gave the ideally unified vocal material the most varied and constantly changing forms."[84]

Danilin continued the role, formerly occupied by Orlov, of the foremost interpreter of the new Russian choral repertoire. Among his most notable premieres were Rachmaninoff's monumental *Liturgy* (1911) and *All-Night Vigil* (1915). The premiere of the latter was called an event "almost Shaliapinesque in its magnitude" by critics.[85] Danilin's ability to place his own inimitable stamp upon performances was likened to Shaliapin's "leonine grip," by which the latter transformed long-familiar operatic roles into new images of compelling power.

Klavdy Ptitsa, who first met Danilin in 1932, obviously recalls an older master than the one who conquered European audiences in 1911; yet many of the traits he describes are recognizable from that earlier period. Writes Ptitsa:

Nikolai Mikhailovich [Danilin's] artistic giftedness was profound and multi-faceted. In a choral performance Danilin the conductor could transmit a broad and colorful gamut of human emotions and movements of the soul. In his interpretations he masterfully succeeded in embodying philosophic meditativeness, epic breadth, the musical depiction of naturalistic imagery, and many other things. His gift was just as boundless in the world of heartfelt lyricism or the sphere of enchanting poetic contemplation. But perhaps closest to his heart was the expression of dramatic intensity.

Danilin was the bard of tempestuous emotions and ultimate emotional forces. His artistic unbridledness, his constant rebellious striving were manifestations of a strong, life-affirming Russian nature—a longing towards the constant renewal of emotion.

In his ability to create a dramatic situation and fill the sonority with the power of pathos Danilin had few equals.... Maintaining an unerring sense of measure in expending his performing resources, Nikolai Mikhailovich always used them boldly, to ultimate saturation. In works of a dramatic nature his fortissimo arrested the breath, while the subito piano, plunging into the abyss of silence, filled the soul with apprehension and dismay.[86]

Like his teacher Orlov, Danilin achieved his results by exercising total control over his singers. He did this, apparently, not only by means of conducting technique, but even more by the force of his will. To his students he would say: "If the conductor is able, like a general, with a single glance, a single movement, to transport the choir along the path of his intentions, then his place is behind the podium. If not, you must change professions."[87] In contrast to Orlov, whose preparation was most intense in rehearsal, Danilin's greatest flights of creativity occurred in the actual course of the performance. "Depending on his creative mood," continues Ptitsa, "he could induce the choir to perform the same work in different ways, ... to change the established dynamic plan, to speed up or hold back a previously established burst of tempo, to elicit from the choir a new interpretive brush stroke, to transform drastically the character and mood of a work." Rachmaninoff used to say that in the numerous performances of the *Vigil* under Danilin, the work appeared to him, the composer, every time in a different light, and he was hard pressed to say which performance he liked best.

Inasmuch as changeability and spontaneity of interpretation were part of his artistic temperament, Danilin undoubtedly had a highly developed conducting technique by means of which he could communicate his wishes to his singers. This fact is corroborated by Ptitsa:

> Danilin's "magical hand" was the object of adulation in the choral world and at times, a source of envy among rival choral conductors. . . . Particularly remarkable was his legato, in which his free hand with an extremely supple wrist wove the musical texture in smooth, silky flexible motions. . . . Most memorable is his manner of showing legato in a full, rich sonority: guiding his maximally tensed arm evenly and freely from the shoulder, with a constant connecting movement of the wrist, Danilin vividly expressed the fullness of the sound with additional tension in the fingers, which seemed to hold and pull the sound, as if overcoming the resistance of rubber or a highly coiled spring. At a diminuendo, the physical exertion left the arm absolutely organically, remaining only to indicate the evenness of the beat and to connect the sound. The flexibility and expressiveness of the wrist in legato were astounding.
>
> At the same time, in the midst of the most calm and smooth movement he could instantaneously and totally reorient the physical state of the hand to indicate some sudden nuance such as *sf*, subito *f*, or a change of tempo. . . .
>
> Danilin was always exceptionally thorough in communicating everything contained in the score that could be expressed in a conductor's actions. . . . "If you can't show everything, don't do the piece," [he would say to his students]. The most minute strokes found in the score were translated by Danilin into conducting gestures. He never left the chorus [to its own devices], by claiming that it was impossible to show some detail or by relying on [their] thorough knowledge of the work. . . . The combination of a broad, general performance plan and the thorough, precise communication of all the details of choral execution made his conducting extraordinarily convincing.[88]

Given the powerful and highly individualized personalities of Orlov and Danilin—the two foremost interpreters of Russian choral literature—one is naturally led to compare and contrast them in search of possible consistencies and differences. Unfortunately, specific references to this effect are very few in number. One may safely say that Danilin was a follower of Orlov in that the latter was his main teacher and model; Danilin's only training in conducting was received at the Synodal School. Reviews note that Danilin's manner of accenting and underscoring the text, almost to the point of excess, was the same as Orlov's. However, in the words of one contemporary, A. Preobrazhensky, Orlov's text was "mellow" while Danilin's was "harsh."[89]

Some comparisons of the two are not entirely consistent. For example, both Orlov and Danilin practiced total control over their chorus, both emphasized matching timbres to achieve blend, and both used a vivid palette of dynamic nuances. But according to Aleksei Naumov, Danilin was not as concerned as Orlov with matching timbres, and hence enlarged the variety of color in the Synodal Choir.[90] Nikolai Matveev, on the other hand, states that Orlov was mostly preoccupied with vertical tuning, while Danilin's main concern was horizontal tuning within each section and from interval to interval[91]—which would require no less concern for unanimity of timbres within a section. Matveev's statement that Orlov worked almost exclusively without the keyboard or any other instrument is contradicted by Nikol'sky's description of Orlov's method of rehearsing. Danilin, however, is definitely known to have used the keyboard as an important tool for communicating choral interpretation. According to Ptitsa,

> [Danilin] rarely used his voice for demonstration at rehearsals, due to a [vocal] defect acquired while still a student at the Synodal School, and he considered this to be his weakness. However, his illustrations at the piano were amazing. In Danilin's hands the piano sounded like the finest vocal instrument. He was able to transmit all the characteristic features and specific nuances of the vocal score. After his demonstration no further explanations were necessary.[92]

For all of Danilin's interpretive originality and creativity, Ptitsa observes that Danilin took a strictly "academic" approach to choral performance: "He did not permit any license that contradicted the intentions of the composer, particularly if it would disrupt the style of the composition. He was a vehement opponent of cheap effects that bordered on poor taste [and] all manner of 'creative fictions'.... Only in rare cases, on the basis of his vast experience, would he introduce slight modifications in the voicing of a score to enrich the sonority."[93] Ptitsa pays fitting tribute to Danilin when he calls him "one of those remarkable, difficult-to-explain phenomena that have arisen [from time to time] in Russia, and have left a marked imprint upon the history of a culture,... embodying and manifesting, in all its richness and multi-facetedness, some particular indigenous trait of the [Russian] people."[94]

The above observations exhaust the information currently available concerning the creative personality of Nikolai Danilin. Undoubtedly he possessed a remarkable set of qualities that were highly individual and impossible to imitate. His very presence among the composers whose works he performed—most notably Rachmaninoff and Kastal'sky—revealed the virtually boundless dimensions of musical content and expression attainable in a choral performance. The model that Danilin provides for subsequent interpreters of Russian choral music is an extremely lofty and challenging one. It combines inspired imagination with ultimate refinement of technical execution—and does so within the limits of the style. It is this model that one must strive to emulate if the music is to have the same impact as it did under Danilin's direction.

Pavel Grigor'evich Chesnokov

To complete the chapter on prominent Russian choral conductors of the pre-Revolutionary period one must mention Pavel Chesnokov (1877–1944), the only composer of the Moscow Synodal School who was also an eminent choral conductor.[95] Many of Chesnokov's views regarding the choral art have been preserved in his book *The choir and how to direct it*; and some additional insights appear in a monograph by Ptitsa, who was Chesnokov's student in the choral department of the Moscow Conservatory.

Chesnokov, who graduated from the Moscow Synodal School in 1895, remained there until 1905 as a teacher of church chant in the elementary grades. Concurrently, he taught singing in several Moscow schools and directed amateur church choirs at the Church of the Holy Trinity "na Griaziakh" (1902–13) and the Church of St. Basil of Caesaria (until 1928). In 1913, having already attained a reputation as a prominent church composer, Chesnokov entered the Moscow Conservatory. He remained there until 1917, studying conducting and composition under Ippolitov-Ivanov. He joined the Conservatory faculty in 1920, and also conducted a number of major choral ensembles in the post-Revolutionary period—the State Chorus (1917–22), the Moscow State Academic Cappella (1922–28), the Bolshoi Theater Opera Chorus (1931–33), and the Cappella of the Moscow State Philharmonia (1932–33).

Chesnokov's conducting earned him plaudits from the days when he worked with a church choir—a group of amateurs that rehearsed once a week. Starting in 1905, he began performing several concerts per year with this choir, which occasionally attracted the attention of critics. In a review written in 1909, Nikol'sky noted that Chesnokov the conductor was "purposeful, clear, expressive, and without any self-centered showmanship, . . . —all signs of an excellent school."[96] In 1913, the review of a concert marking the ten-year anniversary of Chesnokov's tenure with the choir noted that "it is difficult to

Figure 5.5.   Pavel Grigor'evich Chesnokov (1877–1944).

imagine greater control in conducting or a more intelligent sense of measure in the balance not only of the respective sections, but also of the individual voices.... In the field of choral conducting P. Chesnokov is both a marvellous virtuoso and an exceptionally subtle artist."[97]

Many of Chesnokov's views concerning the relationship of chorus singers to the conductor have already been cited. Above all else, Chesnokov emphasized the need for a relationship based upon mutual respect and trust: only then would arise the "oneness of mind" necessary for all successful performance.

In *The choir and how to direct it*, Chesnokov made the first major attempt in Russia to systematize the art of choral conducting. The sections of the book devoted to conducting technique contain a number of generally accepted principles, and do not add significantly to our understanding of Chesnokov as a creative conductor. More valuable in this regard are several excerpts from Ptitsa's monograph, beginning with the following description of Chesnokov's conducting gestures: "Chesnokov's conducting was marked by freedom, breadth, and smoothness of movement. Works containing the sound of a broad cantilena were more akin to his nature as a performer. He was less successful in negotiating gestures that were small, sharp, and fast. His long, powerful arms—those of a tall and broad-boned individual—were capable of great physical intensity whenever an expressive and powerful sonority was required."[98]

Throughout their student and professional days Chesnokov and Danilin were both colleagues and rivals; Chesnokov's diary contains entries about rehearsals of his choir to which he invited Danilin to give critical comments. For most of their lives after the Revolution, the two worked side by side on the choral faculty of the Moscow Conservatory. Yet their temperaments were evidently quite different: in contrast to the fiery, almost gruff emotionalism of Danilin, Chesnokov's artistic personality was characterized, in Ptitsa's words, by "a profound poetic nature and sensitivity. The absence of grandiose climaxes and broad, elemental epic qualities in his performances were supplemented by a great subtlety and genuineness of live human sentiment, which always won the listeners' affection."[99]

Chesnokov was a superb master of unaccompanied choral sonority. Danilin maintained that Chesnokov had no equal in the art of making a choir sing in tune. Having an excellent knowledge of the human voice and its potential, Chesnokov believed that work on vocal development in the chorus was among the most challenging tasks a conductor could undertake, and that such work required a special approach in each individual case.

Chesnokov the methodist divided the process of working on a piece of music into two distinct phases—the technical and the artistic. Attempting to pursue his theoretical principles, he would punctually divide the rehearsal process by days and hours into periods of technical and artistic work. But in practical situations, Ptitsa says, he compensated for the somewhat artificial schematism of his theories.

The three men—Orlov, Danilin, and Chesnokov—who dominated Russian choral performance in the late nineteenth and early twentieth centuries, and who were the definitive interpreters of the new Russian choral school, certainly possessed individual character traits that set them apart from one another. More important, however, are the many similarities in their technical and interpretive approaches.

All three regarded the task of the conductor as one of maximum creativity within the limits of the style and good taste. While attending to meticulous detail in the score in their search for maximum expression, and achieving those details through superlative technical execution, these conductors never pursued external effects solely for their own sake. Rather, they always strove to channel the emotional resources of the music and the singers so that the listener carried away with him an unforgettable musical and spiritual experience. What remains to be examined are the stylistic and technical features of the music to which these conductors applied their unique interpretive gifts.

6

The Style of the New Russian Choral School

The problems of performance practice in the music of the new Russian choral school are intimately related to questions of style and genre—a subject that has not yet received extensive treatment in either Western or Russian scholarly literature. In the years immediately preceding the Revolution a few church musicians, most notably Aleksandr Nikol'sky and Nikolai Kovin, began examining the new choral literature from a theoretical and analytic standpoint. However, the onslaught of the Bolshevik Revolution effectively curtailed all such activity; since then, the focus in Russian church music has shifted from creative and analytical pursuits to salvaging and preserving the sacred choral heritage from further destruction. Today in the Soviet Union, while the historical study of ancient musical monuments has been steadily increasing, the vast sacred choral literature of more recent times remains largely untouched by music scholars. The occasional performances of this music by present-day Soviet choirs often reflect serious deficiencies in the understanding of its style.

Russian choral music of the late nineteenth and early twentieth centuries is more difficult to categorize in terms of style than are other large bodies of choral music in the West. While individual composers of the Renaissance, for example, undoubtedly had their own personal characteristics, the style of Renaissance polyphony was essentially uniform, following certain established "canons" of compositional technique and stylistic propriety. In the minds of some Russian theoreticians, Russian choral composers of the late nineteenth century, particularly those writing sacred choral polyphony, were destined to undertake an historical step analogous to Western Renaissance masters—rendering polyphonically what had formerly been unison chant (or improvised heterophony) through various techniques of counterpoint and harmony. In the words of music historian Nikolai Kashkin, "In Western European music, choral composition attained its highest development in the fifteenth through seventeenth centuries, i.e., in the period of strict and, later, free counterpoint. This epoch was completely bypassed in Russian church music, but it must become the foundation of that independent development to which the newest composers of Russian church music are aspiring...."[1] In Kashkin's view, after becoming familiar with the contrapuntal techniques of Western masters, Russian composers would apply these independently to the chants of the Russian church, which are "completely different in nature than the melodies used by Western composers."

At the end of the nineteenth century, however, Russian choral composers not only had at their disposal the entire musical vocabulary of the "common practice" period, but they had also, in large part, internalized the attitudes of individualistic and subjective creativity that were the hallmark of the Romantic Century. While these attitudes were clearly in conflict with the long-standing traditions of the Orthodox Church, the Church itself was ill-equipped to offer any serious guidance in the matter, having relinquished the responsibility of stylistic censorship to a secular institution (the Imperial Court Chapel). Meanwhile, the Chapel's system of censorship had served a negative rather than a constructive role: the only criterion for an acceptable church style appeared to be the arbitrary personal taste of the Chapel's director. Consequently, there were few if any recognized "canons" for writing polyphonic church music, and had there been, composers would hardly have been interested in them. After Tchaikovsky's victory in the court case against Chapel Director Bakhmetev (which opened the field of sacred music composition) composers seized the occasion to express their own subjective ideas of appropriate church style. Thus began what Kastal'sky so aptly described as "the 'dawning' (following Tchaikovsky's fortunate example) of the 'each-to-his-own' style ... which flourishes to this day."[2]

The Classification of Russian Choral Music

The most obvious criterion for categorizing the music of the new Russian choral school is on the basis of whether the text is sacred or secular. Within each category, however, there are important subcategories. In the secular category one must distinguish between choral part-songs composed on high-quality poetic texts and "artistic arrangements" of folk songs that use previously existing folk melodies and texts. The primary contributors to the part-song repertoire were Tchaikovsky, Rimsky-Korsakov, Arensky, César Cui, Grechaninov, Sergei Taneev, Pavel Chesnokov, Viktor Kalinnikov, and to a lesser extent, Kastal'sky. The most prominent composers of folk-song arrangements were Rimsky-Korsakov, Anatoly Liadov, and Aleksandr Nikol'sky, as well as Kastal'sky, Chesnokov, and Kalinnikov. Within both subcategories one finds a great variety of compositional techniques—forms, textures, expressive devices—and literary themes (lyric, epic, humorous, etc.).

Both subcategories, particularly the arranged folk song, have continued to be staples of choral repertoire in the Soviet period.

With the exception of some works that use characteristic Russian epic or historical texts, the majority of Russian part-songs do not present any special interpretative problems. A work such as Tchaikovsky's well-known *"Legenda"* [A legend], on a text by Pleshcheev, is composed in a style that is thoroughly comprehensible to any choral musician. On the other hand, in a work such as Kastal'sky's *"Bylinka"* [A little epic] (see ex. 6.1), it is the specificity of the language and subject matter (here, a poem about Prince Vladimir of Kiev in a characteristic nine-syllable meter, replete with archaic words and allusions), rather than any musical features, that make the piece somewhat more difficult to interpret. With a little research of the sort one would do in the case of an obscure or archaic Western European text, even these difficulties could be surmounted.

In the case of artistic folk song arrangements the main problem is the degree of stylization that would be required or desirable in "academic" choral performance—a problem very similar to that encountered by an all-white American chorus in performing Negro spirituals, for example. As with any stylization, one must consider not only the appropriate style, but also the limits and boundaries of good taste. To stylize a Russian folk song arrangement properly, one would have to be familiar with the complex field of Russian folklore, including the numerous genres and subgenres of folk song and the specificities of numerous local manners of folk singing. Not only does a discussion of these questions lie beyond the scope of the present study, but the question of stylization has not been unequivocally resolved among choirs and conductors that specialize in this area.[3] Even professional folk choruses in the Soviet Union sometimes do not agree on the proper manner of stylizing "authentic" versions of folk songs, relative to the way they are recorded in the field by musical ethnographers.

However, most folk song arrangements by composers of the new Russian school are written in a style that does not demand extensive stylization. The vocal and harmonic resources used in a work such as Chesnokov's arrangement of *"Vo pole berezon'ka"* [In the field a birch-tree stood] clearly indicate that it is intended for performance by an "academic" rather than a folk chorus. This work would be appropriately performed in the same manner as a composed part-song, without taking into account the complex issues of folk stylization (see ex. 6.2).

By contrast, the stylistic issues in the field of sacred music—wherein one finds the greatest masterpieces of the new Russian choral school—are much more complex. The categorization of styles in Russian sacred choral music may be approached in a number of different ways; none of these systems, however, is without its complexities and ambiguities.

Example 6.1. Aleksandr Kastal'sky—"*Bylinka*" [A little epic].

(*Not the tiny, little stars lit up the span of heaven,*
Not the bright moon shone high above in the sky,
But the fair sun illumined our land...)

Example 6.2.   Pavel Chesnokov, arr.—*"Vo pole berezon'ka stoiala"* [In the field a birch tree stood].

(*In the field a birch tree stood,
In the field the leafy one stood.
Who will prune the birch tree?
Who will trim the leafy one?*)

Texts alone cannot serve as a clear-cut stylistic criterion, since all sacred compositions made exclusive use of Church Slavonic texts as they appeared in the service books and in the Scriptures. Even after the musical censorship of the Imperial Chapel was abolished, sacred works were reviewed by church officials to ensure that the text was rendered correctly. Church tradition did not allow for paraphrases or updated translations of texts unless they were originated by the Church.[4]

Nevertheless, texts of sacred musical compositions may be grouped in two categories: "liturgical"—those specifically prescribed to be sung during the Divine Liturgy and Offices, and "nonliturgical" or "paraliturgical"—those that are not prescribed but are drawn freely from Scripture or various devotional prayers.[5] Although a strict interpretation of the Orthodox liturgy does not allow for paraliturgical texts and, even in periods of less stringent adherence to liturgical order, such works were sung only in one place in the service (i.e., during the communion of the clergy), the genre of the *kontsert* or "concerto" proved to be extraordinarily enduring and popular with both composers and congregations.[6] But merely identifying the concerto as a nonliturgical genre does not help to classify the works that at various times have been sung as concertos, for they themselves display a great variety of musical styles. Moreover, hymns from other Offices, such as Vespers and Matins, were frequently sung as concertos. Thus, the distinction between liturgical and nonliturgical texts by itself does not serve as a criterion for identifying the various styles of Russian sacred choral music.

The Musical Structure of the Orthodox Liturgy

The liturgical year of the Orthodox Church is organized according to daily commemorations of events in the life of Christ, His Mother, and various saints. While every day commemorates some person or event, only certain days are designated as feasts of greater or lesser solemnity. The greatest feast of the year, in a category by itself as the "Feast of Feasts," is Pascha (Easter)—the Resurrection of the Lord. Pascha, as a movable feast, regulates the days of several other Great Feasts of the Lord: the Entrance into Jerusalem (Palm Sunday), the Ascension, and Pentecost. The other Great Feasts of the Lord are immovable: the Elevation of the Cross, the Nativity of Christ, the Theophany (the Baptism of the Lord), and the Transfiguration. Next in rank are the Great Feasts of the Mother of God—the Nativity of the Mother of God, the Presentation of the Mother of God in the Temple, the Presentation of the Lord in the Temple, the Annunciation, and the Dormition of the Mother of God, all of which are immovable. Liturgically and musically, Pascha and the twelve Great Feasts demand the greatest number of special hymns. Next in rank are several lesser Feasts of the Lord and the Mother of

God, as well as feasts of major saints—St. John the Baptist, St. Michael the Archangel, Sts. Peter and Paul, St. Nicholas, et al. These feasts also require special hymns but in smaller numbers than the Great Feasts.

Superimposed on the regular, immovable liturgical year are the movable periods associated with Pascha—Great Lent (including five pre-Lenten Sundays), Holy Week (or Passion Week), and the post-Paschal period. Great Lent, as a period of fasting, repentance, and spiritual preparation, has its own special liturgical commemorations, as well as special services not celebrated at other times of the year: the Great Kanon of St. Andrew of Crete, the Akathistos to the Mother of God, and the Liturgy of Presanctified Gifts. Holy Week, which commemorates the events of Christ's Passion, Crucifixion, and Entombment, is perhaps the most liturgically intense period of the year, when the usual format of services is considerably modified and enlarged by additional hymns and readings. Pascha, because of its special nature, also stands apart liturgically from all the other days of the year. The celebration of Pascha is most intense during Bright Week, the week immediately after the feast, but Paschal hymns continue to be sung throughout the forty-day period until Ascension.

In addition to the yearly cycle, the liturgy of the Church is governed by a weekly cycle of commemorations: Sunday, the Lord's Day, always celebrates the Resurrection of Christ (in fact, the Russian name of the day is *Voskresenie*, meaning Resurrection); Monday commemorates the Angelic Host, Tuesday—St. John the Baptist, Wednesday—the Mother of God and the Cross, Thursday—St. Nicholas, Friday—the Cross, Saturday—the righteous saints and the departed. Every day, therefore, has certain special hymns. Moreover, the musical content of each week changes according to the cycle of Eight Tones, the *Octoechos*, which in Russian practice regulates only certain hymns, namely troparia, kontakia, stichera, prokeimena, alleluias, and kanons. Each category of hymn thus has eight melodies that change from week to week, beginning with Tone One on the second Sunday after Pentecost and ending on the Fifth Sunday of Great Lent. If a major feast falls on a given weekday, however, the daily commemorations, as well as the Tone of the week, are usually superseded by the feast, which has its own configuration of Tones.[7]

The final element that regulates the musical format of the liturgy is the daily cycle. Of the nine Offices in the liturgical day,[8] only three are important musically: Vespers, Matins, and Divine Liturgy. During Great Lent and on the Feasts of the Nativity, Theophany, and Annunciation, the Office of Grand Compline also becomes musically important. Vespers and Matins in Russian practice are served together on Saturday evening and on the eves of major feasts, constituting what is referred to as the All-Night Vigil (in parish practice lasting slightly over two hours). The hymns sung during these services are divided into those that do not change—the ordinaries—and those that change according to the yearly cycle, the weekly cycle, and special seasons such as Great Lent, Holy Week, and the period from Pascha to Ascension—the propers.[9] Tables 6.1, 6.2, and 6.3 show the most important musical elements of these three services, as practiced in late nineteenth-century Russia.[10] For the sake of convenience, English titles have been used.

Table 6.1. The Musical Elements of Vespers

O—The Introductory Psalm, "Bless the Lord, o my soul"
(Psalm 103 [104])[11]

O—The First Kathisma of the Psalter, "Blessed is the man"
(Psalms 1, 2, 3)[a]

P—The Vesper Psalms, "Lord, I call" (Psalms 140, 141, 129, and 116 [141, 142, 130, 117]) and Stichera of the Day[b]

O—The Evening Hymn, "Gladsome Light"

P—Stichera Aposticha[c]

O—The Song of St. Symeon, "Lord, now lettest Thou" (*Nunc dimittis*)

P—The Troparion "Rejoice, O Virgin" (*Ave Maria*)[d] or the Troparion of the Feast

---

O = ordinary, P = proper

(a)On Sundays (i.e., Saturday evening) and on most major feasts.

(b)While the psalm texts remain the same, the melodies change from week to week and on feasts according to the Eight Tones of the Octoechos, as do the Stichera of the Day that are interpolated between the psalm verses.

(c)Change according to the Eight Tones. On major feasts the Stichera Aposticha are preceded by the Lity, a procession around the church or to the rear of the church, accompanied by the singing of festal stichera.

(d)On Sundays.

The scheme of Vespers does not show such minor musical elements as the opening call to worship, the litanies, the vesper prokeimenon (following "Gladsome Light"), and the closing sentence, "Blessed be the name of the Lord." Of the major musical elements only the Introductory Psalm is linked with a liturgical action—the censing of the entire church by the celebrant. Since only a few verses of the psalm are customarily set to music, a moderately melismatic setting is needed to allow sufficient time for the censing. By contrast, the First Kathisma, the Vesper Psalms, and the interpolated stichera, contain greater amounts of text (which is therefore usually delivered in a syllabic fashion). Only the final sticheron of the set, on Saturdays—the Theotokion-Dogmatikon in the Tone of the week,[12] and on feasts—the sticheron following "Glory . . . now and ever" (*slavnik*), is sung in an elaborate, melismatic manner; a similar scheme is followed in the stichera aposticha. The

Table 6.2.   The Musical Elements of Matins

P—The refrain "God is the Lord," the Troparion of the Day and corresponding Theotokion, or the Troparion of the Feast

O—The Polyeleos, "Praise the name of the Lord" (Psalms 134, 135 [135, 136])[a]

O—Five Resurrectional Troparia, each preceded by the refrain "Blessed art Thou, O Lord" (v. 12 of Psalm 118 [119])[b]

or

P—The Magnification as a refrain to selected psalm verses[c]

P—The First Gradual Antiphon in Tone 4, "From my youth"[c]

O—The Hymn "Having beheld the Resurrection"[b]

or

P—Stichera of the Feast[c]

P—The Kanon of the Day, consisting of 9 Odes (except that Ode 2 is usually omitted). Each ode consists of an Heirmos, which is sung, and several troparia (which in Russian practice are recited except on Pascha); the final troparion is usually followed by another Heirmos called a Katabasia. Before the Heirmos of the 9th Ode, the Canticle of the Mother of God (*Magnificat*) is sung, except on major feasts, which have their own proper refrains.

P—The Psalms of Praise, "Let every breath praise the Lord" (Psalms 148, 149, and 150) and Stichera of the Day[d]

O—The Great Doxology, "Glory to God in the highest"

P—One of two Resurrectional Troparia[b] or the Troparion of the Feast[c]

O—The Kontakion "O Victorious Leader" (actually the conclusion of the First Hour, which is appended to Matins)

(a)On Sundays and major feast days.

(b)On Sundays only.

(c)On Feasts only.

(d)The psalm verses remain the same, while the melodies change according to the Eight Tones, as do the Stichera of the Day. These stichera are usually not the same as interpolated into the Vesper Psalms.

musical treatment of the hymn "Gladsome Light" and the canticle of St. Symeon varies depending on the occasion, the latter being simply recited on ferial days.

The hymns of Matins, even more than those of Vespers, are text-oriented. Only the Polyeleos, which usually comprises only four psalm verses, each followed by the refrain "Alleluia," allows for musical elaboration. Of the stichera propers, the Festal Stichera (just before the Kanon) and the final sticheron before the Great Doxology—on Sundays, always the Theotokion "Most blessed art Thou, O Virgin," and on feasts, another *slavnik*—are intended to be sung in an elaborate fashion. The Great Doxology, which

Table 6.3.   The Musical Elements of the Divine Liturgy

O—The First Antiphon, "Bless the Lord, o my soul" (Psalm 102 [103])[a]

O—The Second Antiphon, "Praise the Lord, o my soul" (Psalm 145 [146])[b]

O—The Hymn "Only-Begotten Son"

O—The Third Antiphon, "In Thy Kingdom" (St. Matthew)[a]

O—The Introit verse, "Come, let us worship"[c]

P—Troparia and Kontakia of the Day

O—The Trisagion Hymn, "Holy God"[d]

O—The Cherubic Hymn[e]

O—The Creed

O—The Eucharistic Canon (Anaphora), comprising:
  (a) Three short sentences, beginning with "A mercy of peace"
  (b) The Hymn of praise, "It is meet and right to worship"
  (c) The Hymn "Holy, holy, holy" (*Sanctus* and *Benedictus*)
  (d) The Hymn of the Epiklesis, "We praise Thee"

O—The Hymn to the Mother of God, "It is truly meet"[f]

O—The Lord's Prayer

P—The Communion Hymn;[g] usually followed by a paraliturgical concerto

O—Hymns of Thanksgiving, "We have seen the true light" and "Let our mouths be filled"

O—The "Many Years"

(a)On a typical Sunday; on Great Feasts of the Lord, replaced by proper psalm verses and refrains.

(b)Often omitted in 19th-century Russian practice.

(c)The wording varies slightly on Feasts of the Mother of God and of Saints; replaced by proper Introit verse on Great Feasts of the Lord.

(d)Replaced on certain Great Feasts by "As many as have been baptized" or "Before Thy Cross."

(e)Replaced on only two days a year: on Holy Thursday by "Of Thy mystical supper" and on Holy Saturday by "Let all mortal flesh keep silent."

(f)On Great Feasts of the Lord and of the Mother of God, replaced by the Refrain and Heirmos of the 9th Ode of the festal Kanon from Matins. The Hymn to the Mother of God also changes on the first five Sundays of Great Lent ("All of creation rejoices") and from Pascha to Ascension ("The angel cried to the Lady").

(g)On a typical Sunday the text is "Praise the Lord from the Heavens" (Psalm 148:1); otherwise varies with the feast and the day of the week.

begins with the same text as the *Gloria in excelsis* of the Roman Mass but contains a considerable amount of additional text, does not lend itself to extensive musical elaboration due to the large amount of text.

Like the schemes of Vespers and Matins, the scheme of Divine Liturgy does not show various litanies and short responses, which are found between nearly every major musical element in the table. The major hymns of Divine

Liturgy are much more dependent on liturgical actions: e.g., the Cherubic Hymn must allow the celebrant time to prepare the transfer of the Communion Gifts from the table of oblation to the main altar and the singing of the Hymn is interrupted by a procession with the Gifts. A smaller procession precedes and follows the Introit. The Communion Hymn, supplemented by the concerto, must cover the time required by the celebrants to take communion, which in the case of a cathedral service with a large number of priests can be quite long. Moreover, in Russian practice the hymns of the Anaphora (as well as some others) must extend long enough to allow the celebrant to read some lengthy prayers silently. These hymns therefore lend themselves to elaborate musical treatment. On the other hand, the opening Antiphons, the Creed, and the Hymns of Thanksgiving at the end, which contain a large amount of text, are more suited to syllabic musical treatment.

Whereas the Roman Mass Ordinary was set to music much more than other Offices, both the Orthodox Vigil and the Divine Liturgy commanded the attention of Russian composers in the late nineteenth century. Most of their efforts, however, focused on the unchanging hymns, while the melodic diversity of the Eight-Tone cycle and the textual variety of the festal cycle received only sporadic musical treatment. Besides the two major services, composers set the hymns associated with Great Lent, Holy Week, and Pascha—for the most part, seasonal propers that replaced various elements of the three services outlined above. Other services that were set to music included the "private offices" or "needs"—the Intercessory Prayer Service (*moleben*), the Memorial Service (*panikhida*), and the Wedding Service (*venchanie*). Altogether, the Vigil, Liturgy (including their seasonal variants, propers, and paraliturgical insertions), and the private offices account for ninety-nine percent of sacred Russian choral music.

Attempting to approach the question of style through the various liturgical genres and hymn types can nevertheless be problematic. While familiarity with the liturgical system of the Orthodox Church can certainly be helpful to choral musicians (just as familiarity with the Roman or Lutheran liturgy aids in the concert performance of music from those traditions), knowledge of the liturgy only partially helps to determine the style and the appropriate performance of a given piece of Russian Orthodox sacred music. This is due, in large part, to the great variety and individuality with which late nineteenth-century composers treated the various elements of the liturgy; they often followed their own subjective perceptions of church ritual and liturgical texts rather than any type of canonical explanation found in a church catechism or book of rubrics.

As Johann von Gardner points out, every Orthodox service with a large amount of singing ought to display a distinctive musical "tension curve," resulting from the interaction of the various musical styles found in the numerous hymns and readings.[13] This tension curve may vary for the same Office depending on the solemnity of the occasion being celebrated, or whether the service is celebrated in a cathedral, a village parish, or a monastery. Detailed indications of these levels of solemnity are contained in the *Typikon* (*ustav*), which in Russia has remained essentially unchanged since the fourteenth century, and in various uses (*chinovniki*) of individual cathedrals and monasteries. More importantly, however, these differences are embodied in the canonical chants of the Russian Church—systems of melodies for the entire yearly, weekly, and daily liturgical cycles—in which hymns sung on various occasions are differentiated by the degree of musical complexity.

According to aesthetic principles developed in Byzantium from the early days of Christianity, somber hymns were sung slowly and in a lower vocal range, while joyful hymns were sung more rapidly and in a higher range. Festal hymn propers generally received more elaborate melodic treatment than ordinaries, and ordinaries on feast days were more elaborate musically than on ferial days. To reflect these requirements, the Russian Church first adopted and then developed several distinct bodies of chant. Most complex from a melodic standpoint were great znamennyi chant (*bol'shoi znamennyi rospev*), putevoi chant, demestvennyi chant, and Bulgarian chant; next were (middle) znamennyi chant,[14] Kievan chant, and Greek chant;[15] on the simplest side of the musical spectrum were the little znamennyi (*malyi znamennyi*), abbreviated Kievan, and abbreviated Greek chants, loosely referred to as "common" (*obychnyi*) chant. In addition, various monasteries and some particularly ancient cathedrals developed their own distinctive bodies of chant.

It is within this complex and varied chant repertoire and in the melodic diversity of the Eight Tones that one might expect to find clues for categorizing Russian sacred choral music in terms of style. Unfortunately for the modern-day choral conductor (and for Orthodox church precentors), this is not the case. The incursion into Russian church music of the Polish and Italianate styles during the seventeenth and eighteenth centuries tragically disrupted the stylistic wholeness of the chant system that had fulfilled the aesthetic requirements of the liturgy. As composers began to focus on the unchanging hymns of the Vigil and Liturgy, the richly poetic, image-filled propers of the festal cycle were relegated to the mind-numbing dullness of common chant harmonized in four parts by means of a few trite chord progressions. At the Imperial Court in St. Petersburg services were minimized by eliminating most melodic elaboration in favor of chordal recitative. The resulting unartistic abomination, known as the Court Chant, was disseminated throughout Russia by the authority of the Imperial Court Chapel, assuming a prominent position next to the highly elaborate but nonliturgical sacred concertos of Bortniansky and his Italianate contemporaries. This juxtaposition (which certainly did not favor the liturgical elements of the service music) first of all catered to the opinion, held by some, that church music by its nature ought to be simple and devoid of artistic content; secondly, if artistic content was to be found, it most certainly resided in the hymns of the ordinary, rather than in the changing hymns of the weekly and festal propers. By the late nineteenth century the traditional system of musical aesthetics in the Church was in a shambles—vastly incomplete and in many ways distorted. To make matters worse, historians and theoreticians, refusing to recognize this state of affairs, often described things as they once were or as they should be under ideal circumstances.[16]

As Tchaikovsky had demonstrated, one could write and publish a setting of the Divine Liturgy without any specialized knowledge or preparation. In a letter to his brother he wrote: "I have already done certain things [in the field of church music], but all by feeling around in the dark. I don't have a thorough knowledge of either the history of church singing, or the service, or the relationship of what is in the [chant] *Obikhod* to what is sung in churches. In all these matters there exists a great deal of chaos."[17] Tchaikovsky's example inspired numerous imitators, few of whom took the trouble to investigate issues of liturgical style. And since these issues were nowhere spelled out in an obvious fashion, it was easy to conclude that one could proceed simply by following one's personal musical instincts and taste. Among the composers writing church music at the end of the nineteenth century only those few who were in direct contact with day-to-day church work, most notably, Kastal'sky, Chesnokov, and Nikol'sky, recognized the nature and implications of the distortions that had occurred historically, and made attempts to restore the proper equilibrium among the various elements of the liturgy. However, most of their contemporaries, who approached church music simply on musical terms, essentially perpetuated the emphasis on the ordinary hymns of Vigil and Liturgy, setting proper hymns only sporadically and contributing little towards rectifying the overall liturgico-musical system of the Russian Church.

Stylistic Categories in Russian Sacred Choral Music

In the last two decades of the nineteenth century the musicological investigations of Dmitri Razumovsky, Ioann Voznesensky, and Stepan Smolensky, among others, brought the ancient heritage of traditional chant to the attention of composers in the mainstream of Russian music. As mentioned in chapter 3, the lead in the area of setting chants polyphonically was taken by Tchaikovsky in his *Vigil* and Rimsky-Korsakov in the Imperial Chapel's *All-Night Vigil in Ancient Chants*. The "rediscovery" of chant made it clear that not only Russian secular music, but Russian sacred music as well, could tap an indigenous wellspring of melodic material to produce new works in a nationalistic style. The chant melodies were clearly national in character, while the texts and liturgical format of the hymns were fixed immutably by the Church. Seemingly nothing stood in the way of composers who, like Tchaikovsky, wished "to apply one's talents to the needs of the Russian Church."[18] The only question that remained unresolved was: What musical style was appropriate or desirable for the needs of Orthodox worship?

As early as 1894, the musicologist and critic Antonin Preobrazhensky identified two conflicting schools of thought with regard to this question:

> The first [school] is drawn to the ancient chants, the other renounces or simply ignores them. The first [direction] can be characterized by a single word—"[chant] arrangement" [*perelozhenie*], the second, by the word "composition." . . . Into these two forms can be placed the entire content of our sacred musical literature, which, one must admit, is not very distinguished in terms of quality.
>
> Can both of these directions coexist in church musical practice? In principle no one denies the need for both compositions and [chant] harmonizations, but when it comes down to practice, one finds individuals who deny the necessity of either one or the other. [One side] . . . finds that contemporary music with its artfulness, effect, and subtlety cannot serve purely religious needs: . . . only ancient Russian musical theory can [do so]. . . . The Church, in their view, does not require the services of modern music.
>
> The other direction, on the contrary, seeks to bring modern music into the service of the Church. . . . "[19]

Even among the adherents of chant there was no consensus: some believed that polyphonic chant settings ought to employ the simplest technical means, eschewing all expression; others felt that such settings should employ the full arsenal of compositional technique to pursue the highest artistic and expressive goals. In Russia this debate (which is certainly not unique in the realm of liturgical music) also involved issues of musical nationalism: the means offered by the "simplistic" camp—represented by such individuals as Nikolai Potulov, Vasily Metallov, and Dmitri Soloviev—were generally confined to techniques drawn from the so-called strict style of Western polyphony, though devoid of any contrapuntal interest (see ex. 6.3). The hundreds of chant harmonizations produced in this fashion were not only simple, but amazingly dull; worse yet, they represented another infusion into Russian church music of a foreign style.

By contrast, the "artistic" faction included some of the most innovative followers of the Russian nationalist school, who, in seeking to use all available artistic means for church music, were not content to remain within scholastic prescriptions of Western European music theory. The stylistic dichotomy that resulted was enormous: on one hand were the self-consciously simple, artless works intended to fulfill arbitrarily defined standards of "churchliness"; on the other hand were fresh and vibrant but complex works that integrated

Example 6.3. Vasily Metallov—"*Khvalite imia Gospodne*" [Praise the name of the Lord].
(Kievan Chant harmonized in "strict style")

(*Praise the name of the Lord, Alleluia.*
Praise the Lord, you servants. Alleluia.
Blessed be the Lord...)

traditional chant materials with techniques synthesized from the heterophony of the Russian choral folk song. At the time they appeared, both styles were intended to serve the musical needs of the church. Today, however, the works of the "simplistic" school hardly stand up in performance outside a liturgical context because of their calculated artlessness. The works of the "artistic" school, on the other hand, regardless of their original purpose, clearly surpass a strictly liturgical function and therefore stand as candidates for inclusion in the body of the world's great sacred choral music suitable for concert presentation.

As noted earlier, the achievement of opening up the field of church composition was generally attributed to Tchaikovsky, although in truth his *Liturgy* probably attained prominence more as a result of the notoriety surrounding its publication than because of its musical merit. In the words of the critic Larosch, "it is the work of a competent and conscientious artist, in which one perceives an experienced hand, good taste, and a sense of what is proper, more so than mighty inspiration.... In the field of our liturgical music it is capable of producing neither a schism nor meaningful reform."[20]

The first composer whose style was immediately perceived by critics as innovative was Aleksandr Kastal'sky, who to this day stands as a unique and towering figure in the field of Russian sacred choral composition. In 1896, a mere two years after he first tried his hand at polyphonically setting some znamennyi and Serbian chant melodies, Kastal'sky's work was hailed by Nikolai Kashkin in the following terms:

> Wonderful technique, erudition, and a wealth of inventiveness—these are Kastal'sky's virtues..., to which must be added the distinctive features of his creative gift. Technique within a given style, erudition, and inventiveness have been displayed by other composers, but they were still trying to develop a style [for church music], while Kastal'sky has presently established it—both for himself and for others, and this style is not only appropriate for the Orthodox Church, but must be recognized as *the* genuine style for Orthodox church music. It reconciles the requirement of preserving the fundamental church chants with... the demands, posed by the contemporary development of music, for intense musical interest, as well as the requirement that church music in Russia have a national face....
>
> In his amazing ability to use choral voices... he has no equals. His choral orchestration is truly virtuosic...: the four-part choir sometimes expands to eight voices; rich harmony is supplanted by unisons; and all this has the appearance of being not only intelligent, but... natural and inevitable, and in all cases—extraordinarily beautiful.[21]

Two years later, in 1898, the critic Ivan Lipaev singled out in Kastal'sky's work a unique "absence of subjectivity," which ineffably coexisted with striking originality:

In church music [Kastal'sky] is a type of Vasnetsov.[22] One would like to hear his arrangements and compositions under the arches of the Kievan St. Vladimir Cathedral, so permeated are they with incorporeity and asceticism, so dissimilar are they to the extravagances of a lone individual, sounding more like an echo of a composition by an entire people.... Listening to his works, it seems at times that they have burst into this world on their own accord, without the will and effort on the composer's part. It appears that [Kastal'sky] has wholly mastered the inner essence of ancient singing; his instinct has not misled him.[23]

Similar observations about Kastal'sky's music have been made by critics and theorists since that time. As for Kastal'sky himself, he expressed a number of interesting ideas concerning the church style in his article "My musical career and my thoughts on church music":

> And what about style?... Our indigenous church melodies when set chorally lose all their individuality; how distinctive they are when sung in unison by the Old Believers, and how insipid they are in the conventional four-part arrangements of our classic [composers], on which we have prided ourselves for nearly a hundred years: it is touching, but spurious....
>
> In my opinion it is first of all necessary to get away from continual four-part writing—from the hackneyed—since an original musical thought should always be originally expressed....
>
> The future of our creative work for the church can ... be merely surmised, but I feel what its real task should be. I am convinced that it lies in the idealization of authentic church melodies, the transformation of them into something musically elevated, mighty in its expressiveness and near to the Russian heart in its typically national quality.... I should like to have music that could be heard nowhere except in a church, and which would be as distinct from secular music as church vestments are from the dress of the laity.[24]

The question of style was the subject of considerable debate at the First All-Russian Convention of Choral Directors, which met in Moscow in 1908. Here, virtually for the first time, an attempt was made to identify and evaluate critically the new style of choral writing that had been emanating from the pens of Kastal'sky, Grechaninov, and Chesnokov, among others, throughout the preceding decade. In a lecture entitled "The new direction in Russian church music," Reverend Mikhail Lisitsyn focused on the new sonorities in choral writing pursued by the composers of the new school:

> Just as Wagner introduced new sonorities into the orchestra, the composers of the "new direction" have begun to seek new sonorities in the chorus. Primarily this has been achieved by means of new doublings [of voices],... seeking out effects in the choir similar to those of instruments....
>
> In general, one can observe that the church compositions of the new direction are choral pieces composed in a symphonic, orchestral manner.... The church composers of today must know orchestration in general, and specifically, the orchestration of choral voices, which at present is not yet taught in our conservatories....

> In summarizing the ... works of the new direction, one cannot fail to notice the variety and subtlety of musical techniques and expression. Diversity in unity and unity in diversity—this is the maxim of the new direction in church music.... As he harmonizes the same musical phrases and motives [of chant], each composer strives to dress them up in a slightly different attire, but an attire that is nevertheless of the same style.[25]

Lisitsyn criticized the composers Grechaninov and Chesnokov for employing devices of text painting, which he believed were drawn from the operatic and art-song style and exceeded what he called the "limits of abstractness" appropriate for the church style. "Our church melodies," he said, "by and large are characterized by abstract expression, which is why composers of the new direction ... use them to achieve an objective, dispassionate expression in their compositions."[26]

In the course of the same discussion the composer Konstantin Shvedov, disputing Lisitsyn, placed the artistic qualities of a sacred composition uppermost. This is why, in Shvedov's opinion, znamennyi chant was not entirely satisfactory for contemporary church music:

> Any sacred musical composition that aspires to be viable must satisfy certain demands and conditions, namely: (1) artistic quality, (2) churchliness of style, and (3) a clearly and truthfully expressed national quality [*narodnost'*]. Znamennyi chant does not fully satisfy all three criteria for two reasons: it does not always possess artistic qualities, i.e., changes of religious sentiments expressed in the text are not always reflected by a corresponding change in the melody; and, znamennyi chant is epic in character, having the quality of religious-philosophical narrative. Thus, [contemporary] sacred music requires an additional element—the folk song—used, however, in spirit rather than verbatim.[27]

The church choir directors attending the convention, many from small towns and villages, complained that the music of the new school was generally too complex and therefore inaccessible to small choirs. While this was undoubtedly a justified objection, which prompted composers such as Kastal'sky and Chesnokov to write works for smaller vocal forces and offer *ossia*s for small choirs, the overall artistic credo of the new school was expressed by composer Aleksandr Nikol'sky in his speech to the convention:

> [These new works] are characterized by a grand design in the treatment of ancient melodies that is not in line with the ordinary capabilities of our choirs; the works are written as if for instruments, ... [and] not every choir can sing them.... But should we not assume the viewpoint that the chorus is the brother of the orchestra? Indeed, it is an orchestra of human voices. Just as there are no difficulties [that cannot be overcome] by a large modern-day orchestra, so should there be no difficulties for a chorus.... And if grandiose pieces are inaccessible to small choirs, ultimately it isn't the performer who teaches the composer, but on the contrary, the composition, by making demands on the performer, that forces him to rise to the required heights....
>
> I believe this movement [in Russian church music] is destined to assume the same position that has been attained in the history of music by the works of J. S. Bach, for example.[28]

As the artistic identity of the new style became more evident, more and more voices were heard arguing for the development of sacred music that was not confined to strictly liturgical use. In 1909 Nikol'sky noted: "We already have a nascent and ever-growing movement in the area of sacred composition to create works that are not suited for everyday church use, but appear to be intended specifically for the concert stage.... The performance of these works in concerts by exemplary choirs can give programs [of sacred music] the elements of novelty and independent artistic value that they have not had heretofore."[29]

Drawing upon the ancient historical distinction between znamennyi chant, which was governed by the Eight Tones, and demestvennyi singing, which was independent of the Tones, Nikolai Kompaneisky, both as a publicist and a composer, proposed a special category of "demestvennyi" sacred works: settings of liturgical texts intended solely for performance in sacred concerts, which he dubbed "demestvennyi meetings." As a result, he argued, two different critical standards would be applied, one to purely liturgical singing, the other to nonliturgical music on liturgical texts:

> Liturgical singing is an extremely subtle, delicate art; here one careless stroke can offend the sensibilities [of the worshipper] and destroy the [devotional] atmosphere. Thus, church singing should not be dramatic or subjective; its function is to fuse all the worshippers into a single soul, a single heart: it should be pure, maintaining a generalized, lyrical and religious mood, and not distract from prayer by compelling one to contemplate the music.
> The goals of demestvennyi [i.e., extra-liturgical] singing are different. Extra-liturgical sacred music pursues the same goals as independent religious literature or paintings on Biblical or New Testament subjects. This music must cultivate religious and moral attitudes and develop affection for and stimulate interest in the ritual life of the Church, ... as well as markedly affect the development of the people's religious-aesthetic consciousness.[30]

In Kompaneisky's opinion, only in "demestvennyi" works could composers employ the approach advocated by the composer Grechaninov, who claimed that "for [Russian] church music all forms of counterpoint and harmony are appropriate, as long as they are used sensibly and skillfully."[31] Kompaneisky's distinction, however, while valid in essence, found little practical application. Only in the 1910s were a few sacred compositions overtly labelled by church censors as "not permissible for church performance." For their own part, composers apparently were not interested in specifying whether their compositions were intended for church or concert performance, and vehemently opposed the continued attempts by church authorities to monitor the situation.

An even stronger proposal than Kompaneisky's was made by another writer—most likely the composer (and later a priest), Yuri Izvekov[32]—who called for the creation of Orthodox sacred music in "the highest forms," i.e., large-scale choral-orchestral works. "Contemporary Russian church singing," he wrote, does not yet have the right to make serious claims to a place in general music history. What today is called Orthodox church music is a jumble of contradictory viewpoints, irreconcilable ideas, and unsystematized accretions, which in practice result in a mixture of all types of styles and chants, the absence of a definite school or tradition in the direction of church singing, and the scarcity of more or less major cycles of sacred musical works. . . . [33]

All that the West knows of Orthodox music is a series of charming vocal arabesques, whose fame rests more upon the skill of the performers (in former years—the Court Chapel, nowadays—the Synodal Choir) than upon serious intrinsic musical value. . . .

The composers of sacred music themselves have long yearned for new forms and are instinctively pursuing orchestral effects. One need only to look at the works of the majority of contemporary sacred composers. The vocal style has been relinquished by them and has been replaced by one that is orchestral: high notes for voices, difficult modulations, endless doubling of voices, orchestral nuances, vocal [imitation of] bell-ringing effects, musical realism, arias with choral accompaniment, and so forth. [34]

Although the writer's observations concerning the field of Orthodox church music were valid to some extent, his call for more grandiose musical forms did not bring immediate results. Between the appearance of his article in 1913 and the Bolshevik Revolution in late 1917, only three works of major proportions appeared, all hailed by critics as the greatest works in the genre to that point: Rachmaninoff's *Vigil* (1915), Kastal'sky's *Requiem to the Fallen Heroes*, for chorus and orchestra (1916), and Grechaninov's *Liturgia domestica*, for soli, chorus, and orchestra (or organ) (1917). (Several of Grechaninov's later sacred choral works written after he emigrated call for orchestral accompaniment, but they never gained prominence.) Had the Revolution not occurred, the field of Orthodox sacred music undoubtedly would have been enriched by similar large-scale works, and perhaps would have developed greater stylistic unity and order. Under the circumstances, however, the task of seeking out unifying stylistic characteristics and categories in the existing music has been left to historians.

On the basis of musical factors, Russian choral works of high artistic content written around the turn of the century may be classified into the following four categories.

In the first category are works based on the canonical chant melodies of the Orthodox Church—znamennyi, Kievan, Greek, Bulgarian, in all their variants—in which the chant is a structural, form-determining element. The chant may lie in one particular voice throughout or may migrate from voice to voice, but it remains a continuous, unbroken thread that shapes the formal plan of the work. In many instances the Russian terms used to describe such works—*garmonizatsiia* (harmonization) and *perelozhenie* (arrangement)—do not adequately express the nature of the compositional techniques. Particularly in the case of works based on melodically developed chants, the nature of the polyphonic treatment contrasts directly with the technique of "harmonization," since all the added voices exhibit a marked degree of melodic interest and independence. The term "arrangement" is accurate only to the extent that a melody originally performed monophonically has been arranged for polyphonic performance. Such works would be more adequately described by the terms "polyphonization" or "polyphonic setting" (see ex. 6.4).

Works of the second category are those in which identifiable chant melodies are used as motivic material, but where the chant does not determine the overall form of the composition. At times the chant may disappear from the texture altogether or be paraphrased to a greater or lesser extent. Again, the term "arrangement" suffices only partially to describe works of this nature (see ex. 6.5).

In the third group are works that do not employ any identifiable chant melodies, but whose part-writing either uses the melodic building blocks (*popevki*)[35] of chant or exhibits a marked similarity to them (see ex. 6.6). A subcategory of such "quasi-chant" works are those written in the characteristic chordal recitative style, but not using an actual chant formula (see ex. 6.7).

Finally, there is a category of works in a free style that cannot be linked to any of the specific musical qualities found in chant—qualities that will become obvious in the ensuing discussion. Stylistically these works span the gamut of Western European compositional techniques used during that period.

In attempting to classify stylistically the output of the new Russian choral school, it is valuable to bear in mind Kastal'sky's observation that, despite critics' efforts to draw distinctions, for example, between St. Petersburg and Moscow composers, "the directions of the composing fraternity are so very diverse in both [cities], that to talk of 'camps'...is quite unjustified."[36] Nevertheless, on the basis of the musical features outlined above, it is possible to identify the salient features of each major composer's style, and to group composers into several categories as an aid to finding common approaches to interpretation and performance practice. For obvious reasons the present discussion must be limited to an overview: every composer mentioned below could be, and in some instances already has been, the subject of a separate monograph.[37]

In Moscow of the late nineteenth century a composer of church music could not fail to have had his creative orientation influenced by the unique set of circumstances and personalities at the Moscow Synodal School of church singing. Therefore it is not surprising to find a number of common features in the styles of Moscow composers, particularly those directly associated with the Synodal School and Choir: Kastal'sky and Viktor Kalinnikov, who were faculty members, and Pavel Chesnokov, Aleksandr Nikol'sky, Nikolai Tolstiakov, and Konstantin Shvedov, who were graduates and former members of the Choir. Not directly associated with the Synodal School, but

Example 6.4. Aleksandr Kastal'sky—"*Bog Gospod'*" [God is the Lord] (Hymn to the Mother of God for Palm Sunday).
(Chant-determined form in an arrangement of Znamennyi Chant)

(God is the Lord and has revealed Himself to us!
Celebrate the feast and come with gladness!
Let us magnify Christ with palms and branches, crying out in song:
Blessed is He who comes in the name of the Lord, our Savior.)

Example 6.5. Pavel Chesnokov—"*Nyne otpushchaeshi*" [Lord, now lettest Thou],
Opus 11, No. 4.
(Motivic use of Znamennyi Chant)

(*Lord, now lettest Thou Thy servant depart in peace, according to*
Thy word...)

Example 6.6. Aleksandr Kastal'sky—Sacred Concerto "*Miloserdiia dveri otverzi nam*"
[Open unto us the doors of Thy tender mercy].
(Free composition using melodic nuclei of Znamenny Chant)

(*Open unto us the doors of thy tender mercy, o blessed Mother of God...*)

Example 6.7. Aleksandr Grechaninov—Sticheron for Holy Friday "*Tebe odeiushchagosia*" [Joseph with Nicodemus took Thee down from the tree], Opus 58, No. 9. (Free composition in the style of liturgical recitative)

(Joseph with Nicodemus took Thee down from the tree, Who clothest Thyself with light as with a garment, and beheld Thee dead and naked...)

having close personal contacts with members of the faculty were Aleksandr Grechaninov, Sergei Rachmaninoff, and Mikhail Ippolitov-Ivanov. The faculty and students of the Synodal School were also in close contact with the Moscow Conservatory next door, and particularly with Sergei Taneev, the composer and contrapuntal theorist.

Because no corresponding institutional fraternity existed in St. Petersburg, one finds much greater diversity among the styles of Petersburg composers—from the intense Slavophilism of Nikolai Kompaneisky to the unfocused eclecticism of Semyon Panchenko and Mikhail Lisitsyn and the largely Western-influenced style of Aleksandr Arkhangel'sky, which vacillated between the diatonic austerity of the "strict style" and a highly chromatic, sentimental Romantic idiom. Not associated with either Moscow or St. Petersburg was Dmitri Yaichkov, who for a time lived in Tbilisi, Georgia, but whose music clearly lies within the style of Moscow composers.

The Influence of Stepan Vasil'evich Smolensky

The common stylistic features found in the music of Moscow composers have been attributed to the influence and guidance of Stepan Smolensky (1848–1909). Smolensky wrote but a few works and can hardly be considered a composer of major stature (he once requested that Kastal'sky give him lessons in theory). He was, however, the reigning expert on the old canonical chants and notations.

Some disagreement exists regarding Smolensky's exact role. In his autobiography Kastal'sky writes:

> In the press (by Kompaneisky, and following him, by others) it was coolly stated more than once that Smolensky had supervised my labors. I do not know from where this information was drawn. His "supervision" consisted in the fact that both he and [Vasily Sergeevich] Orlov were in sympathy and greatly interested in this work of mine, and encouraged it in every way.... Always alert and energetic, Stepan Vasil'evich, in his directorial capacity, knew how to "fan the flame"; in this he was particularly valuable and sympathetic.[38]

Smolensky evidently offered some critical advice to Grechaninov, whose first *Liturgy*, Opus 13, was given a preliminary hearing in a closed performance by the Synodal Choir. After this initial essay in sacred music (for the most part in a chordal, harmonic style reminiscent of Tchaikovsky), Grechaninov adopted a much more melodic, chant-oriented idiom—undoubtedly, according to Nikol'sky, as a result of "numerous discussions among Grechaninov, Kastal'sky, Smolensky, and Orlov."[39]

Smolensky's influence and guidance can be documented most clearly in the case of Chesnokov's early compositional efforts, as Chesnokov himself relates:

I was writing my first large concerto for chorus with affection and diligence. But every time, at the next theory and composition lesson, S. V. Smolensky would calmly cross out with a pencil what had been written and say: "This just won't do." Finally I was close to despair. But once I was walking down the street, thinking about my unfortunate composition, and suddenly it struck me! It was as if a closed door had opened before me. I stood there for a moment and then took off running. Muscovites probably stared with surprise at the lanky youth with a happy face running along the Kuznetsky Bridge. I wrote all night, and in the morning S. V. Smolensky, after attentively playing what I had wrought, stood up, embraced and kissed me, and said: "I congratulate you." And indeed this turned out to be one of my best compositions. [40]

In Nikol'sky's words, "not one line was written [by Chesnokov] without Smolensky's advice and criticism." At Smolensky's request, Kastal'sky also took a hand in guiding young Chesnokov's compositional efforts. [41]

According to Nikol'sky, Smolensky was the first to suggest that neither Western European harmony nor counterpoint were suitable for the polyphonic treatment of Russian chant melodies. The melodies needed both harmony and counterpoint, Smolensky said, but of an indigenous Russian variety, drawing upon the counter-voiced polyphony (*podgolosochnaia polifoniia*) of the secular folk song and the melodic style of the church chant. Smolensky called this hitherto unidentified technique *"kontrapunktika,"* using the word "counterpoint" with a characteristic Russian ending. The most important features of this style may be identified as follows:

1. The admissibility of parallel voice leading (in fifths, fourths, and octaves)
2. A constantly changing number of voices in the texture, expanding from the usual four to as many as eight and contracting to only two or a unison
3. The possibility of a single melodic line with a drone (the texture of chant with an *ison* used in the Byzantine Church)
4. Formal structures that are word-related rather than determined by purely musical relationships of periods and phrases.

The counterforce to Smolensky's ideas was Sergei Taneev, Professor of Music Theory at the Moscow Conservatory, who at various times taught theory and counterpoint to Kastal'sky, Chesnokov, Rachmaninoff, Nikol'sky, and Vasily Orlov. Taneev believed that Russian church music should emulate the style of Western contrapuntal masters of the fifteenth and sixteenth centuries. Practically speaking, in the area of sacred music his efforts never got beyond a series of contrapuntal etudes in sketchbooks, based on chant melodies. [42] As Sergei Vasilenko, one of his students, relates, Taneev was an ideological foe of Smolensky and the ancient chants the latter was bringing to light. "Nothing good will come of it," he would say. "The tradition itself is not interesting, and all these 'hooks' [neumes] propagandized by Smolensky are unartistic, [since] they do not lend themselves to being developed [musically]...."[43] Taneev's only published choral works were secular, written in a mixture of harmonic and contrapuntal style.[44]

Despite Taneev's attempts to propagate his theories among his students, the Western style of imitative polyphony and fugue did not assume an important role in the works of the Moscow composers and appeared only in exceptional cases. Undoubtedly a major factor in this was the Orthodox Church's traditional emphasis on the intelligibility of the text, which continued to be a stylistic cornerstone of Russian church music. Another factor may have been simply the lack of thorough training in traditional Western counterpoint: Kastal'sky recalls that even though he himself was a Conservatory graduate, his first efforts at chant harmonization were judged unsatisfactory because of Taneev's ideas; but, says Kastal'sky in his own defense, "Of course I had no technical knowledge of [fifteenth and sixteenth century counterpoint], though I sometimes attempted to adapt various contrapuntal devices to our church melodies."[45] Perhaps for that very reason, and also because he was gifted with an innate sensitivity for translating into the language of art music indigenous features of native Russian song and chant (as were Glinka and Musorgsky, for example, in the realm of secular music), Kastal'sky came to be hailed as the founder of a new style in Orthodox church music.

The Style of Aleksandr Dmitrievich Kastal'sky

Kastal'sky came to church music in a very casual, almost offhand manner. As he relates in his autobiography, he regarded his earliest works—arrangements of Serbian chant melodies for *"Milost' mira"* [A mercy of peace] and *"Dostoino est'"* [It is truly meet]—as experiments to which he "did not attribute any artistic merit." Moreover, he says, "it never occurred to me that my works might be published." Yet, upon the insistence of Prince Shirinsky-Shikhmatov, the Synod's overseer of the Synodal School, published they were, and "quite unexpectedly to myself and others I became a church composer and even the founder of a movement...."[46]

Kastal'sky began by writing service music for use in the Moscow Dormition Cathedral where the Synodal Choir sang, but very soon—by his fourth published opus, *"Miloserdiia dveri"* [Open to us the doors] (ex. 6.6)—he clearly began to exceed the limitations of a purely utilitarian approach. The work was a setting of a nonliturgical devotional prayer to the Mother of God (in other words, a "concerto") for which there was no preexisting chant melody. Rather than adopt a completely free approach, Kastal'sky took the unprecedented step of composing the work out of selected melodic formulae of znamennyi chant. The result was a totally new synthesis in Russian church music of traditional melodic material with the creative compositional process.

Shortly afterwards, Kastal'sky discovered, much to his surprise, that some of his works were perceived as unsuitable for use in the liturgy because of their high artistic content. "An incident occurred," he writes, "in connection with *"Blagoobraznyi Iosif"* [The noble Joseph] and the Troparia of Holy Saturday; after eulogizing this hymn and going beyond the bounds of decency by comparing it with the creations of Bach (!), Kompaneisky declared that it was not suitable for the liturgy (?). Among Moscow worshippers there were those who were of the same opinion. . . . "[47] Although he conceived most of his works for liturgical use (only a few, *"Chertog Tvoi"* [Thy bridal chamber] and *"Svete tikhii"* No. 4 [Gladsome light], were expressly written for concert performance), Kastal'sky's masterful technique in writing for voices and his concern for profoundly expressing in musical sounds each liturgical text he set clearly elevated his works beyond the utilitarian realm.

Of Kastal'sky's more than one hundred published sacred pieces, fully eighty percent fall into the category of chant-based works in which the chant melody determines the form of the work. Of these, more than fifty percent are based on znamennyi chant, the most melodically and rhythmically elaborate of all the chants. The other chant-based works use a variety of Kievan, Serbian, Greek, Bulgarian, and Georgian chants, as well as various local cathedral and monastery melodies. In some works—usually short feast-day propers such as troparia, kontakia, stichera, and heirmoi—the chant appears in a single voice throughout. The chant-bearing voice is not always the soprano and/or tenor, as one might expect in *cantus firmus* technique; Kastal'sky was the first Russian composer to place a chant *cantus firmus* in the bass on some occasions. Kastal'sky's greatest skill, however, lay in passing the chant around from voice to voice in the course of a work, creating an immense variety of textures made possible by such a procedure. His works, moreover, were the first to embody Smolensky's ideas of a native Russian counterpoint—a distinct departure from the concept of "harmonization," which had reigned supreme in Russia for nearly two hundred years. As Boris Asaf'ev observes,

A study of Kastal'sky's choral scores . . . leads one to discover step by step Kastal'sky's determined effort to weave a choral texture from the essential melodic elements and not by a mechanical addition of "harmonies". . . .

In working out his basic thematic elements (*popevki*) Kastal'sky rather decisively ignores all formal mechanical techniques of developing these elements (initial imitation, canonic entry and interweaving, inversion, augmentation, diminution). He does not so much develop the basic elements mechanically as *transmutes* one into another. Variant subordinate voices, variations of melodic moves and turns, the transfer of line fragments from voice to voice and from register to register, the utilization of new timbres, and similar techniques, point to a constant concern not so much for maintaining external variety as for unceasingly "cultivating" the vocal fabric in accordance with its inherent tendency to change and branch out.

In his arrangements of church melodies Kastal'sky, at first instinctively, and then with profound insight into the essence of the folk song and the church art of chanting, strove to form the polyphonic fabric out of melodic (horizontal), step-wise, and breath-determined movement. Living sound, and not mechanical underwriting of the middle voices in the space between the upper and lower voices, serves to organize his music. Melodic rather than harmonic functions constitute the voice-leading. Vocal dynamics control the sonority and the techniques of form building.[48]

Kastal'sky's style of vocal writing must be recognized as a new, hitherto unknown type of "homorhythmic polyphony" in which every voice, while deriving its rhythm from the chant, displays the kind of melodic interest and integrity usually found exclusively in imitative counterpoint. Before Kastal'sky, hints of this type of writing could be observed only in some opera choruses of Musorgsky. In sacred music, however, the introduction of this technique belongs solely to Kastal'sky, who remained its foremost practitioner. Among other Russian choral composers, the technique was employed by Rachmaninoff (in his *Vigil* more than in his *Liturgy*), Kompaneisky, and occasionally by Chesnokov, Nikol'sky, and Kalinnikov.[49]

The twenty percent of Kastal'sky's works that are not chant-based are free compositions that are for the most part constructed, like *"Miloserdiia dveri,"* out of the melodic formulae of chant. In composing these works Kastal'sky was in essence reenacting the historical role of the largely anonymous original creators of Russian chants, who, having at their disposal literally hundreds of melodic nuclei (*popevki, kokizy, litsa,* and *fity*), freely combined them to suit the needs of new texts.[50]

In addition to developing new ways of treating chant melodies polyphonically, Kastal'sky brought the art of choral "orchestration" to unprecedented heights. Kastal'sky's archive contains a remarkable list (shown partially in table 6.4)[51] of vocal-choral coloristic combinations, many of which may be found in his works. At the same time, Kastal'sky, more than any of his contemporaries, approached the voicing in many of his works in a flexible, almost utilitarian fashion: over twenty-five percent of his works contain alternative or simplified versions for all-male or all-female choirs, or for monastic choirs with male altos; some works, e.g., the *"Gospodi vozzvakh"* [Lord, I call] in Eight Tones, are arranged to be sung by any combination ranging from two to eight voices. Kastal'sky's followers were not as flexible with regard to voicing, but they certainly seized upon the new coloristic possibilities displayed in his works. Rich and brilliant choral writing, nurtured by the sonorous potential and technical excellence of the Synodal Choir, became a hallmark of the new Russian style. Kastal'sky may have had his critics, but as Asaf'ev points out, "despite everything, the truth ended up on his [Kastal'sky's] side thanks to one concrete factor: his choruses always sounded better than the choral works of his detractors."[52]

The Style of Pavel Grigor'evich Chesnokov

In some respects Kastal'sky stands as a unique figure among his contemporaries; no other composer, except possibly Rachmaninoff in his *Vigil*, was able to capture the distinctive essence of Kastal'sky's melodies, textures, and sonorities. Several others, however, shared his interest in chant as both a source of melodic material and a structural, form-building principle. One such composer was Pavel Chesnokov.

Chesnokov was without question the most prolific composer of church music in his generation, producing close to four hundred titles for the Orthodox liturgy. Of these, approximately one-third are chant-based, while the rest are free compositions. Among the chant-based works, roughly one-half are based on znamennyi chant, the rest—on Kievan, Greek, Bulgarian, and various monastic chants. As Harry Elzinga observes, "In only twelve of the fifty-seven pieces for which the chant source was available [to H. E.] does Chesnokov delegate the *cantus firmus* exclusively to the top voice.... Chesnokov seeks variety in his treatment of the *cantus firmus*...[and] frequently places successive portions of the chant melody in at least two or more voices in the same piece."[53] However, perhaps because of his prolific output and his tendency to set entire categories of liturgical chants at a time (e.g., *all* the znamennyi chant festal Hymns to the Mother of God in a single opus; *all* the Resurrectional Dismissal Troparia in the Eight Tones), Chesnokov often failed to achieve the kind of individualized treatment of each melody and text characteristically found in Kastal'sky's settings. Chesnokov's sonorous formula for polyphonic chant settings was rich, but it remained a formula nonetheless. The ever-perceptive Asaf'ev was on the right track when he called Chesnokov's style "merely luxurious craftsmanship."[54]

Whereas Kastal'sky's style may be regarded as integrated and homogeneous throughout his sacred works, Chesnokov's displays a marked dichotomy between his chant-based works and his free compositions. Among the latter, some employ chant-derived or chantlike motives; but a large percentage of his works are completely free compositions that have little in common with either the melodic style or the expressive aesthetic of chant. These include a complete *Liturgy* (Opus 42), a *Vigil* (Opus 44), and a number of nonliturgical concerto settings of prayers to the Mother of God (Opus 43) and prayers "In time of War" (Opus 45), composed in the years 1913–15. As Elzinga points out, "a definite increase in contrapuntal writing occurs in the composer's works after about 1910,...[very likely] the result of Chesnokov's

Table 6.4. Aleksandr Kastal'sky's "Timbres of Various Combinations of Choral Voices"

Note: All parentheses are in the original. Material in brackets is editorial.

Choral Colors

1. Descants as *solos* (2–4 voices), far removed from the other voices ([e.g.] Wise Men [in "Deva dnes'"])

2. Descants *divisi*, with the firsts as a pedal on a high note ([e.g.] "Deva dnes'")

3. Descants *divisi*, with the second descant forming a three-voiced choir with two alto parts [under an upper pedal held by the first descants]

4. Descants below the altos (in four voices) [i.e.] in a choral texture without doublings [of the first descants and tenors and second descants and tenors]

5. Descants with tenors without altos [in] quartet [texture];

   (a) [descants] with basses without tenors or altos

6. Descants in unison with altos (low register) or [in a] three-voice texture

7. Descants in unison with altos (high register) in *f* and *p*

   [Note:] The most natural bases for regrouping voices [occur at] the repetition of phrases.

8. The chorus without descants: quartet of altos and tenors (high and low) or two- or three-voice [texture]

9. Altos in low register (*p*) (at *f* the sound is coarse); solo between widely spaced descants and tenors

10. The same as above, reinforced by the first tenor in unison

11. The same [i.e., altos], reinforced by the second tenor in unison

12. The same, (with altos) in octaves with second tenors; altos in low register or doubling an octave higher

13. The brilliant timbre of the altos in high register [from A to D] at *f* (without the descants)

14. Altos singing above the whole choir; (episodically) canonarching either on tonic or on dominant

15. Quartet of altos and basses (at *p*) or three-voice [texture]

16. Quartet of altos and tenors: (altos with low first tenors and violoncellos [sic]) or two- or three-voiced [texture]

17. Chorus without basses (character of women's monastic choir)

18. Unison of first tenors, altos, and descants (at forte—very energetic, at piano—profound [and] mysterious)

19. Unison of second tenors, altos, and second descants in the middle [of the texture] (while first tenors sing above; possibly also with first descants)

20. Second tenors, altos, and descants in (double) octaves (tripling of voice part)

21. Altos and basses in octaves (as outer voices, see below)

Table 6.4. (continued)

22. Descants and basses in octaves (as outermost voices in entire choir)

23. The same at *f*; altos and basses in octaves (not too high) as outermost voices

24. First tenors above entire choir (including descants and altos) [e.g., on an E, above middle C sung by descants and altos]

25. Tenors singing falsetto *pp* in high register (first tenors)

26. Tenors in low register at *f*

27. Tenors in octaves with descants at *f* (high register)

28. Tenors doubling the bass part ([e.g.] "Sam edin esi bezsmertnyi")

29. Entire choir at *f* in low register

    [Note to Nos. 26–29:] Solo voices in combination with chorus...

30. Basses *divisi* in three parts ([moving] octaves around a sustained note in the middle)

    [Note:] The singing of the chorus interrupted episodically by canonarchs (solos in various voices) in various ranges, or interrupted simply by recitation (without a discernible pitch)

31. Basses *divisi* at *pp* in high register

32. Basses *divisi* in three parts in low register; close position

33. Basses *divisi* in three parts in low register; wide position

34. Unison in low register [from E to A of great octave]

    [Note—evidently a quote from] V[ladimir] Stasov: the chorus should perform with all verity, caprice, [apparent] incorrectness, and with a constant *change in the complement of the singers*: some begin or join in, others drop out for a time and rejoin at will, while still others sing constantly...with changes in *rhythm, tempo,* and even *mood,* which is natural for people who are alive and in the process of creating something of their very own (the folk manner)....

35. Male quartet in short notes in low register as a background for a flowing melody above (descants and altos), and vise-versa—the men sing the melody, while the children sing short notes

36. Basses and tenors in octaves

37. Basses sing the melody above the tenors (*f*)

38. The entire chorus in two parts with doublings ([e.g. on the words] "i v zemliu otideshi" [in "Sam edin esi bezsmertnyi"])

39. Double-chorus effects:
    (a) First chorus sustains, while second moves [rhythmically] (perhaps, a recitative on a single chord)
    (b) Sequences distributed from one chorus to the other; sequential entrances
    (c) The second chorus as a reserve (for augmenting the body of singers either suddenly or gradually), [used] as a *sf* on a sustained chord, or to increase suddenly the number of independent voice parts
    (d) Contrasts in position of chords, e.g. [the first chorus in close position, and the second—in wide position]
    (e) An effect of animation (fast notes in the second chorus over calmer notes in first chorus)

    [Note:] [Choral] orchestration according with the character of the voices: descants—lightness, innocence... basses—resonance, solidity, strength study of composition with S. I. Taneev and S. N. Vasilenko [at the Moscow Conservatory]."[55] Chesnokov's use of chant decreased markedly in the same period.

Another group of Chesnokov's free compositions not related to the chant style, and having a very slim connection with the Moscow Synodal School's aesthetic reforms, are his twenty-odd compositions for solo voices with choral accompaniment. Works such as *"Da ispravitsia"* [Let my prayer arise], for contralto solo, *"Angel vopiiashe"* [The angel cried], for soprano solo, or *"Spasi, Gospodi"* [O Lord, save Thy people], for baritone solo, are little distinguished from concert arias with choral accompaniment (see ex. 6.8). At their best they evoke an effective dramatic element (e.g., the angelic voice in "The angel cried"), but one that has generally been considered inappropriate for the liturgy. At their worst, they exemplify the most extreme cases of saccharine sentimentality produced by misdirected nineteenth-century piety. Nevertheless, both in Chesnokov's time and more recently, these works have remained the favorites of concert audiences and congregations alike.

Whereas Kastal'sky's harmonic vocabulary is mostly modal and diatonic, Chesnokov's, as might be expected, swings between modality and rich chromaticism, with chords of the ninth and eleventh.

The Style of Aleksandr Vasil'evich Nikol'sky

Somewhat less prolific and less diverse stylistically than Chesnokov was Aleksandr Nikol'sky (1874–1943). Of his one hundred fifty-five works (forty-one of them unpublished) roughly forty percent are based on chant. Unlike Kastal'sky and Chesnokov, however, both of whom tended to favor znamennyi chant, Nikol'sky predominately set melodies of Kievan, Greek, and "common" chant. His free compositions, on the other hand, make extensive use of chantlike motives, frequently in the melodic style of great znamennyi chant. Although Nikol'sky was professor of traditional counterpoint and fugue at the Synodal School, only a few of his works employ imitative counterpoint; the majority are homorhythmic. And while examples of Kastal'skian homorhythmic polyphony may be found in many works, Nikol'sky's style does not display an unequivocal preference for horizontal melodic writing over vertical harmonic combinations. Of all Russian church composers, Nikol'sky goes farthest in the direction of using nonfunctional harmony for purely coloristic purposes (see ex. 6.7).

The Style of Nikolai Ivanovich Kompaneisky

Working in St. Petersburg, removed physically from the Moscow Synodal School but pursuing largely the same principles, was Nikolai Kompaneisky, who—even more than Kastal'sky—may be called "the great Russian

Example 6.8. Pavel Chesnokov—"*Angel vopiiashe*" [The angel cried out], Opus 22, No. 18.

(*The angel cried out to the Lady Full of Grace:*
Rejoice, o most pure Virgin,
And again I say, rejoice...)

original"—a kind of Russian William Billings. An exact contemporary of Smolensky (both were born in 1848 and died within a year of each other, Smolensky in 1909 and Kompaneisky in 1910), Kompaneisky was also a schoolmate, friend, and passionate admirer of Modest Musorgsky. More than any other Russian church composer, Kompaneisky believed in the common origins and character of church chant and the secular folk song, a belief that often led him to describe hypothetical rather than actual stylistic features of the former:

> The church "symphony" is constructed of the melody in the main voice and a series of counter-voices [*podgoloski*] structurally joined with the former. The wealth of counter-voices and a varied and complex rhythm create in Russian singing a feeling of organic life, a series of movements generated one by another. This vitality is reflected in the outward forms of singing created by the force of tradition: the start of the chant (*zapev*), the carrying of the basic melody, the alternation of voices (*antifon*), and the repetition of words in the manner of a refrain.
>
> As a result of these features the participating voices neither accompany the main melody, nor follow it from beginning to end with chords, ... but add themselves on in layers, as necessitated by the declamation of the words, or to augment the beauty of the melody, or to increase the rhythmic movement. The variety of forms is increased even further by the interpolation in the middle or at the end of melismatic ornaments (*fity*), which are sometimes quite complex and require a great deal of soloistic skill from the singer.[56]

It may safely be said that this style is not found in the works of any composer other than Kompaneisky himself. Even Kompaneisky indicates that his description is as yet a nonexistent ideal: "This type of singing *would be* [my emphasis—V. M.] our own—Russian in style and satisfying the requirements of high artistic content."

In his more than fifty published works Kompaneisky attempts to adhere to his principles. Ninety percent of his works are based on chants; the ones that are not he labels "demestvennyi," employing his peculiar understanding of that term to designate a free composition. In every detail, even in the appearance of his published scores, he asserts the independent and indigenous nature of Russian sacred music. Thus, many scores are printed in black and red ink—the colors traditionally used in old Russian neumatic manuscripts; in many instances he gives the names of the znamennyi chant formulae used; dotted bar-lines are used not to indicate measures or stress points but to separate the melodic formulae; archaic Slavonic words, such as *Kosno* (Slow) and *Borzo* (Fast) are used as tempo indications; and so forth (see ex. 6.9). Kompaneisky's highly unconventional style, together with his acerbic journalistic manner, did not win him many admirers among the church musicians of his time. On a purely musical basis, many critics perceived a lack of elementary compositional technique; Kastal'sky probably had Kompaneisky in mind when he wrote that "originality [among church

Example 6.9. Nikolai Kompaneisky—"*Vsemirnuiu slavu*" [Let us praise the glory of the world].
(Theotokion-Dogmatikon in Tone 1 – Znamennyi Chant)

([Let us praise] the glory of the world, born of man...)

composers] frequently manifests itself in an awkwardness of the musical language."[57] On this point, however, Kompaneisky appeared to be unperturbed. In the preface to his cycle of eight znamennyi *Bogorodichny-Dogmatiki* [Theotokia-Dogmatika], which are perhaps his most significant works, he wrote:

> A few words concerning this composer's intentions. I wanted the chant not to lose its transparency due to the addition of other voices, so that every melodic formula would stand out distinctly, and so that the other voices would not hold back the movement of the melody. In accomplishing this I did not use any prejudicial theories—either my own or others'—and wrote down only what my ear suggested to me as I sang the dogmatiks in full voice, something I find great pleasure in doing. In my scores I see many things for which I would criticize another composer, but revising is contrary to my views. The full power of music's effect lies in the genuineness of the composer's spontaneous mood and in the wholeness of the idea, not in beautiful details.[58]

Indeed, when regarded objectively as genuine experiments in the application of Russian folk counterpoint to chant melodies, Kompaneisky's works exhibit remarkable freshness and, moreover, contain passages of exquisite beauty.

The Style of Aleksandr Tikhonovich Grechaninov

A Moscow composer who took an essentially different direction than Kastal'sky was his younger contemporary, Aleksandr Grechaninov (1864–1956). Although he worked in close association with Smolensky and Kastal'sky, Grechaninov from his first essay in church music displayed less concern for the ecclesiastical element; his approach was clearly that of a secular musician who, like Tchaikovsky, was "looking in" on church music from the outside. Significantly, Grechaninov was not directly involved with the Synodal School or Choir, and was never a church precentor.

Grechaninov's first sacred work, the *Liturgy*, Opus 13, was written in an essentially harmonic style, showing a marked influence of Tchaikovsky's *Liturgy* and using no chant motives. Between this first Liturgy and the second, Opus 29, a noticeable stylistic change occurred: in the latter, Grechaninov appears to have "discovered" the melodic potential of chantlike motives. Closer examination shows, however, that the connection between Grechaninov's motives and actual chant melodies is very slim: it is as if the composer was shown some znamennyi melodies, distilled from them a few essential rhythmic and melodic characteristics, and proceeded to write an entire setting of the Liturgy ordinary without pursuing a closer familiarity with either the sources of chant or its performance. His quasi-chant melodies, such as the almost dancelike motives used throughout *"Slava ... Edinorodnyi Syne"* [Glory ... Only-begotten Son] and elsewhere in Opus 29 (see ex. 6.10),

Example 6.10. Aleksandr Grechaninov—"*Slava ... Edinorodnyi Syne*"
[Glory...Only-begotten Son] (from *Liturgy,* Opus 29).

(Glory to the Father, and to the Son, and to the Holy Spirit, now and ever, and unto ages of ages. Amen.)

display a regularity of meter and periodicity of structure that is seldom encountered in genuine znamennyi chant. Even in the hymn *"Dostoino est'"* [It is truly meet] from Opus 29, which is based on an authentic demestvennyi chant, the chant is used freely as thematic material and not as a form-determining element. The same may be said of his other few works that use chant melodies—*"Volnoiu morskoiu"* [By the waves of the sea], Opus 19, *"Blazheni, iazhe izbral"* [Blessed are they whom Thou hast chosen], Opus 44, and several numbers from the *Strastnaia sed'mitsa* [Holy Week] cycle, Opus 58.

By his own words, Grechaninov strived to "symphonize" the forms of liturgical singing, building upon the traditions of Russian operatic and symphonic classics. As Yuri Keldysh points out, "His choral scores are marked by a richness and brilliance of sonorous colors, a variety of textures, and large-scale [thematic] development.... The style of his sacred works often bears characteristics of purely concert-like splendor. Frequently one encounters broadly unfolding soloistic episodes that approach operatic arias in character."[59] Grechaninov obviously was more interested in creating new forms within the field of Russian sacred music than in restoring traditional aesthetic relationships within the liturgy. Thus he pioneered the technique of solo recitation with simultaneous choral accompaniment, e.g., in his famous *"Veruiu"* [Creed] from Opus 29 (see ex. 6.11). From here it was but a short step to employing soloists and chorus with instrumental accompaniment, which is what he did in his *Liturgia domestica*, Opus 79, composed in 1917. By adding instruments in this work, he became the first composer to clearly indicate his intention to write nonliturgical sacred choral music, since the accompaniment violated the traditional prohibition of the Orthodox Church against musical instruments of any kind.

The Style of Viktor Sergeevich Kalinnikov

An approach somewhat similar to Grechaninov's may be found in the works of Viktor Kalinnikov (1870–1927), except that the latter was essentially a miniaturist. Only one of Kalinnikov's twenty-four published sacred works is based on a chant; the others, however, employ part-writing similar in melodic style to chant. Other aspects of Kalinnikov's style may be linked to Kastal'sky: an intense "melodization" of every voice, modal harmonies, plagal cadences and progressions, pedal points, voice leading that allows parallel octaves, fifths, and triads, "empty" sonorities of the fourth and fifth. All these features impart a supremely Russian character to Kalinnikov's choral works.

Kalinnikov, as professor of harmony at the Moscow Synodal School, worked in close contact with the Synodal Choir; and, like his fellow "Synodals," displayed profound understanding of the specificities of choral

Example 6.11. Aleksandr Grechaninov—"*Veruiu*" [I believe] (from *Liturgy*, Opus 29).

*(I believe in one God, the Father, the Almighty, Maker of heaven
and earth, and of all things visible and invisible. And in one Lord
Jesus Christ...)*

writing. As Kleopatra Dmitrevskaia points out, "The most active means of musical expression in Kalinnikov's choruses...are the resources of vocal timbre—choral orchestration."[60]

Other Composers in Moscow and St. Petersburg

The six composers discussed thus far may be considered pioneer explorers in developing a new style of Russian sacred choral music. The first three—Kastal'sky, Chesnokov, and Nikol'sky—worked in close contact with Smolensky and attempted to embody his ideas with regard to the treatment of chant melodies (although Nikol'sky did not begin composing until after Smolensky's departure from the Moscow Synodal School). Despite the considerable individuality of their respective styles, one senses a common thread running through their works, marked, moreover, by the freshness and spontaneity of an experimental approach. To this group may be added Nikolai Kompaneisky, who in terms of sheer originality, surpasses all of them.

A somewhat different picture appears in the music of a slightly younger generation of Moscow Synodal School graduates, who were regarded as the "future direction" of church choral composition: Konstantin Shvedov (1886–1954), Nikolai Tolstiakov (dates unavailable), Nikolai Golovanov (1891–1953), and Aleksandr Chesnokov (Pavel's brother) (1880–1941). Overall, the stylistic character of their works could not have been encouraging to their mentors. Despite the fact that, as a group, these composers display considerable formally acquired compositional skills—the ability to write good imitative counterpoint, to develop musical themes, and to handle remote modulations adroitly—their compositions tend to lack stylistic integrity on the one hand and spontaneity of expression on the other. Shvedov's freely composed works (which predominate among his sixteen published opuses) alternate between a distinctly secular folk flavor (diatonicism, sparse textures) and chromatic "pseudo-orientalism" such as may be heard in the operatic and symphonic works of the Mighty Five. Tolstiakov, while using more chant melodies than Shvedov, is fond of lush harmonies and abrupt modulations. Incredible thickness and complexity of texture characterize the works of Golovanov and Aleksandr Chesnokov. Undoubtedly it was to the works of these composers that Kastal'sky was referring when he wrote in 1913:

> Of late [church music] has tended to become complex, to disregard the difficulty of performance for the sake of effective sonority, to choose harmonic and melodic means without any discrimination, provided only that they be new and beautiful, and if this tendency continues to develop, church music will end in becoming like any other, except that it will have a sacred text. This would be extremely sad....
>
> The national element is implanted in our church melodies themselves, but the vocal turns of [actual] folk songs should be applied to them with extreme caution, as a church is a

church and not a street or a concert hall. The national color of Russian secular music has its origin in the [folk] song, and similarly church music should be created and developed from our church melodies. The refined voluptuousness and spicy harmonies of contemporary music are, again, unsuitable for a church, although...[they] enrapture and stir up the emotions of amateurs....

Good church music can be created only by talented individuals, and then only if they are able to become permeated by the spirit of the liturgical texts and the special atmosphere of the actual church services. We shall wait....[61]

Other composers writing church music during this period may be classified according to the categories already identified. Some, like Dmitri Yaichkov (1882–1953) and Georgy (Yuri) Izvekov (dates unavailable), followed in the direction indicated by Kastal'sky, emphasizing the melodic aspect of chant set in a rich and variable choral texture. Others, like Nikolai Tcherepnin (1873–1945), followed Grechaninov and Kalinnikov in building their works upon vaguely chantlike, Russian-sounding motives. Still others, like Mikhail Ippolitov-Ivanov (1859–1935) and Semyon Panchenko (1867–1937), emulated Tchaikovsky's model of free composition in a harmonic style, although the latter wrote a number of homophonic reharmonizations of traditional Petersburg Court Chants. While these composers produced some attractive works, they contributed nothing essentially new or original in terms of style. Some highly unusual experiments in a style that might best be described as "musical primitivism" are found in the works of Vladimir Rebikov (1866–1920), particularly in his *All-Night Vigil*, Opus 44; his style, however, did not attract any followers.

The Style of Sergei Vasil'evich Rachmaninoff

The pre-Revolutionary renaissance of sacred choral composition in Russia found its culmination in the works of Sergei Rachmaninoff (1873–1943). Although his contributions to the sacred choral repertoire are not numerous, comprising only the *Liturgy*, Opus 31 and the *All-Night Vigil*, Opus 37 (a concerto-style work entitled *"V molitvakh neusypaiushchuiu Bogoroditsu"* [The Mother of God, ever-vigilant in prayer] written in his student days remained unpublished until recently), they are certainly among the most visible, not only because of Rachmaninoff's stature as a composer, but also because of the monumental nature of the two works.

The *Liturgy*, written in 1910, is an entirely free composition in a richly sonorous choral style that has little thematic connection with canonical chant melodies. Guided not so much by previous models as by his own personal understanding and interpretation of each liturgical text, Rachmaninoff created a large-scale a cappella choral cycle that explores numerous emotional states ranging from pathos to prayerful meditation. The *Liturgy* may be regarded as a culmination of the free approach to setting the ordinary of this service, first essayed by Tchaikovsky.

Five years later, in the *All-Night Vigil*, Rachmaninoff took a different approach, masterfully demonstrating the full artistic potential of chant melodies in combination with indigenous Russian contrapuntal techniques. As Kastal'sky wrote in a preview article to the premiere of the *Vigil*, not only had Rachmaninoff used authentic chant melodies in many sections of the work, "but one should hear what has become of the simple, straightforward melodies in the hands of a major artist!"[62]

Guided in his choice of chants by Kastal'sky, Rachmaninoff composed a cycle of fifteen hymns for a Sunday (Resurrectional) Vigil, nine of which are based on znamennyi, Kievan, and Greek Chants. However, as Yuri Keldysh points out, "between the movements of the *Vigil* based on ancient chant melodies and those freely invented by the composer there is no essential stylistic difference, and a listener familiar with the znamennyi cycle of chant cannot distinguish themes composed by Rachmaninoff himself from those he borrowed."[63] This is equally true with regard to themes of entire movements as it is to subordinate themes and supporting voices in movements based on chant. Moreover, Rachmaninoff's treatment of the actual melodies is quite diverse, sometimes employing the chant as a structural feature and other times using it as thematic material to be treated motivically.

The *Vigil* may also be regarded as a culmination in the use of choral orchestration, which composers of the Moscow Synodal School had been continually developing. Rachmaninoff's palette of choral timbres is greater than that of any composer before him, as is the consistency with which he employs divisi (not infrequently à 3) in each section of the chorus. Yet all of the textural devices display a great sense of purpose: voices are never present merely to thicken the texture, but are always divided with the view of emphasizing an additional aspect of the music. And Rachmaninoff's textures display a greater variety and independence of motives and events than those of any previously written works.

Finally, in terms of both form and expression, Rachmaninoff's *Vigil* exceeds all previously existing dimensions for individual liturgical hymns as well as for entire cycles. Although in the *Vigil* he assumes a less personal, more epically objective stance than he does in the *Liturgy*, he nevertheless scales new heights of expressive intensity, such as have been achieved in only a few choral masterpieces in the entire history of music.

Problems of Performance Practice in the Sacred Music of the New Russian Choral School

Russian sacred choral music composed in the late nineteenth and early twentieth centuries displays a number of technical features that are unfamiliar to Western musicians, indeed, even to Russian musicians trained at musical institutions patterned after Western European models. These features primarily involve chant, which, as has been shown, plays a fundamental role in the works of the new Russian choral school.

As mentioned in chapter 6, the canonical chants of the Russian Orthodox Church have been used in three major ways in polyphonic arrangements and compositions: (1) as a structural, form-determining *cantus firmus*; (2) as a source of thematic material treated more freely than in *cantus firmus* technique; and (3) as a musical prototype for newly composed material that serves as thematic basis of a freely composed work or as added voices in a chant-based work.

Chants used in the above fashions display at least three gradations of melodic complexity. In the ensuing discussion these will be referred to as

1. *Neumatic chant*—chant that has an essentially neumatic structure, with two to four notes per syllable and occasional melismatic inclusions (ex. 7.1)
2. *Syllabic chant*—chant that is syllabic but has a well-defined melodic contour (ex. 7.2), and
3. *Recitative chant* or *liturgical recitative*—chant that comprises long stretches of monotoning upon a single note, which changes in pitch from time to time (ex. 7.3).

While all three types of chant had been used in the Russian Church prior to the infusion of Western polyphony, it was the neumatic chants—the great znamennyi, putevoi, and demestvennyi—that had fallen from use in favor of

Example 7.1. Neumatic Znamennyi Chant—Theotokion-Dogmatikon in Tone 3.
(Note values halved)

Ka - - ko_____ ne_ di - vim - - - sia

bo - go - muzh - no - mu rozh - de - stvu tvo - e mu,_____ pre - chest - na - - - ia;...

*(How can we not wonder at thy mystical childbearing, O Exalted
One?...)*

Example 7.2. Syllabic "Greek" Chant—Resurrectional Troparia at Matins.
(Note values halved)

Bla - go - slo - ven e - si Gos - po - di, na - u - chi - mia o - prav - da - ni - em Tvo - im.

An - gel' - skii so - bor u - di - vi - sia, zria Te - be vmert - vykh vme - niv - sha - sia...

*(Blessed art Thou, O Lord, teach me Thy statutes. The angelic
council was amazed, seeing Thee numbered among the dead...)*

Example 7.3. Abbreviated "Greek" Recitative Chant—Troparion.
(Note values halved)

Bo - go - ro - di - tse De - vo, ra - dui - sia, blagodatnaia Marie, Gospod'

s to - bo - iu; bla - go - slo - ven - na ty v zhe - nakh, i blagosloven Plod

chre - va tvo - e - go, iako Spasa rodila esi dush na - shikh.

*(Rejoice, O Virgin Mother of God,
Mary, full of grace, the Lord is with thee.
Blessed art thou among women,
And blessed is the fruit of thy womb,
For thou hast borne the savior of our souls.)*

composed part-music, and it was mainly their rediscovery by scholars in the second half of the nineteenth century that renewed interest among composers in using chant as a basis for new polyphonic arrangements. Neumatic chant, therefore, is the most appropriate place to begin the present consideration of performance practice problems.

The Sources of Neumatic Chant

Composers seeking neumatic chant melodies at the end of the nineteenth century had three major resources to draw on. A vast number of melodies could be found in five codified chant-books, covering the entire liturgical year, which had been published since 1772 by the Holy Synod in numerous editions.[1] Copies could be found in virtually every church, although in practice they were used only by the chanters (*d'iachki* or *psalomshchiki*) who sang at week-day services in parish churches and in some monasteries that adhered to a more ancient style of singing. The notation in these chant-books (shown in ex. 7.4) was in every respect identical to the original five-line staff notation first introduced in southwestern Russia in the late sixteenth century[2] and brought to central and northern Russia in the latter half of the seventeenth century.

Example 7.4. Square-Note "Kievan Notation" and Equivalent Italian Notation.

The Synodal chant-books were neglected by serious composers until the end of the nineteenth century mainly because of the general estrangement of musicians from the sphere of church music. Musorgsky, for example, wrote to Vladimir Stasov concerning his search for material to use in *Khovanshchina*: "Here's something else: spoke with a commonsensical priest about the character of the Old Believer tunes. Said he: should you, while living in a village, locate and hear the old chanters [*d'iachki*]—that's the way, set your Old Believers like them, using tunes from the *obikhod* [chant-book]. I located and listened to the chanters, but forgot about the priest's advice until I needed a motif for Dosifei's chant and for the baptismal chant at the self-immolation."[3] Ultimately, Musorgsky did not use any authentic chants from the *obikhod* in *Khovanshchina*, but instead adapted a nonliturgical Old Believers' tune supplied to him by his friend, the singer Liubov' Karmalina.

Another source of chant material arose as a result of the renewed scholarly interest in the history and theory of ancient Russian church singing. Dmitri Razumovsky's *Tserkovnoe penie v Rossii* [Church singing in Russia], Ioann Voznesensky's *Tserkovnoe penie Pravoslavnoi Greko-Rossiiskoi*

Tserkvi: Bol'shoi i malyi znamennyi rospev [The church singing of the Orthodox Graeco-Russian Church: The great and little znamennyi chant] and *Osmoglasnye rospevy trekh poslednikh vekov Pravoslavnoi Russkoi Tserkvi* [The Eight-Tone chants of the last three centuries in the Russian Orthodox Church], and Nikolai Potulov's *Rukovodstvo k prakticheskomu izucheniiu drevnego peniia Pravoslavnoi Rossiiskoi Tserkvi* [A manual for the practical study of the ancient singing of the Russian Orthodox Church],[4] all contained additional examples of chants not found in the Synodal chant-books. Towards the end of the century codices containing the collected chants of certain monasteries[5] and the Moscow Cathedral of the Dormition were also published. In these publications the chant was set forth in the same five-line, square-note notation as in the Synodal books; only the Valaam Monastery chant was published in round-note notation.

The third source was the few surviving traditions of live performance that could still be found among the Old Believers and, more significantly, at the Moscow Cathedral of the Dormition, where the choir of cathedral clergy sang ancient unison chants at certain portions of the services. This tradition was most readily accessible to composers connected with the Moscow Synodal Choir.

Two hundred years had passed, however, from the time when unison chant was a living tradition throughout the Russian Church. Beginning with the mid-seventeenth century, when harmonic part-singing in the Western style became the prevailing mode of performance, the neumatic chant was swept aside and relegated to a position of secondary importance. Moreover, the magnitude of the stylistic differences between the chant and the brilliant eight- and twelve-voice Baroque "concertos" and later, Italianate motets, had given rise to the view that chant was totally devoid of artistic value. A major factor that contributed to this view was the manner in which the monophonic chants were renotated from the staffless neumatic notation into five-line staff notation in the late seventeenth and early eighteenth centuries.

There is ample evidence that the neumatic znamennyi (or stolp) notation expressed not only pitch and rhythm, but also a full spectrum of expressive nuances, dynamics, and variations of vocal production and articulation. The staffless neumes were esentially an ideographic, mnemonic device to remind the singer of melodies with which he was already familiar, but their meaning involved more than just the pitches and rhythms. Fragmentary evidence from lexicons of znamennyi neumes indicates that some signs contained specific instructions for technical execution, e.g.: *Golubchik garknout' iz gortani* [the *golubchik* (lit., "a little dove") is shouted from the throat]; *A dva v chelnu kachnout' dvazhdy* [the *dva v chelnu* (lit., "two in a boat") is rocked twice]; *A derbitsa podrobit' glasom vverkh* [the *derbitsa* is fractured with the voice upwards], and so forth.[6] Many neumes of different shapes had the same diastematic meaning, which further suggests that they contained more than purely intervallic and rhythmic information. Neumatic notation also included various interpretational signs (*ukazatel'nye pometki*), which pointed to tempo changes and ornaments, e.g.: ⌐ or ⊤ stood for *tikho* ("quietly," meaning "slowly" in Old Slavonic), ♭ for *borzo* ("quickly"), and ♭ for *zevok* (lit., a yawn), performed by adding two short ornamental notes to the main note.[7] In 1668, Aleksandr Mezenets, the author of the last important treatise on neumatic notation, had argued that "for us Great Russians [as opposed to the Southwesterners, who were known as Little Russians], who know directly the sound of this mysteriously regulated [znamennyi] notation and the many images contained therein, and the measure and power of its forms in every detail and subtlety, there is no need for...staff notation."[8]

However, the relative simplicity of staff notation, which was already being used for part-singing, led to the transcription of the chants, first in binotational manuscripts known as *dvoznamenniki* (ex. 7.5), and then exclusively into staff notation. Only the pitches and rhythms were transcribed, evidently omitting the "detail and subtlety" of which Mezenets spoke. In this form, devoid of all markings of tempo, dynamics, expression, or articulation, the chants were printed in the Synodal chant-books of 1772 and ostensibly preserved for future generations. It is hardly surprising, therefore, that in the middle of the nineteenth century, the Director of the Imperial Chapel Aleksei L'vov, approaching chants from the standpoint of a secular musician, wrote that "ancient chants should be performed absolutely simply and evenly, with all attention directed solely towards making the notes accurate."[9]

Towards the end of the nineteenth century, some scholars began to question this view of chant. Concerning the process of transcription Ioann Voznesensky wrote:

> [In the collections of chants] the melodies are notated in five-line staff notation in a most primitive fashion, with the intent that the artistic side of performance be supplemented by a living oral tradition, the experience of choir masters, and the parallel notation [of the chants] in staffless neumes to the extent [the latter] are still known in Russia. However, in view of the fact that today the ancient oral tradition of singing has been lost, singers experienced in ancient chant are lacking, and staffless notation has fallen into oblivion, this system is clearly insufficient....
>
> The introduction of present-day [round-note] notation resulted in the loss of the [notational] signs indicating nuances of expression, not only of loud or soft, marked or gentle singing, but also sounds that are connected or detached, smooth or wavering and vibrating, nasal or throaty, bright or muted, produced with a greater or lesser opening of the mouth, etc., which are very important for the artistic rendering of the ancient melodies, and which were expressed both by the Greeks and by our forefathers in their staffless notation. It is clear that for the correct and artistic performance of the ancient chants these nuances of melodic expression must either be restored or at least replaced by other corresponding nuances.[10]

Example 7.5. Binotational Manuscript (*Dvoznamennik*) in Stolp and Kievan Notation.

In the same vein, the Reverend Sergei Protopopov criticized those latter-day composers who took the square notation literally and wrote polyphonic arrangements devoid of all expressive markings:

> Church music cannot be separated from general musical principles (as some purists would have it). This is why all attempts to invent a special ecclesiastical scale or tone-row, or to create exclusively ecclesiastical principles of harmonizing [chants] have proven futile. Similarly, one must consider the notation of liturgical hymns without time signatures and the correct division into measures [and, one might add, marks of tempo, dynamics and articulation—V.M.] to be less than useful. This bears the mark of musical sloppiness and nothing else. [11]

However true Voznesensky's and Protopopov's observations may have been, the scholars studying the structure and notation of chants did not attempt to reconstruct their expressive aspects. As Vasily Komarov [12] observed: "The [present-day] compilers of manuals [of neumatic notation] employ the same system of transcribing the neumes to staff notation that they encountered in existing manuscripts, but what was sufficient for our ancestors cannot be considered sufficient in our present state of affairs. . . ." [13] What is needed, says Komarov, is direct, first-hand experience with the practical performance of the chants, something he claims to have gained through contact with old and knowledgeable church chanters and other individuals familiar with the practical performance of chant—members of the Moscow Society of Fanciers of Church Singing. On the basis of this experience Komarov made some extraordinarily valuable observations on the nature of chant performance, particularly with respect to rhythm and tempo.

Komarov is the only writer known to have written about the practical side of chant performance. But he was not the only church musician who knew the chant tradition from a practical standpoint. Another was Stepan Smolensky, who gained a thorough familiarity with chant and staffless notation from Old Believers he met while growing up in the city of Kazan'. As Nikol'sky relates, Smolensky placed great emphasis on knowing the neumes practically: at the Synodal School his students had to not only know them theoretically, but also be able to sing from them and write down dictations. [14] Smolensky's efforts to interest other musicians in the intricacies of neumatic notation, however, were not overly successful. Sergei Vasilenko in his memoirs gives an unflattering description of Smolensky's course in Russian musical paleography at the Moscow Conservatory:

> Although church music was a required subject at the Conservatory, few were interested in it. Out of our class only two or three people studied it, I among them. In class Smolensky behaved in an extraordinarily noisy and undignified manner. Tall, awkward, covered with an overgrown beard, he sang and shouted, listening to no one. . . . His examinations were

fiascos, [since] almost no one knew how to sing the neumes. Smolensky hollered along to make up for everyone, drowning out the assistant professors, and then entered a satisfactory grade for the examinee.[15]

Even Kastal'sky, for all his interest in chant, confesses that when (after Smolensky's departure from the Synodal School) he himself sought out material for historical concerts, he laboriously had to draw up tables in order to read the neumes and found the task to be "sheer drudgery."[16]

The Old Believers, who still used unison chant in their services, remained completely segregated from developments in the official Orthodox Church and in musicology until they were granted religious tolerance in 1905, which enabled them to publish books and journals. As Gardner points out, the history of liturgical chant among the Old Believers after the Schism of 1668 is a total void.[17] Any changes that may have occurred in the performance practice of the Old Believers remain undocumented.

After 1905, however, articles concerning singing in Old Believer churches began to appear in music periodicals. One such article, written by an anonymous Old Believer, laments the low estate of singing both from a professional standpoint (due to the lack of knowledgeable singers) and from a musical standpoint: at the Rogozhsky Cemetery, the center of Old Believerdom in Moscow, the singing is described as "nasal, with unnatural yelps and moans."[18] Nevertheless, some attempts were made by Old Believers to bring their singing to the attention of the rest of the musical world. A choir of over one hundred voices, established under the patronage of the wealthy merchant A. Morozov, gave two concerts in Moscow and two in St. Petersburg in the spring of 1908 and several more concerts in 1910 and 1911. The director, Pavel Vasil'evich Tsvetkov, was a student of I. A. Fortov, a well-known Old Believer singer, but had also studied at the Moscow Philharmonic School. One review described him as being "familiar with conducting technique" and capable of producing "a very polished performance."[19]

In a review of the concert on 6 April 1908, Aleksandr Nikol'sky wrote:

> The concert was of great interest for those who have many questions regarding the performance of chant—the cornerstone of much of the new choral literature ....
>
> We heard the melodies performed in an extremely uncommon rhythmic rendition,... which clearly underscores the faultiness of the strictly measured rhythmic divisions practiced by our choirs in performing ancient chants. This measured character is clearly at odds with the lack of symmetry that characterizes not only entire sections, but even isolated moments of the ancient melodies.... The originality of the rhythm is most noticeable in the execution of short, ornamental notes, which in our [notation] are expressed by means of eighth-notes, and also in those places where our [contemporary] ear perceives either three-quarter-note groups or apparent triplets.[20]

At the same time, the authenticity of these performances may be questioned, particularly in view of the fact that they were prepared and directed by a conservatory graduate. The Old Believers were undoubtedly self-conscious in presenting their singing, which for years had been considered vulgar and unartistic, to the general public. Nikol'sky observes that in the attempt to achieve a clean, three-octave unison of men's, women's, and children's voices, the choir's sound was "somewhat narrow and stilted" and, as he puts it, "too well-groomed," lacking in freedom and power. Another reviewer, Mikhail Lisitsyn, notes that perfect unison singing without any improvisatory subordinate countervoices is "not at all typical of seventeenth-century singing," an observation which, however well-reasoned, remains unverifiable. Lisitsyn also comments that the director attempted to alleviate the monotony of the pure unison with various dynamic effects of the sort practiced by contemporary church choirs.[21]

Another Old Believers' choir, belonging to the Brotherhood of the Holy Cross, under the direction of Ya. A. Bogatenko, gave several performances in the years 1915-17. The choir was described as "well-disciplined," but reviewers questioned the authenticity of this performance as well. "One can hardly agree with the conductor's idea of introducing maximal expression into these dispassionate melodies (crescendos and diminuendos of a moaning quality)," wrote the critic V. Paskhalov. "Equally inadmissible is the raised leading tone in final cadences, which is totally foreign to the diatonic nature [of the chants]."[22] Both the Morozov Choir and Bogatenko's Choir made several gramophone recordings, which will be discussed below.

The above reviews lead one to conclude that by the start of the twentieth century even the Old Believers did not have an absolutely reliable tradition of chant performance. This fact, coupled with the lack of performance indications in the published chant books and transcriptions, in turn suggests that composers who wrote chant arrangements necessarily approached chant more or less with guesswork, supplemented by their own subjective musical instincts. Some chant arrangements were supplied with various performance indications, but in most cases they were not. The performer is therefore confronted with chantlike or chant-based works conceived by composers whose understanding of the nature of chant was probably imperfect. In some works the composer's directions may well be open to reinterpretation on the basis of newly discovered and more complete information, as a result of which the character of a given work may change considerably.

A careful analysis of printed scores and other primary sources reveals a number of major technical questions and interpretive problems that confront a conductor who wishes to perform Russian choral works based on a chant idiom. In some instances these problems may be resolved simply by effective and knowledgeable editing; in others, a thorough familiarity with the style of the music, supplemented by a goodly dose of innate musicality and instinct, is required.

Problems of Pitch

Although some questions concerning the transcription of pitch from staffless notation still remain unresolved, in the chant-based compositions and arrangements under consideration pitch is probably the least ambiguous element. In all latter-day works the notation clearly belongs to the common practice period. Virtually all works are intended to be performed at the notated pitch level; in a few scores composers suggest or give specific instructions for transposition—no more than a half-step higher or lower. Ornamentation and *musica ficta* also are not problematic in arranged works; I have encountered only one work—a znamennyi chant, "Cherubic hymn," by Mikhail Lisitsyn—in which the composer attempted to address the matter of possible ornamentation by writing out somewhat ambiguous ornamental notes to the main melody. Other composers evidently did not envision any ornamentation in their works.

The only questions of pitch notation that arise in some composers' scores have to do with the doubling of certain voice parts—mainly the result of shorthand notational practices. Octave doubling of notated pitches is applicable either to the bass part or to the soprano and tenor parts. With regard to bass doublings, all the visible evidence in the scores indicates that the composers of the new Russian school were extremely scrupulous in writing out doubling by octavists whenever they wanted it. This observation, coupled with Chesnokov's comments concerning the circumscribed use of octavists, suggests that any additional introduction of bass doublings (e.g., following N. Lindsay Norden's prescription cited on pages 152–53) would violate the composers' intentions. Most composers were aware that in writing octave doublings, they were demanding voices that were not always available even in Russian choirs (with a range down to G of the contra-octave, for example). Consequently, many octave doublings, particularly below D or C of the great octave, are given in parentheses.

The practice of doubling voices at the octave in singing common chant in harmony developed sometime in the eighteenth century, at a time when the harmonization was not yet written out but improvised from the basic chant line. Aleksei L'vov, while preparing his *Obikhod* (Book of common chants) of the Imperial Chapel, was the first to describe the practice:

Harmony in four voice parts does not achieve that fullness, that organlike effect, which we hear in the [improvised] performance of plain chant [in harmony]. As I entered into a detailed analysis of the reasons for this, I discovered that according to long-accepted tradition the aforementioned four-part harmony in the Court Choir has further divisions, which stem from our ancient church music, and are quite essential to the proper performance of church music not supported by any instruments.

These divisions are as follows: the main melody is carried by the high basses (baritones), together with the [first] descants (which serves as a very useful means of supporting the inexperienced boys and ensuring the exact mastery of the melodies). The second descants sing with the first tenor; the alto—with the second tenor; the second bass . . . is not doubled. In this distribution the harmony presents itself exactly in the manner we are accustomed to hearing it in Court churches, without the slightest change. . . .

While from the standpoint of classical four-part chorale harmony, where the top voice plays the leading role, . . . the aforementioned distribution of parts is by no means normal, the singular sonority of this combination of timbres imparts a special beauty and energy to the singing of the Imperial Chapel.[23]

The practice of assigning the main melody to a baritone voice (or section) has its roots in an even more ancient style of chant performance, dating back to the time when choirs were led not by a conductor-precentor but the "leading singer" or *golovshchik*. Just like his secular counterpart in the folk chorus, the *zapevalo*, the leading singer in a church choir was responsible for finding the appropriate pitch, setting the tempo, and actually beginning the singing. After this, the rest of the chorus joined in, either in unison or by adding improvised countervoices. While this technique was perfectly suited for neumatic chant, in harmonic singing it produced a thick, overtone-laden texture of the male voices, which led one writer to describe L'vov's notated version as "the preposterous 'Obikhod' . . . with barbarous doublings in the basses."[24]

In Moscow the practice of singing harmonized chant was somewhat different: the chant melody was carried by the top voice—the first tenor in an all-male ensemble or the first tenor and the first soprano in a chorus of male and boys' voices. The second soprano was doubled by the second tenor. The texture was thus divided into six, rather than seven parts, with the altos and basses not doubled (discounting the octavists). This texture is found quite frequently in the works of Kastal'sky and other Moscow Synodal School composers. Kastal'sky in particular often employed a shorthand notation on a two-staff system, writing out the first soprano/tenor part in the top voice and the second soprano/tenor part in the tenor.[25] In printed scores the voicing is usually indicated at the beginning of the first system, although on occasion instructions are supplied by the composer in an explanatory note. The instructions may say to use "customary doublings" (as described above) or point to some passages where these doublings do not apply. In two works (published Nos. 16 and 17) the notes indicate that the doublings "may be used if the size of the chorus permits it," i.e., twenty or more singers, according to Kastal'sky's *Popular self-instructor* (see chapter 4, n. 46). Kastal'sky frequently offers alternative versions for performance by small choruses or all-male (or all-female) choruses: at least twenty-two of his works contain *ossias*. In such instances the *8–va* markings in the score must not be applied in mixed chorus performance, since they pertain only to the alternate versions.

The published works of Kastal'sky are the only ones that present problems having to do with various shorthand devices. All of Kastal'sky's contemporaries wrote out doublings and clearly indicated the voicing of their scores.

Problems of Rhythm and Meter

In every piece of Russian church music that embodies the traditional Orthodox relationship between text and music, the rhythm and meter are text-related. How fundamental and deeply rooted this principle is becomes apparent when one considers that the Orthodox Church has never recognized any music independent of text. Although some Russian sacred works, most notably those of Bortniansky and his contemporaries, contain regular meter and bar lines, one may be certain that these pieces reflect Western European influence. This is true even of some chant melodies, particularly Kievan, Greek, and Bulgarian, that display a regularity of meter and phrase structure. These bodies of chant arose in Slavic lands ruled at the time by Roman Catholic Poland and Lithuania, and date from the late sixteenth or early seventeenth centuries, i.e., a time when the textual basis of rhythm in Western church music was becoming increasingly modified by regularly metered forms.

From the coming of Western-style part-singing to the middle of the nineteenth century, Russian church music all but lost its text-related basis as well. The first individual to reformulate theoretically the principles of irregular, text-oriented meter was Aleksei L'vov. In his work entitled *O svobodnom i nesimmetrichnom ritme* [Concerning free and unsymmetrical rhythm] he expressed views that were bold and unconventional for a time when musical composition was regarded in Western Europe as having attained maximum evolutionary progress. L'vov wrote,

> Is it possible that music in our time cannot and must not exist in a framework other than that of prevailing and inviolable squareness or other uniform periodicity of rhythm? . . . An internal aesthetic instinct loudly proclaimed to me that a free, so-called improper rhythm, i.e., one not measured symmetrically, has the same rights of citizenship in music as what is called proper, symmetrical rhythm. . . .
>
> The labors, deliberations, and researches of many years finally led me . . . to conclude that it was both possible and legitimate to introduce a free, unsymmetric rhythm into music (and

primarily into church music). . . . The language of our prayers has a special character, which must find its appropriate reflection in the character of the singing. Many composers strove to subordinate certain ancient chants to a proper rhythm and definite measures . . . [and in doing so] were forced to resort to various distortions, . . . needless repetition of words, inappropriate elongation of syllables, and, worst of all, nonsimultaneous pronunciation of the text, as a result of which not only the impact but often the very sense of the text was lost. . . . [26]

The "labors of many years" to which L'vov refers were, of course, his work on the harmonized Court Chapel *Obikhod*, in which he rendered in four-part harmony many of the chants found in the Synodal square-note chant-books.[27] In establishing guidelines for the harmonizations (most of the actual work was done by L'vov's assistants), he determined that the rhythmic notation was to be the same as in the chant-books, only transcribed into modern round notes. The harmonizations would have no meter signatures, and the only bar lines would appear between major musical or textual phrases, just as in the chant-books. L'vov did, however, misunderstand one essential feature of the chant melodies—namely, their horizontal, melodic nature. By treating each note of the chant as a chord tone, he shifted the focus from dynamic, forward-moving melodic motion to a series of vertically oriented chord progressions in which the laws of harmonic rhythm were paramount. Despite the objections of some experienced (if musically untrained, by Western standards) church singers in Moscow, L'vov's harmonizations became the standard model in Russian church music at least until the end of the nineteenth century.

A major achievement of Kastal'sky, Kompaneisky, and some of their collaborators lay in recognizing that the melodic essence of chant must not be encumbered or violated by a superimposed harmonic scheme. The recognition of this principle, however, was by no means universal among composers of the new Russian school. Thus one encounters works whose rhythmic structure on the surface resmbles L'vov's unmetered and unbarred harmonized chant; text alone appears to determine the rhythm. A closer analysis of the texture, voice leading, and harmonic rhythm shows, however, that the harmony creates a straightjacket and prevents the melody from moving freely. By contrast, in other unmetered works, the voices of the polyphonic texture flow horizontally with the chant without impeding its natural motion.

In terms of rhythmic and metric notation the scores of the literature in question display a variety of formats. One prevalent type, with bar lines only between phrases, has just been described. Another type of rhythmic organization employing changing meter signatures was pioneered by Tchaikovsky in his *Vigil*, which is based almost entirely on chant melodies. Tchaikovsky's intention was obviously to correlate the meters with the textual stresses; however, since his approach to the chants was essentially harmonic, the changing meters also accommodate the harmonic rhythm. A variation on this technique, found in some works of Kastal'sky and Kalinnikov, consists of using bar lines and measures of different lengths, but without changing meter signatures. In a third type, though a regular meter signature appears at the beginning of the work and the measures remain constant, the textual stresses are independent of the regular metric divisions.

An entirely unique rhythmic layout appears in some of Kompaneisky's works: as a note in the score explains, "Solid lines divide the chant into independent melodic figures [phrases], while dotted lines delineate typical [melodic] groups [i.e., popevki of chant]. There are no divisions corresponding to measures."[28] In Kompaneisky's opinion, the division of chant melodies into any kind of measures, even unsymmetric ones, was "unnecessary and caused distortion of the rhythmic design of chant."[29]

All these systems of rhythmic organization are used interchangeably and without any apparent system or logic in the works of the new Russian choral school. No one system can be called typical for any given composer, and no system can be regarded as ideal for the purposes of conducting. The pedagogical literature contains only a few references to conducting neumatic chants with unsymmetrical rhythms. Kastal'sky's "Methodology of teaching church singing in the school" has a brief section entitled "conducting unmetered church hymns (stichera, dogmatika, heirmoi, etc.)":

> All beats are downward (except for anacruses); duple meter prevails (despite frequent wrong accents), triple [groupings] are rare....
>
> The half-note beat prevails...[and] quarter-notes are given only in the case of anacruses....[see ex. 7.6].
>
> In very slow motion (e.g., magnifications, [the Exaposteilarion of Pascha] "*Plotiiu usnuv*," slow stichera...) one gives ordinary beats down and up (i.e., 2/4 and 3/4) on each quarter....[30]

Example 7.6. Kastal'sky's Example: Theotokion-Dogmatikon in Tone 1
(Znamennyi Chant).
(Original note values)

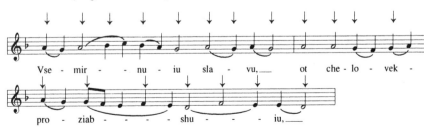

Vse - mir - - nu - iu   sla - vu,___   ot   che - lo - vek -

pro - ziab - - - - shu - - - iu,___

([Let us praise] the glory of the world, born of man...)

Kastal'sky's recommendations are entirely too simple, considering the intricate rhythmic structure of neumatic znamennyi chant. As noted earlier, however, Kastal'sky was not an outstanding conductor himself.

A somewhat more thorough treatment of the subject appears in Nikolai Kovin's *Choral conducting*, although he admits that "The metric structure of our ancient church chants has not yet been studied with sufficient thoroughness and detail. One thing, however, is certain—the presence of complex unsymmetric meters." According to Kovin, "The conductor must in each individual case determine the characteristic meter of a given melodic passage of the chant and indicate it in his conducting"[31] (see ex. 7.7).

Example 7.7.   Kovin's Example: Theotokion Dogmatikon in Tone 2
(Znamennyi Chant).
(Original note values within Kovin's metric scheme)

Prei - de__   sen' za - kon - na - - - - ia._____

(The shadow of the Law passed away...)

In essence, the problems of metric organization presented by chant-based works from the Russian repertoire are quite similar to those found in works of Western Renaissance polyphony. To clarify the rhythmic structure and the textual and melodic stresses, especially for performers who are unfamiliar with the language and the chant idiom, an editing technique is needed that would accomplish this goal without violating the nature of the chant or unduly encumbering the score. In my opinion, such a technique might consist of either dotted bar lines or *Mensurstrichs* between the staves inserted before notes having melodic and/or textual stress. Changing metric patterns may be indicated as well, above or between the staves. The resulting rhythmic organization, while complex, would accurately reflect the supple and flexible text-oriented structure of neumatic znamennyi chant.

While the rhythmic organization of chant on a large scale is clearly governed by textual phrases and individual words, some controversy exists concerning the rhythmic interpretation of the note values of square notation, and, by the same token, of relative note values in chant arrangements. According to Razumovsky,

Although the square notes are explained here in terms of commonly used round notes, this explanation is only approximate.... Round notes represent [proportionally] fixed durations of sound: a whole or full note is always equal in duration to two white or half notes, a white note in turn is always equal in duration to two black or quarter [notes]. By contrast, in the practice of liturgical chant the square notes never implied, and do not to this day imply, such strictly proportioned durations. Concerning the square notes one can only say that a full or whole note (*takt*) represents a long duration, a black note (*chvartka*)—a short duration, and a white note (*poltakta*)—a medium duration. The [actual] duration of notes in church chant depends on the meaning of the words in the text and on their prosodic stresses. If we were to apply a strict (musical) measure to square notes...and to sacred texts, we would immediately notice that, pronounced uniformly [from a rhythmic standpoint], many words lose their prosodic stresses, [and consequently lose] their impact and meaning.[32]

Similar observations are made by Nikolai Potulov in his *Manual for the study of church singing*:

> The overly strict adherence to note values is not only unnecessary, but at times is even detrimental, particularly when long stretches of words are to be performed on a single pitch, i.e., in recitative (*chitok* or *govorok*): for when words are pronounced strictly uniformly, they lose their accents and inevitably lose their impact and sense. The various types of notes (wholes, halves, etc.) indicate only a relatively greater or lesser speed of performance, a greater or lesser degree of accentuating words and syllables; hence, the relationship betweeen the various note values must not always be strictly the same as dictated by the rules of musical theory. In church singing the duration of the notes is determined primarily by the meaning of the word and the spirit of the singer.[33]

The question of proportionality of note values will be discussed in greater detail below, in the section dealing with recitative. In works based on neumatic chant the fundamental question is to what extent the composers writing these works were aware of or followed Razumovsky's and Potulov's pronouncements. Judging from Nikol'sky's review of the Old Believers' concert cited earlier, the practice of treating note values only approximately was *not* commonplace in choral church singing, but rather, the execution was "strictly measured," which is why the Old Believers' performance was such a revelation.

Nikol'sky as a composer was particularly concerned with the accurate rendering of rhythm. Thus his works contain passages marked *Bez razmera* (lit. "without measure"), which he translates as *Senza ritmo* or *Sine ritmo* in the piano reduction (see ex. 7.8), to signify that the note values are not to be treated strictly proportionately. Other composers, namely Grechaninov and Chesnokov, also employed the term *Bez razmera*, but mostly in reference to recitative chant. In one instance, in his Opus 26, Grechaninov used the direction *Con alcuna liberta (quasi Recitatif)*. Only Nikol'sky, however, applied the term *Bez razmera* to broad, melodic episodes, apparently with the intent to counter the prevailing contemporary understanding of neumatic chant as being strictly measured.

Square notation, as well as the staffless neumatic notation before it, contained yet another peculiarity that was transmitted to polyphonic chant

Example 7.8. Aleksandr Nikol'sky—*"Gospod' votsarisia"* [The Lord reigns],
Opus 45, No. 7.

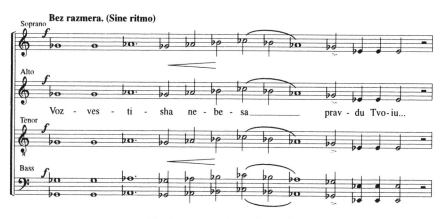

(The heavens proclaim Thy truth...)

arrangements: neither notation had any symbols for rests. According to Kompaneisky, the function of rests was fulfilled by the neume *statiia*—a long, "static" note—placed at the end of melodic and textual phrases. The duration of a statiia varied depending on its position relative to the textual phrase, but after holding the note, the singer almost invariably made a pause. The duration of the pauses also varied, depending on the length of the preceding phrase, the content of the text, and the movement of the melody. "It is very risky for a composer to designate these pauses with rests of specific durational value," writes Kompaneisky. "Rather, he should leave this to the artistic instinct of the conductor."[34]

Most composers of chant arrangements agreed with Kompaneisky's prescription consciously or unconsciously, despite the fact that a certain amount of rhythmic ambiguity resulted. In the square notation the statiia sometimes was indicated by a half-note and sometimes by a whole-note, and these note values were normally preserved in polyphonic arrangements. In performing from round-note notation, however, one tends to make pauses for breaths at the expense of the final note of a phrase, thereby preserving the strictly measured nature of the chant. Based on Kompaneisky's statement, a more accurate procedure would be to insert rests of appropriate duration after holding the final note of each phrase at least its *relative* value. Morozov's Old Believers' Choir follows the latter practice in several recordings.

Another question pertaining to the rhythm of chant has to do with the existence of triplets within what is otherwise duple rhythm. Concerning this question Vasily Komarov states very emphatically:

> On the basis of everything we know about the living tradition of church and folk singing, we may say that one does not find triplets . . . in it. In places where one does encounter them, e.g., in the folk songs collected by [Nikolai] Pal'chikov, it is clearly an error [of the transcriber]. Such singing contains abundant syncopations, both resolved and unresolved, [as well as] other rhythmic combinations not found in Western music and even not recommended by Western theory, but *nowhere triplets*.[35]

The square-note staff notation used for chant contains no examples of triplets anywhere. Chants notated in square notes contained neither time signatures nor proportional changes from duple to triple, even though the composed part-singing notated in the same notation contained both proportional signatures and changes from duple to triple proportion similar to those found in Western polyphonic music of the late sixteenth and seventeenth centuries. According to Komarov, the appearance of triplets in chant arrangements of the late nineteenth century is wholly the result of a misunderstanding by scholars who published lexicons of neumatic notation explaining the neumes in terms of either square or round notes. The analytic methods used to study the notation led scholars to transcribe separately certain neumes that never stood alone in actual practice. But an unsuspecting composer using that lexicon to transcribe some of his own chant material might understand them in an erroneous context. For example, the first short note of the neume *slozhitiia* could be interpreted as a grace note, while the *perevodka s lomkoiu* could be interpreted as a triplet (see ex. 7.9a and 7.9b).[36]

Evidently this is exactly what happened in the case of Kastal'sky, whose early chant arrangements frequently contain triplets (see, e.g., published Nos. 3 and 4 [ex. 6.6]). In later works, e.g., the Kanons for the Nativity of Christ (published Nos. 43 and 44), triplets still appear, but with the instruction: "to be performed almost like simple eighth-notes." Elsewhere in the works of Kastal'sky and others, triplets and other nonbinary fractions of the beat such as quintuplets, are either the result of ambiguous notation (e.g., Kastal'sky's *"Bogonachal'nym manoveniem"* [By the royal command of God], No. 41, contains a notated quintuplet of eighth-notes in one voice while the other voices have a half-note tied to an eighth-note) or stem from the composers' efforts to notate precisely the subtle and complex rhythms of recitative. Overall, one gets the impression that, in dealing with archaic chant, composers trained in the conventions of nineteenth-century music had to struggle with its unfamiliar and complex rhythmic structure.

Additional discussion of triplets and other rhythmic groupings will be found in the section dealing with recitative chant. In the case of neumatic chant arrangements containing notated triplets, however, one could justifiably interpret them, when possible, as three-eighth groupings (with the eighth note remaining constant), which would produce a more accurate rendition of the chant and greater rhythmic interest.

Example 7.9a.   The Neume *"Slozhitiia malaia s chashkoiu."*
(Transcribed separately and in the context of a chant passage)

Example 7.9b.   The Neume *"Perevodka s lomkoiu."*
(Transcribed separately and in the context of a sticheron in Tone 1)

Zhi - vo - pri - em - no - mu   tvo - e - mu_____ gro - bu...

Another problem of square notation with which composers of the time did not deal in a consistent fashion (but which crucially affects the performer's task) is the matter of equivalence between square and round note values. While this question significantly affects the rhythmic nature of neumatic chant, it is more appropriately discussed under the rubric of tempo.

Problems of Tempo

Tempo is one of the most problematic elements of the Russian choral repertoire under consideration. For one thing, the tempo of chant was the one feature most fundamentally misunderstood by both composers and scholars at the end of the nineteenth century. While certain traditions for the proper tempo of various types, styles, and liturgical categories of hymns undoubtedly existed, gramophone recordings show that these were by no means universal. Each composer and conductor had his own subjective notions of a "moderate" or "calm" tempo, for example. Many chant arrangements carry no tempo indication whatsoever, apparently on the assumption that the performer would be familiar with the appropriate tempo. Others have a verbal tempo indication, but no time-signature indicating the note value of the pulse. Few works bear composers' metronome markings.

According to the passage from Razumovsky cited above, a full note (*takt*) in square-note notation corresponds to a whole note in the modern system, i.e., ♩ = 𝑜 , and so forth. This indeed was the opinion of Razumovsky, Potulov, and their contemporaries—who, partly under the influence of Western scholars—thought of chant as something stately, serene, and solemn. As late as 1911, a textbook for parochial schools written by A. Riazhsky and endorsed by Metropolitan Makari of Moscow explained square notes in terms of exact equivalence with round notes (i.e., four beats of the hand to the whole note).[37]

Treatises from the time when square notes were first introduced in Russia indicate, however, that such a view is erroneous. For example, Deacon Ioanniky Korenev's preface to Diletsky's *Musikiiskaia grammatika* [Musical grammar], dated 1681, reads as follows:

> If you wish to understand musical singing . . . you must first comprehend in your mind the six-named signs [i.e., the notes of the hexachord], which properly guide the voice upwards and downwards, in fast or slow motion, and which may be perceived in the raising and lowering of the hand, called a *takt*, written as follows: ♩ . One raising [or lowering] of the hand is a fraction [called] a *poltakta*, written: ✓ . And two fractions on the down[beat] are called *chvartki*, of which there are four in a *takt*, written: ♩ .[38]

Consequently, chant melodies notated in square notes should be performed *Alla breve*, while in transcription to round notes the note values should be halved.

The confusion concerning the note values of chant may even antedate the square-note system, as suggested by a comment in Kompaneisky's arrangement of the hymn in Greek Chant, *"O Tebe raduetsia"* (All of creation rejoices) (published No. 31): "This hymn is joyful and festive, and there is no basis for singing it slowly, as is commonly done, incorrectly interpreting the [neume] ✓ (*kriuk*) as the mensural note ♩ [equal to] two quarter-notes."[39] (This hymn in a widely used arrangement by Pyotr Turchaninov [1779–1856] to this day tends to be performed very slowly, with a half-note pulse equalling no more than 60 according to the metronome.)

In their chant arrangements Russian composers were remarkably inconsistent in applying the principles of equivalence described above and in specifying the value of the pulse. A telling example is found in two sets of troparia and kontakia, for the feasts of the Nativity of Christ and the Theophany, respectively, by Kastal'sky (published Nos. 7 and 8). All four hymns are arrangements of znamennyi chant, very similar in musical style, and were originally published under the same cover. While in three arrangements the note values of the original square-note chant notation have been halved, in the fourth—the Kontakion for the Theophany—the note values are unchanged. The discrepancy is all the more striking in view of the fact that the Troparion for the Nativity (ex. 7.10) and the Kontakion for the Theophany (ex. 7.11) are based on the same chant in Tone 4. In the Troparion the chant lies in the top voice (doubled by the first tenor), while in the Kontakion the chant is in the bass, which perhaps may call for a somewhat heavier articulation, as indicated by the accent marks. Kastal'sky probably did not intend for the Kontakion to be sung at half the speed of the other chant arrangements in this opus, but simply neglected to make the necessary adjustments in the note values of the final arrangement. Similar examples throughout the repertoire suggest that the question of the proper note values and pulse to be used for chant-based works had not yet been clearly and thoroughly understood on a theoretical basis. Only a few composers, most notably Chesnokov and Rachmaninoff, clearly identified the pulse ($\bf d$ or $\bf \downarrow$) in some works; but even then, no tempo is given.

Example 7.10. Aleksandr Kastal'sky—"Troparion to the Nativity," P. N. 7a.

(Thy nativity, O Christ our God...)

Example 7.11. Aleksandr Kastal'sky—"Kontakion to the Theophany," P. N. 8b.

(Today Thou hast appeared to the universe...)

I have found only one explicit discussion of the tempo of znamennyi chant—in Vasily Komarov's *Sredstva k uluchsheniiu tserkovnogo peniia* [Means for improving church singing]. It begins with what Komarov calls "fundamental rhythmic laws," which he believes are derived from ancient Greek and Byzantine laws of rhythm in prosody (and hence, in music). The fundamental unit of time in church chant is the mora (*chronos protos*), "which for the most part corresponds to [the duration of] unaccented syllables . . . and is expressed in staff notation most commonly by the half-note or the so-called 'white note.' "[40] Komarov's first law, therefore, is that the mora by definition is indivisible as a unit of time. The second law pertains to recitative chant: in simple recitative a stressed syllable must be no more than twice as long as an unstressed syllable. (This rule does not apply to chants that contain melismatic passages of several notes.) The third law pertains to the articulation of chant in performance: however extended a melody may fall on a given syllable of text, one must not hear more than a single articulation of the vowel: as the mora is indivisible by syllables, the vowel is indivisible by notes. "In natural Russian singing," says Komarov, "one does not *perceive notes* just as one does not perceive definite vowels and consonants in live speech. To learn the chants one must begin not by studying the notes, but . . . by allowing the living melody to guide the learning of the notes. This is the rule that was followed by our old teachers of church singing." After defining the concept of the mora Komarov takes up the matter of tempo:

> Somewhere we have read that all znamennyi chant may be sung in the tempo of a half-note (the mora) equalling the pulse of an adult, i.e., approximately [one note] per second. Such a tempo may be allowed only at the most elementary stage of note learning. In all natural, purely Russian singing we have never heard such a slow tempo. And indeed, at such a tempo one would hear only separate syllables rather than words. The expressions *"protiazhnaia pesnia"* [lit., an "extended" or "drawn out" song[41]], *"shirokaia melodiia"* [broad melody], do not at all indicate a tempo as slow as a second per mora. The tempos of all Russian singing do not go beyond the limits of 3/4 to 1/8 of a second per mora [i.e., mora = 80 to 480, according to Maelzel's metronome], while church chants lie within narrower limits of 3/4 to 1/4 second per mora [mora = 80 to 240]. Anything faster has developed under the influence of Court Chant.[42]

Komarov deals at great length with the tempos of various hymn categories in different Tones. In some cases his illustrations and examples do not specify to which style of chant he is referring. But properly understood, his discussion offers extremely valuable insights into the performance of various types of Russian chant, particularly with regard to the nearly forgotten art of solo chanting. His observations are of lesser value as a guide to interpreting polyphonic arrangements of chant, as he himself notes: "From what has been said concerning the tempos of common and znamennyi chant it is obvious, incidentally, where the harmonizers of ancient chant made their most fundamental error: the added voices, particularly the bass, are absolutely impossible to perform at this traditional tempo; it furthermore becomes apparent, considering the absence of a [regular] musical meter in these melodies, how inconvenient it is to mark [the meter] with movements of the hand." In a footnote Komarov adds that prior to the *Kliuch* of Tikhon Makarievsky, a treatise dating from the early eighteenth century, manuals of church singing contain no references to marking the tempo with hand motions.[43]

Since Komarov was writing before the chant arrangements of Kastal'sky appeared, his observations apply to earlier attempts to harmonize chants—by Bortniansky, Turchaninov, L'vov, and Potulov (and, one might add, by their followers in terms of style: L'vovsky, Tchaikovsky, Metallov, Arkhangel'sky, Dmitri Soloviev, and Ivan Smirnov). Because these composers neglected the melodic nature of chant, their harmonizations are constructed so that they can only be performed slowly and lugubriously. As an illustration we may consider a znamennyi chant, Cherubic Hymn, a convoluted melody of narrow compass, which perfectly exemplifies Russian folk melodies that "persistently stamp on one spot"[44] (see ex. 7.12), and its arrangement by Grigory L'vovsky in which each note is treated as a chord tone (ex. 7.13). The harmonic chord changes make it impossible to sing this arrangement much faster than $d = 80$, which renders the melody lifeless.

Example 7.12. Znamennyi Chant—"Cherubic Hymn."
(Original note values transcribed in round notes)

(Let us [who mystically represent] the cherubim...)

When Stepan Smolensky heard this chant performed very slowly at a monastery in Novgorod, he reportedly said: "These stolp [znamennyi] pieces must be sung livelier, then they will have greater effect. An overly drawn-out performance only produces boredom. Sing it like you would sing *'Akh vy seni, moi seni'*" [Ah, my front porch][45] (ex. 7.14), a dance song performed at a tempo no slower than $d = 96$–100.

Far from being a personal opinion, Smolensky's analogy was undoubtedly based upon his familiarity with live chant performance among the Old Believers. At a tempo of $d = 100$ the znamennyi Cherubic Hymn is

Example 7.13. Grigory L'vovsky—"Cherubic Hymn," P. N. 47.
(Arrangement of Znamennyi Chant)

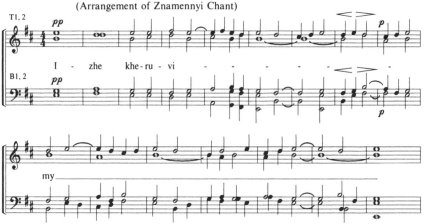

(Let us [who mystically represent] the cherubim...)

Example 7.14. Folk Song *"Akh vy seni, moi seni"* [Oh you front porch, my front porch].

*(Oh, you front porch, my front porch, my new front porch,
New and latticed, made of maple-wood...)*

thoroughly transformed, acquiring energy, vitality, and considerably greater musical interest. Moreover, and this is highly significant in Orthodox church singing, individual words and even entire phrases of text become easily negotiable *on a single breath*, preserving the integrity of the text when performed by a single chanter.

While the tempo of *"Akh vy seni"* may be a little on the fast side, it is by no means inapplicable to the arrangement of the same chant by Kastal'sky (ex. 7.15): here, the character of the part writing and the slow harmonic rhythm do not preclude a fast tempo. Such a tempo, however, would have certainly contradicted the commonly accepted practice of singing the Cherubic Hymn quite slowly. Indeed, during his tenure as conductor of the Moscow Synodal Choir, Kastal'sky was accused by some tradition-minded churchgoers of "introducing frivolous, rollicking tunes resembling folk dances in church."[46]

Example 7.15.   Aleksandr Kastal'sky—"Cherubic Hymn," P. N. 3.
(Arrangement of Znamennyi Chant)

(Let us [who mystically represent] the cherubim...)

Though Kastal'sky gives no tempo marking, his polyphonic treatment of the chant suggests that he would have adhered closely to Smolensky's recommendation for its performance tempo.

An extremely important consideration in determining the appropriate performance tempo for works based on znamennyi and other Russian chants is what Komarov calls the *khod* of a musical work—a term that translates as "pace" or "gait." Although it is not a traditional musical concept, khod refers to a kind of internal dynamism or movement that is inherent and "right" for a given piece of music. Komarov writes,

> Khod is most easily disrupted by mechanical techniques of composition and performance. In composition it is determined by the melody, while in performance [it depends upon] perceiving [the melody] directly with the ear, which results in [the proper] animation and enables the melody to be embellished with natural countervoices, . . . —a live, unaffected harmony that not only does not impede the melodic khod, but flows out of it and supplements it, so that in live performance it takes on the character of an endlessly undulating sea.[47]

Komarov suggests further that clues to the proper performance of the broad, melismatic melodies of great znamennyi chant may be found in "the direct study of live performances of the *protiazhnaia* [extended] Russian [folk] song, . . . not in terms of its melody, . . . but in the manner of its performance by [folk] choruses, [which display] that constant khod from the song's beginning to its end, which, when it is grasped by the ear, explains all: the rhythm, the harmony, and the nuances."[48]

Not all Russian choral works possess that internal dynamic quality called khod. In some liturgical compositions bearing tempo markings of Adagio or Largo, which, to use Ioann Voznesensky's expression, have a "stalling" character, this quality is decidedly lacking. In other compositions, particularly from the Italianate repertoire, the khod resembles that of marches and dances; "but," says Komarov, "the nature of this movement is such that even the singers themselves instinctively sense its impropriety in church and therefore never perform these works in the way that purely musical sense would dictate."[49]

By contrast, khod is present in most chant-based and chant-style works of the new Russian choral school. Writing many years after Komarov and making no references to the former's writings, Boris Asaf'ev described essentially the same quality in the works of Kastal'sky:

> In terms of form-generating principles Kastal'sky's choruses fall into the category of the motet. Their forms are determined not by any [preexisting] scheme, but by the principle of achieving choral movement every time in a new dimension, depending on the nature of the task at hand. An extended, unceasing, slowly unfolding motion is of special concern to Kastal'sky....
>
> Kastal'sky's "typical" composition is a laconic choral "tapestry," whose movement flows steadily and briskly, at an unhurried pace that is at the same time energetic and full of life. The complexity of the polyphonic texture is dependent to a great extent upon the rate of motion.... Especially important in Kastal'sky's works (as in the polyphonic works of the Flemish masters and the Renaissance madrigalists) is the *initial impulse*—the melodic "formula of motion" that serves as the point of departure. Reappearing from time to time in the middle of the composition, it stimulates and supports the movement of the voices whenever the need arises.[50]

This passage, written by an astute theorist who was a student and collaborator of Kastal'sky, gives a better insight into the tempos to be used in performing the latter's works than any discussion of metronome markings. However, due to the relative unfamiliarity of the idiom in which Kastal'sky and his contemporaries wrote, as well as the interruptions suffered by both the chant tradition and the tradition of Russian sacred choral performance, some additional discussion of the metronome markings found in scores and of the tempos heard on available recordings is necessary.

The genuine tradition of chant performance was probably quite obscure in the time of Komarov and the church composers who were his contemporaries. The rubrics of the Orthodox Church rarely prescribed the tempo of a hymn, and then only in general terms, e.g., *"kosno i so sladkopeniem"* (slowly and with "sweet" singing), or *"poskoru, truda radi bdennago"* (quickly, due to the effort in keeping the vigil). Some treatises convey the impression that this type of knowledge was general; for example, Ioannus de Castro, a Roman monk, writes the following in reference to singing in the southwestern and western portions of Russia:

Chant melodies must be performed taking into consideration [each one's] characteristic and particular style, the type of composition, [and] the melody's nature, differentiating the performance of more festive and ornamented melodies from the common and simple. The former must be sung with a certain deliberateness and slowness, extending the notes more than in other chants (but avoiding excess), unfolding the voice more or giving it greater intensity (but without shouting), and trying to observe the elements of good taste and the aforementioned rules, which makes [these melodies] more graceful, articulated, and majestic....

The rate of motion is undoubtedly an important element of expression, and therefore its application to various hymns is dictated by specific rules: a slow and drawn out tempo, *kosno*,... is characteristic of the most festive and ornamented hymns, including hymns connected with time-consuming ritual actions (e.g., the Cherubic hymn and the Communion hymn) and festal hymns, such as the Stichera on *"Slava...i nyne"* [Glory...now and ever], known as *slavniki*. Fast tempo, *poskoru*,... is characteristic of syllabic and recitative-style hymns such as troparia, heirmoi, etc. A third type of tempo, between slow and fast, is not specified in liturgical books but applies to hymns for which no special tempo is indicated.[51]

De Castro's study, a descriptive treatise written primarily for the non-Orthodox reader, saw limited circulation in Russia even though it was translated into Russian by Voznesensky. In church-music circles, however (as far as I was able to determine), no study has ever attempted to correlate the instructions found in the rubrics with specific melodies. Consequently, in assigning tempo markings to chant arrangements or compositions, composers were guided either by vague, general notions of traditional tempos or by their own concept of a given work. In the case of composers like Tchaikovsky (in his *Vigil*), the tempo and metronome marks resemble the procedure of a musical ethnographer attempting to notate and describe scrupulously what he heard in the practice of an unfamiliar body of music.

The actual tempo terms used by Russian composers differ very little if at all from customary Italian terms. The first to introduce Russian tempo terms into choral music was Aleksei L'vov; however, choral composers after him did not exclusively use Russian terms. In fact, most of the translations given below are drawn from textbooks and manuals designed to explain the Italian terms by Russian equivalents. Only with the rise of the new Russian school did the use of exclusively Russian terms become more widespread. Some composers, most notably Tchaikovsky and Nikol'sky, used a dual system of terminology, with Russian above the choral parts and Italian in the piano reduction. Table 7.1 summarizes the most important tempo terms used in Russian choral works.[52]

On the basis of metronome markings in a limited number of works one finds that composers of the new Russian school understood the above terms to include a broad range of tempos: *Medlenno* (Adagio) ranges from 42 to 72 by the metronome; *Pokoino* (Andante) from 52 to 92; *Ne skoro* (Moderato, lit. not fast) from 72 to 126; *Umerenno* (Moderato) from 72 to 116; *Ozhivlenno* or *Skoro* (Allegro) from 108 to 176. Chesnokov's interpretation of tempos tends

Table 7.1.   Russian Tempo Terms and Their Western Equivalents

Russian Tempo Terms	Italian or English Equivalents
Ochen' protiazhno	Largo
Ochen' medlenno	Largo; Grave; Lento
Medlenno	Adagio; Lento
Protiazhno	Adagio
Shiroko	Sostenuto; Broadly
Spokoino	Tranquillo
Pokoino	Andante
Dovol'no medlenno	Andante
Ne spesha	Andante; Moderato
Ne skoro	Andante; Moderato
Ne ochen' skoro	Allegretto
Sderzhanno	Holding back
Umerenno	Moderato
Sredniaia skorost'	Moderato
Torzhestvenno	Maestoso
Stepenno	Stately
Velichestvenno	Maestoso
Dovol'no skoro	Moderato
Neskol'ko ozhivlenno	Allegretto; Poco Allegro
Odushevlenno; S odushevleniem	Animato; Animando
Ozhivlenno	Allegretto; Allegro
Dovol'no ozhivlenno	Allegro assai
Bodro	Briskly
Skoro	Allegro
Dovol'no zhivo	Allegro moderato
Zhivo	Vivace; Allegro
Bystro	Vivace
Ochen' bystro	Presto

to be on the slow side, and Grechaninov's metronome markings are frequently at odds with the tempo terms he employs.

Metronome markings appear in only eleven of Kastal'sky's works, of which six are chant arrangements, four are in the style of chant, and one is a free composition. Of the chant arrangements only three are based on neumatic znamennyi chant: the "Sticheron on 'Glory... now and ever' for the feast of Dormition" (published No. 41), the "Magnification for Dormition" in putevoi chant, a variant of znamennyi chant (published No. 42), and the "Hymn to the Mother of God for Pentecost" (published No. 76). The tempos indicated for these works (in terms of the mora or prevailing pulse) are 80, 74, and 60, respectively; only the Magnification bears also a verbal tempo marking—*Ne zatiagivaia dvizheniia* (Without dragging the tempo). Of the works in chant style, three contain passages constructed of or resembling znamennyi melodic formulae: *"V pamiat' vechnuiu"* [The memory of the righteous] (published

No. 29), and two hymns from the Wedding Service (published No. 32); the metronome markings (per mora) are 92–96, 108, and 120, respectively.

Kastal'sky recorded three of his works based on neumatic chant with the Synodal Choir: *"S nami Bog"* [God is with us] based on znamennyi chant (published No. 9), *"Blagoslovi, dushe moia"* [Bless the Lord, o my soul] based on Greek Chant (published No. 25), and *"Khvalite imia Gospodne"* [Praise the name of the Lord] based on Kievan Chant (published No. 54).[53] The performance tempo in the first two works ranges between 100 and 108 per mora, while in the third work, *"Khvalite,"* the quarter-note equals 100, yielding a mora of 200 in the recitative passages. Kastal'sky also conducts Grechaninov's *"Voskliknite Gospodevi"* [Make a joyful noise], Opus 19, No. 2, a composition in the style of neumatic chant, for which the composer indicated ♩ = 58 (see ex. 7.16). Kastal'sky's tempo, however, is ♩ = 96–100, which in my opinion is more appropriate for this type of chantlike work.

Example 7.16.   Aleksandr Grechaninov—*"Voskliknite Gospodevi"*
[Make a joyful noise], Opus 19, No. 2.

(Make a joyful noise to the Lord, all the earth...)

Very few of Chesnokov's chant-style works bear metronome markings. Of those that do, only one is a genuine chant arrangement, *"Milost' mira"* [A mercy of peace], Opus 3, No. 2, for the Liturgy of St. Basil, which bears a marking of ♩ = 69. In the *"Veruiu"* [Creed] from the *Liturgy*, Opus 15, a znamennyi chant melisma *(fita piatoglasnaia*, see ex. 7.17) appears in the middle of the work and is marked ♩ = 100.

Only two of Nikol'sky's znamennyi chant-based works contain metronome markings: *"Milost' mira"* [A mercy of peace], Opus 3, No. 3, which contains neumatic passages amidst an otherwise syllabic structure—

Example 7.17. Pavel Chesnokov—"*Veruiu*" [I believe], Opus 15, No. 6.
The melisma *"fita piatoglasnaia."*

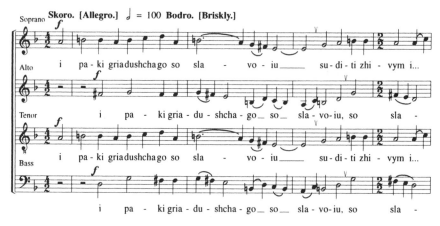

(*...and He shall come again with glory to judge the living...*)

marked $\mathit{d} = 84$, *Dovol'no skoro* (Rather fast); and *"Na rekakh Vavilonskikh"* [By the rivers of Babylon], Opus 7, No. 2—marked $\mathit{d} = 68$, *Ochen' medlenno* (Very slowly).

Grechaninov gives metronome marks for several works employing chant-style motives: $\mathit{d} = 58$ for the aforementioned *"Voskliknite Gospodevi,"* and $\mathit{d} = 72$ for *"Volnoiu morskoiu"* [By the waves of the sea], Opus 19, No. 1, as well as for several works in his *All-night vigil,* Opus 59. Other composers, e.g., Kalinnikov, Rachmaninoff, and Kompaneisky, did not give metronome markings for their chant-based works.

The above metronome markings range from 58 per mora to 120 per mora. Among them, 58 (Grechaninov's *"Voskliknite Gospodevi"*) and 60 (Kastal'sky's "Hymn to the Mother of God for Pentecost") appear to be exceptions. The more prevalent range of tempos is from 80 to 108 per mora, which coincides with Komarov's observations regarding the performance of neumatic chant. This range of tempos also correlates with those found in field recordings made recently among Old Believers in the Soviet Union by a Soviet musicologist studying chant: the tempos range from 84 to 120 for stichera, and from 72 to 100 for Hymns to the Mother of God; only certain hymns, e.g., exaposteilaria (festal troparia following the kanon at Matins) in putevoi chant, are performed quite slowly, with a pulse of 58 to 60.

The determination of tempo in chant-style works is problematic mainly because of composers' inconsistency in designating the note values of the pulse and because of the general vagueness of tempo markings. To arrive at the proper tempo for a given work, one would first ideally consult the original chant to see if the note values have been preserved or halved. Though Russian chant codices are not readily available, a fairly reliable assumption can be made by observing whether the majority of text syllables fall on half-notes (original note values) or on quarter-notes (note values halved). In the former case, eighth-notes will appear rarely and sixteenths not at all, and one should use the half-note as the pulse. In the latter case, melodic turns will generally consist of eighth-notes, sixteenths will have the appearance of embellishments, and the quarter-note pulse should be used.

The second step is to identify the liturgical genre and context, and the character of the text. This, together with the composer's tempo marking (if one is given), should assist in establishing the tempo within the limits given above: 72–80 for particularly solemn or penitential hymns, 108–120 for joyful and festive hymns.

Finally, one must consider Komarov's important concept of khod, or pace, bearing in mind that znamennyi chant melodies are essentially energetic and dynamic. The ultimate criteria for a given tempo are (1) how comfortably and musically the chant can be sung, (2) whether the text is comprehensible, and (3) how well the motion of the accompanying voices correlates with the chant.

One final aspect of tempo must be mentioned—the appropriateness of rubato in performing works in the style of neumatic chant. Concerning this question Voznesensky writes: "In choral polyphonic singing ... one should avoid an uneven tempo, alternately speeded up and slowed down, as well as the prolongation of certain individual notes more than their duration and the prolongation of notated rests. Among the shortcomings of performance practice encountered most often [in the 1880s] are the [undue] acceleration of tempo ... and the excessive prolongation of high notes."[54] Evidently, the period preceding the emergence of the new Russian choral school was marked by a large degree of license in the interpretation of rhythm. Nikol'sky, upon arriving in Moscow from Penza to study at the Synodal School, made the following observations. Today these strike one as self-evident, but at that time were obviously not taken for granted:

> In the performance of composed choral works [e.g., those of Bortniansky] one must definitely distinguish one measure from another, accenting the first note of each measure. Each measure must correspond to a certain fixed portion of time, i.e., if the first measure lasts four seconds [$\downarrow$ = 60 in 4/4], the second measure must take up the same amount of time. To accelerate certain measures and prolong others arbitrarily deprives the ear of what is called rhythmic context.... [The former way] is exactly how the Synodal Choir sings part compositions. For example in Bortniansky's *"Tebe Boga khvalim"* [We praise Thee, O God (in F major)] one can definitely hear: *one*, two, three, *one*, two, three....[55]

Perhaps as a reaction to the looseness of the rhythm and the overabundance of rubato in the sentimental Romantic works from the first part of the nineteenth century, Russian choirs adopted a more rigorous rhythmic approach to pieces based on znamennyi chant. Chant, after all, was regarded as austere, "strict," and devoid of sentimental emotionalism. Yet, from what Nikol'sky has described of the Old Believers' performance and from what one hears on recordings of Old Believers, the treatment of the tempo is not at all steady: indeed, text-related neumatic notation most likely did not presuppose any type of steady, constant pulse, so that the concept of rubato is inapplicable. But the picture presented by a large percentage of chant arrangements in modern notation, often with regularly recurring bar lines, is quite different. Very few composers seem to have been concerned with the rhythmic subtleties inherent in authentic chant performance. The only one to employ the term rubato in relation to chant-style passages was Nikol'sky, who, as noted above, employed terms such as *Sine ritmo.*

Perhaps the best guideline regarding rubato is given by Nikolai Matveev, professor of church music at the Moscow Theological Academy in the Soviet Union, in his text on choral conducting: "Rubato [in church music] is a positive quality only when it is natural rather than artificial, when it displays no abrupt movements or changes, when rhythmic 'liberties' are conditioned by the underlying inner rhythm of the composition.... [Ultimately] the character of rubato is determined by the meaning of the liturgical text and the style and form of a given work."[56]

Problems of Articulation

Articulation, like tempo, is very important in the performance of works in chant style. Here again one finds a variety of notational practices among composers of the new Russian choral school, as well as some conflicting concepts.

Znamennyi chant, by its conjunct melodic movement, lends itself to smooth, cantabile vocal interpretation. Nevertheless, neumatic notation may have implied varied styles of vocal articulation that were not transcribed into square notes and are now irretrievably lost. What remains today is only the intriguing but vague instructions in some old neumatic lexicons, e.g., *golubchik garknouti iz gortani* (the *golubchik* is shouted from the throat). Except for some passages that clearly contain syncopations, the basic choice facing today's performer is between a smooth, legato articulation and one that is more accented or detached.

Several sources speak in favor of smooth articulation, particularly in melismatic passages. For example, Ioannus de Castro writes: "For pleasant effect one must connect all the sounds of a single phrase sung on the same vowel, even if they appear to be separate."[57] Aleksandr Nikol'sky expresses a very similar opinion: "The sounds should not be accentuated,... but on the contrary,... smooth, connected, even *legatissimo*, with one sound flowing into another, forming a single sonorous wave."[58] The most detailed and technical description of articulation in neumatic chant is offered by Aleksei Karasev:

> The performance of the opening psalm [at Vespers, usually in a melismatic Greek Chant] as well as many other arrangements of Kievan and Greek Chants requires *particular smoothness in the notes of the melody....* In singing several notes (mostly in conjunct motion) on a single vowel, one must strive to make each musical sound seem to flow out of the preceding one.... The singing of the chorus must resemble not the playing of a piano, as some mistakenly think,... but the playing of a string quartet or orchestra. To illustrate the necessary smoothness, which is difficult to explain in words, we may compare the various ways of producing the sound on a violin:... The greatest smoothness and *cantabile* is achieved when during the movement of the bow in one direction the fingers [of the left hand] are placed on the strings not from the top, but move from one sound to the next while maintaining consistent pressure upon the string. This is the type of *cantabile* one must achieve in melismatic church singing. Moreover, such connection must be achieved also in singing different vowels, i.e., when the voice moves from one syllable to another....
>
> In view of the above, the performance of harmonizations of ancient chants... presents significant difficulties,... requiring special knowledge, skills, and effort even greater than required to perform the concertos of Bortniansky.[59]

According to Nikolai Matveev, "Legato is the primary form of sound production in church singing, being one of the most important means of rendering the melody expressively." He goes on to say that nonlegato articulation is sometimes used to "underscore each note while maintaining the connectedness of the melody,... but should not contain obvious accents," while "staccato articulation is almost never used in practice."[60]

The above statements belong to the realm of theory. A somewhat different picture is presented by the actual scores and surviving recordings: in fact, most composers of the new Russian school frequently employed the marks > and - in their chant-based and chant-style works. According to Nikolai Kovin, these and other articulation signs had the same meaning as in common Western practice: > or *sf* to indicate an accent, - to indicate a broadending or extension of the note, and · · · or ''' to indicate detached performance. "The correct and precise execution of all the above... nuances depends entirely upon the conductor, his overall taste, musicality, and understanding of what is being performed. Conductors who are poor musicians often exaggerate all nuances to the point of caricature and absurdity. The best way to avoid mistakes and exaggerations is to listen to good examples [and] to exercise good measure and common sense."[61]

In chant arrangements by Kastal'sky, Nikol'sky, and Chesnokov, one frequently encounters entire passages where every note is marked with an accent (>) or tenuto (-). Nikol'sky is particularly liberal in marking chantlike passages (even if freely composed) with accents (see ex. 7.18). The most meticulous and thoroughgoing application of accents and tenutos appears in Rachmaninoff's works, particularly the *Vigil*. This brings up several questions: whether the meaning of these marks is consistent from one composer's works to another's, whether the marks are to be interpreted literally, and if so, how such an interpretation correlates with the cantabile conception of chant?

Example 7.18. Aleksandr Nikol'sky—*"Psalom 109-i,"* Opus 21, No. 2.

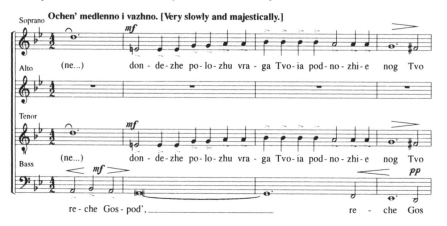

(...until I make your enemies your footstool | The Lord said...)

In Kastal'sky's works, accent marks appear most frequently over the notes of the chant-bearing voice; the other voices, which move homorhythmically with the chant, have only occasional marks of articulation. In an isolated case this might appear to be the result of the composer's carelessness or sloppy music engraving, but its consistent use suggests that Kastal'sky wished to have the chant voice emphasized. In technical terms such emphasis could be achieved by a combination of devices peculiar to the vocal idiom—slightly greater detachment of the notes, more intense articulation of consonants, and slightly greater volume—which are not adequately expressed by the articulation signs used in instrumental music. The fact that Kastal'sky did not regard vocal articulation as being identical to instrumental (pianistic) articulation is indicated by the fact that in several works (most notably, in the Troparia for Holy Saturday Matins, published No. 11) he placed different marks of articulation in the voices and in the piano reduction, i.e., - in the voices and > in the piano. Again, the temptation would be to dismiss these discrepancies as errors, were it not for the fact that Kastal'sky was professor of piano at the Synodal School and was certainly familiar with the pianistic idiom. Another example, *"Nyne otpushchaeshi"* No. 1 [Lord, now lettest Thou] (published No. 48 in the version for baritone solo and chorus), supports the thesis that accents indicate only the emphasis of a given voice. The soloist's part, ostensibly taken from an old manuscript, contains nothing that would suggest anything other than legato execution; yet in the piano reduction the soloist's notes are consistently marked with accents. It is unfortunate that few of Kastal'sky's works contain piano reductions; more examples would have allowed this line of thinking to be developed further.

The possibility that chant lines were marked with accents to indicate dynamic emphasis within the texture rather than marked articulation is also suggested by some of Nikol'sky's chant arrangements, e.g., the Theotokia-Dogmatika, Opus 48, Nos. 1–4. In two arrangements the *cantus firmus* carries the marking marcato, while the other voices bear no marks of articulation. In two other arrangements from the same opus, however, Nikol'sky writes the Russian word *vydeliaia*, meaning "emphasize," above the chant-bearing voice. The type of emphasis suggested by the word *vydeliaia* might include greater accentuation, but could just as easily be accomplished by increasing the volume somewhat. Rendering the term in Italian (marcato), however, tends to shift the focus, perhaps unintentionally, to the manner of vocal articulation. But the abundance of accent and tenuto marks in Nikol'sky's works suggests that, despite his earlier observations concerning the nature of chant (see page 281), in his compositions he wished to elicit a dramatic, intense, and strongly articulated declamation both of the text and of the pitches.

The most careful and detailed placement of articulation marks and other nuances is found in Rachmaninoff's works. Perhaps the abundance of performance details was due in part to the fact that Rachmaninoff, not being a choral church musician, did not take anything for granted. It has also been suggested that the meticulous specification of nuances resulted from consultations with Nikolai Danilin, who was Rachmaninoff's friend from their student days at the Moscow Philharmonic School. Whatever the case, Rachmaninoff apparently understood such terms as marcato and tenuto to mean something entirely different than did Nikol'sky and Kastal'sky. In the *Liturgy*, for example, a note in the Creed reads: *Ochen' ritmichno*; *korotkim zvukom* (Very rhythmically; with a short sound), which is translated in the piano reduction as marcato. In *"Khvalite imia Gospodne"* [Praise the name of the Lord] of the *Vigil*, a note over the znamennyi chant line in the basses and altos reads: *Iarko. S tverdym, bodrym ritmom* (Brightly. With a firm, energetic rhythm)—an effect that Kastal'sky may have indicated by means of accent or tenuto marks. In several other sections of the *Vigil* Rachmaninoff stipulates that the sound be "short and detached" (*Korotkim, otryvistym zvukom*). However, the musical and textual context in which these instructions appear (e.g., at the end of the Great Doxology) by no means suggests lightness or lack of intensity, but rather the opposite.

Rachmaninoff's use of articulation marks, while representative of the highly individualistic approach he brought to all his sacred compositions, is one of the keys to the immense expressive effect of his works. A thoughtful and perceptive artist, Rachmaninoff was perhaps attempting to express in modern notation the declamatory power of archaic chant wedded to and embodying the sacred text, a power not unlike what Caccini and the Florentine Camerata sought in trying to recreate the effects of Ancient Greek drama through operatic recitative. Not only must Rachmaninoff's directions be executed scrupulously, but his works may also be regarded as models of the type of nuancing employed by the conductors Vasily Orlov and Nikolai Danilin.

The notation of other works from the new Russian school does not shed additional light upon the problematic matter of articulation. Side by side with marks of stress or separation composers used terms such as *Sviazno* (Connected), *Pevuche* (Cantabile), and *Plavno* (Smoothly), in chant-style works. Such terms suggest that the prevailing articulation in Russian chant, as it was understood at the end of the nineteenth century, was legato.

Additional evidence is found in existing recordings from the period. The recordings of Kastal'sky conducting the Synodal Choir, deficient as they are, display an absolutely remarkable legato in melismatic passages—a sound that might be described as "slippery" or "sliding," but without portamento. In *"Blagoslovi, dushe moia"* [Bless the Lord, O my soul"], the opening of which contains accents in all the voices, one hears very marked, energetic diction but not mechanical accentuation; the bass line, which carries the chant most of the time, clearly predominates in the texture.

The recordings, not only of the Synodal Choir but others as well, display a very interesting feature that points to a peculiar understanding of the slur (ligature) in vocal music. In Russian choral scores, as in most vocal music, ligatures are used only to link notes sung upon a single syllable of text, rather than for other aspects of phrasing or articulation. Yet several Russian manuals on church singing and choral conducting define the ligature specifically as the symbol for legato: e.g., Kazansky writes, "A ligature placed over notes that differ in pitch, . . . indicates that these notes are to be performed smoothly, without breaths."[62] The corollary of this definition is that notes not linked by a ligature, such as notes sung to several different syllables, are performed nonlegato, which on recordings of the period approaches an intensely chopped staccato. The practice may involve more than a misinterpretation of Italian notation, however. One hears elements of the same choppiness alternating with cantilena in the ekphonetic reading of Moscow clergy, both at the turn of the century[63] and today, as well as in the singing of the great Russian operatic basso, Fyodor Shaliapin.

In recordings, the intense emphasis on certain consonants and syllables imparts to the singing a type of projection and distinctiveness of line that in performances of Orlov and Danilin (and Shaliapin) has been described as "expressive delivery of the text." Curiously enough, in 1898 an anonymous reviewer, possibly Ivan Lipaev, described the manner of articulation employed by the Synodal Choir (under Orlov) as resembling *instrumental* technique, which he nevertheless found most suited to works based on ancient chants:

> The singing of the Choir is now virtuosic in the highest sense. The slightest nuances of sound are executed with remarkable subtlety.... The singing [however,] has a somewhat cool quality; furthermore, the new manner of striking [each note], leaning into each sound, dismembering [the phrase], lends somewhat of an instrumental nature to the choir. Although [the choir] does not abuse this technique, it seems inappropriate for certain pieces. But the technique is wonderfully appropriate for ancient chants, which, I assume, is what was intended.[64]

Other choirs represented on old gramophone records—Arkhangel'sky's Choir; the Choir of the Mariinsky Opera in St. Petersburg, under Georgy Kazachenko; the Choir of Christ the Savior Cathedral in Moscow, under M. Karpov; the Chudov Choir of Moscow, under Ya. Nikol'sky (not A. V. Nikol'sky); Leonid Vasil'ev's private choir of Moscow; Ivan Yukhov's amateur choir of Moscow; and A. Pikman's choir of St. Petersburg[65]—offer some further insights into the question of articulation, despite the poor fidelity of the recordings.

Arkhangel'sky's Choir and Vasil'ev's Choir display a generally good sound and ensemble, and employ a sustained, cantabile articulation in performing works in chant style. A remarkable illustration of the "organlike sonority" for which the Imperial Court Chapel was famous appears in several recordings by the Mariinsky Opera Chorus, particularly in a performance of *"Angel vopiiashe"* (The angel cried out) by Bortniansky, which may be considered a neumatic chant arrangement even though it employs Italianate harmonic vocabulary and an imposed metric scheme. The sound is incredibly steady on sustained notes and in passing from chord to chord, with absolutely no decay of volume or intensity. Quite unexpectedly for an opera chorus, the voices appear to be singing without the slightest hint of vibrato, producing an effect that is indeed reminiscent of organ playing. But what distinguishes the legato sostenuto of the Mariinsky Choir from that of the Synodal Choir is its mechanical quality: the words are treated simply as phonemes of sound, and the legato is relentless and unchanging. The singing of the Synodal Choir, by contrast, seems much more vibrant and "alive," while the legato articulation is perfectly natural—almost naive—in its lack of affectation. Also lacking in the Mariinsky performance is any notion of Komarov's khod, which is present in abundance (one might even say, overabundance) in Kastal'sky's performances.

Problems of Dynamics

As in the case of tempo and articulation marks, no dynamic indications were transcribed in the square-note chant-books from the neumatic notation. Consequently, composers of chant arrangements had to rely upon a combination of traditional church practice and their own musical instincts.

Church rubrics occasionally specify dynamics, as well as tempos, for entire hymns, e.g., *tikho* (softly) or *veleglasno* (in full voice), but they do not provide any clues to the internal dynamics of a chant. Interpreting the lack of dynamic nuances in the chant-books literally, Aleksei L'vov laid down the maxim that "ancient chants should be performed absolutely simply and evenly,"[66] and criticized Lomakin for performing church music with excessive expressiveness and dynamic gradation. Only towards the end of the nineteenth century did the "mono-dynamic" view of chant performance begin to be challenged. Wrote Ioannus de Castro:

> To avoid monotony... the singing must be varied, for example by going from quiet to loud when the melody goes up and, conversely, from loud to soft when the melody descends....
>
> One must distinguish some sounds by a greater or lesser accentuation of the voice; some phrases or sections should have more or less volume or variation.... Such variation must not be constant, but guided by good taste and pleasantness, and should occur at the appropriate time and with moderation, otherwise it may easily go to the opposite extreme, becoming frivolous or absurd, which is even worse.[67]

As described in chapter 4, Russian church choirs in the nineteenth century developed dynamic nuances to a virtuosic degree, first in freely composed pieces and then in chant arrangements. There are abundant dynamic markings in the scores. Thus, the question in chant-style works is not whether dynamic nuances are appropriate, but the degree of intensity and contrast one should employ in executing them. An important observation is made by Komarov: "Church hymns belong to either the lyric or epic category, rather than the dramatic, the latter of which allows for abrupt and striking contrasts; but in the lyric or epic style, even in secular music, such abrupt transitions are not in accordance with the character [of the expression], and are all the more inappropriate in church music."[68]

A number of writers maintain that in church music one must avoid sudden dynamic contrasts. V. M. Orlov, for example, states that there should not be any "extreme effects, not in character with the [liturgy] of the Orthodox Church, such as abrupt changes from forte to piano and vice versa, particularly in the middle of a phrase."[69] Kastal'sky also warns against extreme contrasts, especially when they are unwarranted by the sense and logic of a piece: "[One must exercise] a sense of measure in nuances. One should not try to introduce them in large numbers only for external effect, especially when [the effect] is not justified by anything, e.g., extraordinary *pppp* in well-known pieces, or shouting in place of *ff*, etc. . . . [The guides for] determining the nuances of performance [may be found] in [Mathis] Lussy and [Hugo] Riemann."[70]

Chesnokov wrote: "Without nuances choral sonority is dead."[71] At the same time, he also cautioned against a purely technical approach to dynamic contrasts. In a section of his "Notes of a precentor" entitled "Meaningful and vacuous nuances" he writes:

> Music is the realm of emotion and feeling. If music has neither emotion nor feeling, it is not music, and even if it is music, it is dead. . . . Having achieved various degrees of volume (nuances) wherever necessary, [the conductor] must by the force of his talent also feel, understand, and experience emotionally the overall mood of the work, as well as its every detail . . . *Each outward nuance (p, f, $<$, $>$, etc.) must be imbued with emotion and feeling. Otherwise the outward nuance will be vacuous and meaningless.*[72]

Chesnokov also developed a theory of dynamic nuancing based on choral tessitura, which he explains in detail in his book *The choir and how to direct it.* He identifies five regions of choral tessitura (see ex. 7.19), which he correlates with five dynamic levels: *pp, p, mf, f,* and *ff.* "Each region of chordal distribution in the choral sonority is serviced by a *natural* [dynamic] nuance that is proper to it. . . . A chord will sound well only when the corresponding natural nuance for the region where it is located is applied to it. . . . There may be slight deviations from this general rule, but not significant ones."[73]

In the same chapter Chesnokov discusses minute motivic nuancing based on melodic and harmonic motion and phrasing. "Composers," he writes, "indicate only general nuances, and do not depict the multitude of minute and varied nuances that lie hidden in their compositions. Therefore extracting all the nuances and filling them with artistic content in performance is the task of the conductor, wherein he reveals his giftedness and creativity."[74] Evidence from reviews suggests that Chesnokov's interpretation of his own works and those of other composers were characterized by such detailed nuancing, as were performances by Chesnokov's teacher, Vasily Orlov, and his colleague, Nikolai Danilin.

Nothing in the musical scores suggests that the dynamics of chant arrangements were treated differently from those of free compositions, except in one respect: the matter of balance between the chant-bearing voice and the

Example 7.19.   Five Regions of Choral Tessitura and Corresponding Dynamic Levels (in C Major and G Major).

supporting voices. Chant arangements of the new Russian school are most accurately regarded as genuinely *polyphonic* works, despite the prevailing homorhythm of the text setting. Whereas in Western-style imitative polyphony the principal and subordinate themes are displaced in time, in Russian polyphony they usually coexist homorhythmically, which, however, does not destroy the hierarchy of their relative importance. The importance of emphasizing the chant melody, in this instance in Kastal'sky's works, was noted by the critic Konstantin Nelidov: "The superior qualities [of the chant arrangements] are manifold, but a certain busyness in the arrangements can be counteracted only by constantly emphasizing the chant melody, and if, contrary to common sense, the conductor were instead to emphasize the undisputedly beautiful accompanying voices, the compositions would be distorted, and the performance would stray from the composer's main purpose—to emphasize only the chant melody."[75] Another article, in the journal *Khorovoe i regentskoe delo*, states: "Nothing serves the artistic aspect in the performance of a choral work more vividly than the distribution of light and shadow, dominance and subordination, tension and restfulness. Often there are passages in which a given voice must be brought out to the foreground. The conductor's task is to find the proper degree of this emphasis."[76]

As noted earlier, many composers indicated the emphasis of various voices by means of dynamic and articulation marks. In the znamennyi chant Dogmatikon in Tone 8 (see ex. 7.20), Nikol'sky clearly identifies the *cantus firmus* and gives it a dynamic level three degrees louder than the supporting voices. A note at the beginning of the opus states that the marcato (*vydeliaia*)

Example 7.20.   Aleksandr Nikol'sky—"*Tsar' nebesnyi*" [The King of heaven]
(Theotokion Dogmatikon in Tone 8), Opus 48, No. 4.
(Arrangement of Znamennyi Chant)

(*...He took flesh from the pure Virgin...*)

marking applies only to the *cantus firmus*. Nikol'sky's Opus 48, from which this excerpt is taken, dates from the years of World War I and displays more sophisticated techniques of rhythmic organization and dynamic nuancing than the majority of works written in the two preceding decades. However, the principle of emphasizing the chant line as it moves from voice to voice must be applied to earlier works as well. As Nikolai Matveev has observed only recently,

> Polyphonic ensemble depends on the relative balance of voices and the emphasis of the voice that carries the main musical theme, which may appear first in one voice, then another, or simultaneously in two voices. Each section of the choir must be able to present a theme in the foreground and then flexibly switch to a secondary or tertiary level of importance. This is a very important aspect of performing works in the [Russian] polyphonic style; the thematic material must always sound prominent.[77]

Syllabic and Recitative Chant

The overwhelming importance of the musically rendered *word* in the Orthodox liturgy has resulted in the enduring importance of recitation (also referred to as liturgical recitative) in Russian church music. The rediscovery of the beauties and thematic potential of great znamennyi chant did not lessen the prominence of recitative chant, which continued to be employed for a great number of hymns. There was, however, a renewed interest in syllabic chants—the little znamennyi, as well as Greek and Kievan chant—whose melodic contour was much more varied than that of the abbreviated "common" or "Court" chants made popular by the L'vov-Bakhmetev *Obikhod.*

The composers of the new Russian choral school began to explore the artistic potential of liturgical recitative, which earlier had been considered the most artless type of church music imaginable. They developed new combinations and forms, such as solo recitation with choral accompaniment (Kastal'sky, Grechaninov), and alternation between solo recitation and chorus (Nikol'sky, Chesnokov), which really was not a new form but a revival of the old practice of "lining out" (canonarching) that had been used in Russian monasteries. Syllabic and recitative chants were dressed up in new and more splendid harmonic attire, exploiting to the utmost the richness and contrasts of choral sonority. Finally, recitative became the object of theoretical exploration, as some composers sought more sophisticated techniques for notating its intricate natural rhythms. The performer of Russian choral music can hardly avoid having to deal practically with recitative chant and its execution, which, as most Russian writers admit, is one of the more complex and difficult aspects of Russian sacred music.

Problems of Rhythm in Syllabic and Recitative Chant

Many of the questions pertaining to the rhythmic structure of neumatic chant apply to syllabic and recitative chant as well. The notation of liturgical recitative in square notes presents the same problems with regard to the relative duration of the note values and the equivalence of these note values in round-note notation. In addition, recitative is often not written in specific note values, but is indicated by an extended *longa* (▬▬▬). The vagueness of the notation and the lack of theoretical understanding of the nature of recitative chant resulted in what Kovin called "a universally widespread attitude of carelessness" with regard to its performance.[78]

Important observations on the rhythmic nature of liturgical recitative were made by Komarov:

> Many believe that our recitative-style church chants have no rhythm because they cannot be divided into proper musical measures . . . ; but this is not so, . . . for these chants exhibit other rhythmic aspects, more important [than the division into regular measures]. . . . [The rhythm] is not that of prose, but of poetry . . . in which the number of feet per line varies and the feet themselves are not identical. For the most part the feet are duple with a stress on the first syllable, but some are triple, also with a stress on the first syllable, or duple with a prolongation of the first syllable—something *resembling* a triplet.[79]

Komarov's use of the term "triplet" (*triol'*), qualified by the word "resembling," referred to a major source of confusion among his contemporaries, who were still struggling against the conventions of regular metric schemes. The term may also be a source of confusion to modern-day performers. (I have encountered similar confusion among Anglican church musicians with regard to the performance of Anglican chant, for example.) Komarov goes to great lengths to explain the term:

> Where the number of syllables in a foot is odd there arise so-called triplets, i.e., three syllables per beat, but these triplets are not performed as in other music: whereas in the latter instance the conductor's beat does not change in its duration, but is merely divided into three equal parts, with the notes of the triplet becoming shorter than notes under a duple beat, [in the chant] the notes of the triplet *retain their constant duration* [my emphasis—V. M.] and the beat is lengthened by one note.[80]

This principle was obviously not followed by some composers of the new Russian school. In the works of Kastal'sky and his contemporaries one finds notated triplets and duplets in which the notes of the recitative change in duration; e.g., in Viktor Kalinnikov's *"Blazhen muzh"* (Blessed is the man) (published No. 22), the change of proportion is clearly indicated by the composer (see ex. 7.21). The most confusing instances occur in the works of Grechaninov (e.g., in the *Liturgy No. 1*, Opus 13) and Nikol'sky (e.g., *"Veruiu"* [Creed], Opus 45, No. 3), where the composers have written *Bez razmera* (Without measure) or *Sine ritmo* and yet mark triplets or other

Example 7.21.   Viktor Kalinnikov—*"Blazhen muzh"* [Blessed is the man], P. N. 22.

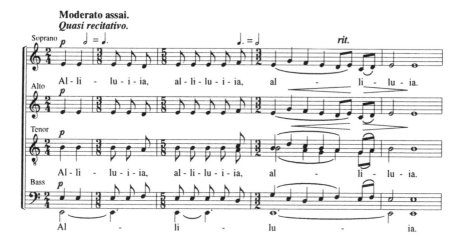

rhythmic groupings (see ex. 7.22). Following Komarov's prescription one should interpret *Sine ritmo* as not having regular meter and not treat the "triplets," "quadruplets," and "quintuplets" as their proportional counterparts in Western music. The specificity of Nikol'sky's notation, however, suggests the opposite interpretation. Nikol'sky's autographs show that he struggled with the question of notating recitative throughout his career, and in his later works developed the notation to a level of great complexity. Other composers evidently decided to leave the matter up to the performer, simply labelling recitative chant passages *"obyknovennym chitkom"* (in the manner of ordinary recitation).

Example 7.22.   Aleksandr Nikol'sky—*"Veruiu"* [I believe], Opus 45, No. 3.

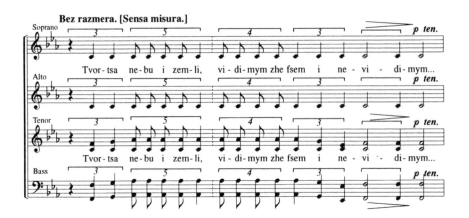

(*...Maker of heaven and earth, and of all things visible and invisible...*)

The rhythmic structure of recitative chant is intimately connected with the problem of conducting it. Most writers around the turn of the century agreed that it should not be conducted one beat to a syllable, although, as the following passages indicate, such a practice was widespread:

> Some conductors . . . give a beat on each syllable of the recitative, but in doing so slow down the proper tempo and deprive the chant of rhythm, since sounds of identical volume and duration have no distinct rhythm. (Komarov)[81]

> In performing [chants with] unsymmetric rhythm . . . one must indicate only the stressed syllables, [and] not attempt to show the movement of each syllable. Only at the beginning of a hymn is it necessary to beat every syllable to establish the rate of motion. (Smolensky)[82]

> [In conducting] the customary tempo of stichera, troparia, and heirmoi, the hand moves *only downward* (in half-notes) or in triple time when such words occur.... In very fast recitative (e.g., the Great Doxology, "We Praise Thee, O God," etc.)... the hand beats *half-notes only downward* (also in triple divisions, as in a fast scherzo). (Kastal'sky)[83]

> The customary practice of showing *every* syllable with a downward motion of the hand is obviously totally unsuitable. In performing recitative at the requisite speed (the average speed of normal human speech, for example, the conductor's hand would meaninglessly flit before the eyes of the choir... [while] in excessively slow singing the beauty, liveliness, and vividness of human speech would disappear. The most useful technique for conducting [recitative chant] chants is one where *entire groups of syllables*, rather than individual syllables are indicated.... To indicate the speed clearly and precisely... the beginning and end of the recitative should be conducted in a [definite beat] pattern, while the middle portion is conducted according to the strong syllables. (Kovin)[84]

Despite this evidence, Nikolai Matveev maintains that the best choirs in pre-Revolutionary Russia developed the following manner of performance, which he calls *chitok*:

> Every syllable of text is performed to a single beat of the conductor conducting "in one." The opening and closing melodic movements of each phrase, which have note values of two or more rhythmic units, are performed strictly in tempo, as the conductor's pulsating motion continues without stopping. Between phrases there should be no breaks. The entire hymn is performed precisely, in tempo, on a [single] "chain" breath. Before the closing phrase a common breath is taken, and the final phrase is performed with some *ritenuto*.[85]

While parts of Matveev's description of chitok are accurate, others are clearly at odds with the historical evidence. At issue are two distinctly different methods of performing recitative chant in terms of rhythmic steadiness: one related to what Matveev is describing (where the pulse, once established, does not vary), and another in which the beginnings and endings of phrases are slower while the middle portion is considerably faster. (Matveev acknowledges that today in the Soviet Union the manner he describes is by no means universal.)

In a conversation with the present writer Matveev identified the rhythmically steady style with Moscow and central Russia and the other style as more characteristic of St. Petersburg and western regions of Russia. However, the former style was also practiced by the Imperial Court Chapel, judging from the following description by Kompaneisky: "We are familiar with the rhythms of plain Court Chant in which all syllables with the exception of stops are equal; this rhythm reminds one of the monotonous clatter of a train engine piston rather than live human speech, much less prayer."[86] To this mechanical singing Kompaneisky contrasts the singing of the Alexander Nevsky Lavra Choir under Yakov Ternov (he does not describe the latter, however), which is one of the "best choirs" Matveev mentions in describing chitok. Matveev's own recordings with the Choir of the "Joy of All the Sorrowful" Church very closely resemble Kompaneisky's unflattering description of the Imperial Chapel.

Evidently rhythmic steadiness by itself is not sufficient to achieve the desired style. According to Komarov, "the shorter notes [of the recitative chant] are not identical in volume, but the first [in a group] of two or three is stronger than the others, although the degree of [relative] loudness... is so slight that in some instances these accents become unnoticeable."[87] Moreover, liturgical recitative is not mono-dynamic. To cite Komarov once again,

> The proper performance of [recitative] chant... requires certain nuances, which... should not be executed mechanically, but in relation to the musical sense of the melody and the text of the hymn.
>
> [Chants] should be performed within certain [dynamic] limits, i.e., not reach *ff* or *pp*, which would be contrary to the simplicity of their structure; furthermore, the increases and decreases in volume should be gradual.
>
> Each phrase of a chant has two main musical stresses: one on the syllable having a textual accent closest to the beginning of the phrase, and a second on the syllable having a textual accent closest to the ending of the phrase.... These main stresses in most melodies are marked by a note twice as long (rarely longer) than the other notes of the recitative....[88]

Komarov's description also contradicts Matveev's assertion that entire hymns in recitative style are to be sung on a single, "patched" breath, which serves to grip the listener's or worshiper's attention in a state of compelling concentration. According to Komarov, "the long note on the last syllable of the phrase... is necessary... both to separate one phrase from the next and to take a breath. It differs from the other two long notes in that it is sung without a *crescendo* in the voice, as required by the other two, and also in that it bears an accent only in isolated instances...."[89]

On the other hand, Matveev's statement concerning the steadiness of the rhythmic pulse is corroborated by several statements in turn-of-the-century sources:

> One must see to it that the syllables of the words flow evenly; the hand moves evenly as well, as if there were measures. (Kastal'sky)[90]
>
> The freedom [of recitative chant] does not constitute... a violation of rhythm. The singing of church chants without measuredness leads to unevenness and irregularity, which in turn destroys the unique beauty of their characteristic rhythm.... Therefore, [the conductor] must not allow a lack of rhythmic definition, but [must] establish the basic duple motion quite clearly for himself and the performers.... (Nikol'sky)[91]
>
> The performance of plain chant must not be too drawn out. It must also not be sung monotonously, uniformly, or "chopped," depriving the verbal rhythm of its natural flexibility....

Marking each group [of syllables] or, what is essentially the same thing, each strong syllable, the conductor maintains the necessary speed. . . . Between the strong syllables the choir performs the passages of text on its own, with the same freedom and flexibility as in common speech, [but] adhering to the rhythm and tempo that the conductor established at the very beginning. . . (Kovin)[92]

In summary, the proper way of performing recitative chant (at least in the works of Moscow composers) is the one described by Matveev, but with some added refinements. Though the pulse must be steady, the articulation of syllables must be differentiated, with greater musical stress on accented syllables. This differentiation is aided when the conductor indicates only strong syllables in his beat; it cannot be easily achieved by giving constant downbeats on every syllable as Matveev suggests.

The evidence from old gramophone recordings with regard to the performance of recitative is inconclusive, since most choirs preferred to record more elaborate compositions rather than plain chant. One recording, *"Gospodi, vozzvakh"* [Lord, I call] in Tone 1, by Vasil'ev's Choir of Moscow,[93] matches Matveev's description exactly with its absolute steadiness of pulse, no common breaths, and strict proportionality of note values. Another recording, the Troparion *"Spasi, Gospodi"* [O Lord, save Thy people] in Tone 1, by the Mariinsky Opera Chorus under Kazachenko,[94] goes to the opposite extreme: long, drawn out melodic notes at the beginnings and endings of phrases, an unsteady pulse in the intervening recitative (with more or less acceleration depending on the length of the text), and abrupt breaths at the ends of phrases. A recording of Arkhangel'sky conducting his recitative-style composition *"Voskresenie Khristovo videvshe"* [Having beheld the Resurrection of Christ],[95] resembles Vasil'ev's performance except for occasional common breaths at the ends of phrases and fermatas on certain important syllables (yet Arkhangel'sky was the quintessential representative of the St. Petersburg, as opposed to Muscovite, style).

With only three examples, none of them by the Moscow Synodal Choir or the Imperial Court Chapel, it is risky to draw any definite conclusions or to assert that there were significant regional distinctions between Moscow and St. Petersburg. Though composers were in the process of formulating theoretical and technical standards of recitative performance, in practice a number of individual interpretations existed.

Problems of Tempo in Recitative

Kovin's claim that recitative should be sung at the speed of "everyday speech," aside from not being very useful, does not agree with evidence from scores, recordings, and other sources. Table 7.2 shows a number of tempos observed by Komarov for various categories of hymns in different Tones. Within these

Table 7.2.   Tempos for Liturgical Recitative according to Komarov

Chant	Tone	Hymn Type	M.M. per Syllable
Little Znamennyi or Common	8	Stichera	120
"	1, 6, 7	"	180
"	2, 3	"	180–240
"	5	"	240+
Greek	8	Troparia	120+
"	4	"	240
Common	1	Antiphons at Liturgy	240
"	4	Heirmoi	240

tempos there is some flexibility, says Komarov, but the relationships among the various Tones remain basically the same.[96]

Another source of metronome markings for recitative chant is Tchaikovsky's *Vigil.* While it is not necessary to list the tempos in detail, the following general observations may be made:

1. The tempo per syllable in the Vesper Psalms "Lord, I Call" in Kievan Chant ranges from 168 to 176
2. The tempo of Dismissal Troparia in Greek Chant ranges from 144 to 200
3. Other recitative-style hymns range from 152 per syllable— "*Voskresenie Khristovo videvshe*" (Having beheld the Resurrection of Christ) in Greek Chant, to 224 per syllable—"*Blagosloven esi, Gospodi*" (Blessed art Thou, O Lord) in little znamennyi chant.

Scattered metronome markings for recitative chant appear in the works of Chesnokov—♩ = 88, 104, 120 (i.e., 176, 208, 240 per syllable) and Kastal'sky—♩ = 82, 84, 100 (164, 168, 200 per syllable).

On the basis of the above evidence one arrives at some general guidelines for determining the tempo of liturgical recitative. The first factor to consider is whether the chant is syllabic or recitative. The former tends to move slightly slower, within a range of 120 to approximately 200 per syllable, while the latter most often proceeds at a tempo of 200 to 240 or more per syllable.

Obviously, a major consideration must be the nature of the text and the liturgical context: e.g., hymns of Holy Week would be sung more slowly than similar melodies at Paschal Matins. Finally, one must determine the tempo at which the text can be delivered clearly and sensibly, bearing in mind the rhythmic qualities described above. At a tempo much faster than 240 per syllable it becomes difficult to preserve the clarity of articulation upon which the rhythmic character of recitative chant depends.

Although the evidence from scores and other sources is often quite specific, the recordings from the period generally do not reflect the tempos outlined above, but are much slower, as table 7.3 shows. Just as a tempo faster than 240 makes it difficult to execute the essential rhythmic qualities of recitative, all rhythmic interest is lost at the extremely slow tempos heard on these recordings. Yet Vasil'ev's tempo almost exactly matches the tempo Matveev specifies for chitok: 120 per syllable.[98] The only recording of recitative chant by Morozov's Old Believers' Choir under Tsvetkov, a Paschal sticheron in little znamennyi chant, proceeds at a tempo of 176 to 184 per syllable.[99]

Table 7.3. Tempos of Recitative on Pre-Revolutionary Recordings

Performers	Title	Performance tempo	Tempo acc. to Komarov
Vasil'ev's Choir	"Gospodi, vozzvakh" (Tone 1)	116	180
Mariinsky Opera Chorus	"Spasi, Gospodi, liudi Tvoia" (Tone 1)	132	240
Arkhangel'sky's Choir	"Voskresenie Khristovo" by Arkhangel'sky	116	120
			Composer's marking
Yukhov's Choir[97]	"Voskresenie Khristovo" by Tchaikovsky	56–60	84

Soloists in Church Singing

As harmonic part-singing became established in the Russian Church, the old rubrical prescriptions calling for certain hymns to be performed either by a soloist entirely or by a soloist with choral refrains became largely neglected. Some hymns formerly sung by a soloist, e.g., *"Da ispravitsia"* [Let my prayer arise] at the Lenten Liturgy of Pre-Sanctified Gifts; *"Chertog Tvoi"* [Thy bridal chamber], the Exaposteilarion at Matins on Monday, Tuesday, and

Wednesday of Holy Week; and *"Razboinika blagorazumnago"* [The wise thief], the Exaposteilarion at the Matins of Holy Friday, began to be composed for solo trio. Soloists within each section also became integral to the solo-tutti texture of sacred concertos from the eighteenth century to the mid-nineteenth century. Another form that entered with Western influence was the solo aria with choral accompaniment. At the zenith of the Italian influence such arias were set to virtually all liturgical texts, often adapted from Western operas and oratorios, with the voices singing the orchestral parts.

Obviously such uses of soloists had nothing in common with the traditional role of the solo voice in Orthodox church singing. By the end of the nineteenth century the traditional "division of labor" between solo and chorus remained only in the responsorial exchanges between the ekphonesis of the clergy and the singing of the choir. But with the passage of time even the ekphonesis lost most of its elaborate melodic nature, becoming reduced to recitation on one or two pitches.

The composers of the new Russian school retained the later uses of the solo voice (i.e., trios, arias, soli-tutti), but also made efforts to reintroduce some of the more ancient traditions of solo singing, most notably, the practice of canonarching or "lining out" that had once been prominent in Russian monasteries. Chesnokov and Grechaninov also attempted to integrate the diverse musical elements of the liturgy into a single artistic whole by composing the solo passages of ekphonesis for the clergy.

The directions left by composers concerning the performance of solos reflect the diversity of their personalities and their often subjective approaches to sacred choral composition. Some composers, particularly Kastal'sky, drew distinctions between the style of solo singing appropriate for church and the theatrical, secular style that had become firmly entrenched during the Italianate era. Kastal'sky's concern for preserving the spirit of the liturgy is reflected in the directions he wrote for soloists in his works, e.g.: "The composer requests that the baritone solo be performed as austerely and simply as possible, and with good sonority. So-called singing with emotion is entirely inappropriate here. (*'Nyne otpushchaeshi'* No. 1 [Lord, now lettest Thou] [published No. 48])." One anonymous reviewer wrote concerning this solo: "The more austerely and dispassionately the solo is performed, the more the work will benefit, since to concern oneself with 'expression' in the commonly accepted sense of the term is entirely inappropriate: what is required is the mood of an inspired prophet who has renounced everything earthly and sees the heavens opening before him."[100] For his *"Nyne otpushchaeshi"* No. 2 (published No. 49), Kastal'sky gave the following instructions: "The tenor solo should be performed simply, without succumbing to emotionalism." Elsewhere Kastal'sky wrote: "[Our church music] may contain unisons and solos, but not such as amateurs delight in. The ideal church solo is the inspired improvisation of the ancient singers of the psalter."[101] Only two of

78. Uspensky, *Drevne-russkoe*, p. 253.

79. I. Zabelin, *Domashnii byt russkikh tsarei v XVI i XVII stoletiiakh* [The domestic life of Russian tsars in the XVI and XVII centuries], vol. I, pt. 1, 4th ed. (Moscow: n.p., 1918), p. 407; cited in Gardner, *Bogosluzhebnoe*, 2:85.

80. As Gardner points out, as yet there exists no complete list of Russian liturgical manuscripts contained in Soviet and Western libraries. The two most extensive anthologies of Russian staffless notations, Metallov's *Russkaia simiografiia* and Smolensky's *Paleograficheskii atlas* [Palaeographischer Atlas der altrussischen linienlosen Gesangsnotationen] (reprint ed., Munich: 1976), contain numerous facsimiles of manuscripts, but do not indicate the size of the originals.

81. The writer wishes to thank Nicolas Schidlovsky, who worked with these manuscripts in the USSR under the auspices of a Fulbright Fellowship, for the information in table 1.

82. I. Kudriavtsev, ed., *Rukopisnye sobraniia D. V. Razumovskogo i V. F. Odoevskogo; arkhiv D. V. Razumovskogo* [The manuscript collections of D. V. Razumovsky and V. F. Odoevsky; the archive of D. V. Razumovsky] (Moscow: Gosudarstvennaia Biblioteka Imeni V. I. Lenina, 1960).

83. Stepan Smolensky, "O sobranii russkikh drevne-pevcheskikh rukopisei v Moskovskom Sinodal'nom Uchilishche Tserkovnogo Peniia" [The collection of ancient-Russian chant manuscripts in the Moscow Synodal School of Church Singing], *Russkaia muzykal'naia gazeta* 13 (1899):401.

84. Aleksandr Mezenets, "Izveshchenie o soglasneishikh pometakh" [A report on the most consonant markings], in Rogov, *Muzykal'naia*, p. 100; see also Vincent Peterson, "The Azbuka of Alexander Mezenets: A Preliminary Study in Znamenny Chant," (M. Div. thesis, St. Vladimir's Orthodox Theological Seminary, 1981).

Chapter 2

1. Antonin Preobrazhensky, *Kul'tovaia muzyka v Rossii* [The music of the cult in Russia] (Leningrad: Academia, 1924), p. 46.

2. Simon Azar'in and Ivan Nasedka, "Zhitie i podvigi arkhimandrita Dionisiia" [The life and exploits of Archimandrite Dionisy], in A. Rogov, ed., *Muzykal'naia estetika Rossii XI–XVII vekov* [Musical aesthetics of Russia in the 11th through 17th centuries] (Moscow: Muzyka, 1973), pp. 68–70.

3. Evfrosin (the Monk), "Skazanie o razlichnykh eresiakh" [The history of various heresies], in Rogov, *Muzykal'naia*, pp. 73–74.

4. Nikolai Findeizen, *Ocherki po istorii muzyki v Rossii* [Essays in the history of music in Russia], vol. 1 (Moscow-Leningrad: Gosudarstvennoe Muzykal'noe Izdatel'stvo, 1928), p. 184.

5. Ioann Korenev, "Predislovie k 'Grammatike musikiiskoi'" [Foreword to *Grammatika musikiiskaia*], in Rogov, *Muzykal'naia*, pp. 126–27.

6. In 1596, a group of Orthodox hierarchs agreed to recognize the canonical authority of the Pope of Rome, while retaining Eastern Orthodox liturgical rites. This brought about a bitter division between the *unia* (as the splinter group came to be called) and the stalwart adherents to Eastern Orthodox ecclesiastical authority.

7. Pylyp Kozyts'skyi, *Spiv i muzyka v kyivs'kii akademii za 300 rokiv ii isnuvannia* [Singing and music in the Kievan Academy in the 300 years since its founding] (Kiev: Muzychna Ukraina, 1971), p. 16. Kozyts'kyi quotes from the *Pamiatniki Kievskogo Bogoiavlenskogo Bratstva* [Monuments of the Kievan Brotherhood of the Theophany] (Kiev: n.p., 1846), p. 38.

8. Somewhat ironically, the curriculum followed the classic plan of a Western liberal arts education, consisting of the *trivium* (grammar, rhetoric, and logic) and the *quadrivium* (arithmetic, geometry, astronomy, and music). In 1632 the Kievan Brotherhood School was combined with the academy of the Kievo-Pechersk Monastery to become a *collegium*—the first institution of higher learning in Eastern Slavdom.

9. Cited in Kozyts'kyi, *Spiv*, p. 21.

10. Cited in I. Malyshevsky, *Melety Pigas* (Kiev: n.p., 1872), p. 89; a similar request was made to the Alexandrian Patriarch Cyril Lukakis in 1614 by the L'vov brotherhood. See Kozyts'kyi, *Spiv*, p. 109, n. 21.

11. Dmitri Razumovsky, *Tserkovnoe penie v Rossii* [Church singing in Russia], vol. 1 (Moscow: n.p., 1867), p. 81; see also, *Arkhiv Iuzhnoi i Zapadnoi Rusi* [Archive of South and West Russia], vol. 1, no. 133 (n. p.), p. 142. The political hegemony of Roman Catholic nations increased the channels for a free flow of trade, travel, and cultural influences. One of the elders and teachers of the L'vov Brotherhood, a Ukrainianized Greek merchant named Konstantin Mezapeti (d. 1650) owned numerous editions of German, Italian, and other Western European music printers, including a treatise on harmony entitled *Tabulatura musices*. As early as 1601, the library of the L'vov Brotherhood contained an instructional treatise by Johann Spangenberg entitled *Questiones musicae in usum scholae Northusanae, oder wie man die Jugend leichtlich und recht im Singen unterweisen soll*, published in Wittemberg in 1542. See Ia. Isaevych, "Bratstva i ukrains'ka muzychna kul'tura XVI–XVII st." [The brotherhoods and Ukrainian musical culture of the 16th and 17th centuries], *Ukrains'ke muzykoznavstvo*, no. 6 (Kiev: Muzychna Ukraina, 1971), p. 50.

12. Kozyts'skyi believes that the square-note "Kievan" notation developed indigenously in southwestern Russia (see *Spiv*, p. 26), on the grounds that the note shapes are "unlike those used in the systems of Guido [d'Arezzo] or Jean de Muris." However, Kozyts'skyi based his observations on the arguments of Razumovsky, who erroneously placed Muris's lifetime at least two centuries later! (Razumovsky, *Tserkovnoe*, p. 85.)

13. Antonin Preobrazhensky, "Ot uniatskogo kanta do pravoslavnoi kheruvimskoi" [From a uniate *kant* to an Orthodox Cherubic Hymn], *Muzykal'nyi sovremennik* (February 1916):11–28.

14. Isaevich, "Bratstva," p. 52. By 1627 the library register of the Lutsk Brotherhood listed "two old part compositions (*partesy*) for the church à 5, three part compositions à 6, and old *osmoglasnyi* compositions," i.e., from the *Osmoglasnik* (the *Octoechos*), or, according to another interpretation, à 8. Kozytskyi suggests that the composer of these works may have been one Pavlo, a teacher of music at the Lutsk Brotherhood School. By 1697 the register of the L'vov Brotherhood School library listed three hundred seventy-three works, ranging in complexity from three to twelve voices. A complete register is found in *Ukrains'ke muzykoznavstvo*, no. 6, Appendix I, pp. 245–49.

15. *Arkhiv*, pp. 435–39; cited in Kozyts'kyi, *Spiv*, p. 31.

16. Kozyts'kyi, *Spiv*, p. 31.

17. Isaevich, "Bratstva," p. 49.

18. Kozyts'kyi, *Spiv,* p. 31.

19. Ibid.

20. Ivan Gardner, *Bogosluzhebnoe penie Russkoi Pravoslavnoi Tserkvi* [The Liturgical chant of the Russian Orthodox Church], vol. 2 (Jordanville, N. Y.: Holy Trinity Monastery, 1980–82), pp. 277–78.

21. The term Greek Singing may refer either to the type of singing practiced at that time in the Greek Orthodox Churches of the Mediterranean, or to Greek Chant (*grecheskii rospev*), a russified, diatonic body of chant written down in southwestern Russia from Greek singers in the sixteenth or seventeenth centuries. Upon becoming patriarch, Nikon invited the Greek deacon Meletios to teach genuine Greek singing to the Tsar's and Patriarchal Clerics. Further research is needed into the nature of Graeco-Byzantine singing of the seventeenth century to determine whether this contact with Greek liturgical chant left any permanent traces in Russia.

22. Ioann Shusherin, "Izvestie o rozhdenii i vospitanii i o zhitii sviateishego Nikona, Patriarkha Moskovkogo i vseia Rossii" [An account of the birth, upbringing, and life of His Beatitude, Nikon, Patriarch of Moscow and All Russia], in Rogov, *Muzykal'naia,* p. 81.

23. Kozyts'kyi, *Spiv,* p. 74.

24. K. Kharlampovich, *Zapadnorusskie pravoslavnye shkoly XVI i nachala XVII v.* [Western-Russian Orthodox schools of the 16th and early 17th centuries] (Kazan': n.p., 1898), p. 74; cited in Kozyts'kyi, *Spiv,* p. 75.

25. E.g., Feodor Rtishchev, who established the Andreevsky Monastery in Moscow, "invited from Kiev and the holy Pechersk Lavra and from the Mezhigorsky and other Little Russian monasteries, fifty monks, well-versed in the [monastic] life, [liturgical] order, church singing, and the rule [of private prayer]; see Kharlampovich, p. 125.

26. E.g., in 1662, eight Kievan singers appealed to Tsar Aleksei in the following words: "In recent years, O Tsar, . . . our land has been torn by civil war, and our fathers, mothers, and brethren have been taken into slavery by the [Crimean] Tatars, and we have been left after them and the Poles totally ruined and insulted; not wishing to compromise our Christian faith, we have escaped Polish persecution under [the protection of] your Imperial name for permanent settlement and service in body and soul, knowing of your unutterable Imperial mercy towards us orphans." Cited by Vukol Undol'sky, *Zamechaniia dlia istorii tserkovnogo peniia v Rossii* [Comments on the history of church singing in Russia] (Moscow: n.p., 1864), p. 26.

27. Kozyts'skyi, *Spiv,* p. 76.

28. Preobrazhensky, "Ot uniatskogo," pp. 12–13.

29. Stepan Smolensky, *"Musikiiskaia grammatika" Nikolaia Diletskogo* [Nikolai Diletsky's "Musical grammar"], transcription and commentary, (St. Petersburg: n.p., 1910), p. 178. A facsimile edition of a manuscript copy from 1723 was published recently: Mykola Dyletsky, *Grammatika muzykal'na* (Kiev: Muzychna Ukraina, 1971).

30. The term "concerto" in Russian sacred choral music underwent several changes of meaning. Initially, when Western-style part singing was first introduced, it referred to a specific compositional device, in which solo voices or groups of soloists were pitted against the entire vocal ensemble (tutti), much as in Baroque instrumental works written in concertato style. In the *partesnyi* singing of the late seventeenth and early eighteenth

centuries, the concerto style was used for various sung portions of the liturgy, as well as for nonliturgical texts selected from the psalms or composed for specific occasions (see n. 72 below).

As the eighteenth century progressed, the term "concerto" increasingly came to be applied to extended compositions, sometimes several movements in length, that were sung by the choir while the clergy were taking communion in the altar. Although these works still tended to use soli-tutti contrasts, they now were composed in a contrapuntal motet-like style of eighteenth-century Italian music. Throughout the nineteenth and into the twentieth century, "concerto" continued to designate a composition, on either a liturgical or nonliturgical sacred text, sung during the communion of the clergy. The concerto was always performed by unaccompanied voices.

31. Preobrazhensky, "Ot uniatskogo," pp. 13–14.

32. Cited in Preobrazhensky, "Ot uniatskogo," p. 13.

33. E.g., Protopopov argues that *partesnyi* singing arose in northern Russia at least as early as the 1630s or 1640s, and was cultivated not only in Moscow, but in numerous cathedrals and monasteries far removed from the capital (see Vladimir Protopopov, *Muzyka na poltavskuiu pobedu* [Music for the Poltava victory], in *Monuments of Russian Music*, vol. 2 (Moscow: Muzyka, 1971), p. 234). At the same time, he admits that "the materials dealing with the history of the Russian *partesnyi* style are still too dispersed to enable one to draw a complete picture of its dissemination in Russia."

34. Another treatise frequently cited is Ioann Korenev's *Musikiia*, which is nothing more than a preface to the 1681 version of Diletsky's treatise, and contains little original material. See Rogov, *Muzykal'naia*, pp. 124–30.

35. Cited in Nikolai Uspensky, *Drevne-russkoe pevcheskoe iskusstvo* [The early Russian art of singing], 2nd ed. (Moscow: Sovetskii Kompozitor, 1971), p. 333.

36. Ibid., p. 343.

37. Protopopov, *Muzyka*, p. 228, n. 1.

38. E.g., Court ledgers for 1682 show that thirty-five singers were attached to serve the co-Tsars Ivan and Peter, while thirty-eight were divided among the Tsarinas Natalia (Peter's mother) and Marfa (Tsar Feodor's widow), and a number of Tsarevnas (sisters and aunts of the Tsars); cited in Protopopov, p. 228.

39. I. Kudriavtsev, ed., *Rukopisnye sobraniia D. V. Razumovskogo i V. F. Odoevskogo; arkhiv D. V. Razumovskogo* [The manuscript collections of D. V. Razumovsky and V. F. Odoevsky; the archive of D. V. Razumovsky] (Moscow: Gosudarstvennaia Biblioteka Imeni V. I. Lenina, 1960), pp. 125–28.

40. From N. Gerasimova-Persyds'ka, *Khorovyi kontsert na Ukraini v XVII–XVIII st.* [The choral concerto in the Ukraine in the XVII–XVIII centuries] (Kiev: Muzychna Ukraina, 1978).

41. Findeizen, *Ocherki*, p. 285.

42. Ibid., p. 277.

43. Olearius, cited in Findeisen, *Ocherki*, p. 276.

44. Protopopov lists no fewer than forty-eight composers of *partesnyi* music who flourished between the last two decades of the seventeenth century and the first half of the eighteenth century; see *Muzyka*, p. 234.

45. The chanters came to be designated by the term *d'iachok*, a diminutive form of *d'iak*, which has a disrespectful or pejorative connotation. (See chapter 1, n. 71.)

46. Cited in Antonin Preobrazhensky, "Iz pervykh let partesnogo peniia v Moskve" [From the first years of *partesnyi* singing in Moscow], *Muzykal'nyi sovremennik* 3 (November 1914):36.

47. Gardner recalls hearing this type of performance in his youth (1910s); see *Russian Church Singing*, vol. 1: *Orthodox Worship and Hymnography*, trans. by Vladimir Morosan (Crestwood, N.Y.: St. Vladimir's Seminary Press, 1980), p. 102.

48. Gardner, *Bogosluzhebnoe*, p. 169.

49. Ibid., 2:169-70.

50. Nikolai Uspensky, "A Wreath on the Grave of Dmitry Stepanovich Bortnyansky," *Journal of the Moscow Patriarchate* (1975), pp. 63ff.

51. A transcription of the full score appears in Protopopov, *Muzyka*, pp. 140-79.

52. Vasily Metallov, "Sinodal'nye, byvshie patriarshie pevchie" [The synodal, formerly the patriarchal singers], *Russkaia muzykal'naia gazeta* 10 (1898):1047.

53. Cited in Izrail' Gusin and Donat Tkachev, *Gosudarstvennaia akademicheskaia kapella imeni M. I. Glinki* [The State Academic Choir named in honor of M. I. Glinka] (Leningrad: Gosudarstvennoe Muzykal'noe Izdatel'stvo, 1957), p. 20.

54. K. Maiburova, "Glukhivs'ka shkola pivchykh XVIII st. ta ii rol' u rozvytku muzychnogo profesionalizmu na Ukraini ta v Rossii" [The Glukhov singing school in the XVIII century and its role in the development of musical professionalism in the Ukraine and in Russia], *Ukrains'ke muzykoznavstvo*, no. 6, p. 133.

55. The term *regent*, taken from the Latin, came to signify the conductor of a church ensemble, replacing the terms *domestik* and *golovshchik*, which were used before the mid-seventeenth century. Although it was probably used earlier in the Ukraine, the first documented occurrence of the term in Russia dates from about 1673: Simeon Pekalitsky is called "arkhiepiskopa Lazariia Baranovicha byvshii muzykiiskii reent [*sic*]" (the former musical *reent* of Archbishop Lazar' Baranovich). In Russia the term *regent* was for some time used interchangeably with the term *ustavshchik*: e.g., Ivan Protopopov, who was the conductor of the Court Choir from 1723 to 1729, bore the official title of *ustavshchik*. However, in 1725, one Ivan Popovsky (possibly the same person) refers to himself as *regent* of the Court Chapel. In 1760, the singer Grigory Khudiakov petitioned to be appointed *ustavshchik* and *regent* of the Moscow Synodal Choir. Thereafter, the latter term became universally applied to conductors of church choirs, although some church choirs even today in the Soviet Union have an *ustavshchik*—a person particularly well-versed in the complexities of the *ustav* (the use). Since the term *regent* specifically denotes a church choir conductor, it will hereafter be translated as "precentor" in this study.

56. Cited in V. Eingorn, *Ocherk iz istorii Malorossii XVIII v.* [An essay in the history of Malorossiia of the XVIII century] (Moscow: n.p., 1899), p. 892.

57. Gusin and Tkachev, *Gosudarstvennaia akademicheskaia kapella*, p. 21.

58. Jakob von Stählin (1712-85), a native of Memminheim, Germany, was invited to Russia in 1735 as a linguist and translator. He spent the remainder of his life in Russia as a newspaper editor, publicist, and theater critic. His "Nachrichten von der Musik in Russland," a very informative account of music in eighteenth-century Russia, appeared in *Haygold's Beylagen zu dem unveränderten Russland* (St. Petersburg: n.p., 1767-68); Russian translation in *Russkaia muzykal'naia gazeta* 11 (1902):322-25.

59. Stählin, cited in Antonin Preobrazhensky, "Pridvornaia kapella 150 let nazad" [The court chapel 150 years ago], *Russkaia muzykal'naia gazeta* 11 (1902):324.

60. Metallov "Sinodal'nye," col. 1047; the opera in question, staged for Empress Anna's birthday, was Francesco Araja's *Il finto Nino, overo la Semiramida riconosciuta.*

61. Gusin and Tkachev, *Gosudarstvennaia akademicheskaia kapella,* p. 16.

62. Stählin, "Nachrichten," cited in Razumovsky, *Tserkovnoe,* 2:225.

63. Metallov, "Sinodal'nye," col. 1048.

64. Stählin, "Nachrichten," col. 323.

65. Ibid., col. 324.

66. Preobrazhensky, *Kul'tovaia,* p. 73.

67. Gusin and Tkachev, *Gosudarstvennaia akademicheskaia kapella,* p. 22.

68. Stählin, "Nachrichten," col. 324.

69. The greater part of the Imperial Chapel's archives was destroyed by fire in 1828.

70. Gusin and Tkachev, *Gosudarstvennaia akademicheskaia kapella,* p. 21.

71. The sacred works written by composers such as Galuppi and Sarti for the Roman Catholic Church were, in most instances, considerably more restrained in style than their works for the Orthodox liturgy. Sacred composition in the West was governed by distinctions between the *stile antico* and the *stile moderno.* However, no similar guidelines existed concerning writing for the Orthodox Church—the Italians were breaking completely new ground.

72. E.g., a text from the brief reign of Emperor Peter III (reigned 1762-63) reads: "Rejoice, exult, thunder joyfully, O Russia, for your God is with you; His most holy grace is magnified in you: for He has blessed you today with a holy and gracious monarch, in whom rests your true hope for your eternal blessings." Cited in Preobrazhensky, *Kul'tovaia,* p. 72.

73. Cited in Gusin and Tkachev, *Gosudarstvennaia akademicheskaia kapella,* p. 17.

74. Ibid., p. 20.

75. Gardner, *Bogosluzhebnoe,* p. 252.

76. Stählin, "Nachrichten," col. 322-23.

77. Payment records from 1710 show that the forty members of the Patriarchal Clerics all received approximately the same salary. Had there been boys in the ensemble, their salaries would have been considerably lower, but would have been supplemented by room and board.

78. *Opisanie dokumentov i del khraniashchikhsia v arkhive sviateishego Pravitel'stvuiushchego Sinoda* [Inventory of documents and cases found in the archive of the Most Holy Ruling Synod], vol. 1 (St. Petersburg: n.p., 1868), p. CCCIV; cited in Gardner, *Bogosluzhebnoe,* p. 143.

79. Metallov, "Sinodal'nye," p. 37.

80. *Delo arkhiva sinodal'noi kontory* [Cases in the archive of the Synodal Chancery], cited by Metallov, *Russkaia muzykal'naia gazeta* 19/20 (1901):513.

81. Although the terms *sopranist* and *altist* sometimes refer to castrati in Western European practice, there is no evidence that castrati participated in Russian church choirs of the eighteenth century. The terms, adopted from Italian, most likely referred to boys, although in some cases, particularly in monastic choirs, the alto part was sung by adult men in falsetto.

82. *Delo*, cited by Metallov, col. 518.

83. In 1685, Metropolitan Simeon of Smolensk was reprimanded by Patriarch Ioakim for cultivating singing "unlike that of other archbishops, . . . polyphonic and not of the Russian consonance," to which Simeon replied that the Patriarch would do well to first eliminate such *partesnyi* singing in Moscow churches if he considered it unsuitable; see Rogov, *Muzykal'naia*, pp. 160–61.

84. Findeizen, *Ocherki*, 2:XIV, n. 70.

85. Ibid., 2:XIX–XX, n. 91.

86. Preobrazhensky, *Kul'tovaia*, p. 75.

87. Cited in Ibid., p. 71.

88. "Vospominaniia E. F. Timkovskogo" [The memoirs of E. F. Timkovsky], *Kievskaia Starina* (April 1894) 11; cited in Gardner, *Bogosluzhebnoe*, p. 229.

89. Gardner points out that, although the Orthodox Church never had a canonical prohibition against women singing in church, several factors effectively prevented women from participating in church singing. First, women could not receive clerical orders, which excluded them at the time when all singing was performed by ordained singers. Also, in many countries women and men traditionally stood in church separately, so for them to stand together on the *kliros*, in plain view of the congregation, would have been considered improper. (When Russian church choirs were moved to a rear gallery, the latter consideration was no longer an obstacle. The requirement that all singers be ordained was also relaxed or eliminated entirely in many churches.) See *Bogosluzhebnoe*, p. 228.

90. Unidentified writer quoted in Preobrazhensky, *Kul'tovaia*, p. 70.

91. Pyotr Tikhov, "Pis'mo neizvestnogo liubitelia tserkovnogo blagolepiia k rektoru Moskovskoi Dukhovnoi Akademii" [A letter from an anonymous defender of church propriety to the Rector of the Moscow Theological Academy], *Muzykal'nyi truzhennik* 1 (1908):5. (For full text, see *Chteniia Obshchestva Istorii i Drevnostei Rossiiskikh* [Readings of the Society of History and Russian Antiquities], n.p.

92. Extremely low bass voices, *bassi profundi*, often sang an octave below the notated pitch; hence they were called "octavists" (*oktavisty*). The origins of this practice are not clear. Although Nikolai Uspensky suggests that it goes back to the period of *strochnyi* polyphony in the sixteenth and early seventeenth centuries, his hypothesis is open to question. It is more likely that the practice arose in the eighteenth century, when Italian composers transferred the stylistic features of the reigning instrumental style (including the doubling of the bass line by cellos and double basses) to the realm of unaccompanied choral music. (See also chapter 4, pages 152–54.)

93. This style was thoroughly rejected both by critics and by serious choral musicians in Russia; however, vestiges of it still remain today in the sound and manner of some Soviet "academic" choirs and many choirs in Russian émigré circles.

94. Preobrazhensky, "Pridvornaia kapella," col. 324.

95. Holy Synod decree No. 4853, dated 22 December 1804; cited in Uspensky, "A Wreath," pp. 63–78.

96. Uspensky, "A Wreath," p. 65.

97. Stepan Smolensky, "Pamiati D. S. Bortnianskogo" [D. S. Bortniansky, in memoriam] *Russkaia muzykal'naia gazeta* 39 (1901):917–25.

98. Uspensky, "A Wreath," p. 66.

99. As Gardner points out, the Court Chant can be characterized as an unsystematic conglomeration of greatly simplified and abbreviated melodies from various other chant systems (mostly from Kievan and Greek chant), as well as melodies of unknown origin. The latest of all Russian chants, it arose between the 1740s and 1800 entirely within the Imperial Chapel, where it was performed in simple improvised harmony. See Gardner, *Russian Church Singing*, 1:110–11.

100. Cited in Findeizen, *Ocherki*, 2:XL, n. 299.

101. Gusin and Tkachev, *Gosudarstvennaia akademicheskaia kapella*, p. 26.

102. P. Chizhevsky, *Tserkovno-grazhdanskie postanovleniia o tserkovnom penii* [Church and civil legislation concerning church singing] (Kharkov: n.p., 1878), pp. 6–7; cited in Gardner, *Bogosluzhebnoe*, 2:269.

103. Preobrazhensky, *Kul'tovaia*, p. 69.

Chapter 3

1. See, e.g., R. Sterling Beckwith, "Aleksandr Dmitrievich Kastal'skii (1856–1926) and the Search for a Native Russian Choral Style" (Ph. D. diss., Cornell University, 1969); Ivan Gardner, *Bogosluzhebnoe penie Russkoi Pravoslavnoi Tserkvi: Sistema, sushchnost', istorii* [The liturgical chant of the Russian Orthodox Church: Its system, essence, and history, vol. 2] (Jordanville, N. Y.: Holy Trinity Monastery, 1980–82), pp. 121–591 passim.

2. Paul Einbeck, *Zur Geschichte des koenigliches Domchors in Berlin* (Berlin: 1893); cited in Ivan Gardner, "Aleksei Feodorovich L'vov," *Pravoslavnyi put'* (Jordanville, N. Y., 1970), pp. 124–34.

3. Cited in Daniil Lokshin, *Zamechatel'nye russkie khory i ikh dirizhery* [Outstanding Russian choirs and their conductors] (Moscow: Gosudarstvennoe Muzykal'noe Izdatel'stvo, 1963), p. 22, n. 1.

4. The German term *Kapellmeister* in eighteenth- and nineteenth-century Russia signified the musical (as opposed to administrative) leader of either a vocal or instrumental establishment, someone who functioned both as a conductor and as a pedagogue. The Imperial Chapel, however, had no such position in its organizational structure. This post was apparently created especially for Glinka, who had no specific duties assigned to him. See Izrail' Gusin and Donat Tkachev, *Gosudarstvennaia akademicheskaia kapella imeni M. I. Glinki* [The State Academic Choir named in honor of M. I. Glinka] (Leningrad: Gosudarstvennoe Muzykal'noe Izdatel'stvo, 1957), p. 44.

5. Mikhail Glinka, *Literaturnoe nasledie* [The literary heritage], vol. 1, (Leningrad: Gosudarstvennoe Muzykal'noe Izdatel'stvo, 1952), p. 175.

6. Fyodor L'vov, *O penii v Rossii* [Singing in Russia] (St. Petersburg: n.p., 1834), pp. 30–42 passim.

7. Antonin Preobrazhensky, *Kul'tovaia muzyka v Rossii* [The music of the cult in Russia] (Leningrad: Academia, 1924), p. 90.

8. Gardner, "Aleksei Fyodorovich L'vov," pp. 112-96.

9. Aleksei L'vov, "Zapiski Alekseia Fyodorovicha L'vova" [The memoirs of Aleksei Fyodorovich L'vov], *Russkii arkhiv* 3 (1884):94.

10. Ibid., p. 93.

11. In reference to liturgical books the term *obikhod* (lit., custom, daily use) corresponds to the Latin *usualis*; however there is no equivalent term in English.

12. P. Chizhevsky, *Tserkovno-grazhdanskie postanovleniia o tserkovnom penii* [Church and civil legislation concerning church singing] (Kharkov: n.p., 1878), p. 10; cited in Gardner, *Bogosluzhebnoe*, p. 330.

13. Ibid., p. 14.

14. Besides his chant harmonizations (which he himself did not regard as compositions), L'vov composed forty-eight liturgical works (published by A. Gutheil). Of these, six or seven are based on chants, while the rest are free compositions.

15. Maksim Berezovsky (1745-77) was a student of Galuppi; Makarov (dates unknown) was a singer of the Chapel in Bortniansky's time; S. Gribovich (dates unknown) joined the Chapel in 1823 as a teacher of singing; Pavel Vorotnikov (1806-76) joined the Chapel in 1843 as L'vov's assistant.

16. Throughout the forty-odd years of L'vov's and Bakhmetev's combined administrations only a handful of minor composers composed Orthodox liturgical works: Gavriil Lomakin (1811-85), the Archpriest Mikhail Vinogradov (1810-88), Mikhail Strokin (no dates), the Priest Vasily Starorussky (no dates). Their works, in most cases very pedestrian, were not approved by the Chapel's censors and were published only when the censorship was relaxed after 1883.

17. Preobrazhensky, *Kul'tovaia*, p. 104.

18. Gusin and Tkachev, *Gosudarstvennaia akademicheskaia kapella*, pp. 31-32. The programs of these concerts were not available. Gusin and Tkachev mention symphonic works by Beethoven, Mendelssohn, Liszt, Weber, and Cherubini, oratorios of Bach, Haydn, Handel, Mozart, and Berlioz, scenes from Gluck's operas, etc., but do not give the exact titles.

19. "Pis'ma kompozitora Adana o svoei poezdke v Peterburg v 1839-om godu" [The letters of the composer Adam about his journey to St. Petersburg in 1839], *Russkaia muzykal'naia gazeta* 38 (1903); see also "Berlioz v Rossii" [Berlioz in Russia], *Russkaia muzykal'naia gazeta* 50 (1903):1254.

20. Ibid. See also P. Perepelitsyn, *Muzykal'nyi slovar'. Entsyklopedicheskii spravochnyi sbornik* [Musical Dictionary. An encyclopedic reference collection] (Moscow: n.p., 1884), pp. 375-76.

21. Gusin and Tkachev, *Gosudarstvennaia akademicheskaia kapella*, p. 46.

22. Ibid., p. 32.

23. Aleksei L'vov, *O tserkovnykh khorakh* [Concerning church choirs] (St. Petersburg: n.p., 1853), p. 3.

24. Pyotr Tchaikovsky, *Muzykal'no-kriticheskie stat'i* [Essays on musical criticism] (Moscow: Gosudarstvennoe Muzykal'noe Izdatel'stvo, 1953), p. 57. In similar terms Tchaikovsky criticizes the performance of the chorus in other operas produced at that time at the Bolshoi, e.g., *Ruslan and Liudmila* (1872) and *Rogneda* (1874); see ibid., pp. 148, 172.

25. Vasily Metallov, "Sinodal'nye, byvshie patriarshie pevchie" [The synodal, formerly the patriarchal singers], *Russkaia muzykal'naia gazeta* 25/26 (1901):636.

26. From 1834: "For a considerable length of time I have noticed the out-of-tune singing of the Synodal Choir...." (Procurator of the Synodal Chancery, Vasily Mikhailov); from 1836: "The Synodal Singers sang quite poorly, specifically, the basses shouted beyond measure, while the sopranos singing solos made many mistakes, all of which was noticed by the Military Governor-General...;" from 1837: "[The former precentor] performed [the chants] according to his own method, with arbitrary distortion of note values, with changes in entire chant melodies, and contrary to the markings in the score." Cited in Metallov, "Sinodal'nye," *Russkaia muzykal'naia gazeta* 25/26 (1901): 639–40.

27. Ibid., 25/26 (1901): 649.

28. Gardner, *Bogosluzhebnoe*, p. 389.

29. N. Zipalov, *F. A. Bagretsov: Opyt biografii v istoriko-muzykal'nom otnoshenii po otzyvam i vospominaniiam ego sovremennikov* [F. A. Bagretsov: A historico-musical biography based on accounts and reminiscences of his contemporaries] (Vladikavkaz: n.p., 1914), p. 17.

30. Hermann Larosch, "Gor'kaia pravda" [The bitter truth], in *Sobranie muzykal'no-criticheskikh statei* [Collected articles of musical criticism], vol. 1 (Moscow: n.p., 1913), pp. 289–93.

31. Aleksandr Nikol'sky, "Dukhovnye kontserty i ikh zadachi" [Sacred concerts and their goals], *Khorovoe i regentskoe delo* 4 (1909):97–101.

32. S[tepan] S[molensk]y, *Ob ozdorovlenii programm dukhovnykh kontsertov v Moskve* [The revitalization of the programs of sacred concerts in Moscow] (Moscow: n.p., 1900), pp. 18–19.

33. [Stepan Smolensky], *Obzor istoricheskikh kontsertov Sinodal'nogo Uchilishcha Tserkovnogo Peniia v 1895 godu* [A review of the historical concerts given at the Synodal School of Church Singing in 1895] (Moscow: n.p., 1895).

34. Cited in Nikolai Kompaneisky, "Protest kompozitorov dukhovnoi muzyki" [A protest by composers of sacred music], *Russkaia Muzykal'naia Gazeta* 23/24 (1906):570.

35. Aleksandr Kastal'sky, "O moei muzykal'noi kar'ere i moi mysli o tserkovnoi muzyke," *Muzykal'nyi sovremennik* 2 (October 1914), p. 36; transl. S. W. Pring, "My Musical Career and Thoughts on Church Music," *The Musical Quarterly* (1925) 232–47.

36. [News brief], *Gusel'ki iarovchaty* 9 (1911):12.

37. Nikolai Kompaneisky, "Dvadtsatiletie kontsertnoi deiatel'nosti A. A. Arkhangel'skogo" [The twenty-year anniversary of A. A. Arkhangel'sky's concert activity], *Russkaia muzykal'naia gazeta* 3 (1903):70.

38. For a complete list of the programs, see Donat Tkachev, "Istoricheskie kontserty khora A. Arkhangel'skogo" [The historical concerts of Arkhangel'sky's Choir], in *Khorovoe iskusstvo* [The choral art], vol. 2 (Leningrad: Muzyka, 1971), pp. 79–87.

39. Anonymous [Concert review], *Nuvellist* 1 (1888):3, cited in Donat Tkachev, *Aleksandr Andreevich Arkhangel'sky (1846-1924). Ocherk zhizni i deiatel'nosti* [Aleksandr Andreevich Arkhangel'sky: His life and works] (Leningrad: Muzyka, 1974), p. 16.

40. Semyon Kruglikov, [Concert review], *Artist* 17 (1891):130-31; cited in Tkachev, *A. A. Arkhangel'sky*, p. 27.

41. Ivan Lipaev, [Concert review], *Russkaia muzykal'naia gazeta* 4 (1897):680-81.

42. Mikhail Lisitsyn, "Iubilei khora A. A. Arkhangel'skogo" [The anniversary of A. A. Arkhangel'sky's choir], *Russkaia muzykal'naia gazeta* 1 (1898):86-88.

43. Anonymous [Concert review], *Die Welt am Abend*, 18 December 1907.

44. Nikolai Golitsyn, "Sovremennyi vopros o preobrazovanii tserkovnogo peniia v Rossii" [The current question concerning the tranformation of church singing in Russia], *Strannik* 1 (1884):555-58.

45. *Sobranie dukhovno-muzykal'nykh sochinenii* [Collection of sacred musical works], E. Azeev, editor (St. Petersburg: Akkord, 1916).

46. Cited in Preobrazhensky, *Kul'tovaia*, pp. 107-8.

47. Nikolai Rimsky-Korsakov, *Letopis' moei muzykal'noi zhizni* [My musical life] (Moscow: Gosudarstvennoe Muzykal'noe Izdatel'stvo, 1955) pp. 152-53.

48. Ivan Lipaev [Concert review], *Russkaia muzykal'naia gazeta* 4 (1897):678-79.

49. Anonymous, "Muzykal'naia zhizn' Moskvy" [The musical life of Moscow], *Russkaia muzykal'naia gazeta* 4 (1898):399-400.

50. Stepan Smolensky, "Vospominaniia" [Memoirs], vol. 2, MS, Golovanov Collection, no. 527-28, p. 260, Glinka State Museum of Musical Culture, Moscow.

51. [Anonymous review], "Chestvovanie pamiati Bortnianskogo Pridvornoi Pevcheskoi Kapelloi" [The celebration of Bortniansky's memory by the Imperial Court Chapel], *Russkaia muzykal'naia gazeta* 40 (1901):964-67.

52. Nikolai Kompaneisky, "Kontsert Pridvornoi Pevcheskoi Kapelly" [A concert by the Imperial Court Chapel], *Russkaia muzykal'naia gazeta* 5 (1902):141-45.

53. See, e.g., reviews in *Russkaia muzykal'naia gazeta* 48/49 (1905):1187-89, 16/17 (1907):464-67, 46 (1907):464-67, 1 (1913):20-21. See also reviews in *Muzyka i Penie* 2 (1905):4-5; 3,4 (1906):3-4; 4 (1908):4-5; 3 (1909):3; 1 (1914/15):2. Other examples may be found in reviews in *Gusel'ki iarovchaty* 4 (1907):9; 6 (1908):17; 1 (1913):9-10. See also reviews in *Khorovoe i regentskoe delo* 12 (1909):302-7; 1 (1911):8; 1 (1913):13.

54. *Khronika muzykal'nogo sovremennika* 8 (1915):14-15.

55. Vasily Metallov, *Sinodal'noe Uchilishche Tserkovnogo Peniia v ego proshlom i nastoiashchem* [The Synodal School of Church Singing in its past and present] (Moscow: n.p., 1911), p. 33.

56. Letter of 27 February 1886, cited in L., "V. S. Orlov. Sovremennye muzykal'nye deiateli" [V. S. Orlov. Contemporary musical personages], *Russkaia muzykal'naia gazeta* 52 (1903):1309-13.

57. Metallov, *Sinodal'noe*, p. 49.

58. Dmitri Allemanov, "S. V. Smolensky, kak tserkovno-pevcheskii deiatel'" [S. V. Smolensky's role as a worker in the field of church singing], *Muzykal'nyi truzhennik* 4 (1910):8–9.

59. Smolensky, "Vospominaniia," p. 180.

60. Aleksandr Nikol'sky, [Manuscript notebook], entry dated 1895, Nikol'sky Archive, Fund 294, no. 379, pp. 22v–23, Glinka State Museum of Musical Culture, Moscow.

61. Letter of 18 March 1891, cited in Metallov, *Sinodal'noe* p. 55.

62. Smolensky "Vospominaniia," p. 42.

63. Ibid., pp. 76–77.

64. Ibid., pp. 75–77.

65. This is true not only of sacred works, but of some secular works as well. Sergei Taneev, whose published choral output is exclusively secular, is known to have routinely "tested" his works with the Synodal Choir prior to publication.

66. Nikolai Kochetov, "V bor'be—zhizn'!" [In struggle—life!], in *Pamiati V. S. Orlova* [V.S. Orlov, in memoriam] (Moscow: n.p., 1908), pp. 17–20.

67. Ivan Lipaev, [Concert reviews], *Russkaia muzykal'naia gazeta* 7 (1896):760–62.

68. Ivan Lipaev, [Concert review], *Russkaia muzykal'naia gazeta* 15/16 (1899):479–80.

69. Anonymous [Concert review], *Khronika muzykal'nogo sovremennika* 5/6 (1916–17):6–8.

70. Unidentified newspaper, Lipaev Archive, Fund 13, Glinka State Museum of Musical Culture, Moscow.

71. Ivan Lipaev, [Concert review], *Russkaia muzykal'naia gazeta* 11 (1901):344.

72. Ivan Lipaev, [Concert review], *Russkaia muzykal'naia gazeta* 14/15 (1903):411–12.

73. Anonymous, [Concert review], *Muzykal'nyi truzhennik* 25 (1907):12.

74. A. L——n, [Concert review], *Muzyka i zhizn'* 3 (1908):14.

75. Mikhail Lisitsyn, "Velikopostnye dukhovnye kontserty" [Lenten sacred concerts], *Muzyka i penie* 7 (1911):1–2.

76. "Kontsert Sinodal'nogo Khora" [The concert of the Synodal Choir], *Khorovoe i Regentskoe Delo* 3 (1911):12–14.

77. Anonymous, [Concert review], *Russkaia muzykal'naia gazeta* 13 (1911):342.

78. Gr[igory] Pr[okof'ev], [Concert review], *Russkaia muzykal'naia gazeta* 14 (1915):260–61.

79. 17 May 1911; cited in A. Gladky, *Poezdka Sinodal'nogo Khora zagranitsu v 1911 g.* [The Synodal Choir's tour abroad in 1911] (Moscow: n.p., 1912).

80. 20 May 1911; cited in Gladky, *Poezdka.*

81. 23 May 1911; cited in Gladky, *Poezdka.*

82. Review of 26 May 1911 concert in Sophiensaal; cited in Gladky, *Poezdka.*

83. Ibid.

84. Ibid.

85. Ibid.

86. Review of 29 May 1911 concert; cited in Gladky, *Poezdka.*

87. Review of 30 May 1911 concert; cited in Gladky, *Poezdka.*

88. Ibid.

89. Cited in *Moskovsky listok*, 25 May [7 June] 1911.

90. M., "Kontserty Moskovskogo Sinodal'nogo Khora v Drezdene" [The concerts of the Moscow Synodal Choir in Dresden], *Russkaia muzykal'naia gazeta* 30/31 (1911):611–16.

91. Secular *Singvereinen* comprised of German immigrants in Russia date from 1822; however their activities did not significantly influence the development of Russian secular choral singing. See Boris Asaf'ev, *Russkaia muzyka. XIX i nachalo XX veka* [Russian music of the nineteenth and early twentieth centuries] (Leningrad: Muzyka, 1968) p. 128, note.

92. Gavriil Lomakin, "Avtobiograficheskie zapiski" [Autobiographical notes], *Russkaia starina* 50 (1886):318.

93. Aleksandr Serov, "Zalogi istinnogo muzykal'nogo obrazovaniia v Sankt-Peterburge" [The roots of genuine musical education in St. Petersburg], in *Izbrannye stat'i* [Selected essays], vol. 2 (Moscow: Gosudarstvennoe Muzykal'noe Izdatel'stvo, 1957), p. 168.

94. Daniil Lokshin, *Zamechatel'nye russkie khory i ikh dirizhery* [Outstanding Russian choirs and their conductors], (Moscow: Gosudarstvennoe Muzykal'noe Izdatel'stvo, 1963), p. 60.

95. Vladimir Stasov, "25-ti letie Besplatnoi Muzykal'noi Shkoly" [The 25th anniversary of the Free Musical School], in *Izbrannye sochineniia* [Selected works], vol. 3 (Moscow: Gosudarstvennoe Muzykal'noe Izdatel'stvo, 1952), p. 85.

96. Lokshin, *Zamechatel'nye russkie khory,* p. 64.

97. N[ikolai] S[okolov], [Concert review], *Muzykal'noe obozrenie* 12 (1888).

98. The words are presumably Bekker's, although the source does not make this clear. Cited in Nikolai Romanovsky, "Iz proshlogo russkoi khorovoi kul'tury" [From the past of Russian choral culture], in *Khorovoe iskusstvo* [The choral art] vol. 2 (Leningrad: Muzyka, 1971), pp. 70–71.

99. Rybakov, "Dukhovnyi kontsert Besplatnogo Khorovogo Klassa Mel'nikova i Bekkera" [A sacred concert by the Free Choral Class of Mel'nikov and Bekker], *Russkaia muzykal'naia gazeta* 4 (1897):654–57.

100. Anonymous, [Concert review], *Russkaia muzykal'naia gazeta* 3 (1898):307.

101. Ivan Lipaev, [Concert review], *Russkaia muzykal'naia gazeta* 9 (1899):288.

102. Dmitri A[rakchiev], [Concert review], *Muzyka i zhizn'* 4 (1908):10–11.

103. Grigory Prokof'ev, [Concert review], *Russkaia muzykal'naia gazeta* 9 (1914):243.

104. Lokshin, *Zamechatel'nye russkie khory,* p. 65.

105. Cited in A. Kondrat'ev, *Russkaia pesnia i ee ispolnitel', narodnyi pevets Dmitri Aleksandrovich Agrenev-Slaviansky* [The Russian song and its performer, the folk singer Dmitri Aleksandrovich Agrenev-Slaviansky] (Ekaterinburg: n.p., 1898); p. 29.

106. Sergei Taneev, cited in Lokshin, *Zamechatel'nye russkie khory,* p. 69.

107. Supplement for 25 December 1885; cited in Ibid., p. 68.

108. 30 December 1869; cited in Ibid., p. 72.

109. M. Yurkevich, *D. A. Slaviansky v ego chetvert 'vekovoi khudozhestvennoi i politicheskoi deiatel'nosti* [D. A. Slaviansky in his quarter-century artistic and political activity] (Moscow: n.p., 1889), p. 108; cited in Ibid., p. 68.

110. Yurkevich, *D.A. Slaviansky,* pp. 183–84; cited in Ibid.

111. *Sovremennaia letopis',* 12 April 1871; cited in Ibid., p. 72.

112. Nikolai Kashkin, "Vecher muzykal'nykh anakhronizmov" [An evening of musical anachronisms], *Russkoe slovo,* 25 October 1907; cited in Ibid., p. 74.

113. M. Gil'din, "Dva kontserta Slavianskogo" [Two concerts by Slaviansky], *Baian* (Tambov) 6 (1907):91.

114. Pyotr Tchaikovsky, *Muzykal'nye fel'etony* [Musical feuilletons], pp. 306, 300, cited in Pyotr Tikhov, "D. A. Slaviansky kak russkii muzykal'nyi deiatel'" [D. A. Slaviansky as a Russian musical celebrity], *Gusel'ki iarovchaty* 9 (1911):10–12.

115. Yuri Arnold, *Vospominaniia* [Memoirs], vol. 2 (St. Petersburg: n.p., 1893), pp. 148ff.

116. Aleksei L'vov, *O svobodnom i nesimmetrichnom ritme* [Concerning free and unsymmetrical rhythm] (St. Petersburg: n.p., 1858), p. 5.

117. See Malcolm Hamrick Brown, "Native Song and National Consciousness in Nineteenth-Century Russian Music," in *Art and Culture in Nineteenth-Century Russia,* ed. Theofanis George Stavrou (Bloomington, Indiana: Indiana University Press, 1983), pp. 57–84.

118. Cited in Anna Rudneva, "Russkoe narodnoe khorovoe ispolnitel'stvo" [Russian folk choral performance], in *Khorovoe iskusstvo* [The choral art], vol. 1 (Leningrad: Muzyka, 1967), p. 186.

119. "Zarubezhnaia gastrol' Leningradskoi Kapelly v 1928 g. Dnevnik M. G. Klimova i otzyvy pressy" [The foreign tour of the Leningrad Cappella in 1928. M. Klimov's diary and newspaper reviews], in *Khorovoe iskusstvo* [The choral art], vol. 2 (Leningrad: Muzyka, 1971), p. 112.

120. N., "Kontsert russkogo khora v Zheneve" [A Russian choir concert in Geneva], *Khorovoe i regentskoe delo* 12 (1913):202–4.

121. H. K. M., "The Russian Choir, A Remarkable Recital in New York," *New York Times,* 1 December 1913.

Chapter 4

1. Pavel Chesnokov, *Khor i upravlenie im* [The choir and how to direct it], 2nd ed. (Moscow: Gosudarstvennoe Muzykal'noe Izdatel'stvo, 1953), p. 16.

2. Nikolai Kovin, *Podgotovka golosa i slukha khorovykh pevtsov* [Preparing the voice and ear of choral singers] (Moscow: n.p., 1916), p. 1.

3. Aleksandr Nikol'sky, "Dukhovnye kontserty i ikh zadachi" [Sacred concerts and their objectives], *Khorovoe i regentskoe delo* 4 (1909):97–101.

4. Chesnokov, *Khor,* pp. 13–17.

5. Nikolai Uspensky, "Problema metodologii obucheniia ispolnitel'skomu masterstvu v drevnerusskom pevcheskom iskusstve" [The problem of methodology in the teaching of performance skills in early Russian chant], in *Musica antiqua Europae orientalis. Acta scientifica* (Bydgoscz: 1976), pp. 467–501.

6. Vsevolod Bagadurov, *Ocherki razvitiia vokal'noi pedagogiki v Rossii* [Essays in the history of vocal pedagogy in Russia] (Moscow: Gosudarstvennoe Muzykal'noe Izdatel'stvo, 1956), p. 20.

7. K. Nikol'skaia-Beregovskaia, *Razvitie shkoly khorovogo peniia v Rossii*, [The development of a school of choral singing in Russia] (Moscow: Muzyka, 1974), p. 6.

8. Bagadurov, *Ocherki*, p. 5.

9. Aleksandr Varlamov, Preface to *Polnaia shkola peniia* [Complete school of singing], ed. with commentary by Vsevolod Bagadurov (Moscow: Gosudarstvennoe Muzykal'noe Izdatel'stvo, 1953), p. 8.

10. Bagadurov, *Ocherki*, p. 132.

11. S. Bulich, "A. E. Varlamov. Neskol'ko novykh dannykh dlia ego biografii" [A. E. Varlamov. Several new facts concerning his biography], *Russkaia muzykal'naia gazeta* 45–46 (1901):1111–20, 1142–51.

12. Bagadurov, *Ocherki*, p. 126.

13. Edited by Nikolai Kompaneisky (St. Petersburg: n.p., 1903).

14. Cited in Bagadurov, *Ocherki*, p. 126.

15. Cited in Vladimir Stasov, "25-ti letie Besplatnoi Muzykal'noi Shkoly" [The 25th anniversary of the Free Musical School], in *Izbrannye sochineniia* [Selected works], vol. 3 (Moscow: Gosudarstvennoe Muzykal'noe Izdatel'stvo, 1952), p. 81.

16. P. Bronnikov, *Uchebnik peniia* [A textbook of singing] (St. Petersburg: n.p., 1880).

17. Stanislav Sonki, *Teoriia postanovki golosa v sviazi s fiziologiei organov dykhaniia i gortani* [The theory of vocal training in connection with the physiology of the breathing organs and the larynx] (Moscow: n.p., 1886); Aleksandr Dodonov, *Rukovodstvo k pravil'noi postanovke golosa* [A manual for the correct training of the voice] 2 vols., (Moscow: n.p., 1891, 1895); Ippolit Prianishnikov, *Sovety obuchaiushchimsia peniiu* [Counsels to those studying singing] (St. Petersburg: n.p., 1899); Caspar Křižanovsky, *Prichiny upadka vokal'nogo iskusstva* [Reasons for the decadence of the vocal art] (Moscow: n.p., 1902) and *Vokal'noe iskusstvo* [The vocal art], vol. 1 (Moscow: n.p., 1909).

18. Vasily Karelin, *Novaia teoriia postanovki golosa* [A New Theory of Voice Training] (St. Petersburg: n.p., 1912), cited in Bagadurov, *Ocherki*, pp. 175 ff.

19. Cited in Bagadurov, *Ocherki*, p. 131.

20. See n. 2 above.

21. Aleksandr Nikol'sky, *Golos i slukh khorovogo pevtsa* [The voice and ear of the choral singer] (Moscow: n.p., 1916).

22. Stählin, cited in Antonin Preobrazhensky, "Pridvornaia kapella 150 let nazad" [The court chapel 150 years ago] *Russkaia muzykal'naia gazeta* 11 (1902):324. See also chapter 2, p. 000.

23. Nikolai Findeizen, "Sinodal'noe Uchilishche Tserkovnogo Peniia v Moskve" [The Synodal School of Church Singing in Moscow], *Russkaia muzykal'naia gazeta* 4 (1898):345–49.

24. Pavel Vorotnikov, *Rukovodstvo k prepodavaniiu khorovogo peniia* [A manual for the teaching of choral singing] (Moscow: n.p., 1894), p. 21.

25. Gavriil Lomakin, "Avtobiograficheskie zapiski" [Autobiographical notes], *Russkaia Starina* 50 (1886):315.

26. *Programmy muzykal'nykh predmetov i istorii iskusstv v Moskovskom Sinodal'nom Uchilishche Tserkovnogo Peniia* [Programs in musical subjects and arts history at the Moscow Synodal School of Church Singing] (Moscow: n.p., 1910), p. 56.

27. Paul Einbeck, *Zur Geschichte des Koeniglichen Domchors in Berlin* (Berlin: 1893), cited in Ivan Gardner, "Aleksei Feodorovich L'vov," *Pravoslavnyi put'* (Jordanville, N.Y., 1970), p. 133–34.

28. Izrail' Gusin and Donat Tkachev, *Gosudarstvennaia akademicheskaia kapella imeni M.I. Glinki* [The State Academic Choir named in honor of M.I. Glinka] (Leningrad: Gosudarstvennoe Muzykal'noe Izdatel'stvo, 1957), p. 40.

29. It is unlikely that the Rubini mentioned by Rosliakov was Giovanni Battista Rubini (1794–1854), who performed in Russia in 1843–45 and again in 1847 as a member of the Italian Opera in St. Petersburg. Possibly, the Rubini in question was Ivan Alekseevich Rupin (1792–1850), a Russian who Italianized his name to Rupini and gained prominence as a vocal pedagogue in St. Petersburg in the 1830s and 1840s. Dmitri Rosliakov, "Vospominaniia o Pridvornoi Pevcheskoi Kapelle" [Reminiscences about the Imperial Court Chapel], *Muzyka i penie* 7 (1909): 1–2.

30. Gusin and Tkachev, *Gosudarstvennaia akademicheskaia kapella,* p. 29.

31. G. Serebriakov, "O 'postanovke' golosa u tserkovnykh pevchikh" [Concerning the vocal 'training' of church singers], *Baian* (Tambov) 4 (1907):51–52.

32. Nikolai Kochetov, "Neskol'ko slov po voprosu o postanovke golosa v tserkovnykh khorakh" [Several words on the question of vocal training in church choirs], in *Vtoroi Vserossiiskii S"ezd Khorovykh Deiatelei; Protokoly i doklady in extenso* [The Second All-Russian Convention of Choral Directors; Minutes and extended summaries of reports] (Moscow: n.p., 1909), pp. 9–10.

33. Viacheslav Bulychev, *Khorovoe penie kak iskusstvo* [Choral singing as an art] (Moscow: n.p., 1910), pp. 17, 34ff.

34. Cited in Vasily Metallov, *Sinodal'noe Uchilishche Tserkovnogo Peniia v ego proshlom i nastoiashchem* [The Moscow Synodal School of Church Singing in its past and present] (Moscow: n.p., 1911), p. 88.

35. Franz Wilhelm Abt (1819–85), *Practische Gesangschule,* Opus 474, 4 vols., German edition: (Braunschweig: Henry Litolff, n.d.); Mathilde Marchesi (1826–1913), *L'art du chant,* Opus 21, (Hamburg: A. Cranz, 1877) or Salvatore Marchesi de Castrone (1822–1908), *Résumé de l'art du chant pour toutes les voix,* Opus 15, (Offenbach/J. Andre [ca. 1865]); Paul Garnault, *Cours théorique et practique de physiologie, d'hygiène et de thérapeutique de la voix, parlée et chantée, hygiène et maladies du chanteur et de l'orateur,* (Paris: A. Maloine, 1896); Prianishnikov, Sonki, see n. 17 above.

36. Mily Balakirev, *Sbornik russkikh narodnykh pesen* [Collection of Russian folk songs] (1866); Nikolai Rimsky-Korsakov, *100 russkikh narodnykh pesen* [One hundred Russian folk songs] (1877); Anatoly Liadov, *Sbornik russkikh narodnykh pesen* [Collection of Russian folk songs], Opus 43 (1898).

37. Aleksei L'vov, *O tserkovnykh khorakh* [Concerning church choirs] (St. Petersburg: n.p., 1853).

38. Einbeck, *Zur Geschichte*, cited in Ivan Gardner, "Aleksei Feodorovich L'vov," p. 134.

39. A. Vander Linden, "Un collaborateur Russe de Fétis: Alexis de Lvoff (1798–1870)," *Revue Belge de musicologie* 19 (1965):64–81.

40. *Sobranie mnenii i otzyvov Filareta Mitropolita Moskovskogo* [The collected opinions and pronouncements of Filaret, Metropolitan of Moscow], vol. 3 (St. Petersburg: n.p., 1885), pp. 472–76; cited in Gardner, "Aleksei Feodorovich L'vov," pp. 183ff.

41. Gavriil Lomakin, *Kratkaia metoda peniia* [A brief method of singing] (Moscow: n.p., 1882), p. 21.

42. Lomakin, "Avtobiograficheskie zapiski," pp. 647, 653.

43. Ivan Kazansky, *Obshcheponiatnoe rukovodstvo k izucheniiu notnogo tserkovnogo khorovogo i odinochnogo peniia* [A common-sense manual of choral and solo church singing], 2nd ed. (Moscow: n.p., 1875), p. 104.

44. Vasily Zinov'ev, *Prakticheskoe rukovodstvo dlia nachinaiushchego uchitelia-regenta* [A practical manual for the beginning teacher-precentor] (Moscow: n.p., 1905), p. 84.

45. Aleksandr Kastal'sky, *Obshchedostupnyi samouchitel' tserkovnogo peniia* [A popular self-instructor of church singing] (Moscow: P. Jurgenson, 1910) p. 4.

46. Ibid., p. 37.

47. Aleksandr Kastal'sky, "Metodika prepodavaniia shkol'nogo khorovogo peniia" [The methodology of teaching choral singing in the schools], MS notebook, Kastalsky Archive, Fund 12, no. 246, Glinka State Museum of Musical Culture, Moscow.

48. First published in 1909, serialized in the journal *Khorovoe i regentskoe delo* (The choral conductor's and precentor's art), and then separately in 1916.

49. Nikolai Kovin, *Upravlenie khorom* [Choral conducting] (Petrograd: n.p., 1916), pp. 3–4.

50. Ibid., p. 5.

51. Chesnokov, *Khor*, p. 5.

52. Ibid., p. 23.

53. A. P[ashchenk]o, "Peterburgskie tserkovnye khory" [St. Petersburg church choirs], *Khorovoe i regentskoe delo* 1–4 (1910):8–13, 41–44, 70–72, 97–103.

54. Anonymous, "Pridvornaia Pevcheskaia Kapella" [The Imperial Court Chapel], *Khronika muzykal'nogo sovremennika* 12 (1915–16).

55. A. P[ashchenk]o, "Peterburgskie tserkovnye khory."

56. *Muzykal'nyi spravochnik na 1914 g.* [Musical handbook for 1914] (Moscow: n.p., 1914), pp. 160–61.

57. These figures are drawn from Vasily Metallov, *Sinodal'noe Uchilishche Tserkovnogo Peniia v ego proshlom i nastoiashchem* [The Moscow Synodal School of church singing in its past and present] (Moscow: n.p., 1911), pp. 6, 16, 34–35.

58. [Newsbrief,] *Khorovoe i regentskoe delo* 10 (1913):162.

59. N. Rozanov, "Ob ustroistve chudovskogo khora pevchikh" [Concerning the organization of the Chudov Choir], *Chteniia Moskovskogo Obshchestva Liubitelei Dukhovnogo Prosveshcheniia* 5 (1868):91–118; A. Miroliubov, *Obraztsovyi tserkovnyi khor vremen Mitropolita Filareta*, [An exemplary church choir from the time of Metropolitan Filaret] (Moscow: n.p., n.d.), p. 6.

60. *Muzykal'nyi kalendar'* [Musical calendar], supplement to *Muzykal'nyi truzhennik* (1909).

61. Pavel Chesnokov, MS notebook, Chesnokov Archive, Fund 36, no. 38, Glinka State Museum of Musical Culture, Moscow.

62. V. Postnikov, "Perechen' tserkovnykh pesnopenii s ukazaniem kompozitorov proizvedeniia kotorykh ispolnialis' khorami pod upravleniem N. M. Danilina v khramakh Moskvy" [A list of church hymns and composers performed by choirs under the direction of N. M. Danilin in Moscow churches], unpublished typescript, Moscow, 4 April 1973. A complete cross-reference by liturgical titles appears in Appendix D of my dissertation, Walter Vladimir Morosan, "Choral Performance in Pre-Revolutionary Russia" (D.M.A. diss., University of Illinois at Urbana-Champaign, 1984).

63. [Ivan Mel'nikov], *Obzor deiatel'nosti khorovogo klassa I. Mel'nikova, pod rukovodstvom F. F. Bekkera* [A summary of the activities of I. Mel'nikov's choral class, under the direction of F. F. Bekker] (St. Petersburg: n.p., 1897).

64. The various aspects of the modern-day Soviet folk chorus have been analyzed in Anna Rudneva, *Russkii narodnyi khor i rabota s nim* [Working with the Russian folk chorus] (Moscow: Gosudarstvennoe Muzykal'noe Izdatel'stvo, 1960).

65. *Raspevanie narodnogo khora* [Vocalizing the folk chorus] (Moscow: Russian Choral Society of the RSFSR, n. d.).

66. Kovin, *Upravlenie*, pp. 12–14.

67. Ibid., p. 14; Kastal'sky, "Metodika," p. 32; Chesnokov, *Khor*, p. 24.

68. Chesnokov, *Khor*, p. 24.

69. Kastal'sky, "Metodika," p. 32.

70. L'vov, *O tserkovnykh*, p. 7.

71. F. E. S[tepanov], "Pis'mo v redaktsiiu" [Letter to the editor], *Muzyka i penie* 3 (1903):6–7.

72. See, e.g., Victor Alexander Fields, *Training the Singing Voice: An Analysis of the Working Concepts Contained in Recent Contributions to Vocal Pedagogy* (Morningside Heights, N. Y.: King's Crown Press, 1947).

73. Cited in Izrail' Gusin and Donat Tkachev, *Gosudarstvennaia akademicheskaia kapella*, p. 37.

74. Cited in Metallov, *Sinodal'noe*, p. 12.

75. *Baian* (St. Petersburg) 4 (1889):53.

76. Kazansky, *Obshcheponiatnoe rukovodstvo*, pp. 53–54.

77. Gavriil Lomakin, *Rukovodstvo k obucheniiu peniiu v narodnykh shkolakh* [A manual for teaching singing in the people's schools] (St. Petersburg: n.p., n.d.), pp. 14–15.

78. Moscow: n.p., 1911.

79. Dmitri Allemanov, *Metodika tserkovnogo peniia* [The methodology of church singing] (Moscow: P. Jurgenson, 1908), p. 9.

80. Kastal'sky, *Obshchedostupnyi samouchitel'*, p. 6.

81. Kastal'sky, "Metodika," p. 32.

82. [Mel'nikov], *Obzor*, pp. 5–6.

83. Notes taken down at rehearsals with the Russian Students' Choir in Prague, Arkhangel'sky Archive, Fund 184, no. 32, Glinka State Museum of Musical Culture, Moscow; cited in Donat Tkachev, *Aleksandr Andreevich Arkhangel'sky (1846–1924). Ocherk zhizni i deiatel'nosti* [Aleksandr Andreevich Arkhangel'sky (1846–1924): His life and works] (Leningrad: Muzyka, 1974)

84. Klavdy Ptitsa, *Mastera khorovogo iskusstva v Moskovskoi Konservatorii* [Masters of the choral art at the Moscow Conservatory] (Moscow: Muzyka, 1970), pp. 27–28.

85. Chesnokov, *Khor*, pp. 46–47.

86. Pavel Chesnokov, "Zapiski regenta" [Notes of a precentor], MS, Chesnokov Archive, Fund 36, no. 322, Glinka State Museum of Musical Culture, Moscow.

87. Chesnokov, *Khor*, pp. 37ff.

88. E. Vitoshinsky, "Khor Kalishevskogo v Kieve," [Kalishevsky's choir in Kiev], *Muzyka i penie* 1–2 (1902/03):4.

89. Rudneva, *Russkii narodnyi khor*, p. 26.

90. See the editions of Russian choral music edited by N. Lindsay Norden, published by J. Fischer & Bro.

91. Elwyn Wienandt and Robert Young, *The Anthem in England and America* (New York: 1970), p. 412.

92. Paul of Aleppo, "Puteshestvie Antiokhiiskogo Patriarkha Makariia v Rossiiu v polovine XVII veka" [The Patriarch of Antioch Makarios' journey to Russia in the mid-seventeenth century], in A. Rogov, ed., *Muzykal'naia estetika Rossii XI–XVII vekov* [Musical aesthetics of Russia in the 11th through 17th centuries] (Moscow: Muzyka, 1973), pp. 169.

93. Octavists, as comparatively rare voices, became the objects of special pride and competition among the various "owners" of choirs. In the days of serfdom, the owner had the power to conscript any one of his serfs into his choir. One recalls Frederick William I of Prussia, who "collected" giants for his Imperial Guard.

94. Rosliakov, "Vospominaniia," pp. 1–2.

95. Vasily M. Orlov, *Iskusstvo tserkovnogo peniia* [The art of church singing] (Moscow: n.p., 1910), p. 11.

96. Kovin, *Upravlenie*, pp. 5–6.

97. Chesnokov, *Khor*, p. 22.

98. Chesnokov, MS notebook, Chesnokov Archive, Fund 36, no. 38, Glinka State Museum of Musical Culture, Moscow.

99. Ivan Lipaev, [Concert review], *Russkaia muzykal'naia gazeta* 7 (1896):760–62.

100. Ivan Lipaev, [Concert review], *Russkaia muzykal'naia gazeta* 10 (1901):314–15.

101. [Vladimir Odoevsky], "Mnenie kniazia V. F. Odoevskogo po voprosam, vozbuzhdennym Ministrom Narodnogo Prosveshcheniia po delu o tserkovnom penii" [Prince V. F. Odoevsky's opinions concerning questions pertaining to church singing raised by the Minister of Education], *Domashniaia beseda* (July 1866): 666.

102. See, e.g., E. Benz, H. Thurn, and C. Floros, *Das Buch der heiligen Gesangen der Ostkirche* (Hamburg: 1962), p. 204, cited in Ivan Gardner, *Bogosluzhebnoe penie Russkoi Pravoslavnoi Tserkvi* [The liturgical chant of the Russian Orthodox Church], vol. 2 (Jordanville, N. Y.: Holy Trinity Monastery, 1980–82), p. 228.

103. [Letters to the Editor], "Zhenshchiny v tserkovnykh khorakh" [Women in church choirs], *Muzykal'nyi truzhennik* 16 (1907):5.

104. Ibid., pp. 5–6.

105. Ibid.

106. Ibid., no. 19, pp. 10–11.

107. M. Stepanov, "Zavety S. V. Smolenskogo regentu tserkovnogo khora" [S. V. Smolensky's testament to a church precentor], *Khorovoe i regentskoe delo* 12 (1915):221.

108. "Zhenshchiny," *Muzykal'nyi truzhennik* 14 (1907):3–6.

109. Ibid., pp. 2–3.

110. Anonymous, [Concert review] of 16 March 1909, *Gusel'ki iarovchaty* 8 (1908/09):14.

111. Quoted in Gusin and Tkachev, *Gosudarstvennaia akademicheskaia kapella*, p. 46; see also, Einbeck, *Zur Geschichte*, in Gardner, "A. F. L'vov," p. 134.

112. Stepan Smolensky, "Vospominaniia" [Memoirs], vol. 2, MS, Golovanov Collection, no. 527–28, p. 180, Glinka State Museum of Musical Culture, Moscow.

113. Aleksandr Nikol'sky, "Vasily Sergeevich Orlov," *Khorovoe i regentskoe delo* 12 (1913):195ff.

114. Ivan Lipaev, [Concert review], *Russkaia muzykal'naia gazeta* 4 (1897):680–81.

115. Nikol'sky, "Vasily Sergeevich Orlov," pp. 198–99.

116. H. K. M., "The Russian Choir, A Remarkable Recital in New York," *New York Times*, 1 December 1913.

117. Bulychev, *Khorovoe penie*, pp. 37–39.

118. Chesnokov, *Khor*, p. 110.

119. Ibid., Tables 94 and 94a.

120. Aleksandr Nikol'sky, *Izbrannye khory* [Selected choruses], ed. by V. Sokolov (Moscow: Sovetskii Kompozitor, 1974).

121. Chesnokov, *Khor*, pp. 14–16.

122. Chesnokov Archive, Fund 36, no. 163, Glinka State Museum of Musical Culture, Moscow. As he was attempting to get his book published under the Soviet regime (a process that evidently was delayed for years), Chesnokov could not openly identify the fact that his source of inspiration and methodology was the Moscow Synodal Choir. As other materials in his archive show, the essential elements of *The choir and how to direct it* were laid out as early as 1912 in a manuscript entitled "Zapiski regenta" [Notes of a precentor]. At some later point Chesnokov entered the following note on the title page of the manuscript: "I look upon this brochure as the precursor of a book." (Chesnokov Archive, no. 322).

123. Among the noteworthy present-day exceptions are the Choir of the St. Alexander Nevsky Russian Orthodox Cathedral in Paris, under its current conductor, Evgeny Ivanovich Evetz, and the Moscow Chamber Choir, under the direction of Vladimir Minin.

Chapter 5

1. Vasily Zinov'ev, *Prakticheskoe rukovodstvo dlia nachinaiushchego uchitelia-regenta* [A practical manual for the beginning teacher-precentor] (Moscow: n.p., 1905), quoting Lisiansky, p. 92.

2. Pavel Chesnokov, "Zapiski regenta" [Notes of a precentor], MS, Chesnokov Archive, Fund 36, no. 322, Glinka State Museum of Musical Culture, Moscow.

3. Nikolai Kompaneisky, "Po povodu 9-go punkta 44-go paragrafa ustava Tserkovno-pevcheskogo Obshchestva v Sankt-Peterburge" [Concerning the 9th point of paragraph 44 in the by-laws of the Church-Singers' Association in St. Petersburg], *Russkaia muzykal'naia gazeta* 17/18 (1903):471–72.

4. Mikhail Ippolitov-Ivanov, *50 let russkoi muzyki v moikh vospominaniiakh* [Fifty years of Russian music in my reminiscences] (Moscow: Gosudarstvennoe Muzykal'noe Izdatel'stvo, 1934), pp. 112–13.

5. Synodal Decree No. 5117, 24 May 1847; P. Chizhevsky, *Tserkovno-grazhdanskie postanovleniia o tserkovnom penii* [Church and civil decrees concerning church singing] (Kharkov: n.p., 1878), p. 9; cited in Ivan Gardner, *Bogosluzhebnoe penie Russkoi Pravoslavnoi Tserkvi* [The liturgical chant of the Russian Orthodox Church], vol. 2 (Jordanville, N. Y.: Holy Trinity Monastery, 1980–82), pp. 324–25.

6. Synodal Decree No. 14040, 11 December 1847, ibid.; cited in Gardner, *Bogosluzhebnoe*, pp. 325–26.

7. Anonymous, "Regentskii klass pri Pridvornoi Pevcheskoi Kapelle" [The precentors' course at the Imperial Court Chapel], *Russkaia muzykal'naia gazeta* 19/20 (1904):516–19.

8. Aleksei L'vov, *O tserkovnykh khorakh* [Concerning church choirs] (St. Petersburg: n.p., 1853), p. 6–7.

9. Anonymous, "Regentskii klass," col. 518.

10. Nikolai Rimsky-Korsakov, *Letopis' moei muzykal'noi zhizni* [My musical life] (Moscow: Gosudarstvennoe Muzykal'noe Izdatel'stvo, 1955), pp. 152–53.

11. Anonymous,"Regentskii klass," *Russkaia muzykal'naia gazeta* 23/24 (1904):584.

12. Nonakk., "Zametka o regentskikh klassakh Pridvornoi Pevcheskoi Kapelly" [A note about the precentors' courses of the Imperial Court Chapel], *Russkaia muzykal'naia gazeta* 11 (1896):1421–24.

13. Vasily Zolotarev, *Vospominaniia o moikh velikikh uchiteliakh, druz'iakh, i tovarishchakh* [Reminiscences about my great teachers, friends, and comrades], letter of 5 August 1891 (Moscow: Gosudarstvennoe Muzykal'noe Izdatel'stvo, 1957) p. 119.

14. N[ikolai] K[ovin], "Regentskoe obrazovanie" [The education of precentors], *Khorovoe i regentskoe delo* 3–5 (1911):66–69; 81–85; 109–15.

15. Daniil Lokshin, "Muzykal'no-pedagogicheskie vzgliady A. D. Kastal'skogo" [A. D. Kastal'sky's views on musical pedagogy] in Dmitri Zhitomirsky, ed., *A. D. Kastal'sky: Vospominaniia, stat'i, materialy* [A. D. Kastal'sky: Memoirs, articles, materials] (Moscow: Gosudarstvennoe Muzykal'noe Izdatel'stvo, 1960) pp. 85–98.

16. Vasily Metallov, "Sinodal'nye, byvshie patriarshie pevchie" [The synodal, formerly the patriarchal singers], *Russkaia muzykal'naia gazeta* 12 (1898):1049.

17. Vasily Metallov, *Sinodal'noe Uchilishche Tserkovnogo Peniia v ego proshlom i nastoiashchem* [The Synodal School of Church Singing in its past and present] (Moscow: n.p., 1911), pp. 12–13.

18. Ibid, pp. 70–71.

19. Ibid, pp. 88–89.

20. Stepan Smolensky, *Kurs khorovogo tserkovnogo peniia* [A course in choral church singing], 5th ed. (Moscow: n.p., 1900), p. 148.

21. In 1885, K. Veber wrote: "A teacher of church singing may not necessarily be a virtuoso, and still do a lot of good if he merely has good taste.... A teacher of secular [choral] singing [by contrast] ought to know everything that a singer, in the full sense of that word, should know, i.e., he must be sufficiently educated musically to be able to interpret the character of numerous composers' works..., have a trained voice, know musical theory, [and be able to] conduct various [types of] choirs...." (K. Veber, *Kratkii ocherk sovremennogo sostoianiia muzykal'nogo obrazovaniia v Rossii* [A brief essay on the current state of musical education in Russia], quoted in Daniil Lokshin, *Khorovoe penie v russkoi shkole* [Choral singing in the Russian school] (Moscow: Gosudarstvennoe Muzykal'noe Izdatel'stvo, 1957) p. 104.)

     Aleksandr Maslov, in his article entitled "On conducting," wrote in 1910: "For the earlier type of church music [i.e., before the new style of the Moscow Synodal School] it was not necessary to have conductors who possessed any technique.... Precentors' courses usually stress the church rule, church singing (chants), and other practical knowledge, to the exclusion of the technical side [of conducting]." ("O dirizhirovanii," *Muzyka i zhizn'* 12 (1910):3–7.)

     That same year, Vasily Mikhailovich Orlov (not V. S. Orlov) wrote that "The precentor's skill does not require extensive musical knowledge. All that is required are a good ear and the ability to play the violin in tune." (*Iskusstvo tserkovnogo peniia* [The art of church singing] (Moscow: n.p., 1910), p. 15.)

22. Cited in Metallov, *Sinodal'noe Uchilishche*, pp. 108–14.

23. The texts included Aleksei Puzyrevsky, *Metodicheskie zametki po prepodavaniiu peniia v narodnykh shkolakh* [Notes on the methodology of teaching singing in people's schools] (Moscow: n.p., 1891); Dmitri Allemanov, *Metodika tserkovnogo peniia* [Methodology of church singing] (Moscow: P. Jurgenson, 1908); Vasily Metallov, *Tserkovnoe penie kak predmet prepodavaniia v narodnykh shkolakh* [Church singing as a subject in people's schools], 3rd ed. (Moscow: n.p., 1903); Vasily Komarov, *Penie v nachal'noi russkoi shkole*

[Singing in the Russian elementary school], 2nd ed. (Moscow: n.p., 1899); Aleksandr Kastal'sky, *Obshchedostupnyi samouchitel' tserkovnogo peniia* [A popular self-instructor of church singing] (Moscow: P. Jurgenson, 1910); Aleksandr Kastal'sky, *Rukovodstvo k vyrazitel'nomu peniiu stikhir pri pomoshchi razlichnykh garmonizatsii* [A manual for the expressive singing of stichera, using various harmonizations] (Moscow: P. Jurgenson, 1909); Nikolai Kashkin and Aleksandr Nikol'sky, *Nachal'nyi uchebnik khorovogo peniia* [A beginning textbook of choral singing] (Moscow: P. Jurgenson, 1909).

    See *Programmy muzykal'nykh predmetov i istorii iskusstv v Moskovskom Sinodal'nom Uchilishche Tserkovnogo Peniia* [Programs in musical subjects and arts history at the Moscow Synodal School of Church Singing] (Moscow: n.p., 1910); see also, Metallov, *Sinodal'noe uchilishche,* pp. 123-25.

24.   Nikolai Findeizen, "Sinodal'noe Uchilishche Tserkovnogo Peniia v Moskve" [The Synodal School of Church Singing in Moscow], *Russkaia muzykal'naia gazeta* 4 (1898):345.

25.   *Programmy muzykal'nykh predmetov.*

26.   Ibid.

27.   See *Programmy Regentskogo Uchilishcha, osnovannogo v 1907 S. V. Smolenskim v Sankt-Peterburge* [The programs of the Precentors' School established in 1907 by S. V. Smolensky in St. Petersburg] (St. Petersburg: n.p., 1908); *Polozhenie o regentskikh klassakh Pridvornoi Pevcheskoi Kapelly* [Decree concerning the pecentors' courses of the Imperial Court Chapel] (St. Petersburg: n.p., 1911).

28.   Komarov, *Penie,* p. 24

29.   Kastal'sky, *Obshchedostupnyi,* p. 9.

30.   Maslov, "O dirizhirovanii," p. 5.

31.   Aleksandr Nikol'sky, [Lecture], *Trudy Pervogo Vserossiiskogo Regentskogo S''ezda v Moskve* [Proceedings of the First All-Russian Precentors' Convention in Moscow] (Moscow: n.p., 1908), pp. 50-51.

32.   Orlov, *Iskusstvo,* p. 18. The last phrase of Orlov's "advice" often goes unheeded to this day. In 1979 I heard choir directors in some Moscow churches using both "ts..." and "tishe" to make their choirs sing softer.

33.   Nikolai Kovin, *Upravlenie khorom,* [Choral conducting] (Petrograd: n.p., 1916).

34.   Ibid., p. 16.

35.   Ibid., p. 17.

36.   Ibid., p. 50.

37.   Ibid., p. 51.

38.   N. Zipalov, *F. A. Bagretsov: Opyt biografii v istoriko-muzykal'nom otnoshenii po otzyvam i vospominaniiam ego sovremennikov* [F. A. Bagretsov: a historico-musical biography based on accounts and reminiscences of his contemporaries] (Vladikavkaz: n.p., 1914); Aleksei Karasev, *Grigory Fyodorovich L'vovsky i ego dukhovno-muzykal'nye proizvedeniia* [Grigory Fyodorovich L'vovsky and his sacred musical works] (Moscow: n.p., 1914); Gavriil Lomakin, "Avtobiograficheskie zapiski" [Autobiographical notes], *Russkaia starina* 49-51 (1886); Yu. Goriainov, *G. Ya. Lomakin: Dirizher, kompozitor, uchitel'* [G. Ya. Lomakin: Conductor, composer, pedagogue] (Moscow: Muzyka, 1984).

39. The instructor in question must have been Antonio Sapienza the Elder (1755–1829), since his son, Pietro Antonio Sapienza (1794–1855), was studying in Naples from 1822 to 1827, i.e., during the time Lomakin was singing in the Count's Chapel. Upon returning to St. Petersburg, Sapienza the Younger also worked in Sheremetev's Chapel in the 1830s.

40. Lomakin, "Avtobiograficheskie", p. 650.

41. Ibid., p. 658.

42. Vladimir Stasov, "Kontsert gg. pevchikh grafa Sheremeteva" [A concert by the singers of Count Sheremetev], *Muzykal'nyi i teatral'nyi vestnik* 9 (1856).

43. Vladimir Stasov, "Tri russkikh kontserta" [Three Russian concerts], *Sankt-Peterburgskie vedomosti*, 30 April 1863.

44. E.g., the program of the concert reviewed by Stasov in 1856 consisted of: Bach—2 Passion Chorales, Leo—"Iudica me Deus," Carissimi—"Plorate filii Israel," Nanini—"Hodie nobis caelorum Rex," and Bach—"Crucifixus" from the *Mass in B minor*. See Stasov, "Kontsert."

45. Among Bekker's assistants was Nikolai Kedroff (the elder), who, along with his son Nikolai Jr. and the Kedroff Quartet, was a prominent musical figure in Russian émigré circles in France after the Revolution.

46. Cited in Karasev, *Grigory Fyodorovich L'vovsky*, pp. 19–20.

47. Daniil Lokshin, *Zamechatel'nye russkie khory i ikh dirizhery* [Outstanding Russian choirs and their conductors] (Moscow: Gosudarstvennoe Muzykal'noe Izdatel'stvo, 1963), p. 40.

48. Rakhlitsky, cited by Zipalov, *F. A. Bagretsov*, p. 11, n. 2.

49. Ibid., p. 12.

50. Ibid., p. 17.

51. All the quotations on pp. 182–83 are taken from Zipalov, *F.A. Bagretsov*, pp. 20–25.

52. Orlov, *Iskusstvo*, p. 18–19.

53. S[tepan] S[molensk]y, *Ob ozdorovlenii programm dukhovnykh kontsertov v Moskve* [The revitalization of the programs of sacred concerts in Moscow] (Moscow: n.p., 1900), pp 7–8.

54. Cited in Zipalov, *F.A. Bagretsov*, p. 6.

55. Wrote Smolensky in his "Memoirs": "In Moscow our success [in Vienna, in 1899] created most favorable impressions among the connoisseurs of church singing and clergy. Even the stubborn partisans of the Chudov Choir, who had criticized our dryness, the 'operatic quality' of our singing, our irreverence towards the compositions of Bagretsov, and the heretical nature of our own direction, represented by the compositions of Kastal'sky, Grechaninov, and Chesnokov, turned in our direction. The rise in the reputation of the [Synodal] Choir and Orlov's authoritativeness forced silence upon critics such as Urusov, Gnusin, Durnovo...." (Smolensky, "Vospominaniia" [Memoirs], vol. 2, MS, Golovanov Collection, no. 527–28, p. 114, Glinka State Museum of Musical Culture, Moscow.)

56. Donat Tkachev, *Aleksandr Andreevich Arkhangel'sky (1846–1924). Ocherk zhizni i deiatel'nosti* [Aleksandr Andreevich Arkhangel'sky (1846–1924): His life and works] (Leningrad: Muzyka, 1974).

57. Arkhangel'sky Archive, Fund 184, n. 32, Glinka State Museum of Musical Culture, Moscow; cited in Tkachev, *Aleksandr Andreevich Arkhangel'sky,* pp. 57–59.

58. Klavdy Ptitsa, *Mastera khorovogo iskusstva v Moskovskoi Konservatorii* [Masters of the choral art at the Moscow Conservatory] (Moscow: Muzyka, 1970), p. 23.

59. Arkhangel'sky Archive, cited in Tkachev, *Aleksandr Andreevich Arkhangel'sky,* pp. 57–58.

60. Tkachev, ibid., p. 56.

61. *Pamiati V. S. Orlova* [V. S. Orlov, in memoriam] (Moscow: n.p., 1908).

62. Nikolai Kashkin, "Vospominaniia o V. S. Orlove" [Remembering V. S. Orlov] in *Pamiati V. S. Orlova,* pp. 10–11.

63. Ibid., p. 13.

64. Cited in Metallov, *Sinodal'noe Uchilishche,* pp. 43–44.

65. Aleksandr Kastal'sky, "O moei muzykal'noi kar'ere i moi mysli o tserkovnoi muzyke" *Muzykal'nyi sovremennik* 2 (October 1915); transl. by S. W. Pring, "My Musical Career and Thoughts on Church Music," *Musical Quarterly* (1925): 240.

66. Nikolai Kochetov, "V bor'be—zhizn'!" [In struggle—life!], in *Pamiati V. S. Orlova,* p. 12.

67. Vladimir Stepanov's monograph "Vasily Sergeevich Orlov," written in 1954, is often cited by Soviet scholars as a major source of information about Orlov. Although Stepanov did, in fact, graduate in 1908 from the Moscow Synodal School, his monograph contains scarcely an original word! All the material is "borrowed" from Aleksandr Nikol'sky's "Vasily Sergeevich Orlov" (*Khorovoe i regentskoe delo* 11–12 (1913):172–77, 195–201), and other sources without a single citation.

68. Semyon Kruglikov, "Regent-master" [A master conductor], in *Pamiati V. S. Orlova,* p. 22.

69. Smolensky, "Vospominaniia," p. 104. The practice of mouthing the words undoubtedly stemmed from the long-standing practice of Orthodox precentors to sing along with the choir, which one may observe even today sometimes. As a more refined approach towards conducting developed, writers pointed out that the precentor must not sing. Smolensky writes, for example: "The precentor must unfailingly conduct the choir silently, i.e., without singing along, since only then will he clearly hear what is being sung and will thus be the full master of the choir." (*Kurs khorogovo tserkovnogo peniia,* p. 148.) In Russian choral practice this apparent truism was not at all self-evident, since for centuries, groups of singers had been led by a *golovshchik*—the lead singer, who, by definition and by tradition, led the others with his voice, rather than by means of gestures. One suspects that even though the repertoire changed with the coming of the Italianate style, the practice of singing along did not stop until as late as the end of the nineteenth century—and even then, not universally.

70. Ivan Lipaev, [Concert review], *Russkaia muzykal'naia gazeta* 13 (1906):348.

71. The preceding excerpts are all taken from Nikol'sky, "Vasily Sergeevich Orlov," pp. 172–77.

72. Aleksandr Nikol'sky, MS Notebook (entry under 1894), Nikol'sky Archive, Fund 294, no. 379, pp. 24–25, Glinka State Museum of Musical Culture, Moscow.

73. Nikol'sky, "Vasily Sergeevich Orlov," *Khorovoe i regentskoe delo* 12 (1913):195–201.

74. See, e.g., ibid., pp. 198–99; also Ivan Lipaev's reviews of the 14 October 1901 concert in *Kur'er* and *Novosti dnia.*

75. Nikol'sky, "Vasily Sergeevich Orlov," p. 197.

76. Nikolai Kompaneisky, "A. D. Kastal'sky (po povodu 4-go vypuska ego dukhovno-muzykal'nykh sochinenii)" [A. D. Kastal'sky (concerning the 4th issue of his sacred musical works)], *Russkaia muzykal'naia gazeta* 13/14 (1904):360.

77. Mikhail Lisitsyn, "Moskva i Sinodal'nyi Khor" [Moscow and the Synodal Choir], *Muzyka i penie* 12 (1906):1.

78. Ivan Lipaev, [Concert review], *Russkaia muzykal'naia gazeta* 46 (1908):1032.

79. A. L——n, [Concert review], *Muzyka i zhizn'* 3 (1908):14.

80. Mikhail Lisitsyn, "Velikopostnye dukhovnye kontserty" [Lenten sacred concerts], *Muzyka i penie* 7 (1911):1–2.

81. Ptitsa, *Mastera.*

82. In 1979, when this writer was in Moscow, material on Danilin was being assembled by one of the researchers at the Glinka State Museum of Musical Culture. However, it was not yet available.

83. Reviews of 29 May and 30 May 1911; cited in A. Gladky, *Poezdka Sinodal'nogo Khora zagranitsu v 1911 g.* [The Synodal Choir's tour abroad in 1911] (Moscow: n.p., 1912).

84. Review of 2 June 1911 concert; cited in Gladky, *Poezdka.*

85. Grigory Prokofiev, "Opera i kontserty v Moskve" [Opera and concerts in Moscow], *Russkaia muzykal'naia gazeta* 14 (1915):260.

86. Ptitsa, *Mastera,* pp. 18–19.

87. Ibid., p. 22.

88. Ibid., p. 24.

89. Interview with Nikolai Mikhailovich Matveev, a prominent church precentor in Moscow and professor of choral conducting at the Moscow Theological Academy, February 1979.

90. Interview with Aleksei Aleksandrovich Naumov, a researcher on choral performance at the Glinka State Museum of Musical Culture, May 1979.

91. Nikolai Matveev, *Khorovedenie* [Choral conducting], typescript (Zagorsk: Moskovskaia Dukhovnaia Akademiia, 1976), p. 45.

92. Ptitsa, *Mastera,* p. 26.

93. Ibid., p. 34.

94. Ibid., p. 9.

95. Other composers who occasionally performed as choral conductors were Grechaninov and Rachmaninoff. However, one review of a concert by the St. Petersburg Imperial Opera Chorus under Grechaninov's direction called Grechaninov's conducting "one of the major obstacles" to the success of the concert *(Khorovoe i regentskoe delo* 4 (1913):64. Only one review dealt with Rachmaninoff as a choral conductor: reviewing the composer's performance of his *Liturgy* several weeks after the Synodal Choir performed it under Danilin, Mikhail Lisitsyn merely notes that Rachmaninoff did not employ "such striking

effects" as Danilin, perhaps referring to the intensity of accents and dynamic constrasts (*Muzyka i penie* 7 (1911):2). Among the lesser composers associated with the Moscow Synodal Choir who were also conductors, one must mention Nikolai Tolstiakov, Konstantin Shvedov, and Nikolai Golovanov. The latter became an outstanding symphonic and operatic conductor after the Revolution, when opportunities to conduct sacred compositions became much rarer and politically undesirable.

96. Aleksandr Nikol'sky, [Concert review], *Khorovoe i regentskoe delo* 4 (1909):112–14.

97. D., "K desiatiletiiu upravleniia P. G. Chesnokovym khorom liubitelei peniia pri tserkvi Sv. Troitsy chto na Griaziakh v Moskve" [Commemorating the ten-year anniversary of P. G. Chesnokov's conducting of the amateur choir at the Church of the Holy Trinity at the mud-baths in Moscow], *Khorovoe i regentskoe delo* 4 (1913):68–70.

98. Ptitsa, *Mastera*, p. 70.

99. Ibid., p. 65.

Chapter 6

1. Nikolai Kashkin, "Ob"iasnitel'naia zapiska k kursu po istorii muzyki" [Explanatory note to the course in music history] in *Programmy muzykal'nykh predmetov i istorii iskusstv v Moskovskom Sinodal'nom Uchilishche Tserkovnogo Peniia* [Programs in musical subjects and arts history at the Moscow Synodal School of Church Singing] (Moscow: n.p., 1910).

2. Aleksandr Kastal'sky, "Metodika prepodavaniia shkol'nogo khorovogo peniia" [The methology of teaching school choral singing], MS, Kastal'sky Archive, Fund 12, no. 246, pp. 16ff, Glinka State Museum of Musical Culture, Moscow.

3. See, e.g., Fyodor Rubtsov, *Stat'i po muzykal'nomu fol'kloru* [Essays in musical folklore] (Leningrad and Moscow: Muzyka, 1973), esp. "Russkie narodnye khory i psevdonarodnye pesni" [Russian folk choirs and pseudo-folk songs], pp. 182–208, and pp. 209ff.

4. The All-Russian Church Council of 1918 was scheduled to consider a proposal that would have significantly updated the liturgical Slavonic language, bringing it closer to modern Russian. However, the Council was dispersed before it was able to act upon this proposal. In the 1900s some liturgical books (e.g., the *Lenten Triodion*) underwent minor revisions, updating particularly obscure or obsolete expressions. However, the major texts of the liturgy remained unchanged.

5. One must further distinguish between "para-liturgical" and "extra-liturgical" texts, the latter being texts related to events commemorated liturgically by the Church (e.g., the birth of Christ, the Resurrection) but not intended to be sung in the course of church services. These texts, known as *dukhovnye stikhi* (sacred verses), progressively disappeared in central Russia during the eighteenth century, remaining only among the Old Believers. In the Ukraine and in Carpatho-Russia extra-liturgical verses remained in the form of carols. Though these were mostly for Christmas, there were a few for other feasts of the Church year.

6. See chapter 2, p. 68, and chapter 3, pp. 83–84.

7. The Russian system of Eight Tones, while superficially based on the Byzantine system, is different in musical structure. Whereas in the Byzantine *Octoechos* each *echos* is a distinctly different scale or mode, all eight Russian Tones (*glas*'s) are based on the same tone row or gamut and are differentiated only by characteristic melodic formulae.

8. (1) Vespers, (2) Compline, (3) Nocturn, (4) Matins, (5) First Hour, (6) Third Hour, (7) Sixth Hour, (8) Divine Liturgy, (9) Ninth Hour.

9. Although the principle of categorizing hymns into ordinaries and propers is somewhat different in the Orthodox Church than in the Roman Church, these terms will be used for the sake of convenience.

10. The services are described in their most usual forms, as they were commonly practiced in parish and cathedral churches, and for which composers wrote their polyphonic choral compositions. For the other, more complex variants, see Gardner, *Russian Church Singing,* vol. 1: *Orthodox Worship and Hymnography,* trans. Vladimir Morosan (Crestwood, N.Y.: St. Vladimir's Seminary Press, 1980), pp. 71–98.

11. The Orthodox Church numbers the psalms according to the Septuagint (as does the Latin Vulgate). The numbers in brackets indicate the numbering used in the Hebrew Bible and the King James version.

12. Stichera which expound the dogma of the incarnation of Christ and the virginity of the Mother of God (Theotokos). The Theotokia-Dogmatika change according to the Eight Tones.

13. Gardner, *Russian Church Singing,* p. 77.

14. The adjective "middle" is never actually used in designating a chant. However, a distinct level of medium melodic complexity can be observed between melodies of the great znamennyi and little znamennyi chants. See also ibid., p. 103.

15. The exact relationship of Russian "Greek" Chant (*grecheskii rospev*) to Byzantine Chant has not yet been determined. Gardner's statement—that it has "nothing in common" with the liturgical singing of the Greeks—is too strong, since the chant melodies were most likely written down by Slavic singers from Greek singers known to have been in the Ukraine and Muscovy in the late sixteenth and seventeenth centuries. See ibid., pp. 105–6.

16. Although he is a ranking authority on the subject of Russian Orthodox church music, Gardner is guilty of this practice as well. One would be very hard pressed to find any Orthodox church in which services are performed exactly the way he describes them.

17. Pyotr Tchaikovsky, cited in Ivan Gardner, *Bogosluzhebnoe penie Russkoi Pravoslavnoi Tserkvi: Sistema, sushchnost', istoriia* [The liturgical chant of the Russian Orthodox Church: Its system, essence, and history], vol. 2 (Jordanville, N.Y.: Holy Trinity Monastery, 1980–82), p. 431.

18. Pyotr Tchaikovsky, *Letters to Madame N. von Meck,* vol. 1 (Leningrad: Gosudarstvennoe Muzykal'noe Izdatel'stvo, 1934), p. 314.

19. Antonin Preobrazhensky, "Trudy P. I. Chaikovskogo v oblasti tserkovnogo peniia" [The contributions of P. I. Tchaikovsky in the area of church singing], *Ekaterinoslavskie eparkhial'nye vedomosti* 23, 24 (1894):571–80, 589–605.

20. Cited in ibid., p. 598.

21. Nikolai Kashkin [Concert review], clipping from unidentified newspaper, Kastal'sky Archive, Fund 12, Glinka State Museum of Musical Culture, Moscow.

22. Viktor Mikhailovich Vasnetsov (1848–1926), a Russian painter who synthesized techniques of modern painting with nationalistic subjects and iconography, painted most of the frescoes and icons of the St. Vladimir Cathedral in Kiev—a remarkable edifice in

neo-Byzantine style. In the frescoes of the St. Vladimir Cathedral, Vasnetsov sought to introduce a spiritual and emotional content into the traditional system of monumental church painting, which had completely deteriorated by the late nineteenth century.

23. Ivan Lipaev [Concert review], *Russkaia muzykal'naia gazeta* 4 (1898):400.

24. Aleksandr Kastal'sky, "O moei muzykal'noi kar'ere i moi mysli o tserkovnoi muzyke" *Muzykal'nyi sovremennik* 2 (October 1915); transl. by S. W. Pring, "My Musical Career and Thoughts on Church Music," *Musical Quarterly* (1925):231–47.

25. Mikhail Lisitsyn, "O novom napravlenii v russkoi tserkovnoi muzyke" [The new direction in Russian church music], *Muzykal'nyi truzhennik* 10–13 (1909):10–11.

26. Ibid., p. 8.

27. Konstantin Shvedov [Reply to D. Zarin], *Trudy Pervogo Vserossiiskogo S"ezda Khorovykh Deiatelei* [Proceedings of the First All-Russian Convention of Choral Directors] (Moscow: n.p., 1908), p. 29.

28. Aleksandr Nikol'sky [Speech], ibid., p. 7.

29. A[leksandr] N[ikol'sk]y, "Dukhovnye kontserty i ikh zadachi" [Sacred concerts and their objectives], *Khorovoe i regentskoe delo* 4 (1909):101.

30. Nikolai Kompaneisky, "Sovremennoe demestvo" [Modern-day demestvo], *Russkaia muzykal'naia gazeta* 6 (1902):165–70.

31. Aleksandr Grechaninov, "O dukhe tserkovnykh pesnopenii" [The spirit of church hymns], quoted in Nikolai Kompaneisky, "O stile tserkovnykh pesnopenii" [The style of church hymns], *Russkaia muzykal'naia gazeta* 37 (1901):854–60.

32. The article, entitled "Novye zadachi pravoslavnoi tserkovnoi muzyki v Rossii. Vnimaniiu kompozitorov tserkovnoi muzyki" [New objectives of Orthodox church music in Russia. To the attention of church music composers], was reprinted in the music journals *Gusel'ki iarovchaty* and *Khorovoe i regentskoe delo* from the Russian church periodical *Tserkovnaia pravda*, published in Berlin, signed only with the initials Yu. I. The Reverend Georgy (Yuri) Izvekov, who published some interesting sacred works in the 1910s, is known to have been stationed at the embassy church in Berlin in the 1910s.

33. By 1913 there already existed a number of large-scale liturgical works, including Grechaninov's two Liturgies, his *Vigil* and *Holy Week*, Rachmaninoff's *Liturgy*, among other works.

34. Yu. I., "Novye zadachi."

35. Znamennyi chant melodies were constructed using a flexible system of melodic nuclei—*popevki*. In the original znamennyi system of Eight Tones, as in the Byzantine *Octoechos*, certain *popevki* belonged to specific Tones, which the chant composer strung together to create new melodies for various hymns within the Tone. A detailed study of znamennyi *popevki* was made by Vasily Metallov in his *Osmoglasie znamennogo rospeva* [The Eight Tones of znamennyi chant] (Moscow: n.p., 1899); other studies include Johann von Gardner and Erwin Koschmieder, *Ein handschriftliches Lehrbuch der altrussischen Neumenschrift*, 3 vols. (Munich: Bayerische Akademie der Wissenschaften, 1963, 1966, 1973), and Constantin Floros, *Universale Neumenkunde*, 3 vols. (Kassel: n.p., 1970).

36. Kastal'sky, "My Musical Career," p. 244.

37. See, e.g., R. Sterling Beckwith, "Alexander Dmitrievich Kastal'skii (1856-1926) and the Search for a Native Russian Choral Style," (Ph. D. diss., Cornell University, 1969); Harry Elzinga, "The Sacred Choral Works of Pavel Grigor'evich Chesnokov (1877-1944)," (Ph. D. diss., Indiana University, 1970); Stephen Prussing, "Compositional Techniques in Rachmaninoff's 'Vespers, Opus 37'," (Ph. D. diss., The Catholic University of America, 1980).

38. Kastal'sky, "My Musical Career," p. 234-35.

39. Aleksandr Nikol'sky, "S. V. Smolensky i ego rol' v novom napravlenii russkoi tserkovnoi muzyki" [S. V. Smolensky and his role in the new direction of Russian church music], *Khorovoe i regentskoe delo* 10 (1913):151-56.

40. Cited in Klavdy Ptitsa, *Mastera khorovogo isskusstva v Moskovskoi Konservatorii* [Masters of the choral art at the Moscow Conservatory] (Moscow: Muzyka, 1970), pp. 59-60.

41. Kastal'sky, "My Musical Career," pp. 234-35.

42. See Beckwith, "Alexander Kastal'sky," p. 190.

43. Sergei Vasilenko, *Stranitsy vospominanii* [Pages of reminiscences] (Moscow-Leningrad: Gosudarstvennoe Muzykal'noe Izdatel'stvo, 1948), p. 108.

44. One should not confuse Sergei Ivanovich Taneev of Moscow with A. S. Taneev, a minor composer of church music in St. Petersburg.

45. Kastal'sky, "My Musical Career," p. 234.

46. Ibid., pp. 234-35.

47. Ibid., p. 236.

48. Boris Asaf'ev, "Kharakternye osobennosti iskusstva Kastal'skogo" [Characteristic features of Kastal'sky's art] and "Khorovoe tvorchestvo Kastal'skogo" [Kastal'sky's choral works], in Dmitri Zhitomirsky, ed., *A. D. Kastal'sky: Vospominaniia, stat'i, materialy* [A. D. Kastal'sky: Memoirs, articles, materials] (Moscow: Gosudarstvennoe Muzykal'noe Izdatel'stvo, 1960), pp. 13-16.

49. Other twentieth-century composers of choral music who made prominent use of a similar type of "homorhythmic polyphony" were Francis Poulenc and Igor Stravinsky (prior to his adoption of dodecaphonic technique).

50. See, e.g., the citation of a seventeenth-century treatise given in chapter 1, p. 20 above.

51. The table appears in a manuscript notebook found in Aleksandr Kastal'sky's Archive (Fund 12, no. 383, Glinka State Museum of Musical Culture, Moscow). Statement No. 39e concludes the section labelled "Choral Colors." Immediately afterward there follow another fifty-four statements describing various devices of "choral orchestration," some of them identical to the earlier ones. The fact that the first set of statements is written in purple ink with numerous notes added in red, black, and green ink, while the second is largely in black ink with only a few notes in red, suggests that the latter is a revision of the former. The first list, however, conveys the variety of choral colors found in Kastal'sky's works much more vividly, which is why it was included here. Both lists appear in full in Appendix F of my original dissertation (University of Illinois, 1984).

52. Asaf'ev, "Kharakternye osobennosti iskusstva Kastal'skogo," p. 16.

53. Elzinga, "Sacred Choral Works," p. 135.

54. Asaf'ev, "Kharakternye osobennosti iskusstva Kastal'skogo," p. 16, n.

55. Elzinga, "Sacred Choral Works," p. 200.

56. Kompaneisky, "O stile," *Russkaia muzykal'naia gazeta* 38 (1901):895.

57. Kastal'sky, "My musical career," p. 244.

58. Nikolai Kompaneisky, Preface to *Bogorodichny-Dogmatiki* (Moscow: P. Jurgenson, n. d.).

59. Yuri Keldysh, *Rakhmaninov i ego vremia* [Rachmaninoff and his times] (Moscow: Muzyka, 1973), p. 385.

60. Kleopatra Dmitrevskaia, "Viktor Kalinnikov. K 100–letiiu so dnia rozhdeniia" [Viktor Kalinnikov. Commemorating the 100th anniversary of his birth], in *Khorovoe iskusstvo* [The choral art], vol. 2 (Leningrad: Muzyka, 1971), p. 63.

61. Kastal'sky, "My Musical Career," pp. 245–46.

62. Aleksandr Kastal'sky, "'Vsenoshchnoe bdenie' S. Rakhmaninova" [S. Rachmaninoff's "All-Night Vigil"], *Russkoe slovo*, 7 March 1915, cited in Keldysh, *Rakhmaninov*, p. 399.

63. Keldysh, *Rakhmaninov*, p. 414.

Chapter 7

1. The five chant-books included the *Obikhod notnago peniia* [The Common hymns in staff notation], the *Oktoikh notnago peniia* [The Octoechos in staff notation], the *Irmologii notnago peniia* [The Heirmologion in staff notation], the *Prazdniki notnago peniia* [The Feasts in staff notation], and the *Triod' postnaia i tsvetnaia* [The Lenten Triodion and Pentecostarion].

2. The earliest known Slavonic MS written in staff notation is the Suprasl' Heirmologion, which dates from 1601.

3. Modest Musorgsky, *Pis'ma i dokumenty* [Letters and documents], Letter to Vladimir Stasov, 23 July 1873, (Moscow and Leningrad: Gosudarstvennoe Muzykal'noe Izdatel'stvo, 1932), p. 260.

4. Dmitri Razumovsky, *Tserkovnoe penie v Rossii* [Church singing in Russia], 3 vols. (Moscow: n.p., 1867–69); Ioann Voznesensky, *Tserkovnoe penie Pravoslavnoi Greko-Rossiiskoi Tserkvi: Bol'shoi i malyi znamennyi rospev* [The church singing of the Orthodox Graeco-Russian Church: The great and little znamennyi chant], 2 vols. (Riga: n.p., 1890); Ioann Voznesensky, *Osmoglasnye rospevy trekh poslednikh vekov Pravoslavnoi Russkoi Tserkvi* [The Eight-Tone chants of the last three centuries in the Orthodox Russian Church], 3 vols.: 1. *Kievskii rospev* [Kievan chant], 2. *Bolgarskii rospev* [Bulgarian chant], 3. *Grecheskii rospev v Rossii* [Greek chant in Russia], (Kiev and Moscow: n.p., 1891–93); Nikolai Potulov, *Rukovodstvo k prakticheskomu izucheniiu drevnego peniia Pravoslavnoi Rossiiskoi Tserkvi* [A manual for the practical study of the ancient singing of the Russian Orthodox Church] (Moscow: n.p., n.d.).

5. E.g., chants from the Solovetsk and Valaam Monasteries.

6. Cited in Nikolai Uspensky, *Drevne-russkoe pevcheskoe iskusstvo* [The early Russian art of singing], 2nd ed. (Moscow: Sovetskii Kompozitor, 1971), p. 292.

7. Nikolai Findeizen, *Ocherki po istorii muzyki v Rossii* [Essays in the history of music in Russia], vol. 1 (Moscow-Leningrad: Gosudarstvennoe Muzykal'noe Izdatel'stvo, 1928), p. 142.

8. Aleksandr Mezenets, "Izveshchenie o soglasneishikh pometakh" [A report on the most consonant markings], in A. Rogov, ed., *Muzykal'naia estetika Rossii XI–XVII vekov* [Musical aesthetics of Russia in the 11th through 17th centuries] (Moscow: Muzyka, 1973), p. 102.

9. Aleksei L'vov, "O vvedenii edinoobraznogo tserkovnogo peniia vo vsekh zhenskikh uchebnykh zavedeniiakh" [Concerning the introduction of uniform church singing in all women's educational institutions], Fund 759, inventory 21, no. 351, Archive of the Imperial Court Chapel, Leningrad.

10. Ioann Voznesensky, *O sovremennykh nam nuzhdakh i zadachakh russkogo tserkovnogo peniia* [Contemporary needs and problems of Russian church singing] (Riga: n.p., 1891), pp. 17–18.

11. Sergei Protopopov, *O khudozhestvennom elemente v pravoslavnom tserkovnom penii* [Concerning the artistic element in Orthodox church singing] (Sergiev Posad: n.p., 1901); 2nd ed. (St. Petersburg: n.p., 1905), p. 13.

12. Vasily Fyodorovich Komarov (1838–1901) was a professor of church music and mathematics at the Moscow Theological Seminary.

13. Vasily Komarov, *Sredstva k uluchsheniiu tserkovnogo peniia* [The means of improving church singing] (Moscow: n.p., 1890), p. 19ff.

14. Aleksandr Nikol'sky, "Kriukovaia sistema; ee smysl i znachenie" [The neumatic system; its meaning and significance], *Khorovoe i regentskoe delo* 3–4 (1912):41–47; 65–72.

15. Sergei Vasilenko, *Stranitsy vospominanii* [Pages of reminiscences] (Moscow-Leningrad: Gosudarstvennoe Muzykal'noe Izdatel'stvo, 1948), p. 106.

16. Aleksandr Kastal'sky, "O moei muzykal'noi kar'ere i moi mysli o tserkovnoi muzyke" *Muzykal'nyi sovremennik* 2 (October 1915); transl. by S. W. Pring, "My Musical Career and Thoughts on Church Music," *Musical Quarterly* (1925): 241.

17. Ivan Gardner, *Bogosluzhebnoe penie Russkoi Pravoslavnoi Tserkvi: Sistema, sushchnost', istoriia* [The liturgical chant of the Russian Orthodox Church: Its system, essence, and history], vol. 1 (Jordanville, N. Y.: Holy Trinity Monastery, 1980–82), p. 373.

18. Staroobriadets, "Staroobriadcheskoe penie i pevchie" [Singing and singers among the Old Believers], *Muzykal'nyi truzhennik* 6 (1909):2–3.

19. Nikolai Kompaneisky, "Staroobriadcheskii dukhovnyi kontsert" [A sacred concert of the Old Believers], *Russkaia muzykal'naia gazeta* 17 (1908):407–11.

20. Aleksandr Nikol'sky, "Staroobriadcheskii dukhovnyi kontsert" [A sacred concert of the Old Believers], *Muzyka i zhizn'* 5 (1908):12–13.

21. Mikhail Lisitsyn, "Staroobriadcheskii kontsert" [An Old Believers' concert], *Muzyka i penie* 7 (1908):3–4.

22. V. Paskhalov, "Staroobriadcheskii kontsert" [An Old Believers' concert], *Khronika muzykal'nogo sovremennika* 19 (1917):13. See also [Anonymous], [Concert review of 22 February 1915], *Muzyka* 222 (1915).

23. Aleksei L'vov, "Zapiski Alekseia Fyodorovicha L'vova," [The memoirs of Aleksei Fyodorovich L'vov], *Russkii arkhiv* 3 (1884):84–85.

24. *Grove's Dictionary of Music and Musicians*, 5th ed., s.v. "Russian Church Music," by A[lfred] S[wan]. The esteemed Professor Swan was, no doubt, reacting with the ears of a modern-day musician, accustomed to part-writing that takes into account the principles of acoustical theory. L'vov, on the other hand, was writing down the performance practice of his day.

25. Thirty-three of Kastal'sky's chant arrangements are written in this format, as is the *Obikhod* of the Synodal Choir, which he edited.

26. Aleksei L'vov, *O svobodnom i nesimmetrichnom ritme* [Concerning free and unsymmetrical rhythm] (St. Petersburg: n.p., 1858), pp. 3–4. Always mindful of his reputation among his Western European colleagues, L'vov had the work translated into German and sent it to them for their evaluation. See Alexis von Lwoff, *Über der freien Rhythmus*, (St. Petersburg: n.p., 1859).

27. The chants selected by L'vov are somewhat different from those found in the latest editions of the Synodal chant-books (1909 and later). A discussion of these differences lies outside the scope of the present study.

28. See Nikolai Kompaneisky, *Dukhovno-muzykal'nye sochineniia* [Sacred Musical Works] (Moscow: P. Jurgenson, 1901–10).

29. Nikolai Kompaneisky, "A. D. Kastal'sky (po povodu 4-go vypuska ego dukhovno-muzykal'nykh sochinenii)" [A. D. Kastal'sky (concerning the 4th issue of his sacred musical works)], *Russkaia muzykal'naia gazeta* 15 (1904):393. Kompaneisky specifically criticizes the system of unsymmetric measures employed in Kastal'sky's "Heirmoi for the Elevation of the Cross" (Published No. 34).

30. Aleksandr Kastal'sky, "Metodika preopodavaniia shkol'nogo khorovogo peniia," MS, Kastal'sky Archive, Fund 12, no. 246, pp. 58ff, Glinka State Museum of Musical Culture, Moscow.

31. Nikolai Kovin, *Upravlenie khorom* [Choral conducting] (Petrograd: n.p., 1916), pp. 38–40.

32. Dmitri Razumovsky, *Bogosluzhebnoe penie Pravoslavnoi Greko-Rossiiskoi Tserkvi*, vol. 1: *Teoriia i praktika tserkovnogo peniia* [The liturgical singing of the Orthodox Graeco-Russian Church, vol. 1: The theory and practice of church singing] (Moscow: n.p., 1886), p. 30.

33. Nikolai Potulov, *Rukovodstvo*, p. 111.

34. Kompaneisky, "A. D. Kastal'sky," p. 393.

35. Komarov, *Sredstva*, p. 18, n.

36. Ibid., p. 18.

37. A. Riazhsky, *Uchebnik tserkovnogo peniia* [A textbook of church singing], 5th ed. (Moscow: n.p., 1911), p. 4.

38. Stepan Smolensky, editor, *"Musikiiskaia grammatika" Nikolaia Diletskogo* [Nikolai Diletsky's "Musical Grammar"] (St. Petersburg: n.p., 1910), p. 56.

39. Nikolai Kompaneisky, *"O Tebe raduetsia"* [All creation rejoices in Thee] (Moscow: P. Jurgenson, n.d.).

40. Komarov, *Sredstva*, p. 26.

41. The term *protiazhnaia* in reference to Russian folk songs has caused English-speaking scholars no small amount of headaches, since it is very difficult to translate exactly into English. In his article, "Native Song and National Consciousness in Nineteenth-Century Russian Music" (chapter 3, n. 122), Malcolm Brown suggests the use of the term "leisurely song" to translate *protiazhnaia pesnia*. According to Komarov the "leisurely" pace of such a song would approach Andante commodo, rather than Adagio. Richard Taruskin has suggested the term "melismatic." Indeed, the protiazhnaia pesnia is usually melismatic; that determination, however, says little about the tempo at which it should be performed.

42. Komarov, *Sredstva*, pp. 33–34.

43. Ibid., p. 35. On this last point Komarov was off by no more than a couple of decades, since Ioanniky Korenev's Preface to Diletsky's *"Musical grammar"* (written in 1681) already refers to movements of the hand to mark the time (see n. 38). What is clear, however, is that beating time came to Russia together with the Western style of part-singing.

44. This apt characterization was made by Alfred Swan. See *Russian Music and Its Sources in Chant and Folksong* (New York: W. W. Norton, 1973), p. 112.

45. A. P[okrovsky], "Vospominaniia o S. V. Smolenskom" [Remembering S. V. Smolesnky], *Gusel'ki yarovchaty* 7/8 (1910):13.

46. [Anonymous article], Veche 12 September 1906; cited in Dmitri Zhitomirsky, ed., *A. D. Kastal'sky: Stat'i, vospominaniia, materialy* [A. D. Kastal'sky: Memoirs, articles, materials] (Moscow: Gosudarstvennoe Muzykal'noe Izdatel'stvo, 1960), p. 31.

47. Komarov, *Sredstva*, p. 37.

48. Ibid.

49. Ibid., p. 39.

50. Boris Asaf'ev, "Kharakternye osobennosti iskusstva Kastal'skogo" [Characteristic features of Kastal'sky's art], in *A. D. Kastal'sky:Stat'i, vospominaniia, materialy,* p. 14.

51. Ioannus De Castro, *Methodus cantus ecclesiae Graeco-Slavici* (Rome: n.p., 1881). Russian translation by Ioann Voznesensky (n.p., n.d.), chapter 5, p. 2.

52. Based on tables found in Lomakin's *Rukovodstvo k obucheniiu peniiu v narodnykh shkolakh* [A manual for teaching singing in people's schools] (St. Petersburg: n.p., n.d.) and Kastal'sky's *Obshchedostupnyi samouchitel' tserkovnogo peniia* [A popular self-instructor of church singing] (Moscow: P. Jurgenson, 1910), as well as a comprehensive perusal of the scores themselves.

53. Zonofon label, Nos. X-2-64756 and X-2-64760. The recordings confirm everything that was said by critics about Kastal'sky's poor conducting. Even through the extremely poor fidelity (the recordings were made probably sometime between 1907 and 1910), one can detect poor intonation and raggedness of ensemble. The tempo is also extremely unsteady, most likely due to poor leadership on the part of the conductor.

54. Ioann Voznesensky, *Obshchedostupnye chteniia o tserkovnom penii,* vol. 3: *Tekhnicheskaia storona sostava i ispolneniia tserkovnykh pesnopenii* [Popular readings about church singing. vol. 3 - The technical aspect of the makeup and perfomance of church hymns] (Kostroma: n.p., 1895), p. 64.

55. Aleksandr Nikol'sky, [Manuscript notebook], entries from 1894–95, Nikol'sky Archive, Fund 294, no. 379, Glinka State Museum of Musical Culture, Moscow.

56. Nikolai Matveev, *Khorovedenie* [Choral Conducting], typescript, (Zagorsk: Moskovskaia Dukhovnaia Akademiia, 1976), pp. 23–24.

57. De Castro, *Methodus*, p. 4.

58. Aleksandr Nikol'sky, "Melodichekoe penie po Obikhodu" [Melodic singing from the Book of Common Chant], *Penzenskie Eparkhial'nye vedomosti* (1897): 232.

59. Aleksandr Karasev, *Besedy o tserkovnom penii* [Discourses concerning church singing] (Moscow: n.p., 1898), p. 81.

60. Matveev, *Khorovedenie*, p. 55.

61. Nikolai Kovin, *Kurs teorii khorovogo tserkovnogo peniia v primerakh i obraztsakh* [A course on the theory of choral church singing in examples and excerpts], 2nd ed. (Moscow: n.p., n. d.).

62. Ivan Kazansky, *Obshcheponiatnoe rukovodstvo k izucheniiu notnogo tserkovnogo khorovogo i odinochnogo peniia* [A common-sense manual of choral and solo church singing] 2nd ed., (Moscow: 1875) p. 75.

63. E.g., the protodeacon of the Moscow Dormition Cathedral, K. V. Rozov, Gramophone label, 4–22289/90, or Protodeacon A. I. Zdikhovsky of the Christ the Savior Cathedral in Moscow, Grammofon label, 2–24803, et al.

64. Anonymous, "Muzykal'naia zhizn' Moskvy" [Musical life in Moscow], *Russkaia muzykal'naia gazeta* 4 (1898):399–400.

65. The latter two, Yukhov's and Pikman's, by far the least distinguished, are represented on the greatest number of recordings. Although Yukhov received a diploma from the Moscow Synodal School (by outside examination) in 1908, neither his repertoire nor his interpretation displays any of the qualities for which the Moscow Synodal Choir was deservedly famous.

66. See n. 9 above.

67. De Castro, *Methodus*, cited by Voznesensky, *Obshchedostupnye chteniia*, p. 62.

68. Vasily Komarov, *Penie v nachal'noi russkoi shkole* [Singing in the elementary Russian school], 2nd ed. (Moscow: n.p., 1899), p. 18.

69. V. M. Orlov, *Iskusstvo tserkovnogo peniia* [The art of church singing] (Moscow: n.p., 1910), p. 17.

70. Kastal'sky, "Metodika," p. 58.

71. Pavel Chesnokov, *Khor i upravlenie im* [The Choir and how to direct it], 2nd ed. (Moscow: Gosudarstvennoe Muzykal'noe Izdatel'stvo, 1952), p. 16.

72. Pavel Chesnokov, "Zametki regenta," MS, Chesnokov Archive, Fund 36, no. 322, Glinka State Museum of Musical Culture, Moscow.

73. Chesnokov, *Khor* pp. 86–90.

74. Ibid., p. 80.

75. K. N[elidov], [Review of A. Kastal'sky's published Nos. 1–11], *Russkaia muzykal'naia gazeta* 16/17 (1899):519.

76. [Anonymous], "O khudozhestvennosti v khorovom penii" [Artisticity in choral singing], *Khorovoe i regentskoe delo* 2 (1912):25.

77. Matveev, *Khorovedenie*, p. 28.

78. Kovin, *Upravlenie*, p. 35.

79. Komarov, *Penie*, p. 11.

80. Ibid., p. 23.

81. Ibid., p. 21.

82. Stepan Smolensky, *Kurs khorovogo tserkovnogo peniia* [A course in choral church singing], 5th ed. (Moscow: n.p., 1900), p. 148.

83. Kastal'sky, "Metodika," p. 58ff.

84. Kovin, *Upravlenie*, p. 36.

85. Matveev, *Khorovedenie*, pp. 93–4.

86. Nikolai Kompaneisky, "Stikhiry Paskhi" [The Stichera of Pascha], *Russkaia muzykal'naia gazeta* 20/21 (1902):558.

87. Komarov, *Penie*, p. 15.

88. Ibid., p. 18.

89. Ibid., p. 18, n. 1.

90. Kastal'sky, *Obshchedostupnyi*, p. 10.

91. Aleksandr Nikol'sky, *Golos i slukh khorovogo pevtsa* [The voice and ear of the choral singer] (Petrograd: n.p., 1916), p. 43.

92. Kovin, *Upravlenie*, pp. 35–36.

93. Zonophone label, No. X-2-64592/3.

94. Zonophone label, No. X-64935.

95. Gramophone label, No. 2-24786.

96. Komarov, *Sredstva*, pp. 34–35.

97. Odeon label, No. 15047-A.

98. Matveev, *Khorovedenie*, pp. 93–94.

99. Zonophone label, No. X-64950.

100. Anonymous review, *Russkie vedomosti*, 13 April 1904; Kastal'sky Archive, Fund 12, Glinka State Museum of Musical Culture, Moscow.

101. Kastal'sky, "My musical career," p. 245.

102. Ibid., p. 243.

103. There are minor exceptions in which the liturgical text is not entirely accurate, e.g., in Ippolitov-Ivanov's Liturgy the text of the "Holy, holy, holy" continues, "Lord *God* of Sabaoth" instead of the correct, "Lord of Sabaoth." However, such deviations are more likely attributed to the composer's and the censor's carelessness, rather than to an attempt to write deliberately a liturgically unsuitable work.

104. See Gardner, *Bogosluzhebnoe*, pp. 428ff; 520ff.

105. See Anonymous, "Novye pravila ustroistva dukhovnykh kontsertov" [New rules for holding sacred concerts], *Khorovoe i regentskoe delo* 10 (1915):177–78.

106. Gardner, *Bogosluzhebnoe*, p. 522.

107. E.g., the recording of Rachmaninoff's *Vigil* by the Johannes Damascenus Choir of Essen, Karl Linke, conductor, and the chorus of the "Russicum" in Rome, Ludwig Pichler, conductor (Christophorus Verlag, SCK 70319). A similar recording of Rachmaninoff's *Liturgy* was made in Bulgaria by the Svetoslav Obretenev Chorus (Angel Records, SB-3864).

108. E.g., a recording of Tchaikovsky's *Liturgy*, Opus 41, by the Galina Grigor'eva Ensemble (Philips label, A 837.928 LY).

109. E.g., Archmandrite Geronty Kurganovsky, *Metod bogosluzhebnykh vozglasov, polozhennykh na noty* [A manual of liturgical exclamations set in notes], 2 vols. (Moscow: n.p., 1897–1900).

110. Kastal'sky, "My Musical Career," pp. 246–47.

111. Protopopov, *O khudozhestvennom*, pp. 5, 12, 19.

112. A. Livin, "Venetsianskaia shkola i otgoloski ee vliianiia v russkoi khorovoi literature" [The Venetian School and echoes of its influence in Russian choral literature], *Muzyka i zhizn'* 6 (1912):1–2.

113. Aleksandr Nikol'sky, [Manuscript notebook], Nikol'sky Archive, Fund 294, no. 379, Glinka State Museum of Musical Culture, Moscow.

114. Nikolai Kompaneisky, "Probuzhdenie ot sna" [Awakening from slumber], *Russkaia muzykal'naia gazeta* 9/10 (1905):271.

115. Pavel Chesnokov, [Manuscript diary], Chesnokov Archive, Fund 36, no. 38, p. 80v, Glinka State Museum of Musical Culture, Moscow.

116. A. M——y, "Nabroski po voprosam tserkovno-pevcheskogo dela" [Essays on questions relating to church music], *Gusel'ki yarovchaty* 10 (1911):4–5.

117. Aleksandr Nikol'sky, "Napev paskhal'nogo troparia v ego podlinnoi redaktsii i obrabotke" [The melody of the Paschal Troparion in its original form and in arrangement], *Khorovoe i regentskoe delo* 1 (1912):10.

118. A. M——y, [Concert review] of 10 March 1911, [unidentified periodical].

119. [Anonymous], "O khudozhestvennosti," *Khorovoe i regentskoe delo* 2 (1912):27.

120. Chesnokov, "Zapiski regenta," MS, Chesnokov Archive, Fund 36, no. 322, p. 11, Glinka State Museum of Musical Culture, Moscow.

121. Nikol'sky, "Napev," p. 2.

122. Robert Brussel, *Le Figaro*, 16 August 1907.

Bibliography

Books, Monographs, Dissertations

[All-Russian Precentors' Convention]. *Trudy Pervogo Vserossiiskogo Regentskogo S"ezda v Moskve* [Proceedings of the First All-Russian Precentors' Convention in Moscow]. Moscow: n.p., 1908.

[All-Russian Precentors' Convention]. *Vtoroi Vserossiiskii S"ezd Khorovykh Deiatelei; Protokoly i doklady in extenso* [The Second All-Russian Convention of Choral Directors; Minutes and extended summaries of reports]. Moscow: n.p., 1909.

Allemanov, Dmitri. *Metodika tserkovnogo peniia* [The methodology of church singing]. Moscow: P. Jurgenson, 1908.

Arnold, Yuri. *Vospominaniia* [Memoirs]. 3 vols. St. Petersburg: n.p., 1893.

Asaf'ev, Boris. *Russkaia muzyka. XIX i nachalo XX veka* [Russian music of the nineteenth and early twentieth centuries]. Leningrad: Muzyka, 1968.

Bagadurov, Vsevolod. *Ocherki razvitiia vokal'noi pedagogiki v Rossii* [Essays in the history of vocal pedagogy in Russia]. Moscow: Gosudarstvennoe Muzykal'noe Izdatel'stvo, 1956.

Beckwith, R. Sterling. "Alexander Dmitrievich Kastal'skii (1856–1926) and the Search for a Native Russian Choral Style." Ph. D. diss., Cornell University, 1969.

Beliaev, Viktor. *Drevnerusskaia muzykal'naia pis'mennost'* [Early Russian musical notation]. Moscow: Gosudarstvennoe Muzykal'noe Izdatel'stvo, 1962.

Brazhnikov, Maksim. *Fyodor Krestyanin. Stikhiry* [Fyodor Krestyanin. Canticles]. Vol. 3 of *Monuments of Russian Music,* Moscow: Muzyka, 1974.

———. *Novye pamiatniki znamennogo raspeva* [New monuments of znamennyi chant]. Leningrad: Muzyka, 1967.

———. *Pamiatniki znamennogo raspeva* [Monuments of znamennyi chant]. Leningrad: Muzyka, 1974.

Bukofzer, Manfred. *Studies in Medieval and Renaissance Music.* New York: W. W. Norton and Co., 1973.

Bulychev, Viacheslav. *Khorovoe penie kak iskusstvo* [Choral singing as an art]. Moscow: n.p., 1910.

Chesnokov, Pavel. *Khor i upravlenie im* [The choir and how to direct it]. 2nd ed. Moscow: Gosudarstvennoe Muzykal'noe Izdatel'stvo, 1952.

De Castro, Ioannus. *Methodus cantus ecclesiae Graeco-Slavici.* Russian translation by Ioann Voznesensky. n.p, n.d.

Dyletsky, Mykola. *Grammatika muzykal'na* [Musical Grammar]. Kiev: Muzychna Ukraina, 1971.

Elzinga, Harry. "The Sacred Choral Works of Pavel Grigor'evich Chesnokov (1877–1944)." Ph. D. diss., Indiana University, 1970.

Findeizen, Nikolai. *Ocherki po istorii muzyki v Rossii* [Essays in the history of music in Russia]. 2 vols. Moscow-Leningrad: Gosudarstvennoe Muzykal'noe Izdatel'stvo, 1928.

Gardner, Ivan [Johann von]. *Bogosluzhebnoe penie Russkoi Pravoslavnoi Tserkvi: Sistema, sushchnost', istoriia* [The liturgical chant of the Russian Orthodox Church: Its system, essence, and history]. 2 vols. Jordanville, N. Y.: Holy Trinity Monastery, 1980–82.

———. *Russian Church Singing*. Vol. 1: *Orthodox Worship and Hymnography*. Translated by Vladimir Morosan. Crestwood, N. Y.: St. Vladimir's Seminary Press, 1980.

Gerasimova-Persyds'ka, Nina. *Khorovyi kontsert na Ukraini v XVII–XVIII st.* [The choral concerto in the Ukraine in the XVII–XVIII centuries]. Kiev: Muzychna Ukraina, 1978.

Gladky, A. *Poezdka Sinodal'nogo Khora zagranitsu v 1911 g.* [The Synodal Choir's tour abroad in 1911]. Moscow: n.p., 1912.

Glinka, Mikhail. *Uprazhneniia dlia uravneniia i usovershenstvovaniia gibkosti golosa* [Exercises for steadying and perfecting the flexibility of the voice]. Edited by Nikolai Kompaneisky. St. Petersburg: n.p., 1903.

Goriainov, Yu. G. *Ya. Lomakin: Dirizher, kompozitor, uchitel'* [G. Ya. Lomakin: Conductor, composer, pedagogue]. Moscow: Muzyka, 1984.

Gusin, Izrail' and Tkachev, Donat. *Gosudarstvennaia Akademicheskaia Kapella imeni M. I. Glinki* [The State Academic Choir named in honor of M. I. Glinka]. Leningrad: Gosudarstvennoe Muzykal'noe Izdatel'stvo, 1957.

Ippolitov-Ivanov, Mikhail. *50 let russkoi muzyki v moikh vospominaniiakh* [Fifty years of Russian music in my reminiscences]. Moscow: Gosudarstvennoe Muzykal'noe Izdatel'stvo, 1934.

Karasev, Aleksei. *Grigory Fyodorovich L'vovsky i ego dukhovno-muzykal'nye proizvedeniia* [Grigory Fyodorovich L'vovsky and his sacred musical works]. Moscow: n.p., 1914.

———. *Tserkovnoe penie. Rukovodstvo dlia organizatsii tserkovno-pevcheskikh khorov dlia regentov i narodnykh uchitelei* [Church singing. A manual on the organization of church choirs for precentors and schoolteachers]. 2nd ed. Kiev: n.p., 1887.

Kastal'sky, Aleksandr. *Obshchedostupnyi samouchitel' tserkovnogo peniia* [A popular self-instructor of church singing]. Moscow: P. Jurgenson, 1910.

Kazansky, Ivan. *Obshcheponiatnoe rukovodstvo k izucheniiu notnogo tserkovnogo khorovogo i odinochnogo peniia* [A common-sense manual of choral and solo church singing]. 2nd ed. Moscow: n.p., 1875.

Keldysh, Yuri. *Rakhmaninov i ego vremia* [Rachmaninoff and his times]. Moscow: Muzyka, 1973.

Komarov, Vasily. *Penie v nachal'noi russkoi shkole* [Singing in the elementary Russian school]. 2nd ed. Moscow: n.p., 1899.

———. *Sredstva k uluchsheniiu tserkovnogo peniia* [The means of improving church singing]. Moscow: n.p., 1890.

Kondrat'ev, A. *Russkaia pesnia i ee ispolnitel', narodnyi pevets Dmitri Aleksandrovich Agrenev-Slaviansky* [The Russian song and its performer, the folk singer Dmitri Aleksandrovich Agrenev-Slaviansky]. Ekaterinburg: n.p., 1898.

Kovin, Nikolai. *Kurs teorii khorovogo tserkovnogo peniia v primerakh i obraztsakh* [A course on the theory of choral church singing in examples and excerpts]. 2nd ed. Moscow: n.p., n. d.

———. *Podgotovka golosa i slukha khorovykh pevtsov* [Preparing the voice and ear of choral singers]. Moscow: n.p., 1916.

———. *Upravlenie khorom* [Choral conducting]. Petrograd: n.p., 1916.

Kozyts'skyi, Pylyp. *Spiv i muzyka v kyivs'kii akademii za 300 rokiv ii isnuvannia* [Singing and music in the Kievan Academy in the 300 years since its founding]. Kiev: Muzychna Ukraina, 1971.

Kudriavtsev, I., editor. *Rukopisnye sobraniia D. V. Razumovskogo i V. F. Odoevskogo; arkhiv D. V. Razumovskogo* [The manuscript collections of D. V. Razumovsky and V. F. Odoevsky; the archive of D. V. Razumovsky]. Moscow: Gosudarstvennaia Biblioteka imeni V. I. Lenina, 1960.

Kurganovsky, Archimandrite Geronty. *Metod bogosluzhebnykh vozglasov, polozhennykh na noty* [A manual of liturgical exclamations set in notes]. 2 vols. Moscow: n.p., 1897–1900.

Lisitsyn, Mikhail. *Pervonachal'nyi slaviano-russkii tipikon* [The first Slavic-Russian Typikon]. St. Petersburg: n.p., 1911.

Lokshin, Daniil. *Khorovoe penie v nachal'noi russkoi shkole* [Choral singing in the Russian elementary school]. Moscow: Gosudarstvennoe Muzykal'noe Izdatel'stvo, 1957.

_____. *Zamechatel'nye russkie khory i ikh dirizhery* [Outstanding Russian choirs and their conductors]. Moscow: Gosudarstvennoe Muzykal'noe Izdatel'stvo, 1963.

Lomakin, Gavriil. *Kratkaia metoda peniia* [A brief method of singing]. Moscow: n.p., 1882.

_____. *Rukovodstvo k obucheniiu peniiu v narodnykh shkolakh* [A manual for teaching singing in the people's schools]. St. Petersburg: n.p., n.d.

L'vov, Aleksei. *O svobodnom i nesimmetrichnom ritme* [Concerning free and unsymmetrical rhythm]. St. Petersburg: n.p., 1858.

_____. *O tserkovnykh khorakh* [Concerning church choirs]. St. Petersburg: n.p., 1853.

L'vov, Fyodor. *O penii v Rossii* [Singing in Russia]. St. Petersburg: n.p., 1834.

Matveev, Nikolai. *Khorovedenie* [Choral conducting]. Zagorsk: Moskovskaia Dukhovnaia Akademiia, 1976. (Mimeographed.)

[Mel'nikov, Ivan]. *Obzor deiatel'nosti khorovogo klassa I. Mel'nikova, pod rukovodstvom F. F. Bekkera* [A summary of the activities of I. Mel'nikov's choral class, under the direction of F. F. Bekker]. St. Petersburg: n.p., 1897.

Metallov, Vasily. *Bogosluzhebnoe penie russkoi tserkvi v period domongol'skii* [The liturgical singing of the Russian church in the pre-Mongol period]. Moscow: n.p., 1912.

_____. *Ocherk istorii tserkovnogo peniia v Rossii* [Essay on the history of church singing in Russia]. Moscow: n.p., 1900.

_____. *Russkaia simiografiia* [Russian semeiography]. Moscow: n.p., 1912.

_____. *Sinodal'noe Uchilishche Tserkovnogo peniia v ego proshlom i nastoiashchem* [The Moscow Synodal School of Church Singing in its past and present]. Moscow: n.p., 1911.

Miroliubov, A. *Obraztsovyi tserkovnyi khor vremen Mitropolita Filareta,* [An exemplary church choir from the time of Metropolitan Filaret]. Moscow: n.p., n.d.

Musorgsky, Modest. *Pis'ma i dokumenty* [Letters and documents]. Moscow and Leningrad: Gosudarstvennoe Muzykal'noe Izdatel'stvo, 1932.

Muzykal'nyi kalendar' [Musical calendar]. Supplement to the journal *Muzykal'nyi truzhennik.* Moscow: n.p. 1909.

Muzykal'nyi spravochnik na 1914 g. [Musical handbook for 1914]. Moscow: n.p., 1914.

Nikol'skaia-Beregovskaia, K. *Razvitie shkoly khorovogo peniia v Rossii* [The development of a school of choral singing in Russia]. Moscow: Muzyka, 1974.

Nikol'sky, Aleksandr. *Golos i slukh khorovogo pevtsa* [The voice and ear of the choral singer]. Petrograd: n.p., 1916.

Orlov, Vasily Mikhailovich. *Iskusstvo tserkovnogo peniia* [The art of church singing]. Moscow: n.p., 1910.

Pamiati V. S. Orlova [V. S. Orlov, in memoriam]. Moscow: n.p., 1908.

Perepelitsyn, P. *Muzykal'nyi slovar'. Entsyklopedicheskii spravochnyi sbornik* [Musical dictionary. An encyclopedic reference collection]. Moscow: n.p., 1884.

Peterson, Vincent. "The Azbuka of Alexander Mezenets: A Preliminary Study in Znamenny Chant." M. Div. thesis, St. Vladimir's Orthodox Theological Seminary, Crestwood, New York, 1981.

Polozhenie o regentskikh klassakh Pridvornoi Pevcheskoi Kapelly [Decree concerning the precentors' classes of the Imperial Court Chapel]. St. Petersburg: n.p., 1911.

Postnikov, V. "Perechen' tserkovnykh pesnopenii s ukazaniem kompozitorov proizvedeniia kotorykh ispolnialis' khorami pod upravleniem N. M. Danilina v khramakh Moskvy" [A list of church hymns and composers performed by choirs under the direction of N. M. Danilin in Moscow churches]. Moscow, 4 April 1973. (Typewritten.)

Potulov, Nikolai. *Rukovodstvo k prakticheskomu izucheniiu drevnego peniia Pravoslavnoi Rossiiskoi Tserkvi* [A manual for the practical study of the ancient singing of the Russian Orthodox Church]. Moscow: n.p., 1872.

Preobrazhensky, Antonin. *Kul'tovaia muzyka v Rossii* [The music of the cult in Russia]. Leningrad: Academia, 1924.

Programmy muzykal'nykh predmetov i istorii iskusstv v Moskovskom Sinodal'nom Uchilishche Tserkovnogo Peniia [Programs in musical subjects and arts history at the Moscow Synodal School of Church Singing]. Moscow: n.p., 1910.

Programmy Regentskogo Uchilishcha, osnovannogo v 1907 S. V. Smolenskim v Sankt-Peterburge [The programs of the Precentors' School established in 1907 by S. V. Smolensky in St. Petersburg]. St. Petersburg: n.p., 1908.

Protopopov, Sergei. *O khudozhestvennom elemente v pravoslavnom tserkovnom penii* [Concerning the artistic element in Orthodox church singing]. 2nd ed. St. Petersburg: n.p., 1905.

Protopopov, Vladimir. *Muzyka na poltavskuiu pobedu* [Music for the Poltava victory]. Vol. 2 of *Monuments of Russian Music*. Moscow: Muzyka, 1971.

Ptitsa, Klavdy. *Mastera khorovogo iskusstva v Moskovskoi Konservatorii* [Masters of the choral art at the Moscow Conservatory]. Moscow: Muzyka, 1970.

Raspevanie narodnogo khora [Vocalizing the folk chorus]. Moscow: Russian Choral Society of the RSFSR, n.d.

Razumovsky, Dmitri. *Bogosluzhebnoe penie Pravoslavnoi Greko-Rossiiskoi Tserkvi.* Vol. 1: *Teoriia i praktika tserkovnogo peniia* [The liturgical singing of the Orthodox Graeco-Russian Church. Vol. 1: The theory and practice of church singing]. Moscow: n.p., 1886.

―――. *Tserkovnoe penie v Rossii* [Church singing in Russia]. 3 vols. Moscow: n.p., 1867–69.

Riazhsky, A. *Uchebnik tserkovnogo peniia* [A textbook of church singing]. 5th ed. Moscow: n.p., 1911.

Rimsky-Korsakov, Nikolai. *Letopis' moei muzykal'noi zhizni* [My musical life]. Moscow: Gosudarstvennoe Muzykal'noe Izdatel'stvo, 1955.

Rogov, A., editor. *Muzykal'naia estetika Rossii XI–XVII vekov* [Musical aesthetics of Russia in the XI–XVII centuries]. Moscow: Muzyka, 1973.

Rozhnov, Aleksandr. *Notnaia azbuka sostavlennaia dlia pevchekikh khorov* [A musical primer for church choirs]. St. Petersburg: n.p., 1861.

Rubtsov, Fyodor. *Stat'i po muzykal'nomu fol'kloru* [Essays in musical folklore]. Leningrad and Moscow: Muzyka, 1973.

Rudneva, Anna. *Russkii narodnyi khor i rabota s nim* [Working with the Russian folk chorus]. Moscow: Gosudarstvennoe Muzykal'noe Izdatel'stvo, 1960.

Skrebkov, Sergei. *Russkaia khorovaia muzyka XVII–nachala XVIII veka* [Russian choral music of the XVII–early XVIII centuries]. Moscow: Muzyka, 1969.

S[molensk]y, S[tepan]. *Ob ozdorovlenii programm dukhovnykh kontsertov v Moskve* [The revitalization of the programs of sacred concerts in Moscow]. Moscow: n.p., 1900.

Serov, Aleksandr. *Izbrannye stat'i* [Selected essays]. 2 vols. Moscow: Gosudarstvennoe Muzykal'noe Izdatel'stvo, 1957.

Smolensky, Stepan. *Kurs khorovogo tserkovnogo peniia* [A course in choral church singing]. 5th ed. Moscow: n.p., 1900.

_____. *O blizhaishikh practicheskikh zadachakh i nauchnykh razyskaniiakh v oblasti tserkovno-pevcheskoi arkheologii* [The most immediate practical concerns for scientific research in the field of church-musical archeology]. St. Petersburg: n.p., 1904.

_____. *Ob ukazaniiakh ottenkov ispolneniia i ob ukazaniiakh muzykal'no-pevcheskikh form tserkovnykh pesnopenii v kriukovom pis'me* [Concerning the indications of performance nuances and vocal-musical forms of church hymns in neumatic notation]. Kiev: n.p., 1909.

Smolensky, Stepan., editor. *"Musikiiskaia grammatika" Nikolaia Diletskogo* [Nikolai Diletsky's "Musical grammar"]. St. Petersburg: n.p., 1910.

Stepanov, Vladimir. "Vasily Sergeevich Orlov." Moscow, 1954. (Typescript.)

Swan, Alfred. *Russian Music and Its Sources in Chant and Folksong.* New York: W. W. Norton and Co., 1973.

Tkachev, Donat. *Aleksandr Andreevich Arkhangel'sky (1846–1924). Ocherk zhizni i deiatel'nosti* [Aleksandr Andreevich Arkhangel'sky (1846–1924): His life and works]. Leningrad: Muzyka, 1974.

Undol'sky, Vukol. *Zamechaniia dlia istorii tserkovnogo peniia v Rossii* [Remarks on the history of church singing in Russia]. Moscow: n.p., 1846.

Uspensky, Nikolai. *Drevne-russkoe pevcheskoe iskusstvo* [The early Russian art of singing]. 2nd ed. Moscow: Sovetskii Kompozitor, 1971.

_____. *Obraztsy drevne-russkogo pevcheskogo iskusstva* [Examples of the early Russian art of singing]. Leningrad: Muzyka, 1971.

Varlamov, Aleksandr. *Polnaia shkola peniia* [Complete school of singing]. Edited by Viacheslav Bagadurov. Moscow: Gosudarstvennoe Muzykal'noe Izdatel'stvo, 1953. First published 1840.

Vasilenko, Sergei. *Stranitsy vospominanii* [Pages of reminiscences]. Moscow-Leningrad: Gosudarstvennoe Muzykal'noe Izdatel'stvo, 1948.

Vitashevsky, N. *Shkol'noe prepodavanie khorovogo peniia* [Teaching choral singing in the school]. Moscow: n.p., 1911.

Vorotnikov, Pavel. *Rukovodstvo k prepodavaniiu khorovogo peniia* [A manual for the teaching of choral singing]. Moscow: n.p., 1894.

Voznesensky, Ioann. *O sovremennykh nam nuzhdakh i zadachakh russkogo tserkovnogo peniia* [Contemporary needs and problems of Russian church singing]. Riga: n.p., 1891.

_____. *Obshchedostupnye chteniia o tserkovnom penii.* Vol. 3: *Tekhnicheskaia storona sostava i ispolneniia tserkovnykh pesnopenii* [Popular readings about church singing. Vol. 3: The technical aspect of the makeup and perfomance of church hymns]. Kostroma: n.p., 1895.

Wellesz, Egon. *A History of Byzantine Music and Hymnography*, 2nd ed. Oxford: Cambridge University Press, 1962.

Zhitomirsky, Dmitri., editor. *A. D. Kastal'sky: Stat'i, vospominaniia, materialy* [A. D. Kastal'sky: Articles, memoirs, materials]. Moscow: Gosudarstvennoe Muzykal'noe Izdatel'stvo, 1960.

Zinov'ev, Vasily. *Prakticheskoe rukovodstvo dlia nachinaiushchego uchitelia-regenta* [A practical manual for the beginning teacher-precentor]. Moscow: n.p., 1905.

Zipalov, N. F. *A. Bagretsov: Opyt biografii v istoriko-muzykal'nom otnoshenii po otzyvam i vospominaniiam ego sovremennikov* [F. A. Bagretsov: A historico-musical biography based on accounts and reminiscences of his contemporaries]. Vladikavkaz: n.p., 1914.

Zolotarev, Vasily. *Vospominaniia o moikh velikikh uchiteliakh, druz'iakh, i tovarishchakh* [Reminiscences about my great teachers, friends, and comrades]. Moscow: Gosudarstvennoe Muzykal'noe Izdatel'stvo, 1957.

Articles in Journals and Collections

[Adan, Adolphe]. "Pis'ma kompozitora Adana o svoei poezdke v Peterburg v 1839–om godu" [The letters of the composer Adan about his journey to St. Petersburg in 1839]. *Russkaia muzykal'naia gazeta* 38 (1903):1816–39.

Allemanov, Dmitri. "S. V. Smolensky, kak tserkovno-pevcheskii deiatel'" [S. V. Smolensky's role as a worker in the field of church singing]. *Muzykal'nyi truzhennik* 4 (1910):4–11.

Beckwith, R. Sterling. "How to Write a Russian Mass." *American Choral Review* 10 (1968):178–85.

Beliaev, Viktor. "Rannee russkoe mnogogolosie" [Early Russian polyphony]. In *Studiae memoriae Belae Bartok Sacra*. Budapest: Academia, 1956.

"Berlioz v Rossii" [Berlioz in Russia]. *Russkaia muzykal'naia gazeta* 50(1903):1250–56.

Brown, Malcolm Hamrick. "Native Song and National Consciousness in Nineteenth-Century Russian Music." In *Art and Culture in Nineteenth-Century Russia*, ed. Theofanis George Stavrou. Bloominton, Indiana: Indiana University Press, 1983:57–84.

Bulich, S. "A. E. Varlamov. Neskol'ko novykh dannykh dlia ego biografii" [A. E. Varlamov. Several new facts concerning his biography]. *Russkaia muzykal'naia gazeta* 45–46 (1901):1111–20, 1142–51.

"Chestvovanie pamiati Bortnianskogo Pridvornoi Pevcheskoi Kapelloi" [The celebration of Bortniansky's memory by the Imperial Court Chapel]. *Russkaia muzykal'naia gazeta* 40 (1901):964–67.

Dmitrevskaia, Kleopatra. "Viktor Kalinnikov. K 100–letiiu so dnia rozhdeniia" [Viktor Kalinnikov. Commemorating the 100th anniversary of his birth]. In *Khorovoe iskusstvo* [The choral art]. Vol. 2. Leningrad: Muzyka, 1971:53–67.

Findeizen, Nikolai. "Sinodal'noe Uchilishche Tserkovnogo Peniia v Moskve" [The Synodal School of Church Singing in Moscow]. *Russkaia muzykal'naia gazeta* 4 (1898):345–49.

Gardner, Ivan [Johann von]. "Aleksei Feodorovich L'vov." *Pravoslavnyi put'* (Jordanville, N. Y., 1970):112–95.

————. "Slovo 'kliroshanin' i ego deistvitel'noe znachenie" [The term *kliroshanin* and its actual meaning]. *Pravoslavnaia zhizn'* 10 (1971):29–35.

Golitsyn, N. "Sovremennyi vopros o preobrazovanii tserkovnogo peniia v Rossii" [The current question concerning the transformation of church singing in Russia]. *Strannik* 1 (1884):555–58.

Grove's Dictionary of Music and Musicians, 5th ed. S.v. A[lfred] S[wan], "Russian Church Music."

Isaevych, Ya. "Bratstva i ukrains'ka muzychna kul'tura XVI–XVII st." [The brotherhoods and Ukrainian musical culture of the XV–XVII centuries]. *Ukrains'ke muzykoznavstvo* 6 (1971):48–57.

Kastal'sky, Aleksandr. "O moei muzykal'noi kar'ere i moi mysli o tserkovnoi muzyke" [My musical career and thoughts on church music.] *Muzykal'nyi Sovremennik* 2 (October 1915). Translated by S. W. Pring "My Musical Career and Thoughts on Church Music." *The Musical Quarterly* (1925):232–47.

Kompaneisky, Nikolai. "A. D. Kastal'sky (po povodu 4–go vypuska ego dukhovno-muzykal'nykh sochinenii)" [A. D. Kastal'sky (concerning the 4th issue of his sacred musical works)]. *Russkaia muzykal'naia gazeta* 13–18 (1904):359–64; 391–98; 425–29; 457–65.

————. "Dvadtsatiletie kontsertnoi deiatel'nosti A. A. Arkhangel'skogo" [The twenty-year anniversary of A. A. Arkhangel'sky's concert activity]. *Russkaia muzykal'naia gazeta* 3 (1903):70.

————. "O privedenii golosa v poriadok" [Getting the voice in order]. *Russkaia muzykal'naia gazeta* 44–45 (1908):968–76; 996–1001.

_____. "Protest kompozitorov dukhovnoi muzyki" [A protest by composers of sacred music]. *Russkaia muzykal'naia gazeta* 23/24 (1906):569–74.

_____. "Sovremennoe demestvo" [Modern-day demestvo]. *Russkaia muzykal'naia gazeta* 6 (1902):165–70.

_____. "Stikhiry Paskhi" [The Stichera of Pascha]. *Russkaia muzykal'naia gazeta* 20/21 (1902):558.

K[ovin], N[ikolai]. "Regentskoe obrazovanie" [The education of precentors]. *Khorovoe i regentskoe delo* 3–5 (1911):66–69; 81–85; 109–15.

_____. "Zametki regenta. Postanovka golosa" [Notes of a precentor. Vocal training]. *Khorovoe i regentskoe delo* 2 (1909):44–48.

Kurdiumov, Yuri. "Ocherk razvitiia sol'nogo peniia" [An essay on the development of solo singing]. *Russkaia muzykal'naia gazeta* 31/32 (1912):625–28.

L. "V. S. Orlov. Sovremennye muzykal'nye deiateli" [V. S. Orlov. Contemporary musical personages]. *Russkaia muzykal'naia gazeta* 52 (1903):1309–13.

Lisitsyn, Mikhail. "O novom napravlenii v russkoi tserkovnoi muzyke" [The new direction in Russian church music]. *Muzykal'nyi truzhennik* 7–13 (1909):1–6; 6–15; 6–11; 10–14; 5–13.

Livin, A. "Venetsianskaia shkola i otgoloski ee vliianiia v russkoi khorovoi literature" [The Venetian School and echoes of its influence in Russian choral literature]. *Muzyka i zhizn'* 6 (1912):1–2.

Lomakin, Gavriil. "Avtobiograficheskie zapiski" [Autobiographical notes]. *Russkaia starina* 49–51 (1886):645–58; 312–21; 676–86.

L'vov, Aleksei. "Zapiski Alekseia Fyodorovicha L'vova," [The memoirs of Aleksei Fyodorovich L'vov]. *Russkii arkhiv* bk. 2, nos. 3–4 (1884):225–60; bk. 3 (1884):65–114.

M—y, A. "Nabroski po voprosam tserkovno-pevcheskogo dela" [Essays on questions relating to church music]. *Gusel'ki yarovchaty* 5–8 (1910):2–5; 3–6; nos. 1, 5/6, 10 (1911):2–6; 3–7; 1–6; nos. 4, 7/8 (1912):1–6; 1–6; and nos. 5/6, 11 (1913):11–15; 5–9.

Maiburova, K. "Glukhivs'ka shkola pivchykh XVIII st. ta ii rol' u rozvytku muzychnogo profesionalizmu na Ukraini ta v Rossii" [The Glukhov singing school in the eighteenth century and its role in the development of musical professionalism in the Ukraine and in Russia]. *Ukrains'ke muzykoznavstvo* 6 (1971):126–36.

Maslov, Aleksandr. "O dirizhirovanii." *Muzyka i zhizn'* 12 (1910):3–7.

Metallov, Vasily. "Sinodal'nye, byvshie patriarshie pevchie" [The synodal, formerly the patriarchal singers], and separately, *Russkaia muzykal'naia gazeta* 10–12 (1898):845–51; 945–50; 1041–49; 17, 19–20, 21–22, 23–24; 25–26; (1901): 489–94; 513–21; 576–81; 606–11; 636–45.

Morosan, Vladimir. "Folk and Chant Elements in Musorgsky's Choral Writing." In *Musorgsky In Memoriam 1881–1981.* Ed. Malcolm Hamrick Brown. Ann Arbor, Michigan: UMI Research Press, 1982:95–133.

_____. "*Penie* and *Musikiia*: Aesthetic Changes in Russian Liturgical Singing During the Seventeenth Century." *St. Vladimir's Theological Quarterly* 23 (1979):149–79.

Moshkov, Valentin. "Nekotorye provintsial'nye osobennosti v russkom narodnom penii" [Some provincial peculiarities in Russian folk singing]. *Baian* (St. Petersburg) 4–5 (1889):49–53; 65–8.

N[ikol'sk]y, A[leksandr]. "Dukhovnye kontserty i ikh zadachi" [Sacred concerts and their objectives]. *Khorovoe i regentskoe delo* 4 (1909):97–101.

Nikol'sky, Aleksandr. "Khorovoe tserkovnoe penie" [Choral church singing]. *Penzenskie eparkhial'nye vedomosti* (1897):179–89.

_____. "Kriukovaia sistema; ee smysl i znachenie" [The neumatic system; its meaning and significance]. *Khorovoe i regentskoe Delo* 3–4 (1912):41–47; 65–72.

_____. "Melodichekoe penie po Obikhodu" [Melodic singing from the Book of Common Chant]. *Penzenskie eparkhial'nye vedomosti* (1897):228–34.

————. "Napev paskhal'nogo troparia v ego podlinnoi redaktsii i obrabotke" [The melody of the Paschal Troparion in its original form and in arrangement]. *Khorovoe i regentskoe delo* 1 (1912):1–10.

————. "S. V. Smolensky i ego rol' v novom napravlenii russkoi tserkovnoi muzyki" [S. V. Smolensky and his role in the new direction of Russian church music]. *Khorovoe i regentskoe delo* 10 (1913):151–56.

————. "Vasily Sergeevich Orlov," *Khorovoe i regentskoe delo* 11–12 (1913):172–77; 195–201.

"O khudozhestvennosti v khorovom penii" [Artisticity in choral singing]. *Khorovoe i regentskoe delo* 1–2 (1912):10–13, 25–27.

[Odoevsky, Vladimir]. "Mnenie kniazia V. F. Odoevskogo po voprosam, vozbuzhdennym Ministrom Narodnogo Prosveshcheniia po delu o tserkovnom penii" [Prince V. F. Odoevsky's opinions concerning questions pertaining to church singing raised by the Minister of Education]. *Domashniaia beseda* nos. 26–28 (1866), pp. 622–26; 642–47; 665–72.

P[ashchenk]o, A[ndrei]. "Peterburgskie tserkovnye khory" [St. Petersburg church choirs]. *Khorovoe i regentskoe delo* 1–4 (1910):8–13; 41–44; 70–72; 97–103.

P[okrovsky], A. "Vospominaniia o S. V. Smolenskom" [Remembering S. V. Smolensky]. *Gusel'ki iarovchaty* 7/8 (1910):13.

Preobrazhensky, Antonin. "Iz pervykh let partesnogo peniia v Moskve" [From the first years of part singing in Moscow] *Muzykal'nyi sovremennik* 3 (November 1914):3–42.

————. "Ot uniatskogo kanta do pravoslavnoi kheruvimskoi" [From a uniate *kant* to an Orthodox Cherubic Hymn]. *Muzykal'nyi sovremennik* (February 1916):11–28.

————. "Pridvornaia kapella 150 let nazad" [The Court Chapel 150 years ago]. *Russkaia muzykal'naia gazeta* 11 (1902):col. 324.

————. "Trudy P. I. Chaikovskogo v oblasti tserkovnogo peniia" [The contributions of P. I. Tchaikovsky in the area of church singing]. *Ekaterinoslavskie eparkhial'nye vedomosti* 23–24 (1894):571–80, 589–605.

"Regentskii klass pri Pridvornoi Pevcheskoi Kapelle" [The precentors' course at the Imperial Court Chapel]. *Russkaia muzykal'naia gazeta* 19/20 (1904): 516–19.

Romanovsky, N. "Iz proshlogo russkoi khorovoi kul'tury" [From the past of Russian choral culture]. In *Khorovoe iskustvo* [The choral art]. Vol. 2. Leningrad: Muzyka, 1971:67–79.

Rosliakov, Dmitri. "Vospominaniia o Pridvornoi Pevcheskoi Kapelle" [Reminiscences about the Imperial Court Chapel]. *Muzyka i penie* 6–12 (1909):1–2; 1–2; 1–2; 1–2; 1–2; 1–2; 1–2.

Rozanov, N. "Ob ustroistve chudovskogo khora pevchikh" [Concerning the organization of the Chudov Choir]. *Chteniia Moskovskogo Obshchestva Liubitelei Dukhovnogo Prosveshcheniia* 5 (1868):91–118.

Sakharov, Ivan. "Issledovanie o russkom tserkovnom pesnopenii" [An investigation into Russian church singing]. *Zhurnal Ministerstva Narodnogo Prosveshcheniia* 61–63 (1849):147–96; 265–89; 1–41; 89–109.

Serebriakov, G. "O 'postanovke' golosa u tserkovnykh pevchikh" [Concerning the vocal 'training' of church singers]. *Baian* (Tambov) 4–9 (1907):50–51; 73–75; 105–6; 152–54.

Smolensky, Stepan. "Iz dorozhnykh vpechatlenii" [Travel impressions]. *Russkaia muzykal'naia gazeta* 42–46 (1908):935–41; 961–69; 998–1007; 1025–33; 1058–61.

————. "Neskol'ko novykh dannykh o tak nazyvaemom kondakarnom znameni" [Several new facts concerning the so-called kondakarian notation]. *Russkaia muzykal'naia gazeta* 44–49 (1913):973–77; 1007–10; 1039–44; 1132–36.

————. "O sobranii russkikh drevne-pevcheskikh rukopisei v Moskovskom Sinodal'nom Uchilishche Tserkovnogo Peniia" [The collection of early Russian chant manuscripts in the Moscow Synodal School of Church Singing]. *Russkaia muzykal'naia gazeta* 13 (1899):401.

————. "Pamiati D. S. Bortnianskogo" [D. S. Bortniansky, In memoriam]. *Russkaia muzykal'naia gazeta* 39 (1901):917–25.

Staroobriadets. "Staroobriadcheskoe penie i pevchie" [Singing and singers among the Old Believers]. *Muzykal'nyi truzhennik* 6 (1909):2–3.

Stasov, Vladimir. "Dvadtsati-piati letie Besplatnoi Muzykal'noi Shkoly" [The 25th anniversary of the Free Musical School]. In *Izbrannye sochinenii* [Selected works]. Vol. 3. Moscow: Gosudarstvennoe Muzykal'noe Izdatel'stvo, 1952:75–81.

————. "Kontsert gg. pevchikh grafa Sheremeteva" [A concert by the singers of Count Sheremetev]. *Muzykal'nyi i teatral'nyi vestnik* 9 (1856):164–66.

————. "Tri russkikh kontserta" [Three Russian concerts]. *Sankt-Peterburgskie vedomosti*, 30 April 1863.

Stepanov, M. "Zavety S. V. Smolenskogo regentu tserkovnogo khora" [S. V. Smolensky's testament to a church precentor]. *Khorovoe i regentskoe delo* 12 (1915):217–21.

Tikhov, Pyotr. "D. A. Slaviansky kak russkii muzykal'nyi deiatel'" [D. A. Slaviansky as a Russian musical celebrity]. *Gusel'ki iarovchaty* 9 (1911):10–12.

————. "Pis'mo neizvestnogo liubitelia tserkovnogo blagolepiia k rektoru Moskovskoi Dukhovnoi Akademii" [A letter from an anonymous defender of church propriety to the Rector of the Moscow Theological Academy]. *Muzykal'nyi truzhennik* 1 (1908):1–5.

Tkachev, Donat. "Istoricheskie kontserty khora A. Arkhangel'skogo" [The historical concerts of Arkhangel'sky's Choir]. In *Khorovoe iskusstvo* [The choral art]. Vol. 2. Leningrad: Muzyka, 1971:79–87.

Uspensky, Nikolai. "A Wreath on the Grave of Dmitry Stepanovich Bortnyansky," *Journal of the Moscow Patriarchate* (1975):63–78.

————. "Problema metodologii obucheniia ispolnitel'skomu masterstvu v drevnerusskom pevcheskom iskusstve" [The problem of methodology in the teaching of performance skills in early Russian chant]. In *Musica antiqua Europae orientalis. Acta scientifica.* Bydgoscz: Academia, 1976:467–501.

Vander Linden, A. "Un collaborateur Russe de Fétis: Alexis de Lvoff (1798–1870)," *Revue Belge de Musicologie* 19 (1965):64–81.

Yu. I. "Novye zadachi pravoslavnoi tserkovnoi muzyki v Rossii. Vnimaniiu kompozitorov tserkovnoi muzyki" [New objectives of Orthodox church music in Russia. To the attention of church music composers]. *Khorovoe i regentskoe delo* 5 (1913):80–85.

"Zarubezhnaia gastrol' Leningradskoi Kapelly v 1928 g. Dnevnik M. G. Klimova i otzyvy pressy" [The foreign tour of the Leningrad Kapella in 1928. M. G. Klimov's diary and newspaper reviews]. In *Khorovoe iskusstvo* [The choral art]. Vol. 2. Leningrad: Muzyka, 1971:78–120.

Concert Reviews. Newsbriefs. Letters to the Editor

Included in this section are various news items, many of them untitled and usually too brief to be considered full articles. In some cases the items were found in archives (see following section), clipped from the original periodical or newspaper, which makes it impossible to give a full bibliographic citation.

A[rakchiev]. D[mitri]. [Concert review]. *Muzyka i zhizn'* 4 (1908):10–11.

Brussel, Robert. [Untitled article]. *Le Figaro* 16 August 1907.

[Concert review of 22 February 1915]. *Muzyka* 222 (1915).

D. "K desiatiletiiu upravleniia P. G. Chesnokovym khorom liubitelei peniia pri tserkvi Sv. Troitsy chto na Griaziakh v Moskve" [Commemorating the 10-year anniversary of P. G. Chesnokov's conducting of the amateur choir at the Church of the Holy Trinity "at the mud-baths" in Moscow]. *Khorovoe i regentskoe delo* 4 (1913):68–70.

Gil'din, M. "Dva kontserta Slavianskogo" [Two concerts by Slaviansky]. *Baian* 6 (1907):91.

H. K. M. "The Russian Choir, A Remarkable Recital in New York." *New York Times*, 1 December 1913.

Kashkin, Nikolai. "Vecher muzykal'nykh anakhronizmov" [An evening of musical anachronisms]. *Russkoe slovo*, 25 October 1907.

Kompaneisky, Nikolai. "Kontsert Pridvornoi Pevcheskoi Kapelly" [A concert by the Imperial Court Chapel]. *Russkaia muzykal'naia gazeta* 5 (1902):141–45.

————. "Po povodu 9-go punkta 44-go paragrafa ustava Tserkovno-pevcheskogo Obshchestva v Sankt-Peterburge" [Concerning the 9th point of Paragraph 44 in the by-laws of the Church-Singers' Association in St. Petersburg]. *Russkaia Muzykal'naia Gazeta* 17/18 (1903):471–72.

————. "Probuzhdenie ot sna" [Awakening from slumber]. *Russkaia muzykal'naia gazeta* 9/10 (1905):271.

————. "Staroobriadcheskii dukhovnyi kontsert" [A sacred concert of the Old Believers]. *Russkaia muzykal'naia gazeta* 17 (1908):407–11.

"Kontsert Sinodal'nogo Khora" [The concert of the Synodal Choir]. *Khorovoe i regentskoe delo* 3 (1911):12–14.

L——n, A. [Concert review]. *Muzyka i zhizn'* 3 (1908):14.

Lipaev, Ivan. [Concert review]. *Russkaia muzykal'naia gazeta* 7 (1896):760–62.

————. [Concert review]. *Russkaia muzykal'naia gazeta* 4 (1897):678–81.

————. [Concert review]. *Russkaia muzykal'naia gazeta* 4 (1898):400.

————. [Concert review]. *Russkaia muzykal'naia gazeta* 9 (1899):288.

————. [Concert review]. *Russkaia muzykal'naia gazeta* 15/16 (1899):479–80.

————. [Concert review]. *Russkaia muzykal'naia gazeta* 10 (1901):314–15.

————. [Concert review]. *Russkaia muzykal'naia gazeta* 11 (1901):344.

————. [Concert review]. *Russkaia muzykal'naia gazeta* 14/15 (1903):411–12.

————. [Concert review]. *Russkaia muzykal'naia gazeta* 13 (1906):348.

————. [Concert review]. *Russkaia muzykal'naia gazeta* 46 (1908):1032.

Lisitsyn, Mikhail. "Ya. S. Kalishevsky i ego khor" [Ya. S. Kalishevsky and his choir]. *Muzyka i penie* 3–4 (1902/03):3.

————. "Iubilei khora A. A. Arkhangel'skogo" [The anniversary of A. A. Arkhangel'sky's choir]. *Russkaia muzykal'naia gazeta* 1 (1898):86–88.

————. "Moskva i Sinodal'nyi Khor" [Moscow and the Synodal Choir]. *Muzyka i penie* 11–12 (1906):4–5; 1–3.

————. "Staroobriadcheskii kontsert" [An Old Believers' concert]. *Muzyka i penie* 7 (1908):3–4.

————. "Velikopostnye dukhovnye kontserty" [Lenten sacred concerts]. *Muzyka i penie* 7 (1911):1–2.

M. "Kontserty Moskovskogo Sinodal'nogo Khora v Drezdene" [The concerts of the Moscow Synodal Choir in Dresden]. *Russkaia muzykal'naia gazeta* 30/31 (1911):611–16.

"Muzykal'naia zhizn' Moskvy" [The musical life of Moscow]. *Russkaia muzykal'naia gazeta* 4 (1898):399–400.

N. "Kontsert russkogo khora v Zheneve" [A Russian choir concert in Geneva]. *Khorovoe i regentskoe delo* 12 (1913):202–4.

N[elidov], K[onstantin]. [Review of A. Kastal'sky's Published Nos. 1–11]. *Russkaia muzykal'naia gazeta* 16/17 (1899):519.

Nikol'sky, Aleksandr. [Concert review]. *Khorovoe i regentskoe delo* 4 (1909):112–14.

————. "Staroobriadcheskii dukhovnyi kontsert" [A sacred concert of the Old Believers]. *Muzyka i zhizn'* 5 (1908):12–13.

Nonakk. "Zametka of regentskikh klassakh Pridvornoi Pevcheskoi Kapelly" [A note about the precentors' courses of the Imperial Court Chapel]. *Russkaia muzykal'naia gazeta* 11 (1896):1421–24.

"Novye pravila ustroistva dukhovnykh kontsertov" [New rules for holding sacred concerts]. *Khorovoe i regentskoe delo* 10 (1915):177–78.

Paskhalov, V. "Staroobriadcheskii kontsert" [An Old Believers' concert]. *Khronika muzykal'nogo sovremennika* 19 (1917):13.

"Pridvornaia pevcheskaia kapella" [The Imperial Court Chapel]. *Khronika muzykal'nogo sovremennika* 12 (1915-16).

Pr[okof'ev]. Gr[igory]. [Concert review]. *Russkaia muzykal'naia gazeta* 14 (1915):260-61.

Prokof'ev, Grigory [Concert review]. *Russkaia muzykal'naia gazeta* 9 (1914):243.

_____. "Opera i kontserty v Moskve" [Opera and concerts in Moscow]. *Russkaia muzykal'naia gazeta* 14 (1915):260.

Rybakov, S. "Dukhovnyi kontsert Besplatnogo Khorovogo Klassa Mel'nikova i Bekkera" [A sacred concert by the Free Choral Class of Mel'nikov and Bekker]. *Russkaia muzykal'naia gazeta* 4 (1897):654-57.

S[okolov]. N[ikolai]. [Concert review]. *Muzykal'noe obozrenie* 12 (1888).

Vitoshinsky, E. "Khor g. Kalishevskogo v Kieve" [Kalishevsky's choir in Kiev]. *Muzyka i penie* 1-2 (1902/03):2-4.

"Zhenshchiny v tserkovnykh khorakh" [Women in church choirs]. Letters to the Editor. *Muzykal'nyi truzhennik* 15-20 (1907).

Archival Materials—Moscow. Glinka State Museum of Musical Culture

Pavel Chesnokov Archive, Fund 36.
    No. 38. Notebook and diary, 1904-1906.
    No. 322. "Zapiski regenta" [Notes of a precentor]. MS.
    Author's copy of *Khor i upravlenie im* [The choir and how to direct it], with marginal notes.

Nikolai Golovanov Collection.
    Nos. 527-28. Smolensky, Stepan. "Vospominaniia" [Memoirs]. 2 vols. MS.

Nikolai Kashkin Archive. Fund 35.
    No. 96. "Zapiski o prepodavanii v Sinodal'nom Uchilishche" [Notes on the instruction at the Synodal School]. MS.

Aleksandr Kastal'sky Archive. Fund 12.
    No. 246. "Metodika prepodavaniia shkol'nogo khorovogo peniia" [The methodology of teaching choral singing in the schools]. MS notebook.
    No. 383. "Tembry razlichnykh sochetanii khorovykh golosov" [The timbres of various combinations of choral voices]. MS.
    Miscellaneous newspaper clippings.

Ivan Lipaev Archive. Fund 13.
    Miscellaneous newspaper clippings.

Aleksandr Nikol'sky Archive. Fund 294.
    No. 379. Manuscript notebook, 1894-95.

Index